JUSTICE FOR ALL: THE TRUTH ABOUT
METALLICA

JOEL McIVER

OMNIBUS PRESS

LONDON / NEW YORK / PARIS / SYDNEY / COPENHAGEN / BERLIN / MADRID / TOKYO

Exclusive Distributors
Music Sales Limited,
8/9 Frith Street,
London W1D 3JB, UK.

Music Sales Corporation,
257 Park Avenue South,
New York, NY 10010, USA.

Macmillan Distribution Services,
53 Park West Drive,
Derrimut, Vic 3030,
Australia.

To the Music Trade only
Music Sales Limited,
8/9 Frith Street,
London W1D 3JB, UK.

Every effort has been made to trace the copyright holders of the photographs in this book
but one or two were unreachable. We would be grateful if the photographers concerned
would contact us.

Printed in Great Britain by Creative Print & Design, Wales.
Typesetting by Galleon Typesetting, Ipswich.
A catalogue record for this book is available from the British Library.

Visit Omnibus Press on the web at www.omnibuspress.com

This book is dedicated to Alice McIver,
born on August 30, 2003.

Contents

Foreword

By Thomas Gabriel Fischer, Celtic Frost/Apollyon Sun

Is it possible to truly capture, by means of mere typed words on dry paper, a feeling as intense and pungent as almost no other, a spirit, a rebellion, an uncontrollable and fanatical adolescent urge? A music? Is it possible to accurately portray the attitude and mood of a time and a generation, if that very generation is propelled by something which cannot be expressed by words? By music?

I am tempted to say, no, it can't . . . Yet at the same time I believe it is extremely important that somebody attempts to do just that.

Metallica changed the face of modern rock music at least twice. The first time in the early Eighties, when they burst onto a brand-new scene of hungry kids looking to exorcise the lingering motionlessness and complacency of late-Seventies hard rock by applying the raw power the punk movement had so brazenly demonstrated. Metallica took this power, already roughly developed by the groups of the New Wave Of British Heavy Metal, and presented it to us in a completely new and utterly infectious form. And the second time came some ten years later, when they proved to that same scene, which itself had become a solid and unreservedly self-indulgent, industry-driven monster, how to still produce a ground-breaking masterpiece by releasing what is popularly referred to as 'the Black Album'.

To some, all this might not seem to be important. Fair enough. But for me, and for hundreds of thousands of others . . . it changed our lives. It became our world, and it remained part of the foundation of how we perceive music for the rest of our lives.

The very first time I heard Metallica, they still barely resembled what later became perhaps the most significant force in hard music. I was a teenager in what was purely an underground scene in 1981, '82, long before the introduction of things like home PCs, the internet or CDs. My friends and I tried to scrape together enough money to buy obscure

ix

new 7″ metal singles from correspondingly obscure insider record stores, and we would spend our Saturdays driving around for hours to find new releases, imported only by a few obsessive store owners in editions of perhaps one or two. I was also part of what had become a flourishing cassette trader network, where kids would copy and exchange new metal tracks by duplicating tapes and sending them to their contacts all over the world. Along with such cassette copies, we also received photocopied fanzines which listed an endless array of names of up-and-coming metal bands. Among these names was Metallica.

Two of my best friends at the time were older than me and already held 'real' jobs and made 'real' money. It was for that reason that they were able to get their hands on some of the hottest new music before the rest of us. They would put together cassette compilations for me, and, some time in 1982, one of these tapes contained a track that was faster and more intense than anything I had ever heard before. It was incredibly modern and included a seemingly never-ending lead guitar section which completely blew our minds. The track was 'Hit The Lights', and the band was Metallica. My friends had taped it for me from one of the first copies of the pioneering *Metal Massacre* compilation album.

There was an air of unpredictability in the era's musical development, and 'Hit The Lights' was a typical exponent. It was implausibly fresh, daring, extreme, and much more advanced than most of the music from the then still dominating British bands. A later edition of the same first *Metal Massacre* compilation album, which I rushed out to buy, contained a re-recorded version of 'Hit The Lights', and it already became apparent that Metallica were a band that wasn't content with staying stationary.

I was in England, and only months away from the release of the first recording of my own band, when I found Metallica's first album in a record store in late summer 1983. It is almost embarrassing, but *Kill 'Em All* remains in many ways my favourite Metallica release to this very day, as simple and spartan as it is and as much as Metallica have proven to be capable of musical invention since then. But *Kill 'Em All* was a revolution, and it is perhaps not so much the music itself which makes it so special, but rather the memory of what it did to a scene to which we all had dedicated our existence. It signifies an aura, an atmosphere, a unique emotion. And yet Metallica went on to record and produce one momentous album after another, and most of us in other bands owe much of our own successes to Metallica's sheer force and the fact that their music was strong and professional enough to once again make heavy rock a household music and a dominant market force.

When I first saw Metallica in concert in February 1984, they were opening for another band, and their performance began with technical problems which forced a re-start of the show. But they kicked ass and blew us all away nonetheless. This was but one of many indications that this band's live performances would become an uncompromising erup-tion of precisely executed music, which would have some bearing on nearly all other contemporary rock bands.

Metallica began and rose as an expression of adolescence, aggression, disagreement, rebellion, frustration – which means that more people were able to relate to their (in some eyes) archaic music than to any supposedly "serious" music of recent years. But how long can a band authentically represent such urges while at the same time turning into adults themselves and becoming hugely successful? Answering a ques-tion Joel posed to me some time ago, I told him something like this: being a musician who has relentlessly experimented and driven his own music to new frontiers, I know how much anybody genuinely creative sometimes needs to enforce a fresh and daring direction. I believe I understand why Metallica did this, too. I believe it was something they had to do, first and foremost for their own sanity. The music industry is an act of balance. You can become successful because you represent the new, the revolutionary, the audacious, yet when you again try exactly that, years down the road, your fans may have made your original revo-lution something household that isn't endorsed for any change. It is easy to appreciate the reasoning on both sides.

I applaud Joel's effort to shed some light on Metallica's rise and the reasons behind their development. I genuinely believe this book will be an enlightenment for all of us whose life has been touched by their music and their muscle.

Tom Gabriel Fischer
Zurich, Switzerland, May 2003

Introduction

This is a book that needed to be written, and there are several reasons for this.

Firstly, in their 20-year career to date Metallica have sold over 85 million CDs and albums, plus huge numbers of singles, videos, DVDs, box sets and merchandise. They are currently the seventh biggest-selling artists in US recording history, and even their closest competitors in the field of heavy rock and metal (enormous sellers in their own right such as Iron Maiden, Guns N'Roses, Korn, Linkin Park and Limp Bizkit come to mind) don't come close in commercial terms.

But these simple statistics give no indication of the cultural changes which Metallica have prompted. Their career has clearly been of two discernible halves – the first as a left-field extreme metal act and the second as a globally successful band with few peers. Somewhere between these two phases lies a ground-breaking album, 1991's *Metallica*, which changed the face of popular music. This record thrust aside all the rules of what heavy metal meant at the end of the 20th century and, in doing so, ushered in a whole range of new bands with a greater or lesser debt to pay to Metallica.

And along the way Metallica changed. They were once a thrash metal band, epitomising the style with highly aggressive, totally uncompromising music played at speeds ranging from fast to extremely fast. Played well, thrash metal is among the most exhilarating, demanding and downright venomous musical genres of all and, for eight years, it was Metallica's chosen speciality. They played it with utter commitment and jaw-dropping expertise, and amassed hundreds of thousands of fans in doing so.

However, the Nineties saw Metallica evolve their music into a slower, more thoughtful, even contemplative hybrid of bluesy, alternative rock and metal, to the confusion and disappointment of the more dedicated headbangers among their fanbase. Simultaneously, the ranks of the faithful were swelled enormously by new fans for whom Metallica's earlier work had been too raucous and who preferred the

new, smoother sounds. Suddenly, Metallica could be heard on the
radio and were seen on TV, a previously unthought-of development.
They released singles in large quantities for the first time. They toned
down their image. They wrote songs with non-metallic instrumentation and introspective, almost philosophical lyrics, only returning to the
older, brasher songs on the ever-more-enormous tours which made
them multimillionaires. They played alongside non-metal artists. They
made high-concept videos. They wore make-up.

To sum up, they shed their skin entirely. As the old-school fans
watched in horror, more and more new converts to the Metallica cause
appeared, and now – in 2003 – they are part and parcel of the establishment. They are a stadium band. They are an MTV band. They are –
wait for it – an *acceptable* band.

Surprisingly, no book on Metallica has yet appeared of sufficient scope
to address the whole of the phenomenon that is this remarkable band.
One or two smaller biographies have appeared over the years, all of
which have their virtues, but Metallica is now a truly heavyweight
institution and deserves a book of similar gravitas if their full story is to
be told. This, I hope, is that book.

Secondly, it's about time an author took the time to investigate every
(and I mean *every*) aspect of the Metallica machine. In order to make
this book as comprehensive as possible, I've gone to great lengths to
speak to as many people close to the band as possible and get the facts
out of them. There's no tabloid rumour-mongering here. This is the
real deal. This is the truth.

Which brings me to the title of this book, and the most compelling
reason why this book needed to be written. There are far too many
rumours about Metallica in circulation – inevitably so, given their size
and the cult popularity which they enjoy. I've read far too many articles
about them which fudge the truth, avoid certain areas of uncertainty or
are simply wrong about certain facts. This isn't the writers' fault: these
things happen because Metallica's roots are now two decades away, and
their genesis occurred in the midst of a confused, alcohol-fuelled music
scene set in a particularly dark, grimy environment: the punk and metal
underground scene in California in the early Eighties. It's only by going
directly to the people who were actually there at the time that the truth
can be revealed – and I've tried to do just that.

Finally, there are loads of irrational opinions flying around about Metallica. Check any website devoted to them. If you believed everything you read there, you'd come away with one of two impressions: either that Metallica are gods whose every word and act is worth intense celebration, and whose every musical note is unsurpassable – or that they are a bunch of sell-outs who lost their balls years ago and who are only interested in money for its own sake. Of course, neither of these views is wholly correct, although there are supporting arguments for either stance (as we'll see, believe me). But Metallica and their fans deserve a more balanced, unbiased view than these two extremes – and this, I truly believe, is it.

With this in mind I've structured the book to allow the story to flow without being held up by intermittent analysis. Like the best of Metallica's music, their story moves fast and unpredictably, so I've allocated the Truth chapters their own separate section every now and then.

This is the most comprehensive book about Metallica ever written, and is likely to remain so permanently unless the band choose to publish their own version a few years down the line. Enjoy the ride, and keep an open mind.

Authorisation
You may be wondering if I approached Metallica to request their authorisation for this book. The answer is no, I didn't. Not because of the likelihood of rejection, but because there are certain constraints which authorisation places on an author which I felt wouldn't have served my approach well, or indeed at all.

As you will see, I have levelled criticism at the band which would probably not have made it into an authorised book. Metallica have made several decisions across the years – musically, strategically and otherwise – which I regard as errors, and have said so in plain terms. These are hardly the stuff of authorised biography.

You may think I've been harsh on Metallica at times, and perhaps I have. But there are no criticisms here which aren't deserved. I'm a huge Metallica fan and am passionate about some of their material to an almost unhealthy degree – which means that where they have made a wrong decision in my view, or released music which is less than their best, I've said so. I hope you will understand why.

Sources & Acknowledgements

This book is based on original research. With the exception of a handful of respected and fully acknowledged sources, all the information contained in the book you are holding is taken from over 70 interviews which I personally carried out between 1996 and 2003. Some of these interviews were arranged as preparation for features which subsequently appeared in *Terrorizer*, *Bass Guitar* and *Record Collector* magazines: no more than 5 per cent of the interview material in this book has been previously published.

The interviewees I spoke to were all, without exception, physically present to witness events in the life of Metallica at first hand, or move in the same circles: many offer unparalleled perspectives on the band-members because they were actually with them as the story unfolded. They were *there*.

The generous people who spoke to me about Metallica were, in alphabetical order:

Musicians: Mikael Akerfeldt (Opeth); Tom Araya (Slayer); Erik Ashley (Unfaith); Jeff Becerra (Possessed); Denis 'Snake' Belanger (Voivod); Glen Benton (Deicide); John Bush (Anthrax); Max Cavalera (Soulfly); Phil Demmel (Vio-Lence/Technocracy/Machine Head); Katon DePena (Hirax); Tony Dolan (Atomkraft, Venom); Billy Duffy (The Cult); Jeff Dunn (Venom); Bobby 'Blitz' Ellsworth (Over Kill); Phil Fasciana (Malevolent Creation); Killjoy (Necrophagia); King Diamond (Mercyful Fate/solo); Ian Gillan (Deep Purple); Billy Gould (Faith No More); Sean Harris (Diamond Head); Steve Harris (Iron Maiden); Gene Hoglan (Dark Angel, Testament and others); Scott Ian (Anthrax); Joey Jordison (Slipknot); Mirai Kawashima (Sigh, Necrophagia); Ian 'Lemmy' Kilmister (Motörhead); Timo Kotipelto (Stratovarius); Dan Lorenzo (Hades); John Marshall (Metal Church); Jim Martin (Faith No More); Eric Meyer (Dark Angel); Dave Miranda (Ludichrist); Mortiis (ex-Emperor/solo); James Murphy (Death,

Testament and others); Dave Mustaine (Megadeth); Jason Newsted (ex-Metallica, Voivod); Eric Peterson (Testament); Mille Petrozza (Kreator); Quorthon (Bathory); Jonas Renkse (Katatonia); Byron Roberts (Bal-Sagoth); Hans Rutten (The Gathering); Samoth (ex-Emperor, Zyklon); Karl Sanders (Nile); Tony Scaglione (Whiplash); Silenoz (Dimmu Borgir); Gene Simmons (Kiss); Robert Sweet (Stryper); Brian Tatler (Diamond Head); Devin Townsend (Strapping Young Lad); Jan Transit (. . . In The Woods); Steve Tucker (Morbid Angel); Jeff Waters (Annihilator); Herr Wolf (Amestigon); Wolfgang Weiss (Cadaverous Condition).

Record company staff: Martin Hooker (ex-Music For Nations, now Dream Catcher); Brian Slagel (Metal Blade); Eddie Trunk (Megaforce); Jon Zazula (Megaforce).

Media: Bernard Doe (journalist); Ross Halfin (photographer); Borivoj Krgin (journalist); Bob Nalbandian (journalist and DJ); Martin Popoff (journalist); Garry Sharpe-Young (journalist); Sylvie Simmons (journalist); Lennart Wennberg (photographer).

Others: John Kornarens (collector); Jessica Litman (author and law professor, Wayne State University, Detroit); Flemming Rasmussen (producer); Ross Robinson (producer); Tomas Skogsberg (producer); Andy Sneap (producer); Torben Ulrich (Lars Ulrich's father).

Any sources other than my own interviews and research are fully credited.

As well as the interviewees listed above, to whom I am grateful for the time and energy they spent talking about Metallica and music in general, I wish to thank the following: Robin; Dad; John and Jen; Lucy, Johnny and Henry; Chris, Nadja and family; Arline, David and Lily; Lorraine and Ben; Phil and Kate; Quinn and Amy; Christian, Anita and family; Woody and Glynis; Belle and Tony; Dave; Jo; Dan; Louise; Bruce; Keith; Richie; Simone; Tim; Babs; the NCT posse; and Rupert (sleep well).

Also Chris Charlesworth and Helen Donlon at Omnibus Press; Thomas Gabriel Fischer (I'm honoured); Ian Glasper; Paul Stenning; Greg Moffitt; Martin Popoff; Garry Sharpe-Young; Colin Larkin; Daryl Easlea; Kas Mercer; Darren Edwards; Ross Halfin; Sylvie Simmons; Andy Turner; Donna O'Connor; Hammy and Lisa; Adrian Ashton; Tim Jones; Patrick Savelkoul; Billy Pilhatsch; Roland Hyams; Steve-O; Gillian Gaar; Alexander Hay; Rachel Clark; Greg Whalen;

Joachim Noske; Johnny Chandler; John Hoare and Mercury Rain; Karl Demata; Kyle Munson; Thor Christiansen; Doug Wright at MFN; Rich at Diamond Head's website; Steven Warner; Molly Martin and Torben Ulrich; Rob Malda at *Slashdot*.

In Sweden, thanks to Paulina at the Ljungby tourist office; Sven-Inge Idofsson at *Smålänningen*; Roland Vagnas of the Ljungby police department; photographer Lennart Wennberg; and the author Carl Magnus Palm for his translations.

Thanks to Cliff Burton and Chuck Schuldiner.

Emma and Alice give it all meaning.

Joel McIver, August 2003
Email: joel@joelmciver.co.uk
Website: www.joelmciver.co.uk

1

Before 1980

If the Metallica story is to begin anywhere, it might as well begin in a jazz club in Rome, where, on a May night in 1973, a bearded, music-loving Dane called Torben Ulrich took his ten-year-old son Lars to listen to a show by his friend, the 50-year-old tenor saxophonist Dexter Gordon.

Thirty years later, Ulrich can still snigger at the memory of that night. "The first time I saw Lars performing on stage was down in Rome," he remembers. "I'd been playing the Italian Open. Dexter was playing in a nightclub and Lars' mother and I went to see him. And all of a sudden, Lars went up on stage and sang into the microphone and ran around on the stage for a few moments." He pauses, shaking his head in amazement at the innate courage of a kid who would do such a thing. "It was like some dog who runs amok for a moment. It was very surprising to everyone."

And so the die was cast.

Lone Ulrich gave birth to Torben's first and only child on December 26, 1963, at Gentofte in Denmark. The boy they named simply Lars was fortunate in the privileges he would enjoy: his father was an internationally recognised tennis star and was active in many other areas as an actor, musician, writer and painter. He played for 20 years at Wimbledon, as did his own father, but he is now deeply philosophical about the talent that took him there. "What does it mean to have that sort of heritage?" he asks. "I try not to see it in very narrow terms — what it means conventionally — but also to view it in greater terms."

The deeply philosophical psyche of Torben Ulrich sheds invaluable light on the character of his son: for example, he has much to say on the nature of the tennis-ball-themed art which he has created over the years: "Cosmology comes up very quickly when you think about the balls, with the spheres and the planets. You investigate the limits of that perception if you try not to take the conventional measures. You say, what is ball-playing about, and you question the concept of winning and losing, and if you question that, you question the nature of play itself."

Torben's extra-curricular interests outside the tennis court included movie-making (he had collaborated on a film called *Motion Picture* in 1969) and acrylic painting, best exemplified by a long-running series of ink and rice-paper works called *Imprints Of Practice*, which he started in 1971 and exhibited in Paris, New York, Los Angeles and Seattle. Add to the résumé his spiritual interests (Torben had visited Indian teachers in music and yoga in the Fifties, as well as studying Japanese Zen in London in the Sixties) and the cultural depth which Lars observed, even as a child, is clear.

The Ulrich family was both well-travelled and well-connected. "Before Lars was born I played music and visited London," recalls Torben. "I was friends with Chris Barber, who is a trombonist who plays traditional jazz music. Humphrey Lyttelton too. I would play with him at 100 Oxford Street, we'd spend a lot of time there." The jazz influences which would mould Ulrich's own playing came from clearly defined sources. "I was a student of Sidney Bechet's work, both before I knew him and later on. Even in the late Forties I was interested in him. I travelled to France and saw some bands who were playing in the style of King Oliver and Louis Armstrong. Bechet was a big hero there, and I tried to get to Paris as often as I could to be around him."

Torben's relationship with the intense Bechet grew, but the tennis star's professional activities caused his mentor some consternation: "Slowly we developed a relationship where he was the teacher and I was the student," says Ulrich, with evident pleasure. "Then he saw in the paper that I had misbehaved on the tennis court and phoned me up and scolded me."

A certain stubborn extrovert quality might be inferred from the way that Ulrich refers so casually to his on-court 'misbehaviour' – but how much of this was the same exuberance shown in the antics of his son on stage with Dexter Gordon that night in Rome? It turns out that there is a reason for Lars' appearance on stage that night after all: Gordon was his godfather.

The Ulrichs and Gordon shared a similar itinerant lifestyle and Gordon settled in Denmark in the Seventies for a while – in Copenhagen, where the Ulrich family were living at the time. "There was an interest in Copenhagen in that kind of music: for example there was a club called the Montmartre," says Torben. "Stan Getz lived there for a while, and so did Bud Powell. Dexter came to Denmark after playing at the London jazz club Ronnie Scott's for a few weeks. There was a whole setting there, if you will, and we were the young guys who would follow it intimately and write about it." It was Ulrich's activities as a journalist which brought them together: "At the time I was writing about jazz for a Danish newspaper called *Politiken*. Dexter became a large figure in the nightlife in the late Fifties, into the Sixties and onwards. We would see him when we were travelling."

The two men developed their friendship and when Lars was born Gordon agreed to be his godfather, but circumstances dictated that they were unable to develop any kind of relationship. Gordon relocated to the USA shortly afterwards, as Torben recollects: "When they could have had a closer relationship, Dexter was either already living in New York, or was in bad shape, or had passed away."* But the memory of his godfather stayed with Lars in some form, it seems: "I remember Lars telling me that he had met Lionel Hampton on the road, and that he had told Lionel that Dexter Gordon was his godfather," adds Torben. "They had a good long talk about that in some breakfast place."

Even in Gordon's absence, Lars began to soak up the music he heard around him from a very early age. "There were always musicians around the house from the day he was born," recalls Torben. An early turning point came when Lars was 10, in 1973, when a family friend visited: "We had a good friend called Ray Moore, a South African player, who was playing in Copenhagen. Ray took Lars to see his first concert," says Torben now.

The nine-year-old boy was so smitten by the show that he went into the city the next day and bought the new album by the group he had seen. The record was called *Fireball*. And the band that had so impressed was Deep Purple.

★ ★ ★

* Dexter Gordon died on April 25, 1990.

Several thousand miles and a whole universe away, a generation of American children and young adolescents were experiencing the same rush that Lars Ulrich felt on seeing Deep Purple for the first time. In the mid-Seventies, American rock fans were in thrall to homegrown stadium fillers such as Kiss, Aerosmith, Ted Nugent and ZZ Top; huge sellers who toured the cities and heartlands with equal diligence until the point came where each new album from any of them wasn't merely a release – it was An Event. They were following in the footsteps of the British rock bands who had spent years establishing vast followings in America, groups in the vanguard, like The Rolling Stones and The Who, then the second tier bands like Black Sabbath, Deep Purple and – most notably of all – Led Zeppelin, whose over-the-top histrionics, spitfire blues and bludgeoning riffs established the idea that heavy rock could be British and cool at the same time.

If you were born in the early Sixties and were living in the more liberal areas of the USA like Los Angeles and San Francisco, and you enjoyed rock music, you would almost certainly have developed a fondness for the music of these acts. The concept of 'heavy metal' was still quite new in the minds of most fans, who would happily listen to Meat Loaf, Kansas, Journey, Vanilla Fudge and Blue Cheer and classify it all as 'rock' without worrying too much (or at all) about which category it belonged to.

One such fan was David Mustaine, born on September 13, 1961 in La Mesa in California, a community east of San Diego. His home life was more or less diametrically opposed to the privileged upbringing which Lars Ulrich was enjoying in Denmark. Dave's father is alleged to have been troubled and unstable, whose erratic behaviour forced Mustaine and his mother to move house frequently. By 1974, Dave had been introduced to the pleasures of pop music via his sister, a Cat Stevens fan, although he was tiring of the gentility of confessional singer-songwriters and beginning to explore the world of rock. Like so many insecure American teenagers, he was drawn to Led Zeppelin, as he told the author in 1999: "*Houses Of The Holy* or *Four Sticks* [sic]* were my favourite records . . . Or The Beatles' *White Album*. I would just listen to them and not even realise that I had gone to the turntable

---

* Presumably Dave is referring to Led Zeppelin's untitled fourth album, which includes the track 'Four Sticks'.

to flip the disc. That was just a mind–melding period for me."

As time passed, Dave began teaching himself to play the guitar, although he made one or two decisions he regretted despite his growing fondness for music: "Led Zeppelin did come through my town once, but this was just after *The Song Remains The Same* had come out and I thought that they were starting to lose it, so I didn't go. I was just becoming a cocky young guitar player at the time, and I had no idea how much I'd cheated myself." But music remained his obsession, and by the late Seventies Mustaine was jamming with other musicians.

His first successful band was an outfit named Panic.

Meanwhile, elsewhere in California, another, less troubled kid by the name of Kirk Lee Hammett was growing up and getting into rock music at the same time as Mustaine, although he wouldn't start learning the guitar until his fifteenth year in 1977. Born on January 18, 1962, Kirk grew up in El Sobrante, a valley community located not far from San Francisco.

Kirk was a rock fan from an early age, recalling via a webchat hosted by Twec.com in 2000: "I loved Jimi Hendrix, Kiss, Aerosmith, and ZZ Top, and I felt that if I learned how to play their music, I'd become closer to them, I'd be unlocking some sort of mystery. When you learn how to play someone's music, it answers questions on a musical level, but it remains a mystery on other levels. I just felt that if I made their music, I'd be making a connection to them."

The half-Irish, half-Filipino Hammett was the middle child between an older brother Rick, who encouraged him to learn the guitar, and a younger sister Tracy; his father was a naval officer and his mother a government employee. The pensive, almost cerebral Hammett was clearly a child of unusual spirituality, even at a young age, although this didn't stop him celebrating the rawer end of heavy rock and working hard to improve his skills and equipment.

Kirk's first guitar was a Montgomery Ward model ordered from a catalogue, which he played through a home-made amplifier, con-structed from a shoebox and a four-inch speaker. After many hours of practice he managed to scrape together the funds for a 1978 Fender Stratocaster, which he constantly adjusted in the hunt for an improved sound. A sojourn at Burger King gave him the money for a Marshall amp and he began looking for other musicians to play with: his hunt ended when he met a singer named Paul Baloff. The pair decided to form a band called Exodus, and started to write material together.

About three weeks after Kirk's birth, a couple who lived just east of San Francisco named Jan and Ray Burton had a son, Clifford Lee. Born on February 10, 1962, the young Cliff was the youngest of three children (he had a brother, Scott, and a sister, Connie) and was an active child, playing Little League baseball for the Castro Valley Auto House team and studying firstly at Earl Warren Junior High and then Castro Valley High School. During his vacations, Cliff was always busy: he worked at an equipment rental yard called Castro Valley Rentals and spent time with his friends, hunting, playing music and fishing.

The biggest change in his teenage life came when Cliff began to learn the bass guitar. He had studied music theory at school and made rapid progress in the lessons he took on the instrument from September 1978 to January 1980, and it wasn't long before he was in demand with local groups. One band he played with was called AD 2 Million, another was Agents Of Misfortune (after the Blue Oyster Cult record of the same name) and consisted of Cliff and a guitarist called Jim Martin, who would later find fame as a member of Faith No More. The only band which Burton and Martin placed much stock in, however, was an outfit called EZ Street, which also featured the future Faith No More/Ozzy Osbourne drummer Mike 'Puffy' Bordin, although his place was sporadically filled by a friend, Dave Donato.

Martin, who is now living away from the public eye after several years in Faith No More, remembers those times clearly: "I started teaching myself electric guitar around 1974 and wanted to find other musicians to jam with," he recalls. "I hooked up with a singer and a guitar player who'd been playing Rolling Stones covers together around the campfire, and we talked about forming a band. My neighbour played drums, so we got him. We found a bass player who later quit and recommended a fella to take his place. His name was Cliff Burton."

The problem of finding suitable rehearsal space was solved when the musicians' parents allowed them – perhaps unwisely – to use their homes to practise in: "We went through a few rehearsals at the homes of our parents, who were good enough to indulge us on a rotating basis," says Martin, before adding: "Generally they would leave the house. Things got broken. Puffy's next-door neighbours' baby went to the hospital and the neighbours accused us of killing the baby." As might be expected, EZ Street didn't create much of a buzz. Martin recalls, "We played a few talent contests, the church fiesta, and parties. Our only paying gig was in Berkeley, a dive called the International Café. It was run by a couple of Greeks. They loved us; all our friends would come out to see us and we'd drink the place dry. We were about 15 at the time."

Cliff had a quixotic personality, which manifested itself in many bizarre ways. He drove a green Volkswagen (which he dubbed 'the Grasshopper') and his musical tastes ranged from Bach and Beethoven to out and out rock. But he had darker influences, too: his elder brother Scott died of cancer at the age of just 16, an event which seems to have affected Cliff's character as he grew older. Asked to elaborate on the character of his friend Cliff, Jim Martin becomes thoughtful: "Cliff and I spent our formative years as musicians together. Dave Donato was also a big part of that. We all three used to go to a remote cabin in the California coastal mountains and experiment with crazy, weird music. We'd just play whatever came up, stuff right from the top of our heads. Some Faith No More and Metallica songs that you are familiar with were germinated during these sessions." The results are rumoured to exist on an unreleased recording called the *Maxwell Ranch Tapes*, although few people claim to have heard them.

Like most of their acquaintances, Martin was both entertained and charmed by Cliff's slight eccentricity – evident not least in his choice of instrument: "He played an old Rickenbacker with a crazy thing called 'Bass Balls' through a Sunn amp with a single 18-inch cabinet. This 'Bass Balls' was like an automatic wah-wah pedal." But despite his unorthodox ways, Cliff had simple tastes. "He liked to fish and drink beer. Shoot and drink beer. We'd go to concerts and see the new metal bands and hang out," says Jim. He also knew when to be polite. "He and his folks lived in an apartment, so we'd have to be real quiet whenever we were there. Cliff would make huge food and we'd rock out real quiet like."

There was a definite air of self-confidence about Cliff. "He figured he could pretty much make things go any way he wanted, and he taught me to think that way," says Martin. Eventually they parted. "Cliff left EZ Street, and I kept the band going for a little while with an ever-changing cast of characters. I started playing in lots of bands; I think I was in four bands at one time, so I was pretty much doing it every night. Cliff and I would still get together to jam, mostly with drummer Dave Donato."

Among the audience at an early EZ Street show was Kirk Hammett, who was putting his own band, Exodus, together and was checking out local musicians. He later recalled that Cliff's amplifier blew up during the set, but rather than leave the stage, the bass player simply sat down in front of the amp and headbanged.

Martin joined Faith No More shortly afterwards, after Cliff suggested to Puffy that he should consider him as a guitarist. But Cliff's Jim Martin connection was not quite laid to rest: together with Puffy, FNM bassist Bill Gould and Burton, the guitarist played a single gig at the Mabuhay Gardens in San Francisco – with an inspired choice of name: "We were called the Chicken Fuckers," laughs Bill Gould now. "There's not much to tell, it was just one show – it was a giant jam. We drank as much and smoked as much weed as we could and went on stage with no real rehearsal." And how did you go down with the audience? "Horribly! That was the idea! It was fun, though."

Burton – whom Gould describes as "a very, very cool guy. Super bright, super perceptive . . . he had a big heart" – had other plans beyond joke bands, though. He left EZ Street to join a San Francisco act called Trauma, a well-known Bay Area band which other groups admired for their musical excellence. The band began gigging locally and Cliff soon developed a reputation for the bass solos which he would perform over the rhythm guitars, unusual at the time. Label interest soon began to grow, with one particularly motivated observer an LA-based metal fan called Brian Slagel.

Around two thousand miles away, a teenager named Jason Curtis Newsted was similarly dedicated to learning how to rock. Born on March 4, 1963 in the town of Battle Creek, Michigan, and raised in the city of Niles until the age of 14, Jason may have been inspired to learn an instrument by his family's relocation in 1977 to Kalamazoo, close to the headquarters of the world-famous Gibson guitar company. The new home was a farm, where Jason enjoyed looking after the horses which the Newsteds kept: he lived an active, sports-filled life alongside his two elder brothers and younger sister. His siblings also introduced him to music (the Osmonds and the Jackson 5 were reportedly family favourites) while his parents, Bob and Jo Newsted, also owned a piano.

Although Jason was a good student, school in Kalamazoo proved to be not to his taste and he dropped out before graduation (he has since gained his leaving diploma). Music was an alternative to study, it seemed: Jason's first attempt at music was a failed effort to learn bass guitar (he had been moved to choose the instrument because of his hero, Kiss bassist Gene Simmons) and a stint at his father's piano. However, a second attempt to learn the bass proved more enduring and he joined a local band, Gangster, with his friend and occasional guitar teacher Tim Hamlin.

While Lars Ulrich remained cocooned in the bosom of his well-off, culturally literate family in Copenhagen, Dave Mustaine's family planned their next move with one eye on the unpredictable Mustaine Senior, Kirk Hammett practised his guitar in El Sobrante, Cliff Burton strolled through the Bay Area woods with Jim Martin, and Jason Newsted cooled his heels in darkest Michigan, another family were getting through the trials and tribulations of life in the Seventies with help that only they could count on: the power of faith, as defined by Christian Science, a branch of the church which cherishes spiritual balance and the strength of self-healing.

Virgil and Cynthia Hetfield lived with their three children, David, James and DeDe in Los Angeles: Virgil was a truck driver with a small distribution company of his own, while his wife was a singer. Their middle son, James Alan, was born on August 3, 1963 and had demonstrated some early musical talent with two years of piano lessons, although these ultimately led to nothing. More successful were his attempts to play the drum kit which belonged to his older brother David, who played in a band, and his decision to turn to guitar in his early teens.

Although James always maintained that his parents loved and supported him, he was shaken by their divorce in 1976. The following year James enrolled at Downey High School in southern LA where he came across others who shared his interest in rock (and in Kiss and Aerosmith in particular): Dave Marrs and Ron McGovney. They met at East Middle School, where James was notable in music class for being the only student who could already play the guitar. In 1993 Ron told *Shockwaves* radio interviewer Pat O'Connor that in September 1977, when the pupils in his year started high school, "Everybody had their little clique . . . there was the cheerleaders, the jocks, the marching band people . . . and you ended up with the laggers hanging around without any real social group, and that included James and I." A misfit even at this early stage, Hetfield took refuge in Aerosmith. According to McGovney, "He was a total Steven Tyler freak. And our friend Dave Marrs was a total Kiss freak . . . they would make fun of the music I listened to, so in return, I would tell them Kiss sucked and Aerosmith sucked, and it went back and forth." As Hetfield's guitar skills improved he began to toy with the idea of joining a band.

James was something of an outsider as a result of his family's beliefs. As he later told *Playboy*: "I was raised as a Christian Scientist, which is a strange religion. The main rule is, God will fix everything. Your body is just a shell, you don't need doctors. It was alienating and hard to understand. I couldn't get a physical to play football. It was weird having to leave health class during school, and all the kids saying, 'Why do you have to leave? Are you some kind of freak?' As a kid, you want to be part of the team. They're always whispering about you and thinking you're weird. That was very upsetting. My dad taught Sunday school – he was into it. It was pretty much forced upon me. We had these little testimonials, and there was a girl that had her arm broken. She stood up and said, 'I broke my arm but now, look, it's all better.' But it was just, like, mangled. Now that I think about it, it was pretty disturbing." Famously, these experiences would go on to colour James' life and work.

By 1980, Hetfield had formed a band called Obsession, which included his friends Ron and Rich Veloz on bass and drums respectively, and a second guitarist, Jim Arnold. During rehearsals in the garage at the home of the Veloz brothers, James sang and played guitar on the band's painfully raw renditions of Black Sabbath, Led Zeppelin and Deep Purple songs such as 'Never Say Die', 'Communication Breakdown' and 'Highway Star', as well as material by Thin Lizzy and UFO. Jim Arnold and Ron Veloz would swap vocal duties with

Hetfield from time to time, as the band tried to ascertain who was its most natural (or least untalented) singer.

McGovney, a close friend of James, roadied for Obsession when they performed at the occasional backyard party and attended their rehearsals at the Veloz house. He told O'Connor that Rich and Ron had set up some stage lights in the garage which he and his friend Dave Marrs would manipulate via a home-made control panel. But the relationship with the Veloz brothers wasn't destined to last, and after around 18 months James, Jim Arnold and the latter's brother Chris broke away to form another band, Syrinx, which specialised solely in Rush covers and didn't last long.

No recordings of either Obsession or Syrinx are known to exist, although hearing any such tapes would be a revelation for Metallica fans accustomed to Hetfield's melodic roar of today. Back then James' voice was fairly weak and his ability to hit and then hold a note was barely adequate. Furthermore, improvements would not take place for some time, as the Hetfield family was struck by a tragedy: not long after James left Syrinx, his mother died of cancer. Ron McGovney had no recollection of his friend mentioning his mother's illness to him: "We had no idea. He was gone for like ten days and we thought he had gone on vacation. When he told us that his mom had just died, we were stunned."

Hetfield, then 16, met his friends by the lockers on his return to school and informed them he was about to move house and school. "Our jaws dropped, we didn't know what to say," says Ron. "He said, 'I have to clean out my locker now and move in with my brother in Brea and go to Brea Olinda High School.' And we were like, no way, this isn't happening."

The move duly took place, although McGovney still saw his friend at weekends. Meanwhile, Dave Marrs attempted to play the drums: "We sounded terrible," recalled Ron. However, while James must have been crushed by the experience he was going through, the move to a new school appears to have motivated him to do something posi-tive about his band. Having met a guitarist at Brea Olinda called Hugh Tanner, James formed another outfit with the typically metallic title of Phantom Lord, encouraging Ron to take up the bass guitar. "I told him I didn't know how to play bass and I didn't even have a bass guitar," said Ron later. "James said, 'I'll show you how to play,' so we rented a bass and an amp at Downey Music Center and James showed me the basics, how to follow him on guitar." As McGovney explained to *Shockwaves*, Phantom Lord was the nearest Hetfield had come to assembling a serious band: "We jammed with Hugh Tanner for a little while, he was actually a pretty good guitar player . . . [and] put out an ad for a guitar player . . . a guy named Troy James answered it and he joined our band."

Nothing stood still for long at this stage, however, and it was only a matter of months before James' band underwent yet another mutation. It was a stroke of luck when McGovney's parents, who owned three houses in the area, allowed them to move into one of them rent free, as it was shortly to be demolished to make way for a new freeway, US 105. "At the time my parents' homes were being taken away by the state in order to construct the new freeway . . . and they told me I could live in it since it was soon going to be torn down," explained Ron. "After we graduated from high school James and I moved into that house and we fixed up the garage into a rehearsal studio. We insulated it and put up dry wall and James painted the rafters black, the ceiling silver, the walls white, and red carpet!"

Phantom Lord, once installed in the McGovney rental house, became Leather Charm, a more glam-rock-influenced band which Ron recalls as, ". . . like Mötley Crüe, Sweet, and this British band called Girl . . . we did a bunch of covers as well, like 'Pictured Life' from The Scorpions, 'Wrathchild' and 'Remember Tomorrow' from Iron Maiden, and 'Slick Black Cadillac' from Quiet Riot."

Hetfield now revealed a previously dormant urge to be a frontman rather than a guitarist tied to a microphone stand: "He wanted to be the singer-frontman, so it was just Troy James on guitar. We started working on three original tunes, one ended up to be 'Hit The Lights', which became a Metallica song, another song called 'Handsome Ransom', and a song called 'Let's Go Rock'n'Roll'," remembered Ron. "We never really played any gigs. Jim Mulligan decided he wanted to play more progressive, Rush-type music. He was a real good drummer, very technical, and I guess he thought we were a little too heavy or too glam for him at the time."

James himself was a stadium-rock fan. As he told *Rolling Stone*: "Probably the most memorable [show I remember] was the California World Music Festival. It was one of those two-day things. The first night was Ted Nugent and Van Halen – no, Aerosmith. I must have been 15 or 16. I remember following around my buddy, who was selling drugs. He tore up a part of his ticket – it had a kind of rainbow edge – and he cut it into bits and sold it as acid. I was like, what are you doing, man? He used the money to buy beer. I was a huge Aerosmith fan. I couldn't believe I was seeing them so close. I worked my way up there as far as I could. There was something magical about seeing them as actual live people, not just pictures on an album. The real coolness of Joe Perry, especially. It's impossible for him to be uncool. And I remember I was blown away by the fact that Steven was calling the crowd motherfuckers. I was like, whoa – are you *supposed* to do that?"

James would look back on his younger years with mixed feelings for most of the next three decades. What does all this turmoil add up to, in terms of the development of the young Hetfield's character? Perhaps, at this stage at least, no more than the usual teenage rebellion and thirst for new experiences. By the time he was in his late teens, James had developed a taste for beer and partying in equal measure, as many of his contemporaries recall to this day. Drummer Gene Hoglan, who would later play with a series of bands including Dark Angel, Death, Testament, Strapping Young Lad and Old Man's Child, has perhaps the earliest recollection of the young Hetfield in action: "I met James at a backyard party one time in 1981," he remembers. "Ozzy Osbourne had just played the week before with Motörhead. I saw this guy walking around this party with a home-made Iron Maiden T-shirt on. I was like, dude! Where did you get that shirt?" Hetfield, who was a few years older than the admittedly precocious Hoglan, responded in a gravelly, unfriendly voice. "He said, 'I made it!' – and he walked away. And I tracked him down and said, 'Where did you make it?' He's like, 'I made it in high school.' So I said, 'I got ten bucks on me right now' – and that was a lot back then – 'Let me buy that shirt from you!' And he went, 'No.'"

Gene, a persistent kid, was not to be swayed so easily, and persevered: "OK, so I said, 'Here's ten bucks, will you make me a shirt?' 'No, fuck off, kid.' And I followed him round the whole party. Like, 'Dude – I am so excited to find anyone who is into Iron Maiden. Nobody's heard of Iron Maiden! Please make me a shirt!' 'No, fuck you!' He was a prick to me all night. In the end I said, 'OK, whatever.'" Chastened, Hoglan left Hetfield with his beer and went off to mourn his lost opportunity. The teenage Hetfield was, it seems, either too haughty to mingle with annoying juniors, or simply too interested in the free-flowing booze to be bothered with the T-shirt conversation. Gene has the last word, however, adding: "And then eight months later I saw him playing a show and I was like, hey, that's the same fucker who wouldn't help me out with the Iron Maiden shirt! Fuck you, I hate you!" although he's laughing as he recalls this.

Eric Peterson, who became the guitarist and principal songwriter in the metal band Testament, remembers James from a little later on: "I used to go to keggers (parties centring on a keg or barrel of beer) with James, he went out with my cousin at one point. He was cool, he was funny, man." What kind of party animal was the young Hetfield? Something of an unreconstructed man's man, it seems: "I'm sure he's a lot different now, of course," recalls Eric, "but back then he burped a lot, was always looking for a good Mexican place to eat, and whenever we went to a party, he would hang out near the keg and just talk hella funny. He would say, 'Goddammit!' all night long. Some people knew who he was and would walk up to him, and he would say, 'Goddammit!' all night long in all these different voices. People would go, 'That guy's a nut!'"

Another die was cast, it appears. James had embraced his first loves: partying and playing the guitar. Nothing would be the same again.

2

1980–1981

As rock and its attendant distractions became the primary focus in the young James Hetfield's life, half a planet away in Copenhagen the Ulrich family were approaching something of a crossroads. For a variety of reasons, in August 1980 Torben, Lone and Lars packed their possessions and moved from their home country to America, specifically to the affluent Los Angeles suburb of Newport Beach.

The reasons for the move have long been supposed to be that Lars' parents wanted him to play tennis professionally, but in fact this was far from the sole or even primary reason. "I think it was a complex of things," Torben explains. "In those years I was beginning to go back and forth and play tennis out of Denmark. I was writing about music for the Danish newspapers, and travelling to London and New York to write, or maybe also to play tennis. All those years we were operating in and out of Denmark. Lars' grandparents had a large house on the coastline west of (the Danish town of) Elsinore, so we could be there a lot and we could also be in town where we had this house. And then Lars went to school there and I would come back there."

So far, so logical. "But then in the late Seventies things changed," Torben continues. "Lars' mother's parents died and I had begun to play more and more in the Grand Masters, a tour for the older players. There were more and more tournaments in Hong Kong and so on, and I felt that it was harder and harder for me to get back to Denmark from these places. And also, as you get older it becomes more stressful to travel so extensively. I felt that I needed more rest in between."

Then there was the question of Lars' own potential as a professional sportsman. The young Dane had shown a remarkable aptitude for tennis – perhaps inevitably, given his pedigree – to the extent that his parents were prepared to support his decision to make it his career if he

15

so chose. But there was a snag: ever since that first fateful Deep Purple concert in Copenhagen, Lars had become fascinated with rock music to the point of obsession. "It was a question at that time of trying to find out if Lars wanted to continue with the tennis, or if he wanted to continue with the music that he was so interested in," says Torben. "So we thought if we moved for a little while that all these things would be addressed, and he could see which way he wanted to go."

Wasn't it a rather drastic move? Couldn't Lars have decided on tennis or music at home in Denmark? Apparently not – individuals in the Ulrichs' circle often took a year out to explore their options: "It was normal in Europe at the time that you could take a year off after school to decide what you wanted to do. And looking at Borg and McEnroe for instance, it was obvious that people were starting earlier and earlier with tennis. You could go to school if you wanted. But we decided that we would take a year and he could decide what he wanted. It was a fair question because he was so into music and the sport. It wasn't too much of a problem to see what he wanted to do and for us to decide what we wanted, especially with all the Grand Masters going on. So the move was a multiplicity of circumstances."

There was an additional incentive for the move to Newport Beach, as Torben explains: "We had very good friends in Newport Beach, including Roy Emerson, the Australian who had won Wimbledon – Pete Sampras became the first player to win more Grand Slams than him a couple of years ago. Roy had two children, one called Anthony, who Lars had known for many years. Lars went to Australia when he was two or three and knew Anthony from then."

The tennis culture was firmly in place in Newport Beach and Lars' parents wasted no time in establishing their son there. "The Emersons moved to that area south of LA and Lars went to school at Corona Del Mar High School in the Newport Beach area: Anthony was playing tennis on the school team there, and Lars thought it would be interesting to link up with Anthony by going to that school. So if he was going to that school, we needed to find a place in the vicinity. The place was ideal from the point of view of practising – there were several courts, plus several players, including Bobby Riggs, who won Wimbledon in 1939, plus the Emersons, with whom we were travelling on the Grand Masters. The Emersons used to receive his copy of *Sounds* magazine for him, and he'd go over there and pick it up."

Ah yes – *Sounds*, the now-defunct British music paper which advanced the cause of heavy metal more than any other publication of the era. The magazine was the perfect accompaniment to Lars' burgeoning interest in rock music, having first championed punk and gone on to cover any kind of rock wherein the beat overshadowed the melody. Furthermore, *Sounds* probably offered a link between the teenage rocker's Danish home and his new environment of California insofar as the British magazine was available only as an import or by subscription in both countries (and was therefore attached to neither), and more importantly because it was the main source of information anywhere on the music which Lars was growing to love more than anything else – the home-grown British heavy metal movement which became known by the turn of the decade as the New Wave Of British Heavy Metal, or NWOBHM (a phrase coined by sometime *Sounds* editor Alan Lewis).

In 1977 Lars had been given his first drum kit by his parents, not (as popular legend has it) by his grandmother. His grandmother did buy him a set, but that came later: by that time he had learned a little technique, but not much. As Torben recalls, "He played melodies on the drums which he would call tunes!" while listening to Deep Purple and Kiss in his bedroom. His father was undisturbed by his young son's increasing interest in heavy music: a liberal and a cultured arts critic, Torben had heard it all before: "I was interested in the music he listened to," he explains now. "I was into Indian music, classical music, John Cage . . . and I'm still interested in listening to British groups like Coil. I listen to all of that." As for metal, the traditionally parent-scaring music, Torben affirms: "I wasn't at all shocked by heavy metal. Not at all!"

It was certainly unusual for anyone living in California to pick up on the NWOBHM at the turn of the Seventies, despite the state's traditionally free-thinking culture. The sunshine-soaked boulevards of Los Angeles and San Francisco were better suited to the lingering strands of Eagles-style country rock and the endless good vibe jams of the Grateful Dead, and the macho stadium rock peddled by Aerosmith and their ilk. The New Wave Of British Heavy Metal was crude, poorly produced and played by musicians with rudimentary talents, at least in its earliest years. Even the punk movement, which had peaked by 1980, was now populated by more competent players than had been the case four years previously. NWOBHM bands such as Venom, Angel Witch, Tygers Of Pan Tang, Anvil and Saxon were hardly acknowledged for their virtuosity or the clarity of their sound, although Iron Maiden were a notable exception on both counts.

What these bands did have, however, was an abundance of passion. Fans picked up on this and admired it, not least because this contrasted sharply with the airbrushed calmness and dry virtuosity of more radio-friendly bands – and for some reason, it was the UK acts which were most welcomed in the US at this time. Many British heavy rock and metal musicians have over the years been pleasantly surprised, not to mention flattered, by the reception they receive in America, particularly on its west coast. Motörhead's Lemmy is one of them: "They still believe in rock'n'roll, the magic of it, and so do I, whereas the audiences [in Britain] have got that blasé 'entertain me' thing, which is not very conducive to a good show, you know. So fuck 'em . . . I've never been a partisan of living in the country you were born in – that's just uninventive, really. To go and live somewhere else is a real turnaround, it makes you think of everything differently. Travel is the only real education, and the only way to find out about the other people in the world, because when you travel you see people as they really are."

Guitarist Billy Duffy of The Cult agrees wholeheartedly, adding specifically that California has much to offer the beleaguered British musician: "We went to America and ended up in LA. And there was everything there that I liked – attractive members of the opposite sex, good weather, and good clothes. We went over with the *Love* album in 1985, which was getting an absolute panning [in the UK]. We were getting totally whipped, so we went to America and everything that was negative here was positive over there. And I won't be the last musician who'll ever say that to you. After growing up in England, it just seemed like an antidote to all that misery and gloom."

Many American metal fans needed the NWOBHM as much as our British performers needed them for their open-mindedness. One band which came after Metallica yet performed with similar passion (if far less success), was Hirax, a powerful outfit fronted by the manic Katon DePena, an adept frontman whose devotion to the cause never wavered and who is to this day an NWOBHM expert to match Ulrich himself. He remembers: "The New Wave Of British Heavy Metal became our new saviour. Anything we could get our hands on . . .

Diamond Head, Angel Witch, Tygers Of Pan Tang, Tank, Motörhead, Saxon, Iron Maiden, Girlschool, Venom, Samson, Trust. We'd search high and low to find those records." Asked if these bands inspire him to this day, DePena vehemently replies: "Hell yes! I'm like a NWOBHM encyclopedia! I love the trivia – even bands that had a 7″ or a 12″ EP. If it's from that period of time, I probably know about it. I think it's so sad that those bands don't get enough credit. Diamond Head for one! I will always remember the bands that have influenced Hirax and will always pay respect to them."

With fans like this worshipping them in America, it seems strange that so few British bands came over and played there. But the reason for this is simple: most of the NWOBHM acts were signed to small UK labels such as Neat, which lacked the funds to support a tour of the US or any other far-flung territory. Although more universally popular metal bands like Judas Priest and Motörhead infiltrated the American touring circuit and took NWOBHM bands along as support, most of the British acts were confined to their home patch, with the occasional European festival slot.

This meant that fans like Lars Ulrich had to be satisfied, for the moment at least, with getting their metal fix from magazines such as *Sounds* and with buying records at the few specialist import shops. However, once Lars had settled in Newport Beach, he began to network a little and in 1981 he struck up a friendship with two LA-based metal fans called John Kornarens and Brian Slagel. As John says: "Brian was a hardcore tape trader: I met him at a record sale and swap meet. He lived out in Willow Hills, and he had a load of bootleg tapes to sell. So I called him in mid-1980, about a month before I met Lars. I was a couple of years older than them."

Kornarens, an affable fellow who has been involved with the heavy metal scene for many years, looks back in amusement at the exact date when he met Lars Ulrich for the first time: "Here's how Lars enters the picture. On December 22, 1980, the Michael Schenker Group was playing at the Country Club. It was a great show, and afterwards every-body's hanging out in the parking lot. My ears are ringing, and I look around and there's a bunch of people, and one of them is this little guy with a Saxon tour T-shirt on. And I say to myself, 'Hey, I'm not the only one who knows about Saxon!' So I walk over and introduce myself and say, 'Hey, where did you get that shirt?' So he says, 'I saw them when I was over in Europe.' And I say, 'You saw Saxon?' And he says, 'Yeah, how do *you* know who Saxon is?' I said, 'I've got their albums.' And his eyes light up and he says, 'Really? What else do you have?' And I said, 'Well, I've just bought the new Angel Witch single' – and he about dropped on the ground! So we spent an hour talking. We hit it off right away."

They wasted no time in checking out each other's music collections: "Lars lived in Newport Beach in a town house with his parents: at the time I met him he either had a paper round or he was working in a gas station. So a few days after that he came up to my house in his mom's 1975 AMC Pacer car, a weird-looking old thing. And once a week we'd go back and forth and bring our tapes." Kornarens also introduced Lars to his friend Brian, which led to the three teenagers making regular visits to record shops all over LA. "After a while I said to Lars, 'Let's go up to my friend Brian's house, he's got a lot of stuff too.' And Brian said, 'Yeah, bring him up.' So after a while we'd all hop in my car and go driving to different record stores. There were three or four around, a couple in the Valley and a couple over the hill, and we would go there to see what new imports they'd got."

John remembers Lars' almost fanatical enthusiasm for imported heavy metal with some amusement: "I wouldn't even have the car fully stopped and shut off before Lars was flying out of the car and into the shop, so he could get in there and get the good stuff before we got there!" Slagel confirms this with a laugh: "We spent the whole of the next year running around the record stores trying to find that stuff. There weren't many stores that imported it, but there were a few. At the time, finding someone who knew the scene and who had been in Europe was awesome! Lars was a good guy, a couple of years younger than John and I and more high-energy than us – we always joked that he'd be out of the car and into the store before I'd even shut off the motor! He lived kinda far away, so it wasn't like we saw each other every day. He had all the records I didn't have, and I had a lot of records he didn't have."

As well as nursing his metal-collecting habit, Lars also had big plans for a band of his own. His drum kit was still set up in his bedroom and he would often talk to John and Brian about his ideas for making music. As Brian recalls: "We used to go over to his house and listen to records. He had this drum kit set up in the corner, and he'd be like,

'I'm gonna start a band! I'm gonna start a band!' and we'd say, 'Yeah, yeah . . . sure you are!' I think he was just starting to learn to play when he first moved here – it took him a while before he first set up the drum set."

Kornarens took Lars' boasting no more seriously than Slagel did, even ignoring Ulrich's outbursts entirely at times: "Lars lived in a three-room town house; his bedroom was in the front, facing the courtyard, and his parents were in the back, and there was this little room in the middle. And he said, 'Uh, I'm gonna start a band, I'm gonna be a drummer.' And he opens this little door up in the middle room and the whole room was a white drum set. It was filling up the room. He stood behind it and started banging away, not really knowing what he was doing – and I said, 'Yeah, yeah, yeah,' and closed the door and went back into his room to look at more stuff!"

While Lars was flailing at his white drum kit, across the city James Hetfield and Ron McGovney's musical ambitions were almost as undeveloped, although at least they had mastered their instruments enough to play coherently with each other. Although Ron's bass skills had improved thanks to some tuition from Hetfield, their songwriting hadn't improved an awful lot, with songs among their repertoire including 'Hades Ladies' and some covers – or, as McGovney later put it, "some really terrible stuff". The house they were living in was now better equipped for music-making and leisure: they had soundproofed the garage (despite the fact that there were no neighbours) and had set up a pool table in their living room.

However, the pair weren't the types to sit back and let their band fail to move forward, so having set up the house as a rehearsal venue they occasionally auditioned new drummers after the skilled Jim Mulligan departed. One such drummer was Lars Ulrich, who came to the house to audition in April 1981, brought along by Hugh Tanner. As Ron remembered: "Hugh brought Lars to our house, and I think Troy James had already quit the band, so James had to go back to playing guitar. When he and Lars first jammed, I thought Lars was the worst drummer I had ever heard in my life!" Far from being a teenage prodigy, Ulrich's limited percussion abilities failed to impress either Hetfield or McGovney. "He couldn't keep a beat, and compared to

Mulligan, he just couldn't play," continued Ron. "So I told James, this guy sucks, dude."

As James later told *Playboy*: "Lars had a pretty crappy drum kit, with one cymbal. It kept falling over, and we'd have to stop, and he'd pick the fucking thing up. He really was not a good drummer . . . When we were done jamming, it was, what the fuck was that? We stiffed him on the bill for the studio, too. There were so many different things about him. His mannerisms, his looks, his accent, his attitude, his smell. He smelled – he smelled like Denmark, I guess. They have a different view on bathing. We use soap in America." Not the most auspicious meeting of minds, then.

McGovney in particular was feeling disassociated from the music scene at the time, and was considering embarking on a career as a photographer. Gene Hoglan: "Ron was wicked, a very nice guy," which perhaps explains why a career in the backbiting world of popular music wasn't for him.

And a backbiting, backstabbing scene it certainly was. In 1981 Los Angeles was the breeding ground for a whole new type of rock'n'roll, typified by bands who wore heavy make-up, high heels, lurid spandex clothes in day-glo colours and big hair sprayed to hold it in place. This movement, latterly known as glam metal (or less politely, hair metal and poser metal), was kickstarted by Mötley Crüe's debut album *Too Fast For Love*. Released in November 1981, it attracted enormous attention from fans who were tired of the slow, antiquated chart-rock typified by bands like Journey. Yet Mötley Crüe received a certain amount of derision from metal fans who simply could not stand their look, their almost self-conscious offstage debauchery (the Crüe were nearly always involved in drug, sex or violence scandals, and their reputation escalated accordingly) or the fact that their stance was based on hedonism rather than aggression, the more usual basis of 'serious' heavy metal.

The music scene soon polarised into glam-metal fans, who followed Mötley Crüe and the wave of bands such as Ratt which followed them, and the hardcore punks, whose heroes (Minor Threat, the Dead Kennedys and a host of grim, nihilistic punk acts) were constantly touring at club level. The split between the two scenes inspired no little violence. John Bush, now the singer in New York metal band Anthrax, remembers that in a few short months the heavier punk music began to focus on San Francisco, while the glam-metal acts mostly remained in Los Angeles: "It was a weird time, and I think there was a division. The hair metal was mostly confined to Los Angeles, although many of them played in San Francisco too and had a large following." Many insults were exchanged from both sides, although ultimately a grudging respect developed: "One side was saying fuck you, pussies! and the other one was saying well, we *get* all the pussy! Stupid comments like that. But there was some mutual respect. People would come to each other's shows."

Bush thinks that the media might have encouraged the bad blood: "That stuff went on in the press, shit-talking about the styles of music. The journalists probably egged it on and brought it out of the musicians." However, he also points out that both scenes had their virtues, even though he personally wasn't a fan of the glam side: "You had to look at the number of records they were selling and give them credit for that, even if they weren't your favourite bands. You had some great singers and musicians on both sides."

Another figure who was in a good position to witness the rise of glam metal was British journalist Sylvie Simmons, who tells the story of how she found herself in California at this pivotal time: "I took myself off to LA because I figured it would be nice to be a rock journalist in a place that was sunny," she recalls today. "The fledgling metal scene out there was very much like the punk scene on the UK: it was very much a grass-roots, DIY movement. LA is this place where people drive around in cars, they don't tend to congregate, there aren't many clubs where you could play. It really wasn't a place like the British industrial Midlands where you would expect heavy metal to appear. It's such a hot place, people don't want to go around in leather, and it's so laid-back that you wouldn't think people would have time for half-hour guitar solos. It really wasn't what you would imagine as the centre of a metal revival." And yet a new form of heavy metal *needed* to appear at this point, she reasons: "The heavy rock scene at that time was incredibly flaccid, it was all Foreigner and that kind of stuff. Kansas, Boston, REO Speedwagon . . . stadium rock was pretty much dead in the water. Led Zeppelin were still revered as gods because they'd had the sense to split up after John Bonham died. It was really Judas Priest and Motörhead who were held up as the only two British bands who'd got it right."

The DIY element that had kept the flag of punk flying for so long began to manifest itself in the glam-metal scene, as Simmons observed: "People started putting out records themselves and raising money in any way they could, going down 7-11s and stealing food to live off, or finding girls with trust funds to keep them. Mötley Crüe came along on the cusp of 1980 to 1981, and before that the only metal band of note in LA was Van Halen, who were almost like a one-off blip – they had come out of Pasadena with this thrust of power which absolutely knocked you sideways. It was absolutely fantastic, they were this completely don't-give-a-fuck band. And of course they toured with Black Sabbath on that last tour they did, and blew them out of the water."

Simmons' first meeting with Mötley Crüe stays with her vividly to this day: "I remember seeing this band on stage who were wastedly skinny, all wearing black and with these ridiculous hairdos, and a very odd stage set, like cardboard boxes in black and white, and they were thrashing out this kind of mixture of garage-rock and punk, a bit New York Dolls, a bit Aerosmith." The catch-all nature of Mötley's music – elements of metal, glam, straightahead rock, punk, garage and even pop – meant that fans of many subgenres of music paid them some attention, and they were certainly a sight to behold in the early days.

Robert Sweet, the drummer of a band called Stryper, who were perhaps the most ridiculed of all the glam-metal bands for their pro-Christian stance (their act included throwing Bibles into their audiences), has clearer memories than most of the roots of the scene: "When Mötley were starting out, I remember seeing them in the clubs when they were basically nothing. I helped pick bassist Nikki Sixx up off the street one time when he'd fallen down drunk. I saw those guys everywhere. The Crüe drummer Tommy Lee was absolutely amazing back then."

I asked Nikki Sixx if he enjoyed the music coming from the emerging thrash scene, and received a surprisingly sanguine answer: "Me personally, I didn't get it. I like it a lot more now than I did back then. To me it wasn't good songwriting. It was great guitars, but it wasn't brilliant in the songwriting department. We really tried to work the hook, you know. It's just a different thing, you know, it's cool. Thank God everyone doesn't sound the same."

Many musicians who went on to play much harder music than that of the glam scene enjoyed Mötley's music, at least initially. Hirax singer

Katon DePena explains: "I loved it. And still do. Most of the hair bands were actually really nice guys, especially Mötley Crüe, we got along with them well. But bands such as Steeler and Stryper played such pussy music that we rarely played with them. We were all drawing big crowds, but there was a dividing line." As he puts it: "Posers on the left. And headbangers on the right. I think it's great because those kinds of bands made us only want to play heavier music. We still co-exist."

Robert Sweet recalls a certain amount of aggression between the two scenes: "Anthrax opened for us and laughed at us a lot. I remember Quiet Riot singer Kevin DuBrow punched my brother [Stryper singer Michael Sweet] out because he thought his hair was too tall, and Great White sabotaged our patch bay. That kind of thing used to plague Stryper. A lot of bands we played with used to enjoy doing really bad things to us – bands were so cut-throat to one another. A lot of jealousy, a lot of competition, a lot of immaturity."

An early convert to the glam cause, but one who left rapidly when the hairspray and lipstick element became too over-the-top, was Eric Peterson of Testament: "Mötley Crüe? I saw them up there before they even had a record out. Me and my friends were the only people who showed up at the first in-store signing they had. We bought them a six-pack of Moosehead and hung out with them all day, it was pretty cool. Their music was heavy and it was outrageous and shocking and very cool. They wrote some good stuff." Later, however, the crossover between the scenes rarely happened – as Peterson says, "The extreme metal guys would bad-mouth the hair-metallers, who wouldn't dare say anything or go to our shows, because we looked like skater-punks."

Gene Hoglan has much to say on the subject of glam metal: "All the hair-metal bands started great and turned shitty – Great White, Ratt, Mötley Crüe and all that. My older sister knew all the bands and was friends with them, so I'd wake up and there'd be the drummer from Great White asleep on the couch!" Hoglan, a committed metal fan from a very young age, saw the Crüe at one of their earlier shows and was surprised at how heavy their music was: "I remember seeing them on October 3, 1981 at the Troubadour, and that happened to be Tommy Lee's 19th birthday. Ratt opened for them and they were actually heavy, chunky guitars and so on." But at that point, as he recalls, their focus was still on the riffs rather than the image: "The whole glam thing hadn't happened yet. Crüe used to have these full-page ads in the local magazines and I thought, they look great, so they must be heavy. It was all leather and studs still, and trying to be heavy like Judas Priest."

When Crüe began to play softer, less aggressive music and increase the glamour element of their look, the young Hoglan wasted no time in venting his displeasure, as he remembers, "I was a very young, opinionated motherfucker and was six feet tall when I was 13, so I had no problems with going up to bands and saying, 'You suck.' What are they gonna do? I'm 13! I'd walk up to Mötley guitarist Mick Mars and say, 'Hi dude, I saw your show.' And he'd say, 'Cool, did you like it?' And I'd say, 'No, you were the worst band I've ever seen, I fuckin' hated your concert and I hate your record!' And he'd be like, 'Get this kid out of here!' "

The glam-metal wave continued despite the complaints of fans such as Hoglan. By 1984 there were dozens of lip-glossed, satin-clothed bands in the charts and on MTV, exciting extreme responses in many different countries. Fans of tougher music hated it, and looked tirelessly for the next wave of metal to replace it. One such teenager was Jason Newsted, who quit high school just three months before graduation (a move he later warned his fans to avoid) and in 1981, as LA rocked to the sounds of glam metal, packed his bags and began a journey from Michigan to California alongside his friend Tim Hamlin, the pair having decided that life in the big city might suit them better than the permanently rural existence they had experienced to date.

By now a competent bassist, Newsted made it as far as Phoenix, Arizona (where he arrived on Halloween, 1981) and took a series of jobs to support himself while setting up a band. He and Hamlin drifted apart, but he did hook up with a drummer, Kelly David-Smith, with whom he worked briefly in a band called Paradox. On moving in with David-Smith in Scotsdale, Arizona, he recruited two guitarists, Mark Vasquez and Kevin Horton, and renamed his band Dogz. Newsted sang on some of the songs they wrote, but soon enough a more solid line-up stabilised when Horton was replaced by Ed Carlson and a singer, Erik A.K. Knutson, appeared. Shortly afterwards the group underwent another name-change and called themselves Flotsam And Jetsam. The music they played owed much to the stadium rockers of the day, but there was a palpable feeling that they could be faster and heavier than that.

Kids like Newsted weren't listening to Mötley Crüe. They were listening to another, far harsher band, whose first album, *Welcome To Hell*, was released in January 1981. The band which had released this album was called Venom, and the music they played was so different to anything that had preceded it that it required a whole new name.

Thrash metal, as a term, didn't exist in 1981. But the music itself was ready to spring to life, with musicians' lust fuelled by Venom's first album, the speed of hardcore punk, the attitude of Motörhead and the fact that metal fans were tiring of the glam-metal scene on the West Coast.

All that was needed for this new music to make the jump to the world stage was a catalyst – a group of musicians with the hunger to make it happen.

3

1981–1982

Unlike many parents Torben Ulrich always approved of what his son Lars got up to. "From early on he'd been used to doing those things on his own," he remembers. "When there were concerts in Denmark, when he was eight or nine, at that time you could go as a boy on the bus to Kiss concerts or whatever, and he would go there and come back on his own, and if he fell asleep on the bus the conductor would wake him up." Unusually, these late-night outings didn't stop Lars from doing well at his classes: "He'd still get up and go to school, he was very good like that," adds his father. "Also I had told him that if you're really interested in music you really have to go to see those players. These were the building blocks: if you were really keen, you had to show that and you had to show up! You couldn't do that long distance."

And so it was that in the summer of 1981, Lars Ulrich informed his parents and friends that he would be travelling to Europe. Specifically, he would be spending time in England, following a tour by one of his favourite metal bands, Diamond Head, who were the darlings of the rock press at the time and whose music he embraced with a fervour that was almost religious. With a tolerance born of many years of fatherhood, Torben explains: "We felt that if Lars wanted to go and check it out in England, that was the right thing to do. He was subscribing to the magazines and reading every line." Asked if he and Lars' mother worried about their 17-year-old son travelling on his own, the elder Ulrich explains that while they often worried about their son's welfare when he was driving an hour each way on California freeways to get to band practice, the concept of him travelling to Europe was less disconcerting. The teenage Lars was, it seemed, a sensible kid.

As it turned out, Diamond Head, a band whose technical music and driving rhythms placed them near the top of the NWOBHM tree,

28

were hardly party animals. Singer Sean Harris recalls today: "We used to play Monopoly after the gigs. We were mama's boys from Birmingham!" They had distinguished themselves with underground and mainstream fans in 1980 by recording and manufacturing their untitled debut album (also referred to as *Lightning To The Nations*) and distributing 1,000 copies to great acclaim: "We had that great Geoff Barton review in *Sounds*: 'Fresher than a bucket of Listermint . . . More riffs on one album than on Sabbath's first five albums!'" remembers Harris with pleasure. The idea, he explains, was to be as good as the big rock acts of the day ("We wanted to be progressive like Purple, but we knew we couldn't be the musicians that they were. We didn't have the Sixties as a background") but they were also influenced by other, rawer music ("We loved punk, we thought that was the catalyst. If you could play three chords and have an attitude, that was enough") and ultimately wound up bringing a depth of heaviness to their sound which transported them to the top of the pile ("We saw Iron Maiden in Birmingham with Samson and a few other bands, and we thought we could easily match them . . . and then later we supported Maiden, Angel Witch and Praying Mantis at the Lyceum"). The recipe was a success: Diamond Head were, for a few brief years, rock stars.

The story of how Lars Ulrich entered the life of Diamond Head is hard to credit nowadays: rumour has long had it that he flew to Britain, walked up to Sean Harris after a show and ended up being invited to stay at the singer's house. This is completely true, as Harris and Diamond Head guitarist Brian Tatler confirm. "Lars had ordered a copy of our album from our mail-order, for which we'd had 1,000 signed copies made," recalls Harris. "Three pounds fifty he got it for! So he came over – that was the winter of discontent, wasn't it – and he came to the Woolwich Odeon. He just showed up one day."

As Harris explains, the band was still underground enough that fans commonly accompanied them offstage ("If anybody had said, could they spend time with us back then, they could have come and lived with us!") but, more than this, Lars was a genuinely charming guy. "He was a very nice chap, very enthusiasic. Very young. He went to Brian's house and my house and slept at the bottom of the bed. We took him round with us."

Asked what the presumably underfunded Ulrich lived on, Sean is at a loss. "I don't think he ate!" he says. "He'd put a record on and go, this is great." It seems that Lars' primary characteristic, one for which he is well known nowadays, was his keenness to learn about music and then discuss it at great length. "We were all amazed at his enthusiasm. He never shut up talking." His love of Diamond Head's music never became tiresome, however. "He just really liked us," says Harris, "and thought we were the bee's knees. But we agreed with him . . . we thought so as well!"

The more softly spoken Brian Tatler recalls: "Lars stayed at Sean's for a month and mine for a week. We must have been nice to him. After he came over he wrote me a letter, saying 'How come Diamond Head aren't the biggest band in the world? What are you up to?'" But there was no mention at this stage that Lars had musical plans himself, although he may well have mentioned that he was studying the drums. Harris: "He didn't say he was going to form a band until later. We stayed in touch after he went back to LA. You gotta give him credit, man. Right at the beginning, there he was – he knew where the inspiration had to be found and he came and got it."

Inspiration was clearly on Ulrich's mind, and judging by what happened next in the life of the young Dane, he found it on that summer tour. At one point his enthusiasm for the music reached as far as Los Angeles, as his friend John Kornarens recalls: "The phone rang in the summer of 1981 and it was Lars. I said, 'Hey Lars, are you back?' and he said, 'No, I'm in England.'" Kornarens never forgot Ulrich's next move: "He said, here, 'I want you to talk to somebody' – and handed the phone to Sean Harris!" The details of the conversation between the Brummie singer and the stunned Californian are lost to history.

On his return from England, Lars seemed to his friends to be a man possessed. He had found something, it seemed: a renewed drive which was leading him towards forming his own band. He began to make contacts and network with musicians as if it was the only thing that had ever mattered.

As it happened, Lars was not the only kid in his circle who had been making inroads into the music industry. His friend Brian Slagel had noticed that European imported vinyl was finding its way into Los Angeles and that the European press had simultaneously picked up on Californian music. His response was to start a fanzine, which he called the *New Heavy Metal Revue*, which he assembled at his house with the help of John Kornarens. The new venture was helped along by the fact that Brian was now working at a record store called Oz Records: his official title, earned due to his vast knowledge of overseas rock and metal, was Import Buyer. As Kornarens remembers, this was a heady time for the American fanzine industry: "*Kerrang!* came out and Brian decided he wanted to start a magazine. He asked me to write for it, and I helped out with the typesetters and so on. Right about that time was when Ron Quintana started *Metal Mania* up in San Francisco, and then Brian got a job at Oz Records, where he was bringing in a lot of cool stuff."

With all this metallic activity, it wasn't long before Slagel and Kornarens crossed paths with Sylvie Simmons, who was still corresponding for *Sounds* about the metal scene in Los Angeles. In fact, before long the two men were helping Simmons with her research, in their position as local experts, as she recalls: "Brian was a very quiet, very laid-back, very un-metal-looking guy, he wasn't a loudmouth with studded bracelets or anything like that. He knew his metal backwards. I wrote an LA Metal round-up with John Kornarens' help. John was going out as a fan to the clubs anyway, so he offered to scout for bands, letting me know which were worth avoiding or checking out."

She remembers Kornarens as 'Heavy Metal John', who was the person to turn to if any information was required about the scene: "Heavy Metal John was a lovely guy, he was about 18 when I knew him. My phone number was in *Sounds*, and he called me up once – as did all sorts of weirdos, I might add – and was quizzing me as fans do, asking me what was happening with new albums and so on. He was a big help and went to shows and recommended bands to me."

Along with Slagel and Kornarens came their friends, prominent among whom was Lars Ulrich. It wasn't long before he impressed his personality on Simmons: "One day John showed up at my flat with Lars Ulrich, who was an absolute hyperactive brat. If they'd have invented Ritalin, they would have given it to him back then. He was absolutely impossible, but sweet. Like a kind of terrier running around the place. He went through all my files and said, 'Have you got pictures of Iron Maiden? Have you got pictures of Diamond Head?' He never shut up."

Kornarens noticed this impossible enthusiasm on Lars' part and was slightly embarrassed by his younger friend: "John was much more laid-back and even a bit apologetic, I remember him calling up a few

31

times and saying, 'I'm really sorry about Lars.' It did drive me a bit mad." Did Lars ever talk about the band he was planning to form? "Yes, he did say he was going to start a band, but it was always between lots of other things – he'd never stay on one subject long enough! He was hyperactive, talked incessantly, never kept still, kept asking questions, was an absolute fan and a massive Anglophile musically. I remember him reeling off lists of NWOBHM bands and going through my papers, picking out promo photos, asking if he could have them. I remember Lars once managing to get from me a signed Xmas card I had from Iron Maiden with a Santa Eddie on the front."

No one really minded Ulrich's infectious eagerness, however, and his friends soon learned to put up with him, although Kornarens remembers one particular event that came close to the limit: "One day we'd been up all day and all night, and then Lars had to drive the 70 miles home from my place in Studio City to his house in Newport Beach. So I finally go to bed, but then 20 minutes later there's somebody throwing rocks at my window, and I'm like, what's going on?" Stumbling to his window, Jon made out the shape in the darkness below of a teenager with long hair: "And it's Lars saying, 'Come on down. I went to get gas but I didn't bring the key for the gas cap, so I can't get home!' So I had him back the car into the garage and I was able to unbolt that whole section. Then he went and got gas, came back and then finally left and I went to bed at 4 in the morning . . ."

As the metal scene grew, groups of teenagers such as Ulrich, Slagel and Kornarens swelled the ranks of the LA faithful and writers such as Simmons faithfully reported on the situation to the UK press. A turning-point came when Brian, who was also writing reviews for magazines by this stage as well as doing some radio work, decided to produce an album commemorating the musical talent he saw every day on the scene. As he remembers, "At the time I was doing the fanzine, working in a record store and helping to programme the local heavy metal radio station. I was writing for *Sounds* and *Kerrang!* in the UK, and there was this really great scene that was going on in LA – with Mötley Crüe, Ratt and Bitch. I was influenced by the whole DIY attitude of the NWOBHM and I thought, nobody's paying attention to the scene here. So I asked all the distributors that I knew from working at the store that if I could put together a local LA compilation, would they sell it? And they said, sure."

These were different times: a self-financed record could not only sell well, but a well-connected individual could get it distributed and promoted without breaking the bank. Slagel continues: "I borrowed some money from my friends and from my aunt, and I had a little bit of money that I had saved from my previous job, and we pooled all our resources and just barely had enough to manufacture a few thousand records." The resources available to Slagel's brand-new label, which he decided to call Metal Blade in the spirit of the times and of the music, were barely adequate ("I never really thought I would start a record label . . . the first three years was pretty much just me in the back of my mom's garage"), as was the professional expertise of Brian and his friends. For instance, when asked how he arranged licences, royalty payments and so on, he simply laughs: "The first record was really just an outgrowing of the fanzine. I made every mistake humanly possible with that record. I licensed it to a guy who ended up ripping everybody off. Then more people wanted the record and I didn't have the money to make any more . . . I was just a kid, I just said, 'Give me a song and I'll put it on there' – there was no mention of an advance or royalties or anything like that."

However, luck was on his side in the form of a rookie lawyer who happened to be living in an apartment above Oz Records: "We had to sign the bands to contracts, but I didn't even have money for that. We had to hire a lawyer, but the lucky thing was that there was a guy living right above the store who was a lawyer and he was just starting out. He came down and said he would charge us ten dollars an hour to do our legal work. So we set it up that we would pay a royalty and do things like proper record companies do. And he's still our lawyer today!"

As Slagel was collecting songs to put on his forthcoming compilation, which he had decided to title *The New Heavy Metal Revue Presents Metal Massacre*, he mentioned his activities to Lars Ulrich, who was immediately enthused by the idea and, on the spur of the moment, asked if he could provide a song for it himself. Slagel agreed, although he didn't know where Ulrich would find such a song in the absence of a band. On such small matters does the thread of history hang . . .

Lars immediately phoned James Hetfield, who he had not seen since the unsuccessful jam session organised the previous year by Hugh Tanner. As Hetfield later told Metal Mike of *Aardschok*: "It wasn't till quite a while later that I heard from Lars again, when he called me. I had finished high school by then and was jamming with Ron McGovney. Hugh Tanner had disappeared from the scene, after only two months he was sick of the musician's life. Hugh's parents wanted him to be a lawyer or something." Hetfield's surprise at hearing from Ulrich again was compounded by the drummer's offer of a recording deal, even if it was only for one song: "Lars said he had a friend named Brian Slagel, who was organising a metal album and had reserved a place on it for him. 'I'll be right there,' I yelled!"

A rehearsal slot at McGovney's house was swiftly organised – at which, to Hetfield's further surprise, Ulrich demonstrated that his drumming abilities had improved several times over. "Lars had improved as a drummer a whole lot," remembered James. "He also had a brand-new drum kit, a genuine Camco. We jammed a few songs which I had written with Leather Charm, 'Hit The Lights' and 'No Remorse'."

The two rapidly became friends and spent time together listening to records, with Hetfield learning more and more about metal from the listening sessions in which Lars drilled him about trends in the music scene. James also accompanied Lars to John Kornarens' house, as John recalls: "James was kinda quiet, kinda pensive: he didn't really invite a lot of conversation. He wasn't that outgoing, he was reserved and not very gregarious. But he was Lars' friend and he was into metal." But Hetfield's quiet demeanour changed when the alcohol began to flow: "I remember them coming up to my house, sitting in my front room eating the chocolate chip cookies my sister had made, and drinking Jack Daniel's from a flask," says John. "And I was like, I hope my dad doesn't see this!" James soon became partial to the European and British music which Lars loved so much, to the occasional dismay of Ron McGovney, as he later said: "Lars told me to buy a Venom LP, but Ron wouldn't let me bring the record into our room. 'Those are devil worshippers, man! Not in my house!' Ron said. 'Fuck you, pussy!' was my answer. 'This is heavy shit!' "

With the bonding of Ulrich and Hetfield, events moved swiftly. Lars was a young, ambitious drummer and James was a beer-drinking, metal-loving party animal whose slightly withdrawn exterior hid a turbulent personality: he had, after all, recently lost his mother. Fuelled by the raw, fast riffing of the NWOBHM and inspired by Ulrich's recent visit with Diamond Head, the pair had everything to play for – and even had a slot on a record to fill. Life must have seemed full of possibilities.

Faced with a deadline, they were forced to move quickly. James and Lars decided that the song they would record for *Metal Massacre* would be the old Leather Charm song 'Hit The Lights', a fast, powerful tune based on a snaky riff and a song which offered all the players the chance to show off their talents. Furthermore, it functioned lyrically as an introduction to the band, with its theme the simple assertion that when they hit the stage, they were ready to play. No more, no less.

One day in practice Lars asked Ron McGovney to sit in on bass for 'Hit The Lights'. As Ron recalled to KNAC in 1993: "I went in there and Lars said, 'Come on man, why don't you just join the band?' So I said, 'OK.' I was in . . . although I never really gained much technical expertise, James was like our mentor, he showed us what to do." As the song gradually came together and approached the stage where it could be recorded competently, the urgent need for some kind of band identity was felt. The trio of Hetfield, Ulrich and McGovney needed a name. John Kornarens remembers that Lars spent a lot of time pondering the problem: "He showed me a list of names for the band. One of them was Lars Ulrich spelled backwards!"

There are several stories as to how Metallica got their name. Some claim that Lars or James took it from a book called *Encyclopaedia Metallica*, a guide to hard rock by the journalists Brian Harrigan and Malcolm Dome, which appeared around this time. This seems unlikely, however, and a popular alternative theory is that the idea came from Ron Quintana, a fanzine editor in San Francisco. As the story goes, the band considered various more or less laughable options such as Grinder, Blitzer and Red Vette, but settled for a different name after Lars spoke with Quintana about the latter's magazine. Ron asked Lars which he thought would be the better name for the publication – *Metal Mania* or *Metallica* – and the drummer, thinking quickly, recommended the former while planning to use the latter for himself.

Either way, by late 1982 Metallica was the chosen name. Kornarens liked the new name: "I liked Metallica – it reminded me of Gigantor, the giant cartoon robot from space." But there was little time to relax and enjoy the newly named band: as McGovney later recalled, Ulrich wanted to expand the line-up with a second guitarist (the logical move for a band with such a focus on both riffs and solos) and placed an ad in a local magazine called *Recycler*. One day, as McGovney recalled, "James told me that they had a guitarist coming over for an audition. I remember opening up the front door and seeing this black dude with a Jamaican accent. He came in and they started jamming to 'Hit The Lights', the old Leather Charm song." The new guitarist's name was Lloyd Grant, and while his playing was competent, he was only, it transpired, intended to fill in temporarily while the band found a permanent recruit.

As Grant explained in 1997, "I answered an ad in the *Recycler* that read 'Heavy Metal Guitarist Wanted for music much heavier than the LA scene'. 'Hit The Lights' was composed by James and one of his friends. I remember the day I went over to Lars' house, he said, 'Check out this song,' and he played me 'Hit The Lights'. We were both into that heavy kind of shit." James and Lars admired Lloyd's lead guitar skills, it seems, and the respect was mutual: "Lars was very easy to get along with, although he had very strong ideas and opinions. I was not around James a lot; the times I was around him he was very quiet."

James' quiet manner was the perfect foil to Lars' outgoing, hyperactive personality, it appeared, as well as proving useful for the times when the band needed to focus on songwriting and rehearsal. But this neat dual set-up wouldn't last for long. Metallica had kept the ad for a lead guitarist running in *Recycler* with the intention of replacing Lloyd Grant when the time came, and one day Ron McGovney took a call from a young, fast-talking teenager who had seen it and was interested. As Ron later recalled: "We put an ad in *Recycler* saying we wanted a way-out, fast lead guitar player. I answered the phone one day and this guy named Dave was on the phone, and he was just spieling this baloney like I could not believe. Said he had like four Marshall stacks, four BC Rich Biches. But we got him over and he really was a good lead guitar player."

The guy on the phone who supposedly had the flash amps and guitars was none other than Dave Mustaine, recently of Panic, who had gained some live experience and a degree of musical competence that the musicians in Metallica could not yet hope to match. He also had an outgoing, confident personality, perhaps a result of the survival skills he had been forced to learn in the absence of a permanently present father. However, the full impact of Mustaine's character would not be felt for some time: for now, the business of recording 'Hit The Lights' had to take precedence over establishing a full rehearsal and live schedule.

Nonetheless, Dave made an impression on the other players with both his playing and his personality. Diamond Head's Brian Tatler recalls that a few months after Lars' sojourn with them in the UK, he received a letter from the young Dane: "He was saying, 'By the way, I've formed a band called Metallica and we're rehearsing six hours a day, six days a week' – or something like that – 'and we've got this guitarist who's pretty good, he's pretty fast.' And I thought wow, they're really going for it." Lars had also been attending live shows and was still inspired by meeting one of his idols: "He said, 'I met Ritchie Blackmore last week' – he was just a fan still!"

As the band had begun, so they would continue. Or at least, that was to be hoped . . .

4

1982

'Hit The Lights' was finally recorded – on, as James later told Metal Mike, a pretty primitive piece of equipment: "We borrowed ourselves a Tascam four-track and recorded 'Hit The Lights'. I played rhythm guitar and bass and sang, while Lars drummed. We were really a duo." With, of course, the addition of lead guitar solos, which Hetfield was not yet developed enough musically to execute. The issue of the solos on 'Hit The Lights' has led to much confusion. Note that James, not Ron, played bass on this recording, which has added to the uncertainty over the years about which incarnation of Metallica recorded the song.

At this stage Dave Mustaine was a member of the band, but a very new one, and Lars and James were still looking to him to prove himself. Although the solos on 'Hit The Lights' were recorded by Dave, Lars thought that Lloyd might be able to do better and decided to give Grant a shot at re-recording one of them, as McGovney related: "Lloyd actually only came over twice, and then they ended up recruiting Dave Mustaine on guitar – they had kept the ad running in the *Recycler*, they only planned on using Lloyd as a fill-in. As I remember, Dave played the two leads on 'Hit The Lights' but they kept the second lead which Lloyd played because they liked it better."

Not that Grant was given much warning. It seems that Lars and James simply drove to his house, set up the recorder and asked him to play the solo. Grant himself later said: "Lars wanted me to play some guitar leads on [the song], but I couldn't make it over to Ron McGovney's house to do the recording. So James and Lars brought the four-track over to my apartment and I did the solo on a little Montgomery Ward amp." The solo was recorded literally hours before Lars and James took the tape to Brian Slagel's studio, it transpires – and the handover was no better planned. As the two walked into the room,

Hetfield took a look around and was nonplussed: "Brian was in the studio polishing up the Bitch track at the mixer. I saw a bunch of equipment for the first time, that I didn't know what were for, and a mixer with hundreds of buttons. Wow! My first time in a studio." Slagel, it turned out, had been expecting a professional recording rather than a four-track cassette: "Where's your 16-track tape?" he asked. "I can see still his face when we put our cassette into his hand. 'Oh, no!' he said, which might make it clear why 'Hit The Lights' didn't sound so good."

Brian himself remembers the incident with some humour: "'Hit The Lights' was the very last song we got for the record. The day we had to master it, Lars had to bring the tape in, and I think he had just done it the night before. He and James just wrote that song and recorded it. The first version was only available on the *Metal Massacre* vinyl and had been recorded on their cassette player."

John Kornarens also remembers this, explaining how the record had initially been conceived: "So we went round a ton of shows. We met Steeler that way, Ratt that way, Mötley Crüe that way. Lars got wind of it and asked if he could be on the album, he was gonna put a band together and it was gonna be heavy. Brian had no problem with it. They were one of my bands that I was looking after for the record."

As for the actual handover of the tape, it emerges that Kornarens played a pivotal role in giving Metallica their shot: "Everything had to be on reel-to-reel tape so we could master it at Bijou Studios in Holly-wood. The deal was that we had a session at three o'clock, and Lars was going to meet us there with the tapes. He met us and pulled out this cassette tape, and Brian said, 'I'll need the fifty bucks we talked about to transfer it over to reel-to-reel so I can master it.'"

Sounds routine? No. Lars didn't have any cash, as John explains: "Lars freaked out and said, 'I don't have fifty bucks.' Brian said, 'Well, I don't have fifty bucks.' So Lars said, 'What about you?' I looked in my wallet and I had fifty-two dollars. So Lars said, 'Please, please, please loan me the money and I'll pay you back.' Otherwise they wouldn't have been on the album. He paid me my fifty bucks back and promised me that on every future Metallica album I'd be known as John 'Fifty Bucks' Kornarens."

And so the *Metal Massacre* recording of 'Hit The Lights' was mastered and cut on the album. Famously, the first pressing of the record listed

Metallica on its sleeve as 'Mettallica'. Later on, the album was re-pressed with the correct spelling and a new version of the song, this time with guitar solos by Dave Mustaine and bass played by Ron McGovney. The first pressing has become extremely desirable among hardcore Metallica fans, as that version of 'Hit The Lights' appears nowhere else – or at least, nowhere else until the release of a Metal Blade box set in 2002, which contained that version. As Slagel explains, "When we put together the box set, Metallica wanted to use the first version because it had never been on CD before – only on that first pressing of the vinyl album."

And so Metallica had made their first steps onto vinyl, before they had even recorded a demo of their own. This event also marked the end of the brief involvement of Lloyd Grant with the band, Slagel remarking that, "Lloyd is still around – actually, last time I saw him was at a Metallica gig four or five years ago and he is still playing in bands," but he has largely faded from view other than an interview he gave in January 1997. Here he pondered on his time with Metallica, saying, "I had several disappointments with previous bands I was in, I guess that's my reason for not pursuing Metallica. There were a lot of flaky musicians; however, this was not the case with Lars, he was 100 per cent intense with the music."

This intensity was a requirement at this stage: any band which wanted to do well at this point in time had a difficult job to do, especially in the metal field. This genre of music, and even more so on America's West Coast, was spiralling in popularity and competition was fierce. All over America there were groups of kids listening to classic rock and reflecting that they themselves could be making it too. I spoke to a long list of musicians about these formative years – the years in which Metallica took their first steps – in an attempt to divine what it was about this period that made it possible for metal to rise so quickly. The secret, it seems, was the passion and diversity which was all over the metal scene back then – and the bands the kids were into weren't solely American or British, either. Vow Wow, from Japan, and European acts such as the Scorpions and Accept, contributed immensely to the scene.

As Hirax singer Katon DePena remembers it, the scene in California was intense at this stage: "The metal scene was very strong. To this day that scene has influenced the whole world. I'm glad I was there to see it!" He explains that the independent record stores were still an important market force in those days: "Growing up as a kid I listened to everything from heavy metal, heavy rock, soul, Motown, jazz, country, and punk. In my later teens I became a heavy metal and punk addict, shopping for records in all the independent stores with my friends."

Rock music came from many sources for the faithful: "Jimi Hendrix was my first introduction. Black Sabbath and Thin Lizzy were instrumental in me wanting to become a musician. You need idols no matter who you are. I was the only black kid in my neighbourhood, so I heard a lot of heavy rock music. When I first saw what Jimi Hendrix and Phil Lynott of Thin Lizzy looked like, I believed I could play heavy metal too."

The scene continued to be fuelled by the rise of the New Wave Of British Heavy Metal, as John Kornarens explains: "About 1980 I started getting a sense of these new heavy metal bands coming out of England. It wasn't on the radio or anything but it was over at a store called Moby Discs in Van Huys in California. They imported a few obscure things, they were a little more eclectic in their tastes than Tower and so on. I remember seeing a singles box on their counter and pulling out a single by this band called Angel Witch, and thinking, damn, this is so heavy! Then they had the first Iron Maiden album and the first *Metal For Muthas* records – all within a few months in mid-1980."

Journalist Martin Popoff remembers those early days very clearly – he and his friends were avid fans of many types of music (as long as it was heavy): "The core experience was Ted Nugent, Aerosmith, Kiss, Zeppelin, Black Sabbath, Rush, Deep Purple, Riot, Moxy, Budgie, Priest, Iggy Pop, Thin Lizzy, AC/DC, Triumph and so on. We were also consumers of punk's first wave, but only the heavy bands – Saints, Sex Pistols, Damned, Lurkers, Drones, Dead Boys, Adverts – and we were experts on everything heavy by the time the NWOBHM came along, regularly buying *Sounds*, *Melody Maker*, getting the imports when they first came out."

Again, the NWOBHM had a profound impact: "The first records were the *Metal For Muthas* albums, Tygers' first, Fist, Diamond Head, Quartz, the *New Electric Warriors* compilation, Saxon's *Wheels Of Steel*. I remember buying Motörhead's *Overkill* the week it came out. I even joined the Motörhead and Saxon fan clubs in '79 or '80."

John Marshall, who grew up a friend of Kirk Hammett in El

Sobrante (he later joined Metal Church and became involved with Metallica in several ways, as we'll see), recalls a whole range of differing acts all sheltering under the metal umbrella: "I remember listening to Kiss, Led Zeppelin, Van Halen, UFO, Thin Lizzy, Aerosmith, Ted Nugent . . . many of the rock bands that were big at the time. My first rock concert was in 1978: the line-up was AC/DC, Van Halen, Pat Travers, Foreigner and Aerosmith. I've played guitar since I was seven years old, and I was really into guitar players. I listened a lot to Michael Schenker, Jimmy Page and Ed Van Halen. Michael Schenker had a huge influence on me. Kirk would always turn me on to new music, and I think he was the one who played me Sabbath, Priest and other bands like that."

Musician Jeff Becerra, who later formed the first death metal band, Possessed, listened to both metal and punk: "I liked stuff like Ozzy, Sabbath, UFO, Rainbow, Blue Oyster Cult, AC/DC, Rush at first – then later I got into punk and metal like TSOL, Agent Orange and Venom. Really anything that was rebellious and heavy. When I was a kid my dad used to turn me on to rock'n'roll, and I think that it all stemmed from there."

The classic rock-to-metal route that so many artists have described here also holds true of hardened extreme metallers such as Malevolent Creation guitarist and songwriter Phil Fasciana. "I started with Kiss in 1977, then moved on to Black Sabbath, Judas Priest, Iron Maiden and Anvil," he says. "My older cousin got me into Black Sabbath when I was 13 years old and I haven't been the same since – after that it was metal forever." The same holds true for Hades axeman Dan Lorenzo: "I listened to old Kiss, Aerosmith, Cheap Trick and the Knack. By the eleventh grade I discovered AC/DC and Judas Priest"; and Whiplash drummer Tony Scaglione, who holds the distinction of briefly playing with the LA thrash band Slayer during the absence in 1987 of drummer Dave Lombardo. As Scaglione explains: "As a teenager I was listening to a variety of music, I was a really big fan of Rush and Journey (and still am) but I also loved the classic metal bands like Sabbath, Iron Maiden and Judas Priest. The first concert I ever attended was Black Sabbath and Blue Oyster Cult at Madison Square Garden in New York. That concert really blew me away and I quickly got more and more into the whole metal scene." As so many others also found, the most extreme act in those days was a certain veteran British band:

"Soon after I discovered Motörhead, which was totally different to the standard metal of the day. It was just so much more raw and powerful to me."

However, the influences worked in both directions: just as American audiences were listening in disbelief to non-American acts, British and European metal fans were hooked on the rock emanating from the USA and Canada. As Kreator's Mille Petrozza recalls: "My first concert ever was Kiss on their Unmasked tour, I think it was in 1980. I was too young to go to the show alone, so I had to go with my older cousin. The band that was opening that night was called Iron Maiden, so I went and bought their record the next day."

In Europe, it was a combination of classic British metal and classic American rock which formed the crucial combination, with Mikael Akerfeldt – of the Swedish progressive death metal act Opeth – explaining: "I got into music at a very early age and listened to every-thing I guess – pop, rock – until I was introduced to heavy metal through Black Sabbath when I was around five years old. I remember, because I was scared of the music when I first heard it. The voice in 'Iron Man' almost made me shit my pants! I was intrigued and scared at the same time. I loved it instantly, I guess."

It was a case of the more visually shocking the better, as Byron Roberts of the British band Bal-Sagoth recalls: "My first experience of heavy metal was when my brother and sister used to make the Kiss logo when I was a kid. I also remember the old Kiss action figures and comic books, even though I never listened to their music." This also extended to the visual impact of classic metal album sleeves.

In these early days in which metal became a widespread force, the distinction between metal and rock was less important, and Motörhead frontman Ian 'Lemmy' Kilmister believes such categorisation can be misleading: "You should be very careful with who's rock and who's metal – there's a terrible difference. This term 'heavy metal' is only rock'n'roll anyway, because metal bands are the logical successors to Eddie Cochran and Buddy Holly. 'Heavy' is a much misunderstood term." As an example, he added: "Black Sabbath were heavy, but I never cared for them. I thought Ozzy's first album was better than all Sabbath's stuff put together . . . and Deep Purple were a really great [rock] band. To just lump them in with heavy metal is grossly unfair."

As the Chinese curse goes, living in interesting times isn't easy. The young Metallica were right in the middle of it, and there was no better place for them to be.

By early 1982 Metallica – now composed of James Hetfield, Lars Ulrich, Ron McGovney and Dave Mustaine – were rehearsing regularly in Ron's garage. Although they had bonded and were gelling as musicians, there was still some doubt about whether James should play guitar as well as sing. Sometimes he would venture that it might be better if he only played guitar, surrendering the microphone to a dedicated (and perhaps better) singer. As McGovney recalled later on: "We would all get together after work. James wasn't working at the time and Lars was working a graveyard shift at a 24-hour gas station, and Dave was . . . self-employed." In fact, Mustaine was dealing drugs to make a living, as he admitted to me in 1999. McGovney: "At the time it was just Dave playing guitar and James was just singing. It got to the point where James had said that he didn't think he was too good of a singer, and he only wanted to play rhythm guitar."

Despite this instability, Metallica succeeded in rehearsing a set of songs to concert-level competence and began to inquire about playing gigs on the LA club scene. The nine-song set they refined (as much as they could, given their amateurish playing skills at this stage) included only two originals: the by-now well-rehearsed 'Hit The Lights', which they planned to use to open the set, and a new song called 'Jump In The Fire', which boasted the lyrics "Moving my hips in a circular way/ Just forward a bit/ Pull your body into my waist/ And feel how good it fits". Not poetry, certainly – but similar to the standard lyrical approach of many metal acts of the era.

Of the other songs in the set, four were by Lars' idols Diamond Head, one came from Savage, another from Sweet Savage and one from Blitzkrieg. Of the Diamond Head songs, 'Helpless' was an immediate standout, with its powerful, very fast riffing in the chorus and the stop-start punch of the verse making it memorable. A laughably 'very metal' song called 'Sucking My Love' was next, and is far less exciting than it sounds, based as it was on a monotonous riff. Lyrically, of course, as Ron later explained, "That song is about exactly what you think it's about."

Perhaps Diamond Head's best-known song to this day is 'Am I

Evil?', a long, multi-layered composition with four distinct sections. It begins with a staccato, ground-out riff in E, which builds ominously until a famous double-tapped lead guitar figure links to the main riff of the song, a classic mid-tempo part which continues (somewhat remorselessly) across two verses and choruses. "Am I evil?" sings Sean Harris here, before reprising "Yes I am!" Next, the song suddenly turns on a dime and speeds up, moving towards a restless chord sequence over which Brian Tatler delivered a truly landmark solo, utilising all the tricks of the day, plus some famously baroque fretboard tapping. Finally the main riff returns and the song grinds to a halt. It was a perfect song for Metallica to cover, with its simple vocal melodies and a long enough solo to allow Mustaine to show off his skills.

The final Diamond Head cover rehearsed by Metallica was 'The Prince', a rather more complex tune based on a fairly tricky riff and including a few moments for a bass solo after the chorus. This, more than the other songs in the set, was probably an over-ambitious choice for a first gig. The three remaining covers, however (Blitzkrieg's 'Blitz-krieg', Savage's 'Let It Loose' and Sweet Savage's 'Killing Time' – the fact that the two bands had such similar names was occasionally a cause of confusion among metal fans), were less tricky to master and were focused far more on riffing power than nimble-fingered dexterity.

After practising unsuccessfully for three weeks with a singer called Sammy Dijon, borrowed from a local band called Ruthless, Metallica decided that for the time being James would indeed continue to sing but that Dave would handle all the guitar parts. A debut concert was booked, and the band-members devoted themselves to preparation. A key event was about to occur.

On March 14, 1982, the nervous band climbed onstage at the Radio City venue in Anaheim, went straight into 'Hit The Lights' and were immediately plagued by problems. John Kornarens was there, and remembers that Dave Mustaine had problems with his guitar distortion pedal – which, as he was the sole guitar player, was absolutely key to the band having any degree of heaviness at all. To add to the problems, he broke a string at one point and, not having thought to bring a spare guitar along, had to restring his instrument right there on stage. An experienced band might have weathered this difficulty by talking to the audience and engaging in some interaction, but not Metallica in March 1982. James was so cowed by the event that he was completely lost for words, and the few minutes which Mustaine required to apply and tune the new string must have seemed like hours.

The set list went as follows: 'Hit The Lights', 'Blitzkrieg', 'Helpless', 'Jump In The Fire', 'Let It Loose', 'Sucking My Love', 'Am I Evil?', 'The Prince' and 'Killing Time'. However, the band chose not to reveal that most of the songs were covers, as Kornarens says: "They did a lot of NWOBHM covers – they did 'Let It Loose' by Savage and didn't tell anyone whose songs they were doing!" Despite the technical troubles and the obvious inexperience of his friends' band, John was pleased with the show: "I liked the music, it had a real European edge to it. It was heavy and it was street, it had a lot of energy to it and it was very aggressive."

Shortly after this first concert, Metallica had a lucky break. Ron McGovney, in his guise as a rock photographer, had snagged the very popular Mötley Crüe as a client. Meanwhile NWOBHM stars Saxon, whose work Metallica worshipped, were due to play a show at LA's famous Whisky A Go-Go club on March 27. Hetfield, Ulrich, McGovney and Mustaine quickly recorded a basic demo tape on their four-track machine of three songs, 'Hit The Lights', 'Killing Time' and 'Let It Loose', to use to persuade the management at the Whisky that they were good enough to be given the Saxon support slot, a major coup for a band so young. Ron took the tape over to the club and waited to see the manager.

As he waited, Mötley Crüe drummer Tommy Lee and singer Vince Neil walked in. As he later recalled: "They said, 'Hey Ron, what's up?' I told them that Saxon was doing a gig at the Whisky and I wanted to try to get my band to open up for them. They said, 'Yeah, we were gonna open up for them but we're getting too big to open. Come on in and we'll introduce you to the chick that does the booking.' So I dropped off the tape."

It was a phenomenal piece of good luck to be introduced to the Whisky booking staff by two of the fastest-rising stars on the scene and, sure enough, the Crüe connection paid off. Ron: "She called me back the very next day. I remember her telling me, 'You guys are pretty good, you remind me of this local band called Black'n'Blue . . . Saxon is scheduled to play two nights; we're gonna have Ratt open for them the first night and your band can open the second night.'"

And so Metallica, green as they were, were scheduled to play the

Whisky, a far weightier prospect than the Anaheim concert, not least because of the pressure of expectation from a crowd of Saxon fans. And on the night, Metallica, much to their credit, managed to win over many in the crowd, even though as before their set consisted of half-covers and half-originals. The new Metallica song was called 'Metal Militia', and was a powerful, Mustaine-composed tune based on a typically snaky riff. The set list – 'Hit The Lights', 'Jump In The Fire', 'Helpless', 'Let It Loose', 'The Prince' and 'Metal Militia' ('Sucking My Love' was added for the slightly longer second set) – went down well with the NWOBHM-loving crowd, although more critical observers weren't too impressed. As Gene Hoglan recalls: "They weren't very good. They were sloppy and kind of ugly . . . poor James, it was only his second show or something, but I remember him kind of crawling behind the amps and letting Mustaine do all the talking. And if Dave Mustaine is your frontman, you've got some whining onstage! That was pretty weak."

A teenager called John Bush, who later became the singer of Armored Saint, and later still of Anthrax (both bands were compatriots of Metallica), was also there, and says with laughter: "I saw Metallica open up for Saxon at the Whisky, when Saxon had their live record out, and James was just singing, no guitar, and wearing leopard-skin pants. They were not very good! It was a trip!" Hetfield was evidently influenced by the hair-metal crowd who had a fondness for leopard-skin. Metallica had also purchased some more appropriate accessories by this stage. As John Kornarens recalls: "They had a bullet belt with a silver skull and red eyes on it. One night James would wear it and the next night Dave Mustaine would wear it!"

Almost a month passed before the third Metallica concert took place. This show was unusual because they had decided to recruit another guitarist, Brad Parker, who went by the stage name of Damien C. Phillips for no adequately explained reason. Rehearsals went smoothly, but just as the April 23 gig at the Concert Factory in Costa Mesa was due to begin, the members of Metallica heard an unexpected noise coming from the stage: "While James, Lars, and myself are getting dressed to go on stage," recalled Ron, "we hear this guitar solo. So we look over the railing of the dressing room, and we see Brad onstage just blazing away on his guitar. So that was Metallica's first and last gig with Damien C. Phillips. Later I think he went on to join Odin." The ambitious Phillips had, it seemed, simply decided to warm up the crowd with his own guitar skills before appearing with the band – a decision far from Metallica's liking, especially Dave Mustaine, who was developing a reputation as something of a prima donna when it came to guitar solos.

The Concert Factory show also saw the debut of a new Metallica song called 'The Mechanix'. As their live repertoire was expanding, they decided to record another demo tape, this time more profession-ally than for the *Metal Massacre* song or for the pre-Whisky recording. This four-song tape, consisting of 'Hit The Lights', 'The Mechanix', 'Jump In The Fire' and 'Motorbreath' (another fast, new song) was to be used to spread the band's name on the LA club scene and became known, bizarrely enough, as the *Power Metal* demo, through a misunderstanding.

McGovney later explained how this had come to pass: "It's funny how that demo was labelled the *Power Metal* demo. The story is, I went to make Metallica business cards to send to the club promoters along with our demo. The card was supposed to just have the Metallica logo and a contact number. But I thought it looked too plain and decided it should say something under the logo. I didn't want to put 'hard rock' or 'heavy metal', so I coined the term 'Power Metal', I thought it had a nice ring to it. No band had used that term before as far as I knew."

It might have been a good idea on paper but the perfectionist Ulrich was not pleased. "I remember bringing the business cards to the band and Lars got so pissed off at me. He said, 'What did you do? What the hell is Power Metal? I can't believe you did such a stupid thing! We can't use these cards with the words Power Metal on them.' So that's how that tape became known as the *Power Metal* demo."

As the tape was distributed, club promoters began to pay Metallica some attention – which makes it all the odder that the very next show should take place at Lars' high school, Backbay High School, another month down the line on May 25, 1982. This time a full ten-song set was played, with five Diamond Head, Savage, Sweet Savage and Blitz-krieg covers plus Metallica's own 'Hit The Lights' (now the standard show-opener), 'The Mechanix', 'Jump In The Fire', 'Motorbreath' and 'Metal Militia'. Unlike the earlier club shows, however, the audi-ence weren't dedicated metal fans and they simply melted away, with Metallica practically emptying the hall before the end of the set, but the gig is notable as it was the first time that James sang and played rhythm guitar live. He had finally acknowledged that a second guitar was necessary and adapted his stage role accordingly.

A line-up which would seem familiar to future Metallica fans had started to materialise but things had still not settled down by any means. James, who would eventually become a guitarist of astonishing precision and power, was still finding his feet on the instrument and was considering a vocals-only role. To this end another guitarist called Jeff Warner was recruited for a show on May 28 at the Concert Factory in Los Angeles where Metallica were scheduled to open for the now almost forgotten bands Leatherwolf, August Redmoon, and Roxy Rollers. The gig took place as planned, but the new line-up couldn't bond (allegedly because Warner was annoyed that Mustaine refused to allow him to play any lead guitar solos) and they were soon back to a four-piece, with Hetfield picking up his guitar again.

Another show at the Radio City Hall in Anaheim took place on June 5 and went well, with the set of covers and originals now becoming honed to competence. The band's expectations were now firmly focused on the forthcoming *Metal Massacre* LP on Brian Slagel's bedroom label, Metal Blade: the record was set to appear on June 14 and represented a step forward for Metallica (or 'Mettallica' as they were billed on its sleeve) and, in fact, meant something more significant to the music community at large than might be supposed. Rather than being just another indie release, *Metal Massacre* was the first time that the underbelly of Californian metal had been exposed to the public outside demo-trading circles and the live club scene. A resolutely fan-produced item (Slagel had also managed to mis-spell Ron's surname as 'McGouney' on the sleeve), it was received with rapturous reviews from fans (but not from the media, unsurprisingly) and would go on to sell about 30,000 copies over the next few years.

In fact, the *Metal Massacre* series would become an institution, although the first volume marked the only time that Metallica were involved. Soon Brian and his friends were working on creating a second album, with a keen eye on the underground scene. Many of the bands which got their first break on an *MM* album went on to greater fame and fortune alongside Metallica, notably Slayer, whose singer Tom Araya explains how the series had inspired his band to greater heights: "We had heard the first two *Metal Massacre* records, and we thought, fuck, we're heavier than that! So we wrote the song 'Aggressive Perfector' for the third one." This song, which became an underground favourite among fans (just as 'Hit The Lights' had done for Metallica) was faster and heavier than the songs which preceded it – a direct result of the material on the *Metal Massacre* albums. That series fuelled the extreme metal wave which was growing at the time, as Araya confirms: "When we wrote 'Aggressive Perfector', that wasn't the kind of music we played at the time. That became a Slayer template. The only reason we wrote it was because of [hearing those records]."

Celtic Frost singer and guitarist Thomas Gabriel Fischer, growing up in Switzerland and culturally light-years away from Metallica's home environment, remembers to this day how profoundly he was struck by that first, seminal album: "I eventually managed to buy both versions of *Metal Massacre*, and one of the reasons for that was to have both the original and the new version of Metallica's 'Hit The Lights': the newer version was featured on a later edition."

What hit Fischer hardest was not the songwriting or the heaviness of the song. Primarily, it was the essence of thrash metal which impacted on him, specifically its tempo. "I remember very distinctively that we were all totally blown away by the speed of Metallica's music. At that time, nobody had ever heard anything like that, and it was an utter revelation. It was air guitar galore . . ." This, it seemed, was the reaction shared by thousands of metal fans. Not only was the new style of metal, thrash, heavier than what went before it; it was much, much faster, and took the listener along with it – or left them sitting in the dust. Rarely has one genre of music inspired so much passion and revulsion in equal measure. Speed was the key – but not everyone wanted to go through the door.

After a June 26 show at the Concert Factory in Costa Mesa once again, Metallica made a pivotal decision. They now had enough original songs to make it worthwhile spending some time, money and effort on committing them to tape. A demo, a professional recording, was about to be made. Little did they know that it would be the spark that ignited an explosion.

5

The Truth About Thrash Metal

Myth 1: Metallica were the first thrash metal band.
Myth 2: Metallica's first album, *Kill 'Em All*, was the first
thrash metal album.

Was thrash metal discovered by accident?

"Like Paul Stanley said," reasons Venom guitarist Jeff Dunn, "when someone asked him how they came up with the Kiss make-up, he said, 'If someone falls into the Mississippi and comes up with 16 gold nuggets, you're not going to call him a fuckin' genius.' What we did was just what we did, it wasn't contrived."

What Dunn (whose stage name is Mantas) is saying is that his band didn't make a conscious decision to play faster than everybody else on their first album. They just decided to play fast one day. "There wasn't a particular moment when it happened," recalls Jeff. "It just *happened*, and the first thrash metal song we did was 'The Witching Hour'." Ah yes – 'The Witching Hour', a high point of *Welcome To Hell* and a song on which Venom drummer Tony Bray (Abaddon) employed a double-speed snare drum pattern for the first time. It's a primitive song, full of raw riffing, roars from singer Conrad Lant (Cronos) and a production that isn't so much basic as indecipherable. But the song is legendary, and has been covered many times, notably by Slayer.

It's that snare drum pattern which is the essence of thrash metal, as well as the palm-muted, rapidly picked single-string riffs or two-string power chords which accompany it (the riffs usually move too fast for full chords to be employed, although many songs do contain slower, heavier sections when these come into play). Abaddon's drum part, which had been employed to good effect on the hardcore punk scene, was much faster than the usual rock and metal drum patterns, and now typifies the basis of all extreme metal (the overarching genre of metal of which thrash metal is just a part).

Of course, many bands said they were the heaviest ever, mostly just for publicity, but the idea that faster equals better didn't really come into play until Venom appeared. Once *Welcome To Hell* had spread through the underground and had enjoyed some media coverage (not that reviews were usually positive: the musicians' skills were far too undeveloped for that), other acts began to emerge, all indulging in some form of accelerated tempo and all sharing a common lyrical theme – Satanism – which brought most observers, at least in the media, out in a cold sweat. Although most observers have worked out by now that the Eighties thrash metal bands employed anti-Christian imagery in a simple attempt to shock rather than because they took it seriously, back then it was genuinely disturbing. And exciting, too.

Venom's initial line-up was influenced by classic rock and metal, but was made unstable by the inclination of some members to play harder and faster than the others. "I was in this band called Guillotine with another guitarist, and a bassist who was a bit of a clever shite," remembers Dunn with some satisfaction. "I said, 'Right, let's get into some heavy stuff, Priest, Motörhead, Sabbath, that kind of music' – and put an advert in the paper for a drummer. Me and Abaddon just got on really well right from the start, but this bassist went, 'If *he's* joining this band, I'm off.' So I said, 'Bye!'"

Venom were based in Newcastle, where the New Wave Of British Heavy Metal had taken hold with a vengeance. "Up here in the early Eighties there was a load of really good NWOBHM bands – Tygers Of Pan Tang, Raven, Fist, Emerson, White Spirit, really good bands. Basically we got successful and they didn't. They did get a certain amount of success, but then suddenly, bang – Venom took over." Asked why his band gained so much recognition while those other acts didn't, Dunn reasons: "I think the metal-buying public was just ready for something different. We had the punk attitude and we were described in the early days as long-haired punks. People used to say, 'You're making such a fuckin' *racket*' . . . we went out there and thrashed it up and the audiences were loving it. The other bands were doing their best to be good musicians and everything."

The same was true of the otherwise diametrically opposed setting of

Los Angeles, where Gene Hoglan, Eric Peterson and the other metal fans were watching the decline of Mötley Crüe from Judas Priest-like respectability into hair-metal clones. A punk and a metal scene existed side by side in LA and Newcastle – and in both cases the nascent thrash metal scene was about to emerge as a fusion of both.

The cause of European thrash metal was advanced in those early days by three bands: Venom, a Danish band called Mercyful Fate and a Swedish act by the name of Bathory. All three recorded dark, aggressive albums laced with demonic imagery on microscopic budgets, leading to a murky, unfinished sound which added much to their grim allure. And that was just the music: the lyrics and song titles (and the artwork which was inspired by them) bore the infamous, Satanic imprint. As Mercyful Fate singer King Diamond explains, the shock-horror influence came from well-known sources: "It was Alice Cooper. I saw the Welcome To My Nightmare tour in Copenhagen in 1975. Even though there wasn't that much make-up, you know, it changed him completely. He became *unreal*. I remember the show so well. I was up front – and I thought if I could just reach out and touch his boot he would probably disappear."

Diamond, more cerebral than many of his colleagues, soon got tired of being asked about his supposed Satanic beliefs, but appreciates that the subject requires some thought: "People say, 'Are you a Satanist?' And I say, 'Well, first of all I need to hear *your* definition of a Satanist before I can say yes or no,'" he muses. There is, after all, an established Church Of Satan in America, with its own Satanic Bible and various associated textbooks, written or co-written by the Church's founder, the late Anton LaVey. "I can relate to the philosophies that Anton LaVey wrote about," continues the Mercyful Fate singer. "When I read his books for the first time, I thought, this is the way I live my life. These are the values I have. But at the same time, there's a big void in there – he doesn't say to anyone, listen here, this is the right god and this is the wrong god. There's *nothing* about gods in there. It simply tells you to pick and choose whatever makes you happy, because no one can prove anything anyway. So if people say I'm a Satanist if I believe in the life philosophy in that book, then sure. But if they're saying, do you believe that baby blood will give you extra energy, and you can conjure demons with it? Then no, I don't believe in that."

Venom managed a second coup in 1982 when they released their second album, *Black Metal*, a record which later lent its name to any metal which dealt with evil or anti-Christian themes. Media and fans began applying this label to more or less any slightly dark metal act, and the bands concerned responded by upping the ante to unprecedented levels. Although two decades later the black metal scene is alive and well, primarily in Scandinavia (Dimmu Borgir, Immortal, Mayhem and many others) and the UK (Cradle Of Filth, Hecate Enthroned), ironically the two bands which are generally acknowledged to have been among the most Satanic of all are Slayer and the death metal outfit Deicide, both American. However, there's an enormous difference between the two, in that Slayer abandoned devilish themes in the early Nineties for more realistic topics such as warfare and social decay (Tom Araya: "A lot of the Satanic stuff was written by our guitarist Kerry King, but from what I understand he's a fictional writer"), while Deicide are firm believers in Satanism. Frontman Glen Benton explains: "I know what I believe, and when I write lyrics I don't write them to offend as many people as I can or to make people become Satanists. I believe a lot of the Satanic philosophies."

In 1981 the anti-Christian topics which Slayer and Deicide sing about would have led to mass outrage and perhaps a ban, but fortunately their heyday was yet to come and at this early stage the relatively mild imagery of Venom, Mercyful Fate and Bathory was more than enough for the industry to deal with. Kreator frontman Mille Petrozza, whose band would head up the B-league of thrash metal by the late Eighties, ponders: "In the early days we would play covers of Raven, Twisted Sister and Priest, but when I heard Venom, our music changed drastically."

The third member of the first thrash wave, Bathory, were somewhat disassociated from the rest of the genre, being isolated in small-town Sweden and influenced primarily by the punk scene. Bathory is primarily the work of one man, Quorthon, whose real name has never been published,* who grew up at some distance from the rest of the music world: "There was one shop in Stockholm called Heavy Sound which would import heavy metal records," he recalls. "Three or four months after our first album appeared in June 1984, the guy showed me one of

---

* Any so-called "real" names you may come across in various magazines and reference works are deliberate fakes, as he told the author in December 2002.

the Venom albums, and I realised that there was a movement going on."

Nonetheless, Bathory became an important influence on the wave of extreme metal which would gather throughout the Eighties and beyond, even though the Satanic themes which Quorthon and the others initially wrote about weren't too popular elsewhere.

In the USA, especially, Christian groups have always had a strong voice in both community and political circles and this was reflected in the reception that the first thrash metal bands received in the early Eighties, as Tom Araya remembers: "We had a lot of shit over our albums *Show No Mercy* and *Hell Awaits* because of those album titles – which were pretty dead on, you know? – and a bit over *Reign In Blood*."

Some musicians even treated the subject with logical ridicule. Anthrax's John Bush told rock writer Xavier Russell: "As for the Satanic thing, well that's crap. It's like, the devil's a boring subject to me. I don't know him and I've never met him, so why should I write songs about him? Anyway, I don't wanna meet him, he's a dickhead. The whole devil thing has just gotten totally out of hand. A good majority of bands who write songs about Satan write songs about him because he's an easy topic to cover." Kirk Hammett himself told *Guitar World* in 1988 that "I'm not into that whole Satanic thing. It's just something to fall back on if you don't have much imagination. Singing your fiftieth song about having lunch with Satan? I'm not into it. It's silly."

Many agreed with these sentiments and, as the years passed, the anti-Christian element of thrash metal faded to the point where such topics were more or less confined to the arenas of black metal and to a lesser extent death metal. Venom themselves, the instigators of all this, the progenitors of thrash metal and the actual inventors of the term 'black metal', remained much-praised by bands and critics within the metal scene but never achieved great commercial success. As Jeff Dunn now recalls, "For the publicity, we said we were going to be the biggest and the fastest and all that shite like every band says – but I think we actually achieved it to a certain degree. I think we opened the flood-gates for a lot of other acts to come through and do this kind of stuff, too." Does he feel that other bands took the thrash recipe which he had patented and took it for their own purposes? Without any bitterness, he

says, "From that point of view, yes . . . but I remember Slayer supported us in around 1985 – I can't remember where we were – and I
watched them and thought, what the fuck are *you* doing, boys?" The
guitarist was struck speechless by the sheer power of Slayer's music:
"They were going so far beyond what we were doing, with all the
black metal stuff. And if you look at the Norwegian metal nowadays,
the orchestral stuff, that's another stage again."

Dunn knows where his band stands in metal fans' esteem, but is
realistic about the cyclical nature of music: "People say, 'How do you
feel, with your place assured in the history books by creating black
metal?' But I credit KK Downing of Judas Priest for influencing me.
He was my big hero. If KK reads this, though, he'll say, 'Fuckin' hell, I
influenced *him*? They sound fuck-all like us!' "

Welcome To Hell and its successors are remembered with affection to
this day by many influential metallers, and, as we shall soon see, by a
certain group of teenagers in Los Angeles. Singer Bobby 'Blitz'
Ellsworth of New York thrash act Over Kill says: "*Welcome To Hell* was
an awesomely ground-breaking record. Bassist DD Verni and I had a
week off just drinking and consuming the opposite sex when we were
kids, and that was the soundtrack to that week." More profoundly,
Kreator singer Mille Petrozza refers to hearing the Venom albums as an
experience that altered his life: "There was this discotheque in Essen
called Kaleidoscope. We used to go there every Monday night because
they would play metal for two hours, before they started their regular
programme. One night the DJ played something I hadn't heard before,
which was almost disturbingly extreme. I went up to his booth and
asked what he had just played. He said that the band was called Venom.
That day changed my life, musically."

Not everyone enjoyed Venom, of course. Mikael Akerfeldt, of the
Swedish progressive death metal band Opeth, says: "I didn't like
Venom, I thought it was done by lousy players and I was more into
The Scorpions. Eventually I found out about bands who could be fast
and extreme but also controlled. Some of the thrash bands were really
good musicians, which was important to me." Despite this not-
uncommon attitude, the thrash virus spread rapidly, with other bands
such as Hellhammer from Switzerland, which featured the young
Thomas Gabriel Fischer among its ranks. The speed of the music, the
essence of its appeal, was increasing too. The reasons for this are unclear

– as John Bush says: "I don't know why everybody suddenly said, 'Let's play faster.' People started going, I can play faster, I can play faster! Then the death metal and black metal bands took it to a whole new world." Bush is, however, one of the few to note an almost classical influence in thrash metal, likening its double-speed snare and kick-drum patterns to traditional European music: "It's the polka, that's what it is, which all of a sudden became entrenched in metal."

However, the most important point that Bush and many others are agreed on is that while the speed of thrash came from Venom, and its lyrical and production rawness came from the punk scene, the one band whose influence is most profound on the emergence of extreme metal is Motörhead. Their attitude alone was an inspiration. As Gene Hoglan recalls, this British trio (occasionally a four-piece) were a revelation when they first played in America: "I saw Motörhead here in 1980 when they were supporting Ozzy Osbourne, and the crowd had no idea what to make of them. They were giving them the bird, which I thought was really cool – I didn't know you could flip off your crowd! Everybody else was waiting for Ozzy but Motörhead kicked my ass." Journalist Bob Nalbandian adds: "The *Ace Of Spades* album was an inspiration to the thrash scene. When I first heard that album, I fuckin' freaked out!"

Ironically, Motörhead frontman Ian 'Lemmy' Kilmister, a veteran of R&B act The Rockin' Vickers and psychedelic bands Sam Gopal's Dream in the Sixties and Hawkwind in the Seventies, is not a fan of extreme metal, nor is he pleased to be credited as an influence. "That's ridiculous," he says. "I cringe when I hear people say that. It's not my kind of music – which, to a layman, might seem to be the same music as ours, but it's not."

But Lemmy is being unduly modest. His attitude alone fuelled the growth of an entire genre.

There is no question that the origins of thrash metal emanated from small, sometimes underground and certainly underfunded record labels, like the pioneering Neat, whose bands honed their craft playing in small clubs. In the early Eighties bands such as Venom and Bathory enjoyed neither radio airplay (heaven forbid!), internet exposure or magazine coverage and as a result the wider world didn't wake up to their music until much later on, when thrash had become the province of bigger bands with bigger record company budgets. The pioneers remain unloved, unappreciated and unacknowledged except by those few fans who were around at the beginning.

Nevertheless many observers credit Metallica with having started the movement. Others insist that the genre was up and running long before Metallica arrived on the scene. So what's the truth? Who applied the word 'thrash' to the word 'metal' for the first time, then?

Eric Peterson, guitarist with Testament, remembers that a different term was prevalent in the beginning, coined primarily after the recreational drug use of many of the musicians. "We used the term 'speed metal' before 'thrash metal'," he says. "A lot of us did a lot of speed. We'd go out on Friday night and come home from, say, Paul Baloff's house on Sunday morning! We were up all night, tripping on dark things. Everything was real dark, Satanic and trippy. And it was definitely a clan." Others were less open about this, as guitarist Eric Meyer of Dark Angel adds: "Our drummer Gene Hoglan called us 'caffeine metal', because he didn't want any illegal substances attached to us."

Neil Turbin, the singer in Anthrax for a short spell, confirmed this in an interview in *Metal Sludge*: "When Anthrax and Metallica were hanging out in the early days the term 'Thrash Metal' had not been used. It was referred to as 'Power Metal' or 'Speed Metal'." Of course, the 'power metal' tag (which nowadays refers to clean, rapid – but not particularly extreme – metal such as that performed by Helloween, Iced Earth and Gamma Ray) might well have come from Metallica's 1982 demo, for which Ron McGovney had added the phrase on its accompanying business cards. Turbin claims that the origin of the term "thrash" can be pinpointed exactly, to the song 'Metal Thrashing Mad' on Anthrax's first album. "I remember seeing it in an early 1984 issue of *Kerrang!* magazine where they reviewed Anthrax and Exciter," he says. "This was the first time I ever saw 'Thrash Metal' used in the media or my singing referred to as 'Thrash Metal'."

This was probably when the term was first used in the media, but fans had yet to pick up on it. Indeed some prominent magazines were initially reluctant to use the term at all, as journalist Garry Sharpe-Young recalls: "I do remember very clearly 'Thrash' being ridiculed mercilessly by the mainstream UK rock press. They soon did a sharp about-turn, and not for the last time!" No one seems to know when fans began using the expression, Brian Slagel confirms: "I've been wondering who thought of that term. It must have been in 1982 or '83, and it might have been someone up in San Francisco, because they embraced that scene."

Even the year of its origin isn't clear. Katon DePena of Hirax suggests that the term came from much further back: "I'd say 1980. It was originally used to explain the nastiest kind of metal. There was already the British New Wave of Metal, so we needed a title for our kind of metal." Conversely, Byron Roberts of Bal-Sagoth thinks that it came much later: "The term 'thrash' was already being bandied about by the US and European metal press by the mid-Eighties, which is where I first encountered its widespread usage." Silenoz of Dimmu Borgir agrees: "I believe the term was starting to take shape sometime during 1984-85. Some bands even had the word 'thrash' in their song titles, and I guess it became more or less synonymous with the fast-paced aggressive metal they were playing at the time." Still others avoid the debate entirely. Jim Martin, sometime guitarist with Faith No More, says: "It seems fat guys wearing sport coats and jeans developed this term behind closed doors at a marketing meeting. I don't think I've ever spoken the term aloud."

Martin has a point. Music journalists seem to be falling over themselves with unseemly haste in their hurry to create new categories for metal, so much so that confusion abounds amongst all but the deeply enlightened. Nowadays, alongside thrash and power metal, the fan can investigate black metal, true metal, doom metal, nu-metal and traditional heavy metal, as well as 'old-school', 'epic', 'brutal', 'symphonic', 'experimental', 'avant-garde' and 'ambient' subgenres of each style. Perhaps the older days were simpler and better, as Glen Benton of Deicide suggests: "There was no such thing as death metal when we were listening to this shit, it was just metal. It was either black metal or it was metal. And what was black metal back then is considered to be death metal now: anything that dealt with Satanism we called black metal, like Venom. I listened to everybody back then, man: Black Sabbath, Venom, Sodom, Destruction, Possessed."

Benton's band is a perfect example of the modern-day confusion. Deicide now fall into the death metal genre despite the Satanic lyrics of their songs, which back in the early Eighties, however, would have made them firmly black metal. Confusing, eh? Benton himself is tired of the relentless pigeonholing, adding: "I don't like the term death metal, really. It's not like when we write the songs we say, man, that's the heaviest 'death metal' song I ever heard! Goddamn! It's not like that." This also applies to Bathory, whose style has been described by various writers as thrash metal, black metal, simple heavy metal or a mixture of all three, as Quorthon explains: "Everything that didn't sound like the NWOBHM in those days was called black metal. In fact, by 1984 when people were asking us how long we'd been into black metal, we were embarrassed because we thought they were referring to the Venom album of the same name." Quorthon also came up with a new genre: "I used to say that we were into death metal, just for fun, and I challenge anyone to show proof that anyone else came up with that subcategory before September 1984." This is an interesting development, if only for the fact that Possessed singer/bassist Jeff Becerra claims to be the inventor of the term at around the same time.

But critics love placing art into boxes and creating buzzwords. By the Nineties the metal scene had fragmented into so many different genres that the catch-all phrase 'extreme metal' had been coined to distinguish the thrash, speed, black and death metallers from traditional heavy metal bands such as Iron Maiden and Judas Priest, as well as glam-metal acts such as Poison, Warrant, Ratt, Mötley Crüe and (briefly) Bon Jovi.

Extreme metal is a vague term with different connotations for everyone, but most pundits don't hesitate to include Metallica under its banner. Writer Martin Popoff reasons: "You might say the first extreme metal was Judas Priest's *Stained Class*. But of course there's a shift when you get to the New Wave Of British Heavy Metal, or, just before that, the fact that there were three Motörhead albums before 1980. That is a very good benchmark for the first extreme music: those three Motörhead albums. Perhaps another benchmark after Motörhead would be Venom. In their own hapless and stupid way, they invented thrash, speed, and black metal. There was also the subtle idea that became a thrash benchmark used sparingly but more than occasionally, and especially in black metal: recording badly on purpose, or at least recording badly and not really caring too much about fixing it. All of that is pretty extreme, along with the graphics, the lyrics, the vomity belching vocals, the look, the poses."

Thomas Gabriel Fischer sees through the surface of metal, extreme

60

or otherwise, to the psychological and political substrata which underpin it, as he explains: "I was fortunate enough to begin experiencing
this form of music consciously as a kid in the early Seventies, at the
tail-end of its inception. This heavy and distorted form of music arose
as one of the expressions of the urge for revolution within the young
generation – revolution against the establishment, against politicians,
against parents, against teachers, against whatever seemed immobile,
antiquated, conservative, and, perhaps most important, uninventive."

Uniquely among the musicians interviewed for this book, Fischer
focused on the beauty of metal hidden beneath the chaos of its epider-
mis: "This screeching music of distorted sounds – noise to all but its
fans – was just perfect to drive all who were hated and despised up the
walls. And this music carried an amazing new energy, it was fresh,
adrenalinised, a cry for vitality and attention, a perfect vent for accumulated frustration. I began to love – and live – this music. I couldn't get
enough of it. That I continuously began to search and yearn for ever
more power and ever fewer limits to it was probably connected to the
circumstances of my youth and the very dark experiences in my daily
life."

The darkness of the music attracted thousands of disaffected youths
like Fischer, as well as the power that drove it. And, of course, there
was the intense speed of extreme metal (and its early-Eighties antec-
dents, thrash and black metal), which, it appears, was born as much of
onstage adrenaline as from songwriting intention. This brings us to
Metallica, as James Hetfield told *Guitar World* in 1992: "Lars was always
nervous on stage, so he'd play faster and faster. Nobody wanted to
wimp out and tell him that he was playing too fast. We just figured,
hell, we'll just play faster too." Tony Scaglione of Whiplash confirms
that speed was the key to extreme metal: "The main bands that I
listened to at that time were definitely Metallica, Exodus, Slayer,
Voivod, Celtic Frost and Megadeth. There were different things that I
liked about each individual band but the common thread had to be the
speed element and the extreme energy these bands projected. That is
what I really liked and what I believe set these bands apart from the
more classic metal bands."

It should be noted, however, that as influential as Metallica would
become, they were already being shadowed by 1982 and 1983 by their
Los Angeles compatriots Slayer, whose phenomenal speed and

aggression even threatened to eclipse Metallica's powerful early work. In fact, one of the long-standing arguments which this book addresses in a later chapter is which of the two bands have created the best extreme metal album ever – the rivalry is *that* close. Even though Metallica emerged quite a while before Slayer, some industry veterans still credit the latter for creating the extreme metal genre, notably Armored Saint guitarist and (ironically) sometime Metallica roadie John Marshall, who remembers: "When I was working for Metallica in late '83 we were on the East Coast doing some gigs. One of the guys had a tape of Slayer's first album, and kept playing it over and over. It seems tame by today's standards, but back then it was the fastest, craziest thing we had ever heard." Dan Lorenzo of Hades traces his enthusiasm for extreme metal to the date when, "A guy from a fanzine called *Sledge-hammer Press* mailed me a tape of Slayer, Exodus, and Celtic Frost . . . I got *way* into Slayer and Exodus." Phil Demmel of Technocracy and Machine Head adds that his first taste of the extreme genre was, "Slayer supporting Laaz Rockit. They came out with 'Evil Has No Boundaries' and I'd never heard anything so fast in my life."

The issue of speed remains a contentious one. Lars allegedly told a fanzine in the mid-Eighties that Slayer only decided to speed up after they supported Metallica at a show in 1982. I asked Tom Araya if this was true: "Oh, no no no!" he responded. "What made us go fast was the Metal Blade *Metal Massacre* series. Brian Slagel approached us and said, 'I want you on *Metal Massacre 3.*' So we went out and got a copy of the first one, with Metallica on it, and we looked at each other and said, 'We can do fuckin' heavier and better and faster than this shit!' And that's exactly what we did. Then we did shows in San Francisco, and what *really* blew us away was Exodus. We did three shows with them at various clubs that weekend, and we came home with a competitive edge. Like, fuck . . . that's what we gotta do to make fuckin' great music! Those live shows blew our minds. Lars can think what he wants, but it was Exodus that blew us away. We figured we could come up with something heavier and faster than what Metallica had done. And we did, and we always have!"

Tom is right about Exodus. As writer Borivoj Krgin, long-time metal journalist and founder of metal news website Blabbermouth.net, remembers: "My first exposure to Exodus, Testament, Forbidden and Vio-Lence took place through tape-trading from 1984 to 1987 and seeing them on tour in the New York area after they released their first albums. It was a very exciting time for the metal scene, because everyone had the feeling that something new and fresh was being created by these bands, and the number of quality acts coming out of the Bay Area was pretty astounding. I always heard stories about how "violent" some of the early Exodus shows were in the Bay Area, and I'm sure some of that was embellished – as is usually the case with these things. But I certainly believe that they had a loyal and rabid following in the early years, and judging from the live tapes I was hearing while on the East Coast, it definitely seemed like the shows were very exciting to be part of."

Nevertheless many do remember Metallica performing the first genuinely extreme music, even if it would soon be superseded in terms of speed and heaviness by Slayer and others. By June 1982, Metallica were on the point of recording a seminal demo tape: and it's this which has made a lasting impact on most old-school observers. Tony Scaglione: "I guess my first really influential experience of extreme metal had to be the first time I heard the *No Life 'Til Leather* demo by Metallica. Up until that time, Motörhead was the most extreme thing I was into, but they were still based in the rock'n'roll bluesy kind of sound. Metallica, on the other hand, was like nothing I had heard before. It was so fast and heavy (maybe not by today's standards) that everyone I knew who had heard it was just blown away. I don't really remember who coined the term 'thrash' but as far as I remember, the first time I saw it used was in conjunction with Metallica."

Eric Peterson of Testament supports this: "Metallica had the *No Life 'Til Leather* demo out and opened up for Laaz Rockit, which was one of the favoured bands round here. It had the NWOBHM riffing, but they added the GBH punk drums to it. At first it reminded me of Motörhead. It was really cool what they did, and all the other bands followed what they did. As soon as I heard Metallica I knew what kind of music I wanted my band to do. It all clicked for me."

Martin Hooker, who later founded the pioneering Music For Nations record label (which would play a large part in Metallica's career), explains: "Initially the most extreme band was probably Motörhead, who I thought were great. Then I heard Metallica's demo and it was a whole new ball game."

Tony Dolan, bassist with Atomkraft and later Venom, says: "I first heard Metallica through a guy called Sam Kress who had come to England with the *No Life 'Til Leather* demo to get the guys a deal. We exchanged tapes. I gave him our *Total Metal* demo and I got said tape in return. Sam also had a mag called *Whiplash* in San Francisco which he was going to use to promote the band. He played me the Metallica demo and my first reaction was, fuck, man, that is so fast! They played like a wall of sound, so tight and so precise. I couldn't believe how tight the band was."

Bernard Doe, later the founder of the *Metal Forces* magazine but at the time a tape-trader, remembers receiving the two Metallica demos: "I was heavily into the underground tape-trading scene in the early Eighties and was discovering some great unsigned bands from all over the world. I guess I had some kind of reputation as being a 'key' tape-trader on the scene at that time and Lars Ulrich wanted to spread the word about his band. Lars was aware of my reputation from a couple of mutual friends, Ron Quintana and Patrick Scott, so he got Pat to send me a copy of a four-song demo they had just recorded. Of course I was blown away by that demo! It was really a breath of fresh air to the underground metal scene at that time. Then came the famous *No Life 'Til Leather* demo. Those early Metallica demos and Exciter's *Heavy Metal Maniac* demo really started to cause a buzz on the underground."

Some observers nail the emergence of the terms 'thrash metal' and 'extreme metal' to the appearance of Metallica's debut album, *Kill 'Em All*, which would be released in 1983. As Phil Fasciana of Malevolent Creation says: "I think the first time I heard thrash metal was when me and my friends bought *Kill 'Em All*. That is what the guys at the local record store were calling it, and that became a new term for metal music for me and my friends. I basically worshipped bands like Slayer, Dark Angel, Exodus, Destruction, Kreator and Metallica. I was attracted to the down-to-earth nature of the bands and the speed of the music, and the hateful-sounding vocals. It just made me freak out." Jan Transit, of the Norwegian avant-garde black metal band . . . In The Woods, adds: "For me, the term popped up when *Kill 'Em All* grew really big. I guess the whole Bay Area period gave birth to it, but just like any other trend, it took a while before it was a term that metalheads added to their vocabulary."

Writer Borivoj Krgin, who has followed the extreme metal scene since its inception, recalls: "I first heard Metallica in early 1983, prior to the release of *Kill 'Em All*. I thought it was the greatest thing I'd ever heard up until that point, basically. It was the first time a band had come along and played ultra-fast (relatively speaking), but didn't simply churn out noise – they actually had intricate guitar picking and were tight as hell. Additionally, they had a very powerful, polished production without being too clean, which only made their music that much more effective. Compared to bands like Venom and Motörhead, Metallica came across as much more musically involved and less punkish-sounding."

One of the songs on *Kill 'Em All*, 'Whiplash', had a notable effect on many listeners, as the most consistently fast song on the record. One such listener was Steve Tucker, vocalist and bassist for Morbid Angel, who reasons: "The term 'extreme' has changed over the years. What was extreme when I first heard it is by no means extreme today. But what really woke me up was when I heard 'Whiplash' for the first time. That was a whole new thing to me when I first heard it, I think I was 12 years old. It made me want to play music. I had been listening to a lot of Iron Maiden, which was great at the time, and then I heard 'Whiplash' and nothing else seemed to compare."

The conclusion? That Metallica's *No Life 'Til Leather* demo of 1982 and their *Kill 'Em All* debut album of 1983 were immensely influential on thrash metal and the broader church of extreme metal. No, they weren't the first thrash metal band; Venom came first. No, *KEA* wasn't the first thrash metal album – *Welcome To Hell* was before it – although it was certainly the first *big-selling* thrash metal album.

But the wider issue is *when* they did these things, and that's all tied up with Metallica's move to another city and their meeting with a man who would change everything.

6

1982

In 1982, if you were in a band anywhere in America or Europe but you weren't lucky enough to have a record company manufacturing and promoting your songs and a distributor getting them into the shops, you still had one invaluable way of getting your songs heard: the tape-trading network.

Like a primitive internet made up of fans and mailboxes rather than computers and phone lines, the scene functioned purely through the distribution of music. Mostly recorded at home or in low-budget studios, cassette tapes would fly back and forth across continents, usually for free (fans tended to exchange rather than purchase tapes), and all in a spirit of punkish co-operation. It didn't matter too much that the sound quality on the cassettes would diminish as later- and later-generation copies were made and exchanged: what mattered was that good music, often unavailable in many countries, found its way to the fans who wanted it. And all for the price of a blank tape and an airmail envelope (although the record companies would bewail the loss of revenue that such trading inevitably entailed).

A similar scene still exists, of course, but thanks to the arrival of four overlapping technologies (the internet itself; file-sharing programs; CD ripping and burning software; and broadband internet access) within five years or so, fans mostly exchange music by creating copies of albums on blank CDs, or by downloading them from each other's computers and distributing them by email or through instant-messaging services. But the principle is the same.

And so Metallica recorded a demo, which they hoped would lead firstly to a reputation among the tape-traders who would inevitably send it to each other, and which would then entice record companies to offer them a deal. The band wouldn't make much money from the cassette, of course (although initial sales at gigs and through mail-order might defray a few recording expenses), but the interest in them generated through word of mouth would be priceless – or so they hoped.

The immediate problem was finance. Recording a master tape and manufacturing sufficient copies to make an impact costs money, and the four musicians were hardly in a position to fund time in a studio, even though McGovney and Hetfield were living rent-free in McGovney's mother's soon-to-be-demolished rental house. However, as usual Lars managed to come up with a way round the issue. He had hooked up with a record label owner called Kenny Kane, who had seen Metallica perform and was interested in financing a recording. As Hetfield told *Aardschok*: "A guy named Kenny Kane scratched together some money for us so that we could go into Chateau East studios in Tustin, California. We had written some songs in the meantime [as well as playing] 'Killing Time', 'Let It Loose' and a few Diamond Head songs in our set."

Ron McGovney wasn't keen on Kenny Kane, telling *Shockwaves*: "Kenny Kane had this punk label called High Velocity which was a division of Rocshire Records, an Orange County record company. He said he would put up the money to have us do an EP. So we went in the studio."

The tracklisting for the recording sessions (which Kane had envisaged as providing material for an EP) was re-recordings of 'Hit The Lights' (the version which would appear on the second pressing of *Metal Massacre*), 'The Mechanix', 'Jump In The Fire' and 'Motorbreath', plus the newer songs 'Seek And Destroy', 'Metal Militia' and 'Phantom Lord'.

There was an immediate problem insofar as High Velocity was into punk, not metal. Kane had heard the covers which Metallica played and had liked what he heard, not realising that the songs were not originals. As James explained: "When we were in the studio and began recording our own songs with Kenny, he said, 'It sounds completely different!' 'Yeah, Kenny, the other songs aren't by us.'"

Unusually, although Kane wasn't inclined to issue the material, he allowed the band to retain the tapes, from which Lars and his friend Pat Scott made copies to distribute to the contacts they had made. As Ron told KNAC in 1993: "That demo went everywhere, even to Japan. We had letters from everywhere."

Among the recipients were Bernard Doe and Tony Dolan, and an advert for the demo was taken out in *BAM* magazine. Ron: "It cost us $600, which was a lot of money back in 1982. It was probably Lars and James' idea. They laid the ad out and showed it to me and said it would cost $600. I said, 'OK, Lars, James, where's your money?' And they said, 'We don't have any money.' I was the only one that had any money, so I wrote out a cheque for $600 to *BAM*. To this day I never got that money back." Ron was, it seemed, becoming a little disillusioned with his bandmates at this time; perhaps a warning of events to come.

Once the demo (dubbed *No Life 'Til Leather* after the first line of 'Hit The Lights' and possibly in homage to Motörhead's seminal live album *No Sleep 'Til Hammersmith*) was out, the word spread rapidly. Copies of the cassette spread through the tape-trading underground very quickly, probably because of the speed, the aggression and the tight, focused performance. James Hetfield's guitar work is especially notable on this cassette, although it hadn't approached the precision it would later achieve, and his vocals are very different from Metallica's later work. His range is limited, of course, but in the field of extreme metal (and in the demo world in general) this wasn't too out of the ordinary. The main difference between his singing then and on later albums is that his vocals are sung, not barked or shouted, making it sound weak in comparison.

Journalist Bob Nalbandian points out that the importance of the *No Life* demo should not be underestimated, at least in terms of the boost it gave Metallica's reputation: "*No Life 'Til Leather* really struck a chord in San Francisco, for example. I know Ron Quintana had a bunch of friends who were into Venom so much, who were like gods on the underground scene . . . *NLTL* was the ultimate demo tape back then. They were one of the first US bands to have an impact with a demo. Before that, no one got reviews from a demo tape. But in the UK and Europe all these bands like Sweet Savage and Mercyful Fate would put out demos and we would trade them. Blitzkrieg, Satan, Deep Machine and all the Neat Records bands did it too. Metallica got wind of that and put one out. But no one had thought a demo tape could make a band big. Bands would put out demos because they couldn't afford to do records."

In PR terms, too, the tape was a real asset: "All these key people had the tape because we sent it out to KJ Doughton in Oregon, and *Aardschok* magazine in Holland, and Bernard Doe at *Metal Forces* in England."

In a matter of weeks the *NLTL* demo was everywhere. And not only this tape. As singer Snake of the Canadian band Voivod recalls, live Metallica bootlegs were circulating too: "I had a demo with Dave Mustaine singing. The attitude of the songs was like . . . this is gonna be big, we were like, whoa! It was a really underground demo, probably a bootleg. It had 'No Remorse' and 'Metal Militia', and we were listening to it and freaking out because of the picking." Again, the precision of Hetfield's riffs (and to a lesser extent the fire of Mustaine's solos) had made a serious impression on a future mover on the metal scene. This knock-on effect is where the true impact of the demo can be seen.

In the summer of 1982 the band were going from strength to strength, but internal relations were becoming fraught. As we've seen, Ron McGovney was unhappy because of the way he felt he was being taken for granted by the others – but the most volatile member, Dave Mustaine, was also walking a fine line. At one point an incident occurred which led to his temporary dismissal, and which has gone down in Metallica's folklore in several conflicting versions. It's the story of Dave, his dogs and Ron McGovney's car.

In 1999 I interviewed Dave Mustaine and was keen to hear his version of events. His exact words were as follows: "I was dealing drugs to keep myself afloat, because my mom had moved out. It had become a way of life for me, and when I would do a concert people knew I was gone, so they'd jump in through my window and steal my stuff. There are only so many places you can hide something in a house, and usually it was an insider, people who had been there. So I had dogs to protect my merchandise."

All clear so far: Dave had a couple of dogs for security. However, the problem occurred when one of his dogs took an interest in Ron's car: "I took one of them with me up to rehearsal one day and the dog put her paws on the bass player's car. I don't know if it scratched it or left paw-prints, or you know, put a fuckin' dent in the car, I don't know." James, it seems, objected to this, and either cuffed the dog, pushed it or otherwise laid his hand or foot on it, whether gently or with some force. "James kicked the dog and we started arguing," said Mustaine. "Push led to shove and I hit him, and I regret it." The latter sentiment is obviously genuine, as Dave reiterated: "If I had the chance to do it all over again, I would not have brought the dog."

Ron McGovney told the same story to *Shockwaves*, if a little more graphically (and unsympathetically to Mustaine). He also omits any mention of James touching a dog: "Dave had come over to my house on a Sunday afternoon and he brought his two pit bull puppies. I think I was in the shower at the time. Anyway, Dave let the dogs loose and they were jumping all over my car scratching the shit out of it, I had a rebuilt '72 Pontiac LeMans. And James came out and said, 'Hey Dave, get those fuckin' dogs off of Ron's car!' And Dave said, 'What the fuck did you say? Don't you talk that way about my dogs!' Then they started fighting and it spilled into the house, and when I came out of the shower I see Dave punch James right across the mouth and he flies across the room, so I jumped on Dave's back and he flipped me over onto the coffee table. And then James gets up and yells to Dave, 'You're out of the fuckin' band! Get the fuck out of here!' So Dave loaded all his shit up and left all pissed off. The next day he comes back crying, pleading, 'Please let me back in the band.'"

Other versions of this story over the years have suggested it was Mustaine who had kicked one of Hetfield's dogs, a spin which betrays the fallibility of the Metallica rumour-mill.

Despite the difficulties among the relationships in the band, Metallica continued their gigging schedule, building a reputation to match the impact generated by the *No Life 'Til Leather* demo. July 1982 saw four shows (the Concert Factory in Costa Mesa, the Troubadour in Hollywood, a private party in Huntingdon Beach and another party at Dana Point) and the band did several more in early August (the Troubadour again, plus another slot at the Whisky opening for Steeler, and a gig at the Bruin Den at Long Beach). The last of these took place on August 7 and was notable for the appearance on the bill after Metallica (the openers) of Hirax, and in headline position, none other than Stryper, the glam-metal band whose Christian stance attracted more derision than any other band of their type. To this day Hirax singer Katon DePena laughs at the memory of Stryper performing on the same bill as two such dedicated extreme metal acts: "Hirax and Metallica were very good friends in the early days. Practising, playing records, and drinking a lot of vodka. We only played together once . . . with Stryper headlining. That's a true story!"

Stryper were certainly the victims of such sustained abuse, but a combination of Bibles thrown into the crowd at gigs and hairspray seems like asking for it. They also dressed in yellow and black stripes (they took their name from a verse in the Bible mentioning the stripes of a whip) and it's a miracle they escaped worse fates. As drummer Robert Sweet recalls, however, Metallica weren't too unfriendly – except for the ever-mercurial Dave Mustaine: "Back in 1982, I didn't know anything about Metallica and they didn't know anything about us, but I remember them laughing about all the yellow and black stripes. In a terrible way! All the guys were really cool except for Dave. Man, I remember him really giving us a hard time. He basically hated us. He hated my brother (singer Michael Sweet), he hated me, he was laughing at the hairspray. But that happens: they came from a different background and they were going for a different thing."

While the vibe backstage wasn't too friendly, the atmosphere out front was non-existent. As Sweet recalls: "There were like seven people in the crowd. The promoter hadn't told anybody we were playing, so nobody showed up!" Still, the now-less-bouffant drummer remembers Mustaine and the band more charitably: "I would have liked to spend more time with Metallica, but Dave made it a little tense that day. I thought they were a good band. They were loose, but we were, too . . . I've heard that Dave is a great guy and that he's had a change of heart recently."

The rest of August was taken up with Metallica's now-regular gigging schedule. August 18 saw them open at the Troubadour for another hair-metal act, Ratt, who – while not quite as popular as the still-fashionable Mötley Crüe – were well ahead of B-league acts like Stryper. More shows at the Woodstock in Anaheim, another slot at the Whisky and a trip to HJs in North Hollywood kept the band's local profile high. But the most crucial show of all was one 450 miles away in San Francisco, a city to which Metallica had not yet thought to venture.

Brian Slagel had not been idle in the months since the release of *Metal Massacre*. For the night of September 18, 1982, he put together a bill of bands to perform at the Keystone in San Francisco under the umbrella title of 'Metal Massacre Night'. A slot for Cirith Ungol, who were scheduled to perform between Hans Naughty and Bitch, suddenly became vacant when the band dropped out. As Slagel recalls:

"One of the bands I had lined up to do the Metal Massacre show dropped out so I called Metallica and said, 'Do you guys wanna come up and play the San Fran gig?' They said, 'Sure.' "

As various eyewitnesses recall, the response to Metallica's performance (the seven songs on the *No Life* demo, plus two Diamond Head covers) was incredible. The audience went completely over the top to a degree that no previous Metallica show had seen. Many of the 200 or so fans in the venue even joined the band on stage for a marathon headbanging session. This came as a surprise to the band themselves, who had had no idea that their music had penetrated as far away from Los Angeles as San Francisco. In fact, as Brian explains, they had only exposed their music to the more glam-metal-oriented audiences of Los Angeles before this point, without ever really finding their genuine fanbase: "At this point Metallica had started playing around LA a bit, but not really to the greatest reaction, because they were playing something a lot heavier than what was going on on the LA scene at that point. People were scared of it, especially the club owners." As Jeff Becerra of Possessed, who was at the show, recalls: "I remember seeing Metallica at the Keystone Berkeley and thinking, wow – these guys are tremendous."

Ron McGovney later told KNAC that, true to form, the logistics of getting to and from the show didn't go smoothly: "I rented a trailer and we loaded our drum riser and all our gear and pulled it with my dad's 1969 Ford Ranger, we all drove up in that one truck. I had never been to San Francisco before, I remember driving around Chinatown with this trailer and I was getting so pissed off trying to find this club. All the other band members are back there in the camper shell drinking and partying and I'm just pissed as shit." But the reaction from the audience made it all seem better: "We had no idea that our *No Life 'Til Leather* demo had gotten up there, they knew all the lyrics to our songs and everything. People asking us for our autographs, it was a trip, we couldn't believe it. When we played in LA with bands like Ratt, people would just stand there with their arms crossed."

Relationships between Ron and the rest of the band were now becoming severely tested. McGovney, who perhaps took life a little more seriously than Ulrich, Hetfield and Mustaine, was starting to find their constant drunken antics more than a little wearing, especially as he was expected to manage the band, as he told *Shockwaves*: "Things started happening back at the house . . . my things would be missing. The worst thing was when we played with my friend Jim's band Kaos . . . apparently one of Dave's buddies stole my back-up Ibanez bass guitar. My leather jacket was missing. I was really getting sick of the situation." What made it more annoying was that McGovney was working hard to keep the band on the road: "I didn't know why this was happening because I did what I could, and what they asked me to do. Lars and I butted heads a lot, I hate when people show up late and use you all the time and that's just what Lars did. . . . Every time we did a gig up in San Francisco I had to borrow my dad's truck, pay for the gas, I had to rent the trailer out of my pocket, I paid for the hotel rooms on my Visa card – and San Francisco is expensive, even for a cheap room. I paid for all of this and they couldn't understand why I was mad, they said, 'Well, you're getting the cheque after the gig,' and we were only getting paid $100 per gig at the most, which didn't even cover the hotel room. Plus we drank a couple hundred dollars worth of alcohol. I always said to them, 'If I'm a part of this band, why is it up to me to pay for everything while you guys get the free ride?' I had suggested we get a manager or somebody that could back us, because I was really getting tired of this. And they just laughed about it and said, 'Have a sense of humour.' They just didn't understand, so they interpreted it as me having a bad attitude."

As Ron explained to KNAC: "I was kind of their babysitter, you might say. They would get stinking drunk all the time but I was the person who was elected to drive them everywhere. I used to tell them not to drink so much, or we'll never get anything done. They didn't like being told what to do, and they had a kind of contempt for me." Not only this, but he had work to do: "I was the one with all the responsibility – I was the road manager and had to book the hotels, drive the trailer, load the equipment, while they sat in the back of the van and drank a gallon of vodka and got totally ripped and said, 'Ron's such a jerk, blah blah blah.' They came to hate me . . . it came to the point where they couldn't stand me any more and I couldn't stand them any more, and they started looking for another bass player."

Ron's irritation was noted by James and Lars and, on Metallica's return to Los Angeles, they hooked up with Brian Slagel again, who was mightily impressed with their performance in San Francisco. On hearing Ulrich and Hetfield's explanation of their problems with

McGovney, he told them about a band he had seen playing a show at the Whisky A Go-Go some weeks before. The band, an otherwise unremarkable rock outfit called Trauma, included among their members a fearsomely talented bass player. His name was Cliff Burton.

Cliff had not been idle since the demise of EZ Streets and the departure of Jim Martin to Faith No More. Trauma, a competent band even if they didn't exactly stand out from the crowd at the time (they had scored a slot on Brian Slagel's second *Metal Massacre* LP, for example), offered an opportunity to perform to the best of his abilities, which he had now honed to the point where his bass playing was breathtakingly nimble. Burton would often use the live shows as a chance to demonstrate his solos, which he would play over the riffs of the two guitarists, an unusual device at the time.

It took Slagel no time to convince Lars and James to take in a Trauma show. As he recalls: "Although Metallica had done a few shows by now, they were still a little frustrated by LA, as well as looking for a bass player. *Metal Massacre II* had Trauma on it, who I'd seen once before when they came down and played in LA. When Lars said they needed a bass player, I said, 'You've got to come and see this band Trauma, because the bass player is awesome.'" What was it about Cliff that had impressed Brian to such a degree? "First of all he was a phenomenal musician, but he was also a maniac on stage. He used to headbang like you've never seen anybody headbanging before. He used to just get up there in jeans and gigantic hair and just bang."

When Hetfield and Ulrich finally saw Burton and his band, they were awe-struck. Cliff's insanely committed headbanging and his fiery playing won them over immediately. Dave Marrs, Metallica's first roadie, later said of Lars and James: "I could just see them go, 'Oh my God! Look at that guy!' The thing that struck them the most was that while you see lead guitar playing, here you had a guy playing lead bass. They thought that was great." James told *Aardschok*: "We were completely impressed by this headbanging, hippie bassist." As Ron McGovney recalls: "We were sitting there watching the band and all of a sudden the bass player goes into a solo as the guitar players were playing rhythm, and he's just thrashing his head all over the place. And James and Lars were just bowing to him."

Lars approached Cliff after the show, introduced himself and asked him if he would join Metallica. Initially, Burton wasn't keen on the idea. Famously, he disliked Los Angeles, particularly its glam-metal scene, and wouldn't consider leaving San Francisco to live there. Although disappointed, Ulrich repeated his offer and resolved to keep working on the bassist.

As it happened, Cliff was thinking of quitting Trauma anyway. As he later told journalist Harald Oimoen: "Trauma went down to LA and did some stuff. While in LA, Lars and James saw us and decided that they would like to have me in their band. And so they started getting ahold of me and calling me, and I came to their shows here when they played Frisco. And eventually Trauma started to . . . annoy me . . . a couple of different ways, so I said, later." It seemed that Trauma's music wasn't going in the direction which Cliff had originally conceived: "They were starting to adopt these attitudes about . . . well, it was starting to get a little commercial in different ways, just different general musical attitudes that I found annoying."

While Lars persisted in trying to recruit Cliff to the Metallica cause, gigs had to be played, including another show at the Woodstock on October 1. However, the success of the San Francisco gig had inspired Metallica to return there and on October 18 they supported Laaz Rockit at the Old Waldorf. This show marked the first appearance of a powerful new song called 'No Remorse', and was very well received. Ron McGovney later recalled, "That was at the Old Waldorf on a Monday night. The people went nuts at that gig," and added with a touch of irony: "In fact I think Cliff Burton came to that show."

After four more hometown shows (a notable support slot to Y&T took place on November 11 at the Woodstock in Anaheim), another show was booked at the Old Waldorf for November 29. This concert was important for three reasons. Firstly, the support band was the San Francisco-based Exodus, whose guitarist was 20-year-old Kirk Hammett. Secondly, the show was recorded and became a demo, which fans labelled *Live Metal Up Your Ass* (its sound quality was appalling; the band had initially intended to record it through the mixing board but were obliged to set up a portable cassette recorder in front of the speakers instead). Finally, the song 'Whiplash', debuted at this concert, inspired the crowd to slam with unprecedented intensity.

The following night Metallica played a show at a second San

Francisco venue, the Mabuhay Gardens. Another successful night, it was a milestone for Metallica, as it would be the last time that Ron McGovney played with them. As he recalled to KNAC in 1993, the journey home was the final provocation which pushed him over the edge and prompted him to leave: "On the way home we stopped at the liquor store, I was driving, and they got a whole gallon of whisky. James, Lars and Dave were completely smashed out of their minds. They would constantly bang on the window for me to pull over so they could take a piss, and all of a sudden I look over and see Lars lying in the middle of Interstate 5 on the double yellow line. It was just unbelievable! And I just said, 'Fuck this shit!'"

Perhaps if Ron's role as band babysitter had been his only burden, he might not have left. But there was more to endure: "Then one of my friends told me that they witnessed Dave pour a beer right into the pickups of my Washburn bass as he said, 'I fuckin' hate Ron.' The next day my bass didn't work. My girlfriend at the time also told me that she overheard that they wanted to bring Cliff in the band."

Ron's reaction was not unreasonable, perhaps: "After Dave fucked my bass up, I confronted the band when they came over for practice and said, 'Get the fuck out of my house!' I turned to James and said, 'I'm sorry, James, but you have to go too.' And they were gone within the next couple of days." Ron was clearly annoyed by what had happened, too: "I was so disgusted with the whole thing that I sold all my equipment . . . I was just so pissed with the whole thing."

And so Ron McGovney and Metallica parted company. He had had some idea that Cliff might be recruited in his place ("After I heard them talk about Cliff, I had some idea . . . I kind of saw the writing on the wall"). Despite various suggestions to the contrary, the conclusion is that he left, rather than being kicked out – although it seems that he would have been replaced anyway. As he said: "If you listen to their version, they claim they kicked me out. But I never, ever heard them tell me 'You're out of the band.'"

As the years have passed, the rancour caused by Ron's departure has dissolved. In a Nineties interview with *Metal Hammer*, Dave Mustaine admitted, "Something that I need to get right with was something I did to Ron McGovney . . . I poured beer into the pickups on his bass. He remembered and I had forgotten, but he was snivelling about it in an interview a while ago and I'm trying to make that up." As for Ron himself, when he was recounting the events he added: "This was so long ago it doesn't even matter today. I'm just telling you what I was feeling then. I want to make it clear that it doesn't bother me now, this was 14 years ago, it's just memories. I get along with all the guys now."

No sooner had the band bid farewell to McGovney,* than they decided to quit LA for good. Cliff Burton finally agreed to join Metallica, as long as they were prepared to move to San Francisco. Looking around at the hairsprayed glam-metal bands and fans who had refused to accept them for so many months, Ulrich, Hetfield and Mustaine saw sense in his offer and packed their bags. The move took a few months to complete, but the first stages were finished by Christmas.

On December 28, 1982, the first jam with Metallica featuring Cliff Burton as a member took place. Now, it seemed, they could begin making serious music with a truly phenomenal bassist. But what was it about him that made him so special?

* McGovney disappeared from the music scene apart from a 1986 appearance on a metal project called Phantasm with Katon DePena.

7

The Truth About Cliff Burton

Myth 3: Lars and James run Metallica, and always have.
Myth 4: Lars and James write all the songs and bring the best musicianship to the band.

Every now and again a truly influential genius comes along, someone whose passion for their art is so all-consuming that it threatens to overwhelm them. Many such artists receive the publicity they deserve. Many do not, and hate it. A very small number don't care either way. Cliff Burton was one of them.

The performing arts are full of extreme personalities that match extreme talents. This is normal. After all, getting up on stage and entertaining demands either extraordinary confidence or the courage to camouflage stage fright. Furthermore, the world of metal, and even more so extreme metal, is overflowing with eccentric characters whose excesses we usually forgive because of the nature of the beast. But Cliff wasn't like this: he was a quiet, pensive, even cerebral individual who enjoyed life and didn't make a fuss unless it was strictly necessary – which is unusual, because his talents were formidable.

Bass players, and especially metal bass players, will tell you that Cliff had several strengths as a player. Firstly, he had absorbed a rigorous musical education: in an interview with Metallica associate Harald Oimoen, Cliff's mother Jan Burton explained: "He didn't take music lessons until he was 13, after his brother died. We didn't think he had too much talent at all. We had no idea! We just thought he'd plunk, plunk along, which he did at first. It was really not easy for him at first. Then, about six months into the lessons, it started to come together. I thought, 'This kid's got real potential,' and I was totally amazed

Metal gurus: Metallica pictured around the time of release of the *Master Of Puppets* album – for many, their finest hour. From left: Cliff Burton (bass), Kirk Hammett (guitar), Lars Ulrich (drums) and James Hetfield (guitar/vocals). *(LFI)*

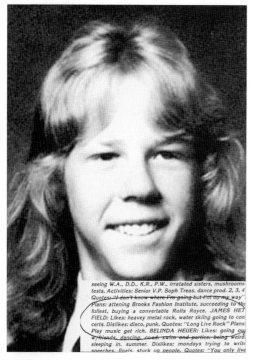
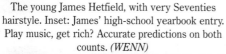

The young James Hetfield, with very Seventies hairstyle. Inset: James' high-school yearbook entry. Play music, get rich? Accurate predictions on both counts. *(WENN)*

The teenage Kirk Hammett, with what can only be described as a haircut with wings. *(WENN)*

Lars Ulrich (left) with his father Torben, a Danish tennis champion, and (right) having metamorphosed from clean-living sports kid to heavy metal teen. *(left – Polfoto and right – WENN)*

Metallica's first stable line-up, pictured in 1982 (from left): Hetfield, bassist Ron McGovney, Ulrich and guitarist Dave Mustaine. "The line-up that we had with Ron and Dave just wasn't happening. When you thought ahead five years, you couldn't picture either of them in the band," said Lars the following year.

Insets: the *No Life 'Til Leather* and *Live Metal Up Your Ass* demos that brought Metallica to the attention of metalheads across the US and beyond.

One of the business cards that Ron McGovney had made for Metallica, much to Ulrich's chagrin. "I remember bringing the business cards to the band and Lars got so pissed off at me," said Ron later. "He said, what did you do? What the hell is Power Metal?"

Dave Mustaine backstage at the Old Waldorf concert hall in San Francisco in 1982. *(Xavier Russel)*

James and Ron in action at the Old Waldorf. Note Hetfield's none-more-metal T-shirt, depicting Venom's *Black Metal* logo, and McGovney's bass, which was later ruined by Mustaine when he drunkenly poured beer into its pickups. *(Xavier Russel)*

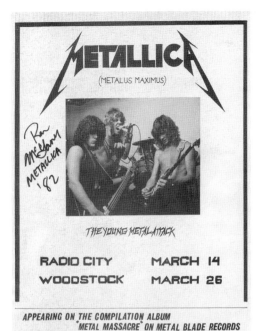

The 'Young Metal Attack' appearing in spring 1982. James was still a vocals-only frontman at this point and wouldn't take up rhythm guitar permanently until later in the year.

A historically important night for metal: Metallica supporting Saxon at the Whisky. Anthrax singer John Bush recalled: "James was wearing leopard-skin pants. They were not very good! It was a trip!"

Jon Zazula (Johnny Z) at the heart of Megaforce Records in New York, the label which signed Metallica and funded their first record, 1983's *Kill 'Em All*. "Metallica delivered themselves to my front door," said Zazula. "It was basically, well, we're here — what do we do next?" *(Frank White)*

With Dave Mustaine kicked out and his replacement Kirk Hammett (far left) drafted in, Metallica embarked on a 1983 drinking and performing spree that took them to every small-town venue in America... *(LFI)*

JIMBELLLLLS !!!
WHAT THE FUCK !?
HOW ARE YOU DOING?
WE JUST GOT DONE TOURING
PLAYING THE LAST GIG A FEW
DAYS AGO HERE IN S.F.
IT WAS GREAT FUN, TREK-
KING ACROSS THE U.S. W/
RAVEN. BY THE WAY, WHERE
WERE YOU AT ROCHESTER???
ARE YOU WIMPING OUT OR
SOMETHING?? THANX FOR
IN JUNE
APPRICIATED !!!   Lars

Post Card
JIM FERRARO
243 A. MELVILLE S
ROCHESTER
NEW YORK
14609

...a jaunt which Lars chronicled in postcards to his buddies. Although he describes the Raven tour here as 'great fun', James recalled life in the communal van less positively: "Halfway through Texas the air-conditioning system broke... you woke up in the morning, and your tongue was stuck to your palate, because it was 200 degrees in there!"

Kirk in full hotel-room-party mode. Compact drummer not pictured. *(Michael Johansson)*

Metallica in (mostly) serious mood. As Ulrich once explained: "If there's anyone who's at the top of the game in terms of doing what we're doing and being professional about it, it's us". *(LFI)*

because none of the kids in our family had *any* musical talent!"

Lessons were the obvious next step, as Jan Burton recalled: "He took lessons for about a year, and then he totally outgrew [the teacher] and went to another place for a couple of years and outgrew him, too. Then he went to the school and took lessons from a very good jazz bassist, a very fine musician. He was the one who made Cliff take Bach and Beethoven and baroque [music], and made him learn to read music and stuff like that. He was with him for a long time, and then he really outgrew him, too. He really got so good that he didn't need that anymore. He really did sit down and study and play Bach. He loved Bach." In fact, one of the most recognisable aspects of Cliff's playing, most evident in his bass solos, was the classical symmetry which he took from composers like Bach, whose famous mathematical balance informed the triads and arpeggios around which Cliff's playing was formed. Jack Bruce, amongst the most distinguished bassists ever, has gone on record as describing Bach as the 'gov'ner of the bass-line'.

Secondly, and equally importantly, was the flipside of Cliff's classical obsessions; his love of punk and heavy metal. James Hetfield recalled once how Cliff would insist on commandeering the stereo in the tour bus, on which he would play crushing, monotonous songs by bands such as Discharge. Burton's passion for heaviness found its way into his playing style at an early age when he discovered the grinding howl he could add to his melodies by running his bass through an overdrive or distortion pedal – most memorably showcased on the solo track he played on *Kill 'Em All*, 'Anesthesia (Pulling Teeth)'.

Thirdly, Cliff was rarely content to sit on the beat and simply emulate a guitar riff, although this minimal approach was usual in thrash metal, which focused on speed and precision rather than expression and melody. He would develop a progression to entwine around a guitar line (a simple example is the *Kill 'Em All* version of 'Jump In The Fire', in which he improved on the original Ron McGovney line by ascending rather than descending the line at the end of every second bar). He also threw in expert fills when a main bass-line didn't permit much ongoing melody (see the upper-register sixteenths just before the lead guitar breaks on 'Phantom Lord'), and had a full arsenal of melodic and harmonic tricks which thrash metal, in the very early days at least, had not seen. Frank Bello of Anthrax was doing similar things by 1986, and by the time the death metal movement took off in the late Eighties there were a series of excellent players such as Steve DiGiorgio (Sadus, Testament) and Alex Webster (Cannibal Corpse) pushing the boundaries. But in the early Eighties on the thrash metal scene, Cliff had no equal.

Finally, there is the issue of Cliff's personality. He was clever without being obscure, driven without being dictatorial and inventive without being eccentric. Added to this his placid, relaxed character, which made him easy to like, as Metallica producer Flemming Rasmussen told me: "Cliff was a really cool, really laid-back kind of guy, really friendly and really nice to be around. He was the only guy at the time wearing bell-bottoms, he liked them and he didn't give a shit and [said that] he'd just wait till they came back in style, which they are now. All the guys gave him shit about them, and me too. He didn't care." Yes indeed: the famous flared jeans, which in the early Eighties, the era of new wave and the drainpipe cut, were tantamount to fashion suicide. The other members of Metallica and the other metal bands on the scene were wearing skin-tight jeans or spandex, but Cliff genuinely did not care.

He had other things on his mind, primarily the music. Rasmussen continues: "Cliff was really into making different sounds, he was into just playing bass and getting the best out of it without having to do a boring down-beat with the drums." Cliff's enjoyment of a smoke and a drink completes the picture of a man who had risen above the petty concerns of the day, and was most interested in the best way to deploy his enormous talents, without ever becoming arrogant or lazy. As his mother told Oimoen, his self-imposed practice sessions verged on obsession: "Between four and six hours a day, every single day, even after he got into Metallica. He was a very modest kid. He always said, 'No, there's somebody in their garage that hasn't been discovered that's better than you are.' Even in the last year with Metallica, when they had made it, it didn't make a difference to him. He still practised every bit as much; he'd stay up all night and sleep late. But then when he got up, that's what he would do, is put on his bass first thing and play."

But if you're getting a picture of a laid-back guy who lived only for his guitar, think again. The other side of Cliff which made him special was his drive to succeed: the commitment which led him to direct the career of his band, even though so many people perceived him as a mere performer. Metallica photographer Ross Halfin is absolutely convinced of this: "The thing that people miss is that at the beginning it was very much Cliff Burton's band. He very much ran the band, he had the major say, and after 1986 Lars took it over. James didn't really have a lot to do with it, it was all very much Cliff Burton."

This single-mindedness, despite his mellow exterior, had been apparent all Cliff's life, reported his parents. As his mother said, he chose his own path early in life: "Even when he was a tiny little kid he would listen to his music or read. He was a big, big reader and he was very bright. In the third grade they tested him and he got 11th grade comprehension. He just heard a different drummer; he never went with the crowd if he didn't want to. He was always popular and had a lot of friends. He was a very kind, very gentle kid but always his own person." He also refused to tell anything but the truth: "He was so honest that sometimes you'd think, 'Oh, Cliff, I wish you weren't quite *so* honest!' We were talking about that once, and he said, 'I don't have to lie for anybody. I don't want to lie.' And that's how he felt about it. God, I think he hated lying more than anything. He was big on just being yourself."

This determination stood Cliff in good stead when he decided to become a musician, as his father told Oimoen: "When he was about 21 or 22 he said, 'I'm going to be a professional musician. I'm going to make my living as a musician.' And that's what he did." His mother continued: "We said, 'OK.' Because Cliff never gave up on anything! I've never seen that boy give up on anything or anybody. So I knew that when he said that, he 110 per cent was going to go into it. Because we loved him very much and we respected him, we really tried to give him 110 per cent because we felt he was very deserving of it. He had been playing with other little local bands up until that time. We said, 'OK, we'll give you four years. We'll pay for your rent and your food. But after that four years is over, if we don't see some slow progress or moderate progress, if you're just not going anyplace and it's obvious you're not going to make a living out of it, then you're going to have to get a job and do something else. That's as far as we're going to support you. It should be known by then whether or not you're going to make it,' so he said, 'Fine.' And, boy, did he make it! Two years later." The Burtons' patience was paid off in spades when Metallica made their first impact. But Cliff refused to change: "He never considered himself a star. He said, 'I'm just a good musician, but I'm not a star.' He *was* a star, but he wouldn't recognise himself as that."

In an earlier Oimoen interview, first published in the American magazine *Thrash Metal*, Cliff talked about his influences: "First off, with bass playing it would be Geddy Lee, Geezer Butler, Stanley Clarke." The influences of these three are clear in Cliff's playing. There's progressive melodic playing like that of Rush player Lee; plenty of near-psychedelic power like Butler, whose inventiveness had been the perfect foil to the doom-laden riffs of Tony Iommi in Black Sabbath; and the pure jazz elements of Clarke, whose experimental work has amazed bassists for years.

Curiously, Burton denied much interest in the work of Iron Maiden bass-player Steve Harris, the only major player on the metal scene whose power and melodic skills could be said to exceed Burton's at this time. Cliff also namechecked guitarists such as Jimi Hendrix, Uli Roth, Michael Schenker and Tony Iommi; an obvious hint at the interest he had in playing solos, rather than simple supporting bass-lines, on his instrument. Asked by Oimoen about his musical tastes, he named punk acts the Misfits and Samhain (he sported a tattoo on his arm derived from a Samhain face design), as well as Thin Lizzy, Black Sabbath and Aerosmith.

But even more revealing – and eclectic – was when Cliff talked about "a band called R.E.M. that I like a lot, strangely enough". At the time of this interview (1986), the Athens, Georgia quartet were critical darlings with three albums behind them and favourites on the limited college and club circuit, but they showed little sign of progressing beyond cult status. They specialised in brittle, intelligent, jangly guitar tunes with obscure, virtually indecipherable lyrics – worlds away from the gothic darkness of The Misfits and the chugging brutality of Discharge. Nevertheless, Cliff not only had the perception to pick them out from the crowd of quirky guitar bands (which in the light of R.E.M.'s subsequent multi-platinum status suggests he would have made a terrific A&R man) but he liked them too. Their bassist, Mike Mills, was formally trained, coming to the instrument after learning piano and sousaphone, and his bass-lines were unusually melodic and free flowing for a band whose influences veered between new wave simplicity and the harmonic grandeur of The Byrds. Cliff appreciated them though: not many other thrash metal musicians would have admitted to liking R.E.M., or been sufficiently broad-minded enough to have listened and learned from them.

And so the different aspects of Cliff Burton shaped the future of Metallica. A true performer, he knew instinctively that his talents needed a formal outlet, as his mother explained: "Trauma wanted him to go plunk, plunk, plunk, plunk. He wanted to play lead bass and they said, 'No way.' He really became so frustrated at wanting to express himself musically." When Lars' calls came, Burton was torn between his loyalty to his band and his need to express himself: "Metallica kept calling every week. They'd call him from LA and he'd say, 'No, no.' When they finally got together he'd say, 'I wanna play lead bass. I want some spot in here where I can go off.' And they said, 'You can play anything you want, just come with us.' They gave him a five-minute solo, and they still do that. I don't know about other bands, but there was never a bass player, unless he was the leader of the band, that took solos and wrote and played like Cliff."

As we will see, the musical talents of Cliff Burton would take his new band in some unexpected directions. But for now, note his entry into their lives, and what it meant for them and for metal.

As for the myths? Ostensibly Lars and James have always controlled the band on the surface. But Cliff's musicianship meant that his influence on the songwriting of the band and the way it sounds is profound: he controlled, as it were, from within. And yes – without a doubt he was the most musianly member that the band has ever had. Much respect is due.

8

1982–1983

And so the move began – away from the freakshow of LA to the much more refined (or at least, so Metallica hoped) environs of San Francisco.

Moving all your belongings to another city isn't easy when you're a musician with no money, and the transfer took a little time. James Hetfield, Lars Ulrich and Dave Mustaine began shifting what little they had to their new home in December 1982 but didn't complete the relocation until March 1983, as events conspired to disrupt the move. Initially Lars and James moved in at 3132 Carlson Boulevard with a friend of theirs named Mark Whitaker, who they had met on the metal scene and who was studying sound engineering. Perhaps bizarrely, the firebrand Mustaine ended up taking a room at Whitaker's grandmother's house.

It didn't take long for Metallica to establish themselves in their Bay Area home and to raise their profile on the local metal scene. As Whiplash drummer Tony Scaglione remembers: "We played our very first gig at a club called Ruthie's Inn in Berkeley, California, with Possessed and Death Angel. The guys from Metallica were at the gig along with Exodus and many of the Bay Area locals. I got a chance to meet and speak a little with James and Cliff Burton. They were both extremely nice, down-to-earth guys and it is a great memory." Possessed frontman Jeff Becerra adds: "Metallica used to show up to the underground shows and hang out when we played. They are really some cool guys."

Within a few months Metallica had settled into the El Cerrito district. Eric Peterson of Testament got to know them fairly early on: "Cliff was a quiet kind of guy and a pretty smart fellow. Maybe a little too intellectual for some people, and didn't even know it. Very nice though. He was always pissed off because we had a studio where Metallica jammed too, and he'd always be sitting out on the couch with a six-pack of Löwenbräu, waiting for the other guys. He was pissed off because he was always the first! I guess he didn't have the keys to the studio."

James Hetfield recalled these early days to *Aardschok* magazine: "We already had a few friends in Frisco: Mark Whitaker was managing Exodus, and Jeff Weller, who was responsible for pyrotechnics at our appearances, was the manager of Laaz Rockit. We moved into Mark's house in El Cerrito. Of course it didn't have enough bedrooms, so Lars and I shared a room. Dave was put in the cellar at Mark's grand-mother's. That was a mad time!" The move took place without an awful lot of forethought, it seems, as James told *Thrasher* magazine in 1986: "Now that I think of it . . . it was really wild that we did that. All of a sudden just move up to SF, no place to stay or nothing. It was cool!"

An unexpected bonus came up when Whitaker needed a band to record a demo which he could submit as part of his course. James: "We made a demo, free of charge, of 'Whiplash' and 'No Remorse'. It sounded great. The best thing we had recorded up to then."

Later, they moved to the Albany district. Jeff Becerra of Possessed recalls that the Metallica party schedule was pretty intense, right from the beginning: "I grew up with these guys. Kirk lived right around the corner from me and we used to go to raging parties at his house. We used to hang at their house, which was just some big shabby house in Albany, and get pretty fucked up. People used to party and get crazy there. If anyone really remembered what was happening back then, then they really weren't there!"

But Metallica weren't simply living the high life, they were rehears-ing a live set with Cliff who soon added a more melodic feel to their existing songs. On March 5, 1983, he played his first Metallica show, at the band's favourite haunt, the Stone. The set list was a mixture of older, *No Life 'Til Leather* tracks, the new ones which Metallica had recently refined, plus some new additions: the expected 'Hit The Lights', 'The Mechanix', 'Phantom Lord', 'Jump In The Fire', 'Motor-breath', 'No Remorse' (which, with its lightning-fast closing section, was rapidly proving to be a high point of the set) and 'Seek And Destroy' were all present – but a wholly new section attracted most attention. Cliff had devised a bass solo called 'Anesthesia', a five- or six-minute flurry of overdriven triads and classical motifs which had the crowd spellbound. With his rapid fingerwork, the ear-shredding distortion of his bass, his violent windmilling hair and his stubbornly outmoded bell-bottomed jeans, Burton was an entirely new face on the metal scene for most people. The solo led directly into Metallica's fastest song to date, 'Whiplash', which had the audience in a frenzy that hardly abated for 'Am I Evil?', 'The Prince', 'Blitzkrieg', a solo spot from Dave Mustaine and a final storm through 'Metal Militia'. A second, shorter concert took place at the venue and was filmed for posterity.

Metallica's relocation to San Francisco was a creative and career rebirth, with the musicians adopting the city as their home and publicly stating their affection for the town in later interviews. The success of the *No Life 'Til Leather* demo there the previous year would have helped smooth the transition of course (as Bob Nalbandian remarks, "Metallica were already huge before they went to San Francisco, because of the tape-trading"), but it seems that there was a vibe or a special atmosphere about the city at that time which made it the perfect home for them. As Eric Peterson of Testament says: "There was definitely something in the air. You didn't know what it was going to be in the future, but it was really cool."

There was a marked difference in personality between the heavier crowd up in Frisco and the glam-metal audience down in LA. "There was the poser scene, which we didn't feel like we fit into because we were younger," says Peterson. "We weren't gorgeous-looking and muscly. Everybody was sleeping with each other on that scene, whereas with us there was more friendship and loyalty. On *that* scene everybody was stabbing each other in the back and ripping each other off. It seemed like that, anyway."

Gene Hoglan noticed the different atmosphere in the city too: "All the wimpy power stuff was in the spotlight already. I hated that stuff, the songs were so plastic and shallow and the bands had nothing to say. When your clothing budget costs more than your instruments, fuck it. But San Francisco did feel like the mecca. All the bands that were halfway decent from LA would go up to play there, come home and say, 'Fuck, that was deadly!' San Francisco knows what's up. They just got into heavier shit." Jeff Becerra goes further still: "The Bay Area is a musician's playground. There were so many great bands out there and everyone wanted a piece of the action. Local heroes were being made and along with that came prestige, pussy, and free beer. As long as I can remember I wanted to be a rock star and the Bay Area was a perfect stomping ground to prove oneself. The Bay Area bands were supportive and they were all my friends at the time."

But why were the people in San Francisco so into heavy music? Ask this question and you'll hear a variety of answers. Writer Martin Popoff attributes this partly to geographical factors: "I know from knowing Brian Slagel and knowing what Lars Ulrich went through that a lot of it has to do with, quite frankly, there being a huge population in California . . . the thrash occurred all over America in proportion to the population." Jim Martin supports this, as well as throwing in a cynical aside about the industry presence: "More people per acre. The West Coast is the media capital of the world, so I think exposure had something to do with it. Really, there were a few guys who knew this thing called metal was happening in Europe, something called the British invasion or whatever, and they figured out how to capitalise on it in Hollywood. Period. Some of those people figured they could expose San Francisco to it and make them pay."

California, especially San Francisco, has traditionally been sympathetic to free-thinking liberals and new ideas than other parts of the USA and this clearly helped Metallica's progress, as Karl Sanders of Nile suggests: "I think California is a progressive, free-thinking kind of area: perhaps during that period metal fans in that area of the country were more willing to embrace something new." Popoff adds: "California is known for being artistic, so I guess many art movements are slightly bigger in proportion out there." Meanwhile, Byron Roberts emphasises that change feeds off itself: "History shows that most art, be it painting, literature, film or music, generally has a localised 'hot bed' of young talent at some point in its development, from which many talented artists spring. People of similar ages, with similar ideas and influences are invariably drawn together and unite to produce such a pop-cultural movement if the circumstances are right. I suppose the Bay Area was destined to be the centre for US thrash metal." Popoff: "Maybe good competition feeds good competition. There was a little hotbed of that stuff all up and down the coast, perhaps fuelled somewhat by Brian Slagel and Oz Records, along with avid consumers like Lars."

The group of people to which Roberts refers would be the hardcore fans and industry movers who encouraged the scene to grow through supporting and buying the music. Jeff Waters of Annihilator pins it down to a small clique of musicians, saying: "The metal scene was a small one then, that they all knew each other and that they were all influenced by each other's playing and songwriting." Writer Garry Sharpe-Young is even more specific about who was responsible: "The personalities involved – Ron Quintana, Lars Ulrich, James Hetfield, Kurdt Vanderhoof, Brian Slagel, Rick Hunolt. These guys were totally devoted to old-school British rock and were then spurred on to create bands and set up labels, radio stations, shops and fanzines by the NWOBHM."

In due course these 'movers and shakers' established venues in which the music could flourish, which themselves became well known. Sharpe-Young says: "Why the Bay Area? Probably the club scene, Ruthie's, Waldorf, the Stone, and the enthusiastic metal community." Phil Demmel of Technocracy was there and remembers it all clearly: "There were three or four clubs – Ruthie's Inn, the Mabuhay Gardens, the Stone – where you could go see four or five killer bands in a night and everybody had Venom vests on. I remember being at a Mercyful Fate show and shouting, 'Fuck you, King Diamond – Exodus!'" Eric Peterson recalls the outdoor events as well as the club scene: "There's always been a lot of metal in the Bay Area. When I was 15 or 16 the Bay Area had this thing called Day On The Green at the Outdoor Coliseum. Every summer we had two of them. My first concert was Ted Nugent, Aerosmith, AC/DC with Bon Scott and Mahogany Rush."

The poodle-permed, high-heeled glam-metal scene of LA was a constant reminder of what metal could become if it was not monitored carefully. Metal Church's John Marshall suggests: "I think it may have been a reaction to the awful hair/poser/make-up bands that were coming out of LA at the time. Having Metallica relocate to the Bay Area was helpful, but even without their huge presence there were still many great bands here." Katon DePena is more forthright than the tactful Marshall: "There is so much shitty music in LA that there are always going to be a few good metal bands that try to break those rules and go against the grain. It's a good environment for heavy bands to come out of. I mean, when we were starting out alongside Slayer,

Megadeth and Metallica, there was Mötley Crüe, Ratt, and Dokken. We wanted to go totally against that kind of music – louder, faster and heavier!"

As for the San Fran crowds, DePena has nothing but praise: "San Francisco is different than LA. They really, really love heavy music. Metallica moved there because they had a bigger following there. Exodus, Possessed and Death Angel all came out of there as well. More great bands followed them. San Francisco is a very special city for heavy metal music, and will always be. For us, Hirax, it is one of the greatest places to play in the world. The fans there are crazy, and we fuckin' love it!"

Maybe, as Eric Peterson suggests, the reason why thrash metal did so well in San Francisco was simply that the musicians helped each other more than their counterparts on the more cynical LA scene. As Mikael Akerfeldt of Opeth reasons: "I reckon they all pushed each other to evolve, as well as to get gigs." Kreator's Mille Petrozza agrees: "What I liked about those bands was the fact that most of the musicians that I met had more of a punk rock attitude instead of being rock stars. You actually had a chance to meet the bands and talk to them."

Interestingly, not every metal musician fell instantly under the Bay Area spell. Quorthon of Bathory recalls: "I remember a friend of mine bought *Kill 'Em All* the same week we recorded our first album. I couldn't separate one Bay Area group from another. It all melted together and we couldn't really connect with it, because between the lines it seemed to have the do-ron-ron-ron surf beat. We'd been growing up with Hammer horror movies and things like that. In fact, our love of the NWOBHM had made us slightly suspicious of anything that came out of America."

Others are cynical about the importance (or lack of it) of locating a place where thrash metal was spawned. Jan Transit says, "As always happens with any movement of this kind – modern, popular music's 'cribs' have always been a big issue with journalists. It's more the media who create an artificial background, rather than the artists themselves. This is what the audience relate to when scanning the jungle for something new to take part in, and thus they become a part of the hype."

And still others don't regard the Bay Area as particularly significant. Steve Tucker says, "I wasn't aware that very much came from there that was worthwhile! There were a lot of bands from there, but not many worth remembering. But the reason I think so much came from there was because bands tend to rip off other bands' styles, and there was a lot of that going on. Usually there are a couple of really great bands in a genre, and hundreds of sub-par rip-offs that follow." Opeth's Mikael Akerfeldt concludes that, "In the end, as with any other 'happening' thing, most of the bands in the scene will get signed. Still, in retrospect, I think the Bay Area scene spawned more shit than good bands. It's classic, though, and I get nostalgic just from talking about these bands!"

Nostalgia is always a powerful force and is clearly still felt by most of the metallers interviewed for this book. The Bay Area thrash scene of the Eighties was, it seems, a whirlpool of creativity and opportunity which happens every once in a while in the world of music, and leaves a lasting impression. As this ocean-side community had once been the fulcrum for the hippie/flower power movement in the Sixties (and as it would go on to be for the hip-hop and G-Funk music of the mid to late Nineties), so it functioned in the Eighties as the area where thrash metal was nurtured and developed. As we've seen, the population density, the proximity to the Bay Area of the world's media, the need to react against the sleazy glam-metal of Los Angeles, and the historical artist-friendly culture of the city itself all contributed. And the music which came out of the area was world-class. No wonder people look back on this time with awe.

The exact date-line of the thrash emergence is still argued over. Metallica's *No Life 'Til Leather* demo of 1982 sparked an explosion of metal, that's for sure; and their physical presence certainly added much fuel to the fire. But San Francisco already had more than its fair share of young, aggressive metal bands ready to go. As Testament's Eric Peterson and many others recall, it was Kirk Hammett's band Exodus which was next in line after Metallica as pioneers of the Bay Area thrash movement – and some even suggest that the line between the two was too close to call who was active first.

Hungry though Metallica were (and they were twice as keen now that the ambitious Burton was in the band), Exodus and their following were not to be trifled with. Phil Demmel of Technocracy remembers that: "Exodus had the crowd who would kill you. If you said anything against them, they would destroy you." Peterson adds: "At Exodus shows, anybody glam-metal in the crowd would get their ass kicked.

They would get beat up." Not pleasant if you weren't a hardcore metal fan, then: but certainly an inspiring environment for the later thrash acts who followed Metallica's lead and set up a live scene of their own in San Francisco. Eric Meyer, guitarist with LA thrashers Dark Angel, confirms this: "One of our first shows was at Ruthie's Inn in SF, because we'd heard that it was a good place for that kind of music. Maybe it was to do with Metallica moving up there and starting that scene. There were a lot of good players up there." He points out that the tape-trading scene which had made Metallica famous in San Fran before they had even played there also worked in the other direction for Exodus, whose debut demo had arrived in LA: "We met the guys from Exodus up there, which was funny because we'd been listening to them on the way up. Their debut album *Bonded By Blood* wasn't even out yet, and they were pissed off, saying, 'How did you get our tape?' And of course everyone had it! It was a pain for them that even people down in LA had it through tape-trading."

The only other realistic candidate for 'second US thrash act after Metallica' was Slayer, of whose early work most observers cannot speak highly enough. They gained ground rapidly through one important advantage, as Bob Nalbandian asserts: the punks, as well as the metallers, loved their music. "Slayer would play Orange County, where all the punks went to see their shows. There weren't many good metal bands in OC, but Slayer got the Suicidal Tendencies crowd. A lot of punks said, 'Oh, they've got long hair, fuckin' hippies!' But the punks who were just into the aggression of the music got into Motör-head, then Venom, and then Slayer. Their guitarist Jeff Hanneman was really into punk, and they really crossed it over. Slayer was the one band who were cool to be on a punk bill."

Nalbandian is insistent that this is the key reason why Metallica were obliged to leave Los Angeles to find a consistent audience: "That's why Metallica never really made it in LA," he explains, "because they didn't get the punk crowd. I think Metallica was too metal, the punks didn't really cross over at that point. Punk and metal were total opposites at the time." Stryper's Robert Sweet, who found himself at the wrong end of the punk and thrash scenes at various times, supports this: "The punks were unto themselves. It was more violent. The violence level at the punk shows in Hollywood at the time was so intense. I saw a lot of people getting stabbed and hospitalised." The violence was real, it seems: John Bush recalls: "After a time bands like DRI managed to bring punk and metal together. But I remember wanting to go to punk shows at a club called the Starwood and being afraid, because I had long hair. You would get beat up, no doubt about it. The punks were more bad-assed, most of the metallers didn't have that about them."

Even in Europe, metal fans perceived the influence which punk had on the metal scene. As Thomas Fischer remembers: "There was a surge of more and more musical intensity at the tail-end of the Seventies, an inspiration which heavy metal very obviously took from the raging punk wave. I couldn't identify with much of the new punk music, but I absolutely loved what it did to heavy metal. It was a rejuvenation which was overdue. The revolutionary spirit had become tired and many of the flexible and aggressive metal bands had become uninspired behemoths." He specifically cites a band who, as it happened, were much loved by Cliff Burton: "A major influence was the band Discharge and their first two albums. At the time, Discharge was considered punk, and they were more extreme than absolutely anything I had ever heard. It is now clear that Discharge were pioneers of much more than just radical punk."

Another important influence on the fledgling thrash metal scene was Armored Saint, whose powerful riffs and tempos had a similar effect on the thrashers as Motörhead. Eric Meyer of Dark Angel says: "One of the first bands I remember seeing in one of my local dive bars was Armored Saint. I was like, oh my God, these guys are so far beyond any punk band!" Bob Nalbandian adds: "Armored Saint started that live vibe. When they played down in LA, Metallica would open for them, and the other way round in San Francisco." In fact, Metallica admired the Saint so much, they began to watch the singer, John Bush, with a certain degree of interest. Would he be the next recruit?

With all this activity, it soon became difficult to track the progress of the various scenes. But if you liked your music heavy and fast and didn't worry too much about categories, it was a golden age. Gene Hoglan remembers with great satisfaction: "I was always delving into the underground of metal. My friend Bob Nalbandian ran one of the first American fanzines, *Headbanger*, which was dripping with all the cool metal patches and stuff like that. I was always giving him tapes and saying, 'Please make me tapes of the latest stuff!' I was really into Iron Maiden at the time of their first album." Not that he listened to everything indiscriminately – he adds: "I always dug Bathory's 'The Return Of Darkness And Evil' on *Scandinavian Metal Attack*, which I thought was really ripping, but after that they were just a terrible copy of Venom."

The exact sequence of events has been tracked by Eric Peterson, who founded Testament and initially gave them the early name of Legacy: "It went Metallica, Slayer, Exodus, Possessed, Death Angel, Legacy. By the time we were ready to play gigs, Death Angel was up and running. They were before us." Later, Eric recalls, there was a follow-up set of thrash acts in the wake of the vanguard: "Vio-Lence didn't come till another three years later. They were the second wave along with Forbidden with Rob Flynn; they popped up and all of a sudden there was something really cool going on every weekend."

As the thrash movement grew, many bands didn't survive, either due to the weight of competition or because they received bad advice. Peterson: "Some bands didn't make the right decisions, we were lucky. We had a manager who was a lawyer, and as a favour to our guitarist Alex Skolnick's parents, who were law professors, he said he would help us out and not let us make the wrong decisions." Others did well and laid down an enduring body of work, but have been forgotten due to confusion over categories: "Possessed were the Bay Area black metal band," states Eric. "The fact that they were later known as a death metal band is probably just a political thing: they were a black metal band. They were a little too much like Slayer, I think."

This is an interesting point for extreme metal observers: the fact that Possessed sang songs with deeply Satanic lyrics made them a black metal band in the eyes of their contemporaries, although in point of fact their debut album *Seven Churches* (1984) was a thrash metal album and, of course, they later invented the term 'death metal' (although Quorthon, as we have seen, disagrees) and became one of the best early bands of that genre. No wonder there is still so much confusion associated with the early scene.

Or, as we should really refer to it, the *two* scenes. Although thrash metal began to grow after the relocation of Metallica to San Francisco in late 1982 and early 1983, the hair-metal scene was much larger and would remain so for some time – at least until the second wave of thrash that Peterson refers to above had begun to take effect. How did the two scenes manage to co-exist? In the industry at least, with ease, as

Martin Hooker recalls: "I obviously worked with both types of metal at the same time because it's not good to be too blinkered into only one type of metal. I thoroughly enjoyed working with Twisted Sister when I owned the Secret record label, and in their own way they were quite extreme themselves. Subsequently at Music For Nations we did Poison, Stryper, Tygertailz, Ratt and so on. We had a great deal of chart action with both types of music, but the fans were usually two distinctly different groups of people. The hair bands were extremely popular with girls, while thrash was predominantly a guy thing."

Interestingly, the whole scene appears to have revolved in its early stages around a small group of individuals, of whom Metallica formed just a part. As Andy Sneap, producer and sometime guitarist with one of the best British thrash metal bands, Sabbat, recalls: "When I was younger I always had this picture in my mind of the Bay Area as this huge scene which was going off, and then later when I was working out there I realised that it's more a collective group of people who all knew each other and were trying to out-shred each other. So it wasn't as big as the magazines hyped it up to be. Really it was a few individuals who were keeping the whole thing going. They've all been in each other's bands. There was a lot of competition in the Bay Area at the time, rather like the Swedish thing which happened much later."*

So who were the prime movers, exactly? The key bands resident in the Bay Area in 1982 and 1983 were Metallica and Exodus, while Slayer were snapping at their heels down in LA. But just as important were the record company founders and fanzine writers such as Brian Slagel and their associates like John Kornarens, as well as the club-owners and promoters. Because of the small number of individuals involved – at least in the early days, before it was widely recognised that thrash metal could make a lot of money – an atmosphere of camaraderie and friendship prevailed (that is, before the corporations moved in). The thrash circle was composed of a small number of acts who looked after each other, it seems: as Over Kill singer Bobby Ellsworth recalls: "The great thing was that it was all sneakers and jeans, just a lot

---

* At the time of writing the extreme metal scene in Sweden is proliferating, with bands on both sides of the thrash and death metal divide such as The Haunted, The Crown, Shadows Fall and dozens of others striving to outdo each other for power and precision – but using a relatively small number of producers, studios and session musicians while doing so.

of beer-drinking and partying and making a lot of noise. Everyone kind of knew each other."

Nevertheless, competition was fierce. Insults being occasionally exchanged between musicians who disliked each other's work. One such confrontation happened between Slayer and James Hetfield, as Gene Hoglan (who worked for Slayer as a lighting and sound technician as a teenager) remembers: "I was at an Exodus, Slayer and Possessed show and James and Cliff Burton came to the show. I was sitting at the side of the stage, doing lights, and they were hanging back. Then Hetfield was down the front and banging for the last few songs."

Then Slayer performed a cover of Venom's 'Witching Hour'. Hoglan: "Slayer kicked into 'Witching Hour', which was the very first time they'd performed it – they were really nervous about performing it and had rehearsed the shit out of it all week. Hetfield just put his head down and shook his head throughout the entire song!" Perhaps, as Hoglan speculates, James disliked the fact that Slayer were a band from LA (even though they went decidedly against the prevailing LA hair-metal style): "Metallica moved to LA just afterwards and were like fuck LA, it's a bunch of posers. And they were right!"

However, the whole LA versus San Francisco controversy didn't last long after Metallica briefly ignited it. Although it seems that LA had a certain audience which simply couldn't understand thrash metal (Ron McGovney told KNAC: "We never really got any recognition here. We played with Ratt and Steeler and poser guys, who didn't know if we were punk or heavy metal bands"), both cities had plenty of fans of both extreme and glam-metal. Anthrax singer John Bush reasons: "Of course you had huge Metallica fans all over LA, plus Exodus and other San Francisco bands: when Vio-Lence played LA, the heavy metal fans came out for them. And I'm sure the hair-metallers came out in San Fran when Poison and Ratt played there."

Broadly, the division between the two communities *was* accurate but in fact Metallica may well have caused this by moving away from LA, rather than escaping it. Bush: "Cliff asked them to move, but I think they used that as leverage to say that LA was not the right place for them. So when they moved from LA – which Armored Saint didn't: we said, 'We don't give a shit, we'll find our fans here' – everybody said, 'Yeah, San Francisco is the place for metal, the Bay Area is where it's happening. LA is for the fuckin' glammers!'" And as James told

95

Thrasher magazine in 1986: "The scene was way better up here, just the overall vibe. People could get into what we were doing as opposed to LA, where they were just hanging out, posing with their drinks and cigarettes."

So much for the West Coast and its divisions. Observers of American music might wonder why the thrash metal scene arose in San Francisco and not a more well-known centre for cutting-edge culture like New York, which certainly made a significant contribution to metal across the years. Scott Ian, guitarist with NY thrashers Anthrax, noticed this himself: "In New York there was Carnivore and Over Kill, but other than them there really wasn't much of a New York metal scene. There always seemed to me to be a lot more bands in the Bay Area and LA than there was coming from NY."

Bobby Ellsworth of Over Kill explains it as psychological: "Maybe the area dictates the kind of music. This was a blue-collar expression of what was going on everywhere else in NY, and perhaps that creativity doesn't lend itself to that blue-collar approach. The whole American thrash thing was almost a conservative, right-wing, middle America thing. Now thrash has taken on social elements and political ideology, and has progressed internally, but back then it was about release. It was action and reaction and explosion. It was about the angry young white guy screaming at the top of his lungs, 'I'm not gonna take this shit.' You only really got that in New York on the punk scene."

However, the next step for Metallica would take place not in Los Angeles, or San Francisco, or anywhere else in California. Despite the absence of a significant extreme metal scene on America's East Coast, their next move would be to New York.

9

1983

"Someone we knew came back from San Francisco with a tape, and said, 'Johnny, Marsha – you have to hear this!' We were playing something in the store, I don't remember what it was, but it was metal, we never played anything else, and I took it off and put the tape on. It was mind-blowing."

Jon Zazula had just slotted a cassette of *Live Metal Up Your Ass* into his tape player in his record store and pressed the play button. The tape Metallica had recorded the previous year had spread nationally and beyond as fast (or faster) than its predecessor, *No Life 'Til Leather*. After playing the tape in his store, a New Jersey business called Rock'N'Roll Heaven, Zazula quickly realised he was onto something completely new. "It had the ingredients of Motörhead and the feeling of the NWOBHM. But it was American, and it felt like it was new and improved. Also, I thought there was a great melodic pound to the rhythm section. But it wasn't melodic as in sell-out, it was a whole new way of approaching a melody line."

Zazula was involved in promoting live shows and managing artists under the Crazed Management umbrella, as well as running his store. As he explains: "My interest was bringing metal to the masses. We were very heavily promoting concerts as well as running the record shop. Anvil and Venom, for example . . . we were the absolutely first people to bring those guys into the States."

This knack for spotting new talent spurred Zazula into calling KJ Doughton, who had written about Metallica and was on the point of taking on the administration of their fan club. "We called KJ Doughton – he had written an article on the boys, the first article I'd seen," recalls Jon. Times were hard back then, as Zazula recalls: "We didn't actually have a phone in the store, we called him from a public phone. It was quite a distance away. He called me back that night and told me that I'd have to speak to Lars Ulrich. And then Lars Ulrich called the next day."

Brian Slagel recalls the Zazulas' initial contact with Metallica, and explains that it was timely: "At that time Jon and Marsha were bringing in bands to New York. Metallica had been in San Francisco for a while, and by then they wanted to get out and conquer the rest of the US. So they said yes, we'll go to New York and spend some time there."

Lars was delighted that word on Metallica had spread as far as New York, and revealed that he in turn had heard of the Zazulas, whose attempts to bring British and European bands over to play in America had earned them the praise of the metal cognoscenti. "Lars was very positive," says Jon. "He had actually heard of us: it had trickled back to the West Coast that there was a whole explosion happening in the north-east and we were leading it. I told him we had a bunch of Venom shows and Rods shows coming up and we said, 'We'd like you to do some shows and talk to you about some business ideas. If you come over we'll discuss it.' "

His sixth sense told John that Metallica were worthy of his attention. "I knew that we wanted to get involved with the band . . . we were gonna let nature take its course. Or let anarchy take its course!"

Lars accepted Jon's invitation to travel to New York but had to confess how broke his band were. If Metallica were to make the coast-to-coast trip, the Zazulas would have to front the money for the fare. As Jon recalls: "They needed some money to get here, which was very tight for us in those days. We weren't wealthy people by any means. So we sent them $1,500 to come across. They got a one-way rental: a U-Haul van and a truck. Literally, they had two drivers and they slept in the back with all their gear, and they delivered themselves to my front door. It was basically, 'Well, we're here – what do we do next?' "

The fact that Metallica were still so broke tells us much about the undeveloped state of the thrash metal movement back then. As Zazula recalls, the corporate will to give the music the exposure it needed to breathe was simply not there: "Nobody would do anything [to promote a show] unless the band was doing covers, and it was very hard to get these bands into clubs in America, because it was all about dancing and playing AC/DC songs and things like that."

This low-budget approach was a common experience for the other new thrash bands, too, as Jeff Dunn of Venom recalls: "In the early days, we were three young lads who didn't know squat, and we were going to Holland and Belgium and playing to thousands of people, and we'd come back and get thirty quid off the record company a week. At one point everybody was saying we were the biggest-selling independent metal band in the world . . . We were mismanaged, let's put it that way."

In late March 1983, Hetfield, Ulrich, Burton and Mustaine, together with their Frisco flatmate and sound engineer Mark Whitaker, collected their U-Haul, loaded in their gear and began the 3,000-mile journey to New York. The trip was not without incident, not least because of Dave Mustaine's disturbing behaviour. Although not an alcoholic, he was certainly prone to drinking to excess and acting unreasonably under its influence, making him not just an irritant but also a positive liability on the road. Lars Ulrich told KUSF a couple of weeks later: "On the big continental trip from SF to NY it all kind of spilled over – there were a few things happening that became too much. The guy couldn't control himself under various situations. And it just didn't . . . on a long-term basis it would have become a problem. We decided [to fire him] somewhere between Iowa and Chicago."

James added that on the journey, Mustaine had been drunk while driving the U-Haul, observing: "If there had been a smash, we could have all got killed." He later told *Thrasher*: "All of a sudden, a straight drive out to New York in a U-Haul. There were five of us and we had a mattress in the back . . . Get in the back. Slam. You're shut in. We'd never been out of California, and we got there to find out we were having some real problems with Dave's attitude. He couldn't really handle being away from home or something . . . we knew it couldn't go on like that, so we started looking at other stuff."

Mustaine's unpredictability while drinking had been annoying his band-mates for some time – not to mention his fiery temper, which appeared in incidents such as the 'dog' fight of the previous year – as had the question of replacing him. "We were just gonna wait around and one day find someone to fill the spot," said Lars. "We were just gonna hang on until someone came along."

True to his word, Lars told Jon Zazula when Metallica arrived that there was a problem with Dave. As he told KUSF: "We came out here and told Johnny that the line-up change should happen as soon as possible". However, nothing could happen immediately as no replacement for Mustaine had been organised and there were two shows to play on April 8 and 9, supporting Vandenburg and the Rods at two New York venues, the Paramount Theater and L'Amours in Brooklyn. After a day or two, Zazula realised how the land lay between the members of Metallica: "Things were really rough between Mustaine and the band. I think the problem was that they were playing for keeps, but there was no certainty with Dave. With him, you never knew what you were going to get. And every day was different: they needed one secure man anchored to the spot to do what he had to do."

The two shows took place, and then the band took a day off before they acted. As Ulrich put it: "We fucked around on Sunday [April 10], then we told him on the Monday morning." As legend has it, Mustaine awoke early one morning to find his bags packed and his band-mates staring down at him with sombre expressions. James told him that he was out of the band, and Dave, struggling to find an appropriate response, merely asked what time his plane was due to leave. His fellow guitarist's answer was that he was booked onto a Greyhound bus in one hour. "He was on the bus an hour later," confirmed Lars to KUSF.

Jon Zazula remembers Mustaine throwing a fit of anger as he left. "They put him on a bus and they sent him home. He was full of venom." Ron McGovney, watching from the sidelines back in Los Angeles, later commented: "I was surprised when they kicked Dave out, I never thought much would happen after I left. I thought James would go back to making stickers and Lars would move back with his rich parents to Europe."

In fact it was just the opposite. The expulsion of Mustaine was the very thing necessary to keep Metallica on an upwardly mobile career path.

The received knowledge is that Mustaine was fired for being unable to behave acceptably while under the influence of alcohol, the drug which fuelled Metallica for so many years. This may well be true: Ulrich and Hetfield, and for a brief period Cliff, were ambitious musicians motivated solely by their desire to push Metallica to the next level of success, whether this meant via a no-budget record deal with Jonny Zazula or to the stadium level which they would reach in another decade. Mustaine's unreliability stood in the way of this, and so he was removed.

And yet there's much more to the Mustaine story than this. Having been fired he channelled his anger into a new band, Megadeth, which went on to become the second most successful thrash act after his old band. As any musician knows, the effort and talent required to push any band to such a level can only come from a person with commitment and deep reserves of motivation. As Zazula commented, "My label was called Megaforce, his band was Megadeth – we share the Mega's for a reason." It's clear that far from the split occurring because of alcohol abuse (after all, the other three drank their fair share and more), Mustaine and Metallica couldn't keep it together because of a clash of personalities. James and Dave had both endured significant losses as children, with the former's mother dying young (and his father retreating to the comfort of Christian Science), and the latter surviving an uncertain upbringing with the presence of neither parent guaranteed. Lars, meanwhile, was a near-hyperactive kid whose presence would fill any space in a matter of moments. While Cliff was quiet and placid, the combination of the three others together was explosive, and in the closed confines of a hired van, with everyone tired by the long journey as well as drunk, the conflict was inevitable. As singer Ian Gillan of Deep Purple told me: "It's like a football team: everybody's got to be comfortable with each other before you can be confident enough to do your best."

Many of the performers I spoke to while researching this book confirm that Mustaine today is intense, cerebral, intelligent and thoughtful, a far cry from the aggressive irritant that he clearly was back in those early days of Metallica. Katon DePena of Hirax says: "I've known Dave Mustaine for years. I didn't know what to think of him when I first met him. Just like me, he was very young, and ready to take on the world. We always got along good. The fire between James Hetfield and Dave Mustaine was amazing for me to see. You can't bottle that kind of energy. I still love listening to the leads on *No Life 'Til Leather*: Dave Mustaine is one of my all-time favourite guitarists. I realise it more now than I did in the early days. I don't think there will be anybody quite like him ever again." Dan Lorenzo of Hades has nothing but good words to say about Mustaine, recounting a meeting with him: "I was at the Ritz to see Megadeth. I go into the men's room to pee and Dave is at the stall moaning. I said, 'What's the matter Dave, have you got VD?' He tells me to fuck off and asks, 'Who the hell are you?' I said, 'I'm Dan from the band Hades.' He screams, 'You guys rule, c'mon bro,' and brings me backstage to hang out."

A general difficulty to manage alcohol seems to have been a feature of Mustaine's behaviour even back in the early days. Brian Slagel confirms that booze was definitely not the best choice of stimulant for Mustaine: "Dave liked to drink a lot. Yes, they all drank a lot but Dave was a little beyond those other guys. When they played the Metal Massacre gig, Dave came up to me after they'd played and said, 'You're gonna hear something but don't believe it, it's not true.' I was like, 'What the hell are you talking about?' And apparently he had gone behind the bar and stolen a case of the best beer that the club had." This petty indulgence almost became a serious problem: "The club owners weren't going to pay them, and there was a whole big thing. I found the empty beer bottles in his dressing room!"

Brian concludes: "He was just a little more extreme in his partying than the other guys," a fact which Morbid Angel frontman Steve Tucker discovered at first hand, reporting: "I met Mustaine on the *Peace Sells* tour and he was a raging asshole. He was a drunk dickhead." And Jim Martin, sometime of Faith No More, recalls: "Every time I saw the guy he was busy putting his foot in his mouth. He was interested in expressing his politics which were naïve and uninformed. The first couple of times I saw Metallica play I asked, 'Who's that guy?' 'Shut up and play yer guitar.' When I saw him with Megadeth, I asked the same questions."

There are few other musicians of Mustaine's technical ability on the guitar, but one of those is Jeff Waters of Annihilator, who received a call from Dave when Megadeth required a second guitarist: "He called me once in 1989 and I was very honoured that he asked me to audition. I politely declined, but what an honour. Good thing though – he says he was very screwed up on drugs and alcohol and, at that time, I was on a lot of alcohol. The combination of egos and addictions would have made that not work out!"

As Eric Peterson wonders, "Who knows why people act like they do? Maybe he was just shy and didn't like dealing with people." Like most of us, maybe Dave is just a combination of good and bad character traits: Bob Nalbandian says, "Dave was a mixed guy. When he was drunk he was a brash, obnoxious asshole, but I always got along with him. He showed respect to me because of *Headbanger* magazine. Metallica had these personalities: between Dave and Lars, that was what got them where they were. That kind of 'I don't give a fuck' attitude – Dave was all about that. I think James worked really hard and really wanted to make it, but he was shy, Dave would go on the microphone and not give a fuck." He quite rightly points out that Mustaine's come-back with Megadeth was little short of miraculous: "Look at the difference between him and Ron McGovney. After Ron got fired he didn't do anything. When Dave got fired he was like, 'I'm gonna fuckin' get back.'"

Canadian journalist Martin Popoff interviewed Mustaine and found him to be, "pretty intense, pretty sure of himself, a bit egotistical and doesn't listen to other people's ideas too well. He's a pretty smart guy and he moves around a point he makes quite quickly; a very talented guitar player, and he seems to have come out of all drug and booze problems with his brain squarely intact. He seems a bit paranoid, but he's a very interesting guy to talk to, no problem there." There is a dark side to him, it seems: "He can be very polite, but can also be cutting. He does leave things between the lines to read. It's kind of an edgy polite, like a psychopathic polite. But by the same token, he knows how to make fun of himself. But you don't really think he's making fun of himself, in any really profound way. What I mean is he knows what parts of himself he can make fun of and be very open about, like drug abuse."

Garry Sharpe-Young explains: "I've interviewed him three times in the flesh and he was very intense. Once a Capitol press officer told me under no circumstances to ask him about Jeff Young or drugs, so guess what my first two questions were? He was fine. I interviewed Jeff Young earlier too and as I wrapped up, Dave came into the room and said, 'Don't believe a fucking word he just told you. The guy is a fuckhead and I hate him.' Yes, Jeff was still in the room!"

The author interviewed Dave in 1999 and found him reasonable, calm and rational: he appeared to have gained some wisdom through the therapy he'd been through as part of his recovery from addiction. He also managed to mock the way he had dressed in the Eighties while presenting a view of how the musical wheel had in some ways come full circle: "There's a lot of music around that's similar to the punk and new wave of 20 years ago . . . I don't think anybody looks too fondly on people wearing skin-tight jeans with turn-ups and hi-tops any more. But there comes a point when you have to ask, is it about the hair or is it about the music?"

For me, his most profound words came when I asked him how his relationship was with Metallica nowadays. "Are you friends," I asked? "Yes. I'd like to think so," he said, and added, quite seriously: "I've got to the stage where I can listen to their music without having to turn it off when it comes on the radio." When had this acceptance come? "I knew I'd come to terms with it when I started stopping wanting to be in the band and being comfortable with my own group," he replied.

And so Dave Mustaine exits the Metallica story, apart from a few brief occasions when they performed together. A strange character in many ways, it's his fiery personality which gives the tale of their first few years as a band much of its colour.

While Mustaine headed westwards on the bus, James and Lars were establishing themselves as leaders of Metallica over the laid-back Cliff. Unsurprisingly they had not fired Mustaine without making preparations. Fully ten days before their errant guitarist was ejected, a surprised Kirk Hammett had received an April Fool's Day phone call from Metallica sound man and Exodus manager Mark Whitaker, asking him to fly to New York to audition for the band. The young guitarist was half-certain that the phone call was a prank and said, "Yes, sure," without thinking too much about it. A second call the next day convinced him that Metallica meant what they were saying and Hammett prepared himself for the audition by playing along with tapes of their songs.

As it happened, Hammett was less than satisfied with the progress of Exodus' career at the time anyway. Although Exodus were very popular in San Francisco (and, as we've seen, had amassed a seriously committed fanbase), they had yet to build on their success on the tape-trading scene and further advancement was still some way off. Add to this some difficulties with the line-up and it's understandable that Kirk was perhaps more willing to be wooed away by Metallica than he might previously have been. As he later told *Thrasher* magazine: "At the time Exodus was having personnel problems, we had this bass player who wasn't really fitting into the direction we were going. The band wasn't rehearsing and we were at a real stale period. I was getting kind of fed up. It's really funny, because one day I was sitting on the can and I got a phone call from Whitaker. He called up and asked me if I'd be interested in flying to New York to try out with the band, because they were having problems with Dave."

Hammett knew the band, having shared a stage with them back in San Francisco, and required little persuasion: "I saw Metallica twice and then we played with them at the Stone. Opportunity knocked, so I thought, what else do I have to do but check this out? So, Mark Fed-Exed a tape out and I sat down with the tape for a couple of days. And then I started to get more calls from Whitaker saying, 'Well, are you into it?' I said, 'Yeah, sure,' and then he said, 'Well, the band wants you to come out to New York to audition with them.' So I thought about it for like two seconds, and said, 'Sure, I'll check it out.'" As for the other members of Exodus, there was a little bitterness but this passed: "At first, but they understood. If any of them had been approached they would have done the same thing," rationalised Kirk.

Strangely enough, it seems that the three members of Metallica never formally welcomed Hammett to their band: his audition was a success and they simply continued to play alongside him. In later times, formal deals would have been signed and contracts stipulating various entitlements would have made his membership of the band a legal reality, but until then it seems that he simply hung in there, a member but not on the same level as the others, perhaps. James acknowledged this state of affairs, also to *Thrasher*: "It wasn't like we really auditioned Kirk. He came in, set up, played and he was there. I don't know what we would have done if we hadn't liked him. We didn't have the money to send him back. We barely had enough money to get Dave home." Odder still, Hammett even temporarily used two of Mustaine's speaker cabinets for his early performances, even though he was still uncertain whether his membership would be long-term or not, as he explained: "I took a big chance because there was always the possibility that they might not have liked me or something. I flew out there with all kinds of equipment and stuff, and I even paid for it. It was real weird because I was in the same situation of being out of California for the first time, and on top of that I barely knew any of them. The only one I knew was Mark."

It was a courageous move by Kirk to leave a band with much potential for a rival act who might not even have taken to him or his playing. But this confidence is part of Hammett's character, it appears: two men who knew him well are Katon DePena, who refers to Kirk as "a great guy. Loves music. He is really nice. He did a hell of a job replacing Dave Mustaine," and John Marshall, who recalls: "Kirk and I have been good friends since we were about 15 years old. When he was in Exodus, I would help set up his gear at their gigs so I could get in for free. When he joined Metallica he convinced them to let me work for them." (Marshall would roadie for them on several occasions.)

Once the audition had taken place and Lars, James and Cliff were satisfied with Hammett's guitar skills, he made his debut performance on April 16 at the Showplace in New Jersey. The band were scheduled to begin a tour supporting none other than their heroes Venom the following week and must have been anxious to prove that the new line-up could match up to the job of playing with the Newcastle trio. Luckily, Kirk's performance was exemplary and the band faced their future with renewed confidence.

At this point Metallica, who had been living as guests at the house of Jon and Marsha Zazula, found themselves forced to move into a new home after their constant party antics upset their hosts once too often. As Hetfield revealed in a later interview, the Zazulas understood that their guests enjoyed a drink and a spot of late-night revelry as much (or more than) the next young band and were contented to let the parties continue to a certain point – but when they awoke one morning to find that a treasured bottle of champagne which they had been saving for a special occasion had been wolfed by the band at some point the night before, enough was finally enough.

Zazula's new home for Metallica was grim. As he remembers: "We put them into this terrible, terrible, *terrible*, legendary place called the Music Building. They shared the rehearsal room with Anthrax, but they actually slept in a terrible area. It was like a storage place, it was a part of the building where they had all the rubbish. It was a terrible scene, but I had really no choice. I didn't know what I was getting myself into either!" Kirk remembered it with even less pleasure: "The Music Building was something else. I found a piece of foam on the ground, and I used that as my mattress to put my sleeping bag on. The people that owned it didn't put any time into it. The place had no hot

106

water. I remember washing my hair in the sink using cold water, it was brutal." Although the Music Building functioned pretty well as a rehearsal space, actually living in it was a tough experience, especially for a band with little or no money. Scott Ian of Anthrax, whose band soon struck up a firm friendship with the San Franciscan firm, explains that he and his band-mates used to help them out wherever possible: "They had no money, they had nowhere to go, so we pretty much went out of our way to help them out in any way we could. We brought them to our houses to shower, and we gave them a refrigerator and a toaster oven so they could cook the hot dogs that they were eating cold. We just hung out as much as possible."

Not only did New York bands such as Anthrax take Metallica to their bosoms, the local metal fans were keen on them too, as soon as a buzz over their performances started to develop. Dan Lorenzo of Hades was a young metal fan in NY at the time, and remembers how a gang of fans of which he was a member would follow Metallica and their contemporaries with some devotion: "The early incarnation of Hades used to run with the Old Bridge Militia, so we knew of Metallica early on. The Militia was a bunch of metal-heads from Old Bridge, New Jersey, who used to take underground metal bands under their wing. Bands like Metallica, Anthrax, Hades, Raven and so on would come to Old Bridge because Jon Zazula lived there."

Zazula, it seems, was a man with far-reaching influence. Not only had he forged links with overseas record labels such as Neat, he had kept in touch with the local metal scene and knew exactly which bands would draw crowds. His decision to put Venom and Metallica on the same bill was a masterstroke, providing as it did the chance for the British band (who were riding the crest of a wave of publicity at the time after two successful albums and legendary live shows) to show the locals how it was done, and the opportunity for Metallica to rise to the challenge of playing in front of their idols.

Jeff Dunn of Venom remembers the two shows they played together at the Paramount Theater on Staten Island, on Friday, April 22 and Sunday, April 24, 1983, very clearly. Venom had been invited to stay at the Zazulas' house, probably to Jon and Marsha's regret ("I remember we wrecked his kitchen one night when we were trying to cook something, and set fire to the fuckin' place!"), and the shows themselves were equally chaotic. James Hetfield managed to celebrate Metallica's successful opening slot for Venom by falling over while clutching a bottle of vodka, cutting his hand and requiring six stitches. The general drunkenness that pervaded the visit was extreme, as Jeff recalls: "On that first US tour I remember Cronos and Lars being in the same bed! Absolutely pissed out of their fuckin' heads and they just fell asleep, then woke up together in the morning and said, 'What the fuck is this!' Everybody just crashed out. We were upstairs and they were downstairs, and it was so fuckin' hot it was difficult to get to sleep anyway. I could hear Lars going nuts downstairs, and I heard my roadie saying, 'I'm gonna go down and knock that cunt out in a minute, I just really want to go to sleep.' Then it was quiet all of a sudden, I guess he just passed out or something."

Venom – who, despite their reputation as seasoned journeymen of metal, were still used to working in low-budget situations – almost managed to destroy the Paramount Theater itself with an accidental overdose of pyrotechnics. To this day Dunn is amazed that no one was killed: "We had a bit of hassle when we played Staten Island. The first show, which was my birthday, we had a hell of a lot of technical problems. The speakers were hanging out of the cabinets. What actually happened was, we had these cast-iron bomb pots, right, about the diameter of a mug and eight inches high, and there were 24 of these along the front of the stage. One guy went along and filled the pots with blasting powder and put the fuses in, right? Then – because communication was so crap – another guy goes, 'Fuck! The bomb pots!' half an hour before the show, gets up and fills them up again, not knowing the first guy had already done it!"

Jeff's voice sinks as he recalls the next moment: "So when these went off . . . *fucking hell*. The explosion was louder than the band. One of the bomb pots – and this is no word of a lie – was found in the balcony embedded in the wall. That fucker could have killed somebody. There was a four-foot hole blown in the wood of the stage, as well. How somebody wasn't injured . . ."

The promoters were livid, although history does not recall whether Venom, Jon Zazula or in fact anyone at all was billed for the damage. The next day was more sober. Dunn recalls: "On the 23rd, the Saturday, we went down to Rock'N'Roll Heaven to sign autographs. I've still got the original poster which says, 'Meet in person: Venom at Rock'N'Roll Heaven' and then in tiny writing at the bottom 'Also

Metallica'." And the Sunday night show barely got off the ground, with the Venom axeman suffering from a common travel ailment: "I remember it now, I had a serious dose of the shits at the time. It was our first time in America, and it was a really hot night so I'd been up all night in the hotel drinking water. Fuck me, the next day, I was ill. I remember running out of the toilet on stage as the intro tape was running. No word of a lie."

Despite these ancillary problems, Metallica and Venom regarded both shows as an unqualified success, as did the fans who had crammed the venue on both occasions. Enthused by the experience, Lars and James told an interviewer from the KUSF radio station that . . . "We might do something with Venom if they can get off their ass and do more than one album every five years." The two bands had got on well, it seemed: "Venom were so fuckin' friendly – you'd think they would be against you but they help you out." The latter comment was inspired by a disappointing experience they had the previous year: "Saxon didn't even say hello, they weren't friendly at all."

Both men were delighted with their relatively new bassist, Burton, as James said, "Oh yes, he's the best bass player I've ever worked with. He's a real musical fuckin' genius. Great guy too, very laid-back. There's a whole different bottom end to the sound now." The comparison between Cliff and Ron McGovney was marked, as Hetfield explained with evident disgust: "Ron was shit, I taught him how to play. He was the player from my old band." Lars added: "The line-up that we have with Ron and Dave, it just wasn't happening. When you thought ahead five years you couldn't picture any of them in the band. Even with Dave, deep inside we never thought it would last that long." The presence of Kirk, too, was an obvious relief to both musicians: "Kirk plays all the time, he gets up in the morning and just jams. For nine days in the band he's real tight . . . he's got a lot of good material that we're gonna start using." Hammett, it emerged, was on the point of swapping his guitar to avoid making the band too clichéd in appearance. His Gibson Flying V, coupled with James' similar guitar, was just too traditional an image for them. "Two Vs is a real cliché, Kirk sold his to get a Marshall cab. I think he's gonna get an Explorer," said James – although in fact he would later be the one to make a Gibson Explorer his chosen instrument, while Hammett would retain his 1971 Flying V for many years.

But the line-up wasn't completely stable, it seemed, as Lars and James still discussed recruiting a 'proper' singer. John Bush of Armored Saint was the man they were after, and they were clearly hoping to wear down his resistance and persuade him to join: "We've been looking for a singer for a long time . . . we're trying to get the singer from Armored Saint. His stage presence would make you freak out, he looks like he means it. He's got a real good voice and he's really young." Lars paid Bush the ultimate compliment for the time by saying: "This guy could be like Sean Harris is now." Ulrich also revealed that Zazula had lined up some singers to audition: "There are about three people that Johnny has hooked up with out here that we wanna try out." Whether the auditions actually came to pass or not is unlikely.

Most excitingly, the Metallica duo revealed that plans were afoot for the recording of a debut album. Lars, who told the reporter that he was training himself to use a double bass pedal, which he had acquired just a couple of days previously, had clear ideas about the record: "Most of the songs we've got lined up aren't as fast as the others. Fast songs all the time tend to sound the same . . . when we do fast stuff we try and have breaks, because it makes it seem faster."

This casual chatter about the imminent recording of an album masked several weeks of hard work which Jonny Z, who was acting as a de facto manager for Metallica by this stage, had put in on their behalf. To this day he recalls the process of getting an album deal ready to go for Metallica as one of the most stressful experiences of his career: "Once they were here, we got them some dates, and then we started talking about what it would be like if we put out a Metallica record . . . something with the best possible production we could do."

The logical first move was to approach record companies who might give Metallica a deal, but nobody was interested in this bunch of West Coast brats who played too fast and looked too normal. Jonny: "I went to some very famous people. I won't name them, but they were all big shots, and presented the band – and they just didn't get it at all. They had no clue as to what it was."

The main problem, as with all things Metallica at this stage in their careers, was money – or the lack of it. Zazula had done his arithmetic ("For the album they had, we figured it would cost us about five thousand dollars, but . . . pennies were miracles in those days") but knew that it would be difficult to raise that amount himself. His income from the record store was minimal, but Jon had two important advantages. Firstly, his faith in Metallica was profound: "I just had this belief that *this* was the band and that eventually everybody would get it. We had the constant support of the people in the record store, they were spreading the word, the word was getting out to the West Coast, all over. It was feeling right, even though there was no money."

Secondly, Jon and his wife were expert business-people and knew how to raise cash when times were hard: "Marsha and I are miraculous at moving one penny here to over there. We did whatever we had to do. Second mortgages. We put our life up, we literally put our life on hold to do this. It was sink or swim." Although stress levels were rising daily ("It was horrible. Some of those days were the worst days of my life. My neck was constantly in a noose. And we'd just had a baby, you know? It was like the Christians in the Colosseum walking out to the lions!"), the band and the Zazulas decided that they would fund the recording, manufacture and release of the record by themselves. "We decided to do it ourselves, and fuck everybody. We just said, to hell with what people say, we're gonna do it. And people thought we were mad. We just did it," he recalls with some satisfaction. Initially the Zazulas decided to christen their fledgling record company Vigilante, perhaps to place emphasis on its independent, rebellious nature; but then the ever-divergent thinker Burton came up with a better idea. "One day we were talking with Cliff, and we came up with Megaforce," recalls Zazula.

Was it weird that Jonny was both the record label head, as a result of this decision, and simultaneously the band's manager? "Yeah, I was their manager and their record label guy, which is a strange position to be in, but I've been there many times," he responds. "At that time nobody could do it better. Nobody understood the sensitivity to it. Nobody understood it more and nobody would take on the task, because the odds were impossible."

Metallica, who had started 1983 with a brand-new bass player, an erratic guitarist whose ever-increasing instability was a constant stress to them, and a brand-new home in an unfamiliar city, had come a long way in only four months. They now had a manager, a record company prepared to fund the recording of a debut album and a supremely talented new guitarist.

All that remained for them to take the next step was to get their brand of fiery eloquence down on tape. Would the results be all they had hoped for?

10

1983–1984

Actually getting Metallica into a studio, with funds available for the making of an album, was a herculean task. The band themselves had gelled into a professional, disciplined unit and had honed their set of songs to a fine degree over the many shows they had performed to date, but as always, cashflow seemed likely to hold them back. Luckily, Jon Zazula managed to convince the management of the New York State-based Pyramid Studios, near Rochester – where Manowar and the Rods had previously recorded albums – to allow him to pay for sessions in instalments spread over a period of time. As he remembers, the man chosen to produce the record, Paul Curcio, took some persuading: "We saved up a few dollars and flew up to Rochester, New York – which is quite a ways – and my job was to convince them that we should do the album on spec. Curcio thought he'd get me there and get me to pay for it! But he did give me terms which were do-able, he gave me time to pay it out, which I felt that we could do."

On May 10, 1983, Metallica began the recording. Fortunately they had practised endlessly. Zazula: "They were ready to go. They did some rearranging of some songs and so on, but these songs were their songs. In fact it was kinda funny because we always said, 'Don't you know any other songs?'" With little in the way of in-studio rearrangement necessary, Zazula's funds would hold out.

During recording breaks, various ideas for a title were tossed around: the original concept had been the rather unsubtle *Metal Up Your Ass*, but the distribution company chosen to handle the album were against it. As Zazula recalls, "We put together an album cover of a guy sitting on the toilet, with a sword coming out and cutting his ass. The distributor didn't want that. He said that nobody would take it up with that title, which was the temperature of the industry at the time."

113

Annoyed at this lily-livered attitude, the band suggested alternative titles, with Burton's idea the immediate winner: "What happened was, Cliff said, 'Just kill 'em all, you know?' And that became the name of the record," chuckles Zazula.

The *Kill 'Em All* sessions resulted in ten completed songs, all of which had been performed live in the preceding year. 'Hit The Lights' opened the album, and was an immediate insight into the speed and the precision of the relatively new line-up. Cliff and Kirk both brought a melodic approach to the band which had been absent in Ron McGovney's playing on the *No Life 'Til Leather* demo and not much more evident in the playing of the young Dave Mustaine. The first song, obviously an early declaration of intent by Metallica (its opening line contained the promise "Gonna kick your ass tonight!"), was based on a fast riff which allowed Hammett enough space for plenty of wild self-expression (although he and others have stated that his playing was enthusiastic rather than accomplished at this stage) and also featured a fade-in, a relatively uncommon device in metal at the time. The next track was 'The Four Horsemen', an interesting choice as it is lengthy, full of unpredictable one-off motifs and a direct predecessor of the much more complex, progressive songs which Metallica would write in the mid to late Eighties. Although its basic premise is a simple, scratched riff, it contains a slow, cleanly picked section which Burton underpins with a classical, ascending progression, reaching the upper registers of his bass in the bar before Hammett's understated solo. Bernard Doe recalls with a smile: "'The Four Horsemen' was a reworking of 'The Mechanix' complete with Lynyrd Skynyrd's 'Sweet Home Alabama' interlude! Ulrich threw a minor fit when I made that comparison in my review in *Metal Forces*, although he did admit later that he did see where I was coming from."

'Motorbreath', the crowd-pleaser which Metallica still pull out in their live sets at the time of writing, is a work of genius, based as it is on a simple, four-chord verse and a stop-start chorus. The lyrics are classic, we're-on-the-road metal ("Motorbreath, it's how I live my life/ I can't make it any other way" and so on), but the lead breaks, based on a genuinely powerful backing riff from Hetfield, also make the song memorable. The very catchy 'Jump In The Fire', which follows it, has nothing to do with thrash metal at all, resembling a Judas Priest or (unsurprisingly) a Diamond Head song: it even has a shout-out chorus of "So come on!" which gives it an almost mainstream rock quality.

The album's centrepiece is Cliff Burton's astounding bass solo, 'Anesthesia (Pulling Teeth)', and Metallica's speedy showcase, 'Whiplash', which follows it. The former has been assessed many times by bass experts and remains a startling fusion of classical triads (groups of three notes), an almost progressive, wah-pedal-infused section and a blast of pure distortion accompanied by Lars' fundamental drum pattern. To this day, the sound of James saying "Bass solo, take one" on the studio mike before Burton activates his overdrive is a spine-chilling moment.

'Whiplash', above all, established Metallica as a thrash metal band. There are no hooky choruses or slow sections here: the song is a solid chug against a very rapid rhythm from Ulrich, an almost supernatural degree of precision in the main riff from Hetfield (although this would be superseded later, on even speedier songs) and memorable moments coming when the band stops suddenly and Hetfield shrieks the song's title. After this, the powerful 'Phantom Lord' (a carefully crafted song with a lead section which introduces itself three times before kicking in fully) and 'No Remorse' (which soon-to-be Metallica tour photographer Ross Halfin reports is "a complete lift from 'Hocus Pocus' by Focus. That's where they nicked the riff from. Kirk told me that!") seem almost relaxed. The latter, however, does equal the ferocity of 'Whiplash' with its closing section, an insanely speedy riff which brings the song to a fiery close.

'Seek And Destroy', above all other Metallica songs, became known as the one in which band and audience would interact: it has a simple, one-line chorus of "Searching . . . seek and destroy!" in which James would encourage the crowd to roar along. Apart from this, it's just a classic early Metallica song, with a speedier second section and a blistering solo from Hammett. The album closes with 'Metal Militia', another statement of intent of sorts: the song likens Metallica to an army of metal on the march, even adding the sound of tramping feet and a ricocheting bullet to its outro.

Although the results of the recording sessions were impressive, the actual making of the record wasn't much fun. As James told *Thrasher* magazine in 1986, "We had no experience whatsoever in the studio when we were recording *Kill 'Em All*. Our so-called producer was sitting there checking the songs off a notepad and saying, 'Well, we can go to a club tonight when we're through recording. Is the coffee ready?' He had nothing to say about any of the songs. I don't think he'd dare say anyway, because we'd have said, 'Fuck you, that's our song.' But production-wise, helping with sound or anything, he didn't contribute. So right away we had a bad reflection of what a producer was."

So much for the production of the record, although in fact both the mix and clarity on *KEA* are fine for a metal album of this budget and era. The key aspect, which surprised many, was the sheer speed at which Metallica played on songs like 'Hit The Lights', 'Whiplash' and the last section of 'No Remorse'. Kirk told *Thrasher*: "We thought that whatever we did, there'd be people who would approach [the record] with a lot of hesitation, because it was so different back then . . . We wrote stuff thinking that we were going to play it at a normal speed and just naturally speed it up." James added that the unprecedented speed of the album came about because . . . "We'd just keep practising, and the songs would get faster and faster, and the energy kept building up . . . It's always faster, [a lot of] shit's going on live. Booze and freaks dinking around, just the excitement."

The artwork of *Kill 'Em All* is its other remarkable feature. The cover is a collage photo of a sledgehammer, a pool of blood and the shadow of a hand; a much subtler image than the original jagged knife protruding from a toilet bowl which still surfaces on T-shirts to this day. The Metallica photo on the rear sleeve is astonishing from this distance: the band are all in their very early twenties, although they're clearly trying to look older and tougher. Kirk is the only one who isn't suffering from the last vestiges of teenage acne, and Lars' attempt to add some years by not shaving for a few days simply does not work. Still, both pictures are iconic, given what the album meant to the fledgling thrash metal scene, and stand up today against the much more graphic sleeve imagery used by many other metal bands of the time.

The issue of whether James' vocals, which he had extended from the early days by adding a harsher, barked tone to his delivery, would match up to the standards required, was clearly resolved with *Kill 'Em All*. Although his vocals are still undeveloped (his delivery of the word 'how' in "Motorbreath, it's how I live my life" in particular is way off-key), the rawness of the style suits the music perfectly. John Bush told me that Metallica were keen to recruit him right up to the recording of *KEA*: "At the time when they were ready to make *Kill 'Em All* there was a little question as to whether or not James wanted to do the singing, and if they were all behind the idea of him being the singer. They had seen Armored Saint play, and I guess they thought – and obviously it's been the ultimate compliment – that I was maybe somebody who could make their sound different." How did they go about chasing him? He recalls: "Back in the days when Jonny Z was managing Metallica, he would call me and then Lars would call me. But in my defence, at that point Armored Saint was starting to happen and get popular. Plus all the guys in Saint and me had grown up together, so for me to say, I'm quitting this band to go join Metallica, a band that I don't know . . . I just wasn't gonna do it, quite honestly."

Bush doesn't regret his decision. "I was not a soothsayer, nobody could have predicted the future for Metallica. It was not my fate, it was not my destiny, and of course who knows what would have happened? It could have changed the whole face of music. I don't want to hold that over my head, though . . . and even after they were done with the record they were still flirting with the idea of getting another singer, and not just with me. But James is James. Talk about someone who turned out to be an amazing vocalist! You can see progression in his singing that is just remarkable."

In fact, the Zazula connection was renewed when, a decade later, Anthrax (who he managed) needed a new singer after Joey Belladonna's departure. Bush: "Ten years after Z started managing Metallica I got a call from him asking me to join Anthrax, and I swear I had never spoken to him in that time! So I called him and he was like, 'How's this for ironic? I'm calling you again about a job!' It was so weird, a bizarre twist of fate."

To coincide with the release of *Kill 'Em All*, Megaforce also issued a 12″ single of 'Whiplash', clearly one of the standout tracks on the album, if not the most obviously marketable one. The A-side comprised the song and a 'Whiplash' remix, although the differences between the two weren't immediately clear: the flipside held live versions of 'Seek And Destroy' and 'Phantom Lord' (later revealed not to be live, but to be merely re-recorded versions of the songs with overdubbed crowd noise). The single sold respectably enough, but in the climate of the time metal singles weren't expected to cause much impact, and this certainly didn't.

Although one or two of Metallica's contemporaries needed a little time to get used to the concept of Metallica on vinyl (for instance, Eric

Peterson of Testament was taken aback by Hetfield's harsher singing style: "I was so used to the *No Life 'Til Leather* demo that when I heard *Kill 'Em All* I thought, why is he screaming now? I didn't like that"), its impact was enormous. Thomas Fischer, at the time with Hellhammer and soon to be with Celtic Frost, nails the specific influence of the album down to James' almost unnatural accuracy as a rhythm guitarist: "There was one major instance in which Metallica were an important inspiration on our own early work. That was the area of precision. Being still somewhat new on our instruments, we were much more sloppy in the execution of our music, and the American bands which flooded the underground scene by means of demos, singles and compilation albums seemed like a million times more professional in that respect. We of course never reached that level of precision, but the standard was set and remained firmly engraved in our consciousness."

Fischer adds that the influence of the album extended as far as the whole metal scene: "There was no doubt in anybody's mind that a new era of heavy music had begun, and what separated Metallica from any other of the fresh young bands was their precision and their (for that time) enormously professional approach and production. Their music was unique, and *Kill 'Em All* was a true innovation. They came with that album and simply set new standards overnight, seemingly effortlessly."

And so Metallica committed themselves to posterity. Jon Zazula wasted no time in getting them on the road while *Kill 'Em All* was being pressed and packaged, not least because his new label, Megaforce, was already starting to attract new business. US distribution for *KEA* came from Relativity, while Roadrunner distributed the album in Holland, Banzai in Canada, RGE in Brazil, King in Japan and Bernett in France.

Zazula had also built links with a UK power trio called Raven, who he thought would make good touring partners for Metallica: "At the time, Raven were having a problem. Nobody in the States wanted them. Also at the time, Anthrax were driving us crazy trying to get a deal with us, and at the same time Manowar were off of EMI and needed a deal. So here we are, a record store – four blokes – and next thing you know it we're signing all these bands, with the biggest pair of brass balls you ever had!"

The result was that Metallica and Raven were scheduled for a

118

two-month tour together from late June to early September, 1983. As the British band was just releasing an album called *All For One*, the package was labelled the Kill 'Em All For One tour – and would go down in history as one of the most riotous ever. All seven musicians and a communal crew were housed in a mobile home procured by Jonny Z. James told Metal Mike of *Aardschok* that Metallica studied Raven's show (a style of music which had been called 'athletic rock', for no obvious reason) and learned from their tourmates' absolute commitment. However, life on the road was tough at times, as he recalled: "Halfway through Texas the air-conditioning system broke, and it was like travelling in an oven. You woke up in the morning, and your tongue was stuck to your palate, because it was 200 degrees in there!"

Living on a bus with several other drink-loving males on a jaunt of this length must have been tough. The tour began on July 27 at the Royal Manor in New Jersey and headed slowly westward, taking in Bridgeport, Connecticut; two shows in Boston, Massachusetts; Yonkers, Jamestown, Buffalo, Rochester, Elmhurst, Brooklyn, Long Island and Morganville in New Jersey and New York, followed by concerts along the lengthy route through Baltimore, Chicago, Milwaukee and then into the American heartlands of Arkansas, Texas, Oklahoma and New Mexico. The tour wound up in late August with a handful of triumphant Californian shows at the Country Club in Reseda and the Keystone and Stone venues in San Francisco. For these final dates Metal Church guitarist John Marshall helped out as a roadie, marking the beginning of a long-standing friendship with the band.

While this tour – Metallica's first of any significant length – exposed them to thousands of metal fans and established them in America, Raven's profile would drop in the following couple of years, leaving them with the status of respected also-rans. Gene Hoglan once interviewed Raven's John and Mark Gallagher, vocalist/bassist and guitarist respectively, for *Shockwaves*, asking them: "Do you realise the influence you had on metal bands in the Eighties?" John responded, "We don't really know how much of an influence we made in America since we're not here much . . . [but] Flotsam And Jetsam, apparently they used to play Raven cover songs. People have told me Billy Sheehan is a big fan of ours, as well as the guys in Skid Row and Phil from Pantera." That his band became a cult rather than one with widespread appeal was, perhaps, down to the inability of many fans to categorise their music: "We toured in Europe with bands like Testament and Kreator, and it went over great, but in certain towns we weren't 'thrash' enough for them. But Raven is more of a heavy rock'n'roll band rather than a thrash band, even though people say that we've influenced thrash metal."

As the tour rolled on, June became July, and on the 25th Megaforce released *Kill 'Em All*. Initially pressed as a run of a few thousand copies, word of mouth generated by the KEAFO tour saw the record snapped up wherever it appeared. By the end of the year it had sold 17,000 copies in America. But this is only a fraction of the story. Zazula had forged links with a British record company called Music For Nations, whose founder Martin Hooker remembers those early days of metal very clearly: "Music For Nations was my company and I founded it at the end of 1982, with the first release coming out on my birthday in February 1983. My job title was Managing Director and Head of A&R. When MFN started we got all our contacts in the US to send us new releases and demos of bands looking for deals in Europe: within weeks we had huge piles of material, as there really weren't many independent companies doing metal at the time. I gradually waded my way through all the piles of material and settled on a handful to get the ball rolling. First up was Virgin Steele, who 20 years later are still enjoying strong sales in Europe, and next came the first Ratt mini-album which I loved."

One day Hooker was sifting through the latest batch of potential releases when his eye fell on a rough copy of *Kill 'Em All*. "I'd become aware of Metallica through the *Live Metal Up Your Ass* demo which I'd got hold of somewhere on a trip to the US," he recalls. "I listened to *KEA* again and again and just thought it was brilliant. At first I saw Metallica as the next step on from the punk scene I'd been doing with my previous label Secret, all aggression and speed, but they eventually became popular because they were doing something totally different from everybody else."

From his office in New Jersey, Jon Zazula remembers Martin Hooker and MFN with respect: "I liked Martin very much, and his staff was wonderful, he had a guy called Gem Howard who was there from the beginning and took care of all the band's needs. There's a whole book about Megaforce's relationship with MFN alone – a lot of history, a lot of stories!" He was keen to do a deal with Music For

Nations for the release of *Kill 'Em All* in Europe, and a contract was rapidly drawn up. "Was it easy to strike the deal," I ask? "Yes. They gave me nought and I gave them none!" he says, laughing. "It wasn't a complex deal: it was complex enough to give them several albums, and for me to have a secure deal, but it really wasn't much. Martin put in a lot of money and a lot of time into them – he spent some good marketing money on them. They really did their job."

Hooker tells his side of the story with the words: "We contacted their manager Jon Zazula and quickly put a three-album licence deal together, where we'd handle the band for the UK and Europe. Initially it was very hard work to get people interested in the band, because they just thought it was a joke. Primarily because of the speed and the way they played, people in the industry refused to take them seriously and I remember taking a lot of stick at the time from friends in the industry."

When he refers to hard work, he means it. "The initial UK ship out of the album was only 1,300 units, and the re-presses were done 500 copies at a time. This really shows how much like hard work it was. We tried to arrange a tour for them with The Rods and Exciter, but the whole thing was cancelled due to lack of ticket sales. Not to be put off, we kept at it and eventually brought Metallica over for a club tour. Once people saw them live the word of mouth really started. By this time the media were starting to get on board and sales were really picking up." The net result, as he recalls it from two decades' distance, repaid all their expectations: "After investing over $100,000 in touring the band, their popularity was really increasing and we ended up with a gold album in the UK and a very successful record all over Europe."

The live tour was the key element. By this stage Metallica had developed into a live presence of considerable power: the four musicians, all experts at their craft and driven by their desire to make their band as good as it could be, created a stage show light on accessories (they famously retained their 'fan' image) but heavy on power and aggression. James had conquered his earlier shyness and now incorporated audience shout-out routines in 'Seek And Destroy': an important part of any concert in popular music but more so in metal, where the need of the crowd for catharsis is high. The sight of the four Metallica members headbanging had also gripped crowds, as it had for contemporaries such as Venom, Anthrax and Exodus. In fact, 'the mosh' (extreme, windmilling headbanging) became such an integral part of

121

the thrash scene that short-haired fans were literally unable to look the part at concerts. A player who took this to extremes is Slayer's Tom Araya, who even tried not to let physical injury prevent him from banging his head on stage, as he told me: "I've never injured my neck bones, but I have snapped muscles in the middle of a show. I'm head-banging away and suddenly it's like, aarrgghh! So I keep my neck and back stiff and see if it hurts too bad, and if it does I just try to rock my head back and forward a little bit."

As Metallica's live abilities grew, so their partying instincts became more honed. Live shows with Armored Saint in November 1983 were followed by huge drinking sessions, with destruction part of the package. James told journalist Xavier Russell of *Kerrang!* of one particularly debauched night: "Well, as usual, we'd spent hours and hours in the bar and then we decided to booze it up with Armored Saint, so we went up to [AS bassist] Joey Vera's room and drank all his beer. We were all getting really ripped and started throwing bottles out the window. They were smashing and it sounded really neat. But that soon got boring, so I threw Joey's black and red leather jacket out and it landed in the pool, which luckily had its cover on. So we went down to get it and on the way back up to the tenth floor I decided to open the elevator doors between floors . . . we then got stuck for half an hour and everyone is like freaking out and I started shouting, 'Get us the fuck out of here!' We finally get up to the tenth floor and by now I'm pretty [mad] so I see this fire extinguisher hanging on the wall. So I kinda took it down and started squirting people with it – all this CO2 or some kinda shit was comin' out of it."

All this madness occasionally spilled over on stage, as when Metallica attended a Mercyful Fate show after a prolonged drinking session. Fate singer King Diamond had become friends with the band through his countryman Lars Ulrich and invited them on stage, but Hammett – somewhat worse for wear – managed to knock the King over. As Diamond told me: "We were standing next to each other. He was leaning on me, and suddenly my balance went. Flat on my ass on stage." Unperturbed, Diamond laughed it off and forgot all about it.

It emerged that after the show Hetfield, Burton and Ulrich told the confused Hammett, as a joke, that Diamond was furious with him for the incident. Although Kirk was clearly worried about this, the others forgot to tell him later that they were just kidding – and it was not until

1999, when Hammett approached Diamond at a backstage party and apologised to the bemused singer, that he realised how he'd been tricked.

But Metallica remained dedicated despite all the games. *Kill 'Em All* had only been out for five months when they began writing material for a second album at a rehearsal room in New Jersey, after six California shows at their old haunts. Gigs in Chicago, Cleveland, New Jersey and New York with Megaforce's new signing (and their erstwhile Music Building co-habitants) Anthrax followed. These shows and the six they had executed back home in California were notable as they saw the debut of songs from the next album – songs which marked the progression of Metallica to another plane in composition terms. The first to appear live was an instrumental tune called either 'When Hell Freezes Over' or 'The Call Of Ktulu': it was not until the following year that Metallica decided to use the latter title permanently. This lengthy, almost epic composition first appeared on September 2 at the Keystone in Berkeley and was a much more fluid, jammed performance than the version which would be recorded the following year. November shows at the Stone, the Keystone again and at the Country Club also marked the appearance of new songs called 'Fight Fire With Fire', 'Creeping Death' and 'Ride The Lightning', all much more structured and precise than the *Kill 'Em All* material.

But the more crafted structure of the new songs wasn't all that distinguished them. One day James was tinkering around on an acoustic guitar in Metallica's rehearsal room, when a sequence of minor chords came to him which, picked as an arpeggio, generated a pensive, almost melancholy effect. This soon developed into a song, which he decided to call 'Fade To Black'.

Another development in Metallica's career was about to happen. 'Fade To Black' was a soft, sweet ballad – perhaps the least expected move Metallica could have made.

11

1984–1985

1984 was even more pivotal for Metallica's upward mobility than 1983. The pace of their progress was staggering with the band going from strength to strength with almost unprecedented speed after the release of *Kill 'Em All*. Extraordinarily, this was accomplished alongside the sudden re-appearance of Dave Mustaine in his new band Megadeth, at the end of 1983.

Dave, it seemed, was not a happy man. The main reason for his ire was the fact that his contribution to many of the songs on *Kill 'Em All* had been uncredited, a dispute between Dave and Metallica which has never been put to rest. He told Bob Nalbandian, "When I joined that band they only had one song, 'Hit The Lights'. James did not write that song, Hugh Tanner wrote it . . . [as well as] the song 'Motorbreath' . . . I wrote the most songs on that whole fuckin' album! I wrote four of them, James wrote three, and Hugh Tanner wrote two!" Adding, "I'm just wondering what Metallica are gonna do when they run out of my riffs," and introducing Megadeth's forthcoming material with the words, "I thought I'd have a helluva lot harder time coming up with something better, but this is three times faster, more advanced and a helluva lot heavier!" Mustaine also told the writer . . . "I already smashed James in the mouth one time, and Lars is scared of his own shadow."

Perhaps most interestingly, Dave seemed most annoyed with the enthusiastic reception that his replacement, Kirk Hammett, had received from the fans, remarking, "Kirk is a 'Yes' man . . . 'Yes, Lars, I'll do Dave's leads'; 'Yes, James, I'll play this' . . . James played all the rhythm on that album and Cliff wrote all Kirk's leads, so it shows you they're having a lot of trouble with this 'New Guitar God'."

More damaging by far to Metallica at this stage, however, was not their erstwhile band-mate's bile but the fact that much of their stage equipment was stolen from a van after a show at the Channel Club in Boston, Massachusetts on January 14, 1984. Their touring partners Anthrax loaned them enough amplification and other gear to allow the shows to continue, but the loss of their cherished equipment was felt deeply, especially by James, who had lost a much-needed Marshall amplifier. However, Zazula and his Crazed Management team had set up Metallica's first European tour, which was scheduled to commence on February 3, so there was no choice but to soldier on with borrowed gear and buy more when the opportunity arose.

The new tour, which would take in Switzerland, Germany, France, Belgium and the Aardschok Festival in Holland, was dubbed the Seven Dates Of Hell tour (a suitably metallic quip). Metallica would be opening for none other than their old friends Venom, who were still riding a wave of publicity caused by their near-conceptual third album, *At War With Satan*, which had appeared the previous June. The route that Metallica had followed to the Venom support was, despite their recent successes, still somewhat home-made in nature: according to Venom guitarist Jeff Dunn, the two bands had not crossed paths since the brief US tour the previous year and communications were sporadic: "They actually sent a demo, which arrived at the fan club address, Eric Cook's house. The next thing we knew, there was apparently a phone call from Lars at the house, asking if they could support us. I think Eric's mum spoke to him! Well, I must admit that in the early days we were quite arrogant and brash about everything, so it was a case of yeah, they can support us again. Nobody worried us."

Had Dunn even heard *Kill 'Em All* by this stage? Apparently not: "The *No Life 'Til Leather* demo was all we'd heard of them. When we went to the US the first time we were just told, there's this band Metallica going to support you, and we were like, yeah, whatever, because we didn't even know who they were at the time. Literally, the conversation was, 'There's your support band.' We weren't in contact with any Americans at the time, Jon Zazula was the first one."

The opening gig of the Seven Dates tour was at the Volkshaus in the Swiss town of Zürich. Metallica's first European show was, logically enough, followed by their first European party, as Dunn recalls: "It was like *National Lampoon's Vacation*. Metallica went fuckin' *nuts* on the first night. What had happened was, there were some fans outside, and one of Metallica had broken a window to get to the fans and say hello. By this time the promoters had decided that they were gonna kill them for damaging the venue, so Gem Howard from Music For Nations, who was looking after them on the tour, brought them into our dressing room and said, 'We'll put the guys in here because the security and everybody's looking for them, there's gonna be hell.' And they just sat there in our dressing room like little rabbits caught in the headlights!"

Although the celebrations continued throughout the tour just as they did on the US jaunt of 1983, the gigs themselves were a big success. Audiences seemed to enjoy Metallica's new material (Dunn: "I would say Metallica always got a good response") and the quartet were simultaneously making plans for recording a new album, discussing how this could be done with the advice of Zazula and Martin Hooker. The tour passed through the Teatro Tenda in Milan, the Hemmerleinhalle in Nuremberg, the Espace Ballard in Paris, before a notable slot at the Aardschok Festival in Ijsselhal, Holland. They finished on February 12 at the Poperinge Festival in Belgium where traditional end-of-tour practical jokes were visited on Metallica by their mentors, as Dunn remembers: "We had some fun . . . I think some of the road crew had covered Lars' drum heads in talcum powder. And we were throwing fruit at them, it was just high jinks. They didn't do anything in return, I think they were too scared to. It was like, that's funny, but we're not gonna do anything back, haha."

Dunn also adds that the two bands always got on very well from the beginning. Perhaps the characters of the musicians complemented each other well: "As far as I can remember, Lars was always the spokesperson and always had the most to say. James was always down to earth, just a genuinely nice guy who seemed to be pleased to be there and was there for the love of it. He loved it on stage and there were no airs and graces about him whatsoever. Cliff was Captain Spaceman. Permanently chilled out. I remember he always had a denim jacket and denim flares and was quiet."

As Megaforce had done for *Kill 'Em All*, Music For Nations decided to issue a Metallica single to promote the tour. In the absence of new material (the new album sessions were still months away), Martin Hooker and his team assembled a single around the *KEA* song 'Jump In The Fire', coupled it with the two 'live' versions of 'Seek And Destroy' and 'Phantom Lord' which had appeared on the US-only 'Whiplash' single and released it in spring 1984. On the cover was a picture of a fearsome-looking demon emerging through a wall of flame, which led to erroneous associations between Metallica and the ascendant black metal movement pioneered by Bathory, Venom and Mercyful Fate. Still, the single served its purpose by making metal fans aware of Metallica and giving a bit of stability to their cash-starved business situation. Indeed, Zazula's Megaforce company lacked the funds to pay for the recording of a second Metallica album, so it would be funded by Martin Hooker's Music For Nations. "The band's manager, Jon Zazula, was having cashflow problems and couldn't afford to pay for the recording, so we stepped in and put the band in the studio and picked up the tab," confirms Hooker.

With funding secured Metallica decided to record *Ride The Lightning* not in America but in Denmark, Lars' home country, at the Sweet Silence Studios in Copenhagen. Producing the record would be Sweet Silence founder Flemming Rasmussen, whose work on Rainbow's *Difficult To Cure* album in 1981 had impressed the band.

In February 1984, the band wound up the Seven Dates Of Hell tour, bid farewell to Venom and drove up to Copenhagen, where they rehearsed the material for the album at Mercyful Fate's practice rooms. As it happened, Mercyful Fate singer King Diamond had left a book of lyrics lying around the rehearsal space and Lars and James couldn't resist taking a peek. Diamond recalls: "There was one day when we were using the room after them, and they saw my book of lyrics and said, 'Shall we look at it?' But then they got scared and said, 'He'll know that we looked at it! He'll sense it!' But they looked at it really quickly anyway. Then I walked in and went straight to it, like I always did . . . and they were terrified!"

Once Metallica were ready to record, they moved into the studio, which had a space where they could sleep. "For *Ride The Lightning* they lived in the studio, because they couldn't afford to stay in hotels," recalls Rasmussen. "We had an upstairs room that we hadn't converted to the B studio yet, so they slept up there. No extra charge!" Metallica had rehearsed their set not quite to perfection, but near enough, he remembers: "They had most of the songs down, but not completely. We used quite a few takes, but they rehearsed a lot in the studio and a lot of the parts we worked out in the studio." A schedule soon established itself, revolving around getting as much done as possible, as fast as possible, while maintaining quality: "We did mostly night sessions, we had two shifts in those days, we started at seven in the evening and went through till four or five in the morning. Yes, they were definitely hard-working."

This time around, Metallica weren't going to let the producer sit back and determine how their album should sound; but at the same time, they wanted a producer with ideas who would come forward and offer suggestions about the music they were recording. It seems that in Flemming Rasmussen they found both these qualities. However, his role was – on the surface, at least – that of engineer rather than producer, as he says: "They'd done their first album in New York and they didn't want to do that again. They had some sound ideas and they needed a studio with a good in-house engineer; they basically booked the session on their own. They heard the Rainbow album and liked it, which is why they used me. Plus Lars and I come from the same country, so he came back home." Did it seem that Metallica enjoyed the sessions? Rasmussen thinks so: "I think they had a pretty good time, I actually think they enjoyed it. We were and still are really friendly. We got along great together. So yeah, we had a good time. We didn't party too much, though, because we had to work most of the time. Everybody else was running round doing disco and shit, and I hated that. Most of the other people in the studio thought that Metallica was the worst piece of shit they'd heard in their lives, but I loved it."

Why such antipathy towards Metallica? Although thrash went down well in certain areas of America, in early 1984 extreme metal in Europe was the province of a few near-underground bands like Venom and Bathory and some sympathetic industry personnel like Martin Hooker. It was hardly ever mentioned in the music press, as Flemming explains: "We were probably the only people apart from a couple of really die-hard metal fans who thought that this music was worth listening to. At that time it was really wild and provocative, I guess. Pop was getting a lot of airplay on the radio, the whole Duran Duran kind of thing. All the keyboards and shit. We hated it!"

It seems that in addition to the generally unfriendly musical atmosphere of the day, James was still suffering insecurities about his voice. Rasmussen: "I encouraged him a bit but he wasn't really receptive to it at that time." He was more focused on his guitar sound, according to the producer, and the quality of the music which was being laid down.

Among the new songs was the ballad, 'Fade To Black', a wistful, depressing song inspired, as one legend has it, by the theft of Metallica's equipment back in Boston. However, far from being worried about their fans thinking they had gone soft, Metallica's thoughts were focused on another of the new tracks: "They weren't too concerned about fans not liking 'Fade To Black', they were more worried about 'Trapped Under Ice', which they thought was maybe a bit too poppy. That was the only concern during the recording. They joked about it almost being a single song!" recalls Flemming.

Due to studio commitments Metallica were scheduled to record *RTL* in two sessions, the first in February and March and the second in June. This gave them a few weeks of spare time in March and April, and Music For Nations set up a tour for them in the UK alongside the Rods and Exciter but, as Hooker recalls, the tour had to be dropped as ticket sales were poor. Nevertheless, Metallica weren't about to spend weeks sitting around doing nothing and two shows were booked at the famous Marquee Club in London for the evenings of March 14 and 27. Both sold out completely: there was clearly a UK fanbase which, thanks to MFN and the 'Jump In The Fire' single, had been alerted to Metallica's presence.

The shows were a great success. Present at the first date was none other than Diamond Head guitarist Brian Tatler, who had stayed in touch with Lars Ulrich since the Dane had visited him almost three years before. Tatler remembers that his initial reaction to Metallica was one of astonishment: "The music was a bit much at first, so fast and relentless," he says. "I just couldn't take it all in, it took me a while to get into it. I stood and watched and thought, how the hell do they play that stuff? And if one of them left, how would you be able to play that set? It just seemed so, well, not just complex, but they were such long songs, with loads of tight bits and little details that they must have spent ages on. I was impressed with the musicianship, but the songwriting just seemed like a bit of a wall flying at me at 100 miles per hour!"

With UK press and fans now alerted to the fact that a new Metallica album would be arriving in their record stores very shortly, the band returned to Denmark, completed the *Ride The Lightning* sessions and immediately headed out on tour again, this time on a brief four-gig jaunt supporting Twisted Sister in Holland and Germany. Their final appearance this time around came at the Heavy Sound Festival on June

129

10, once again at Poperinge in Belgium: a show at which Motörhead were the headliners.

On June 27, 1984, *Ride The Lightning* was released by Music For Nations in the UK, Megaforce in the US and Roadrunner (with whom Zazula had cut a distribution deal) in Holland. If *Kill 'Em All* had been impressive, *RTL* was stunning: the leap in professionalism and song-writing skill from the first to the second record has not been seen between any other two adjacent Metallica albums ever since.

As Martin Hooker puts it, "They basically learnt how to play and structure the songs better. The raw edges were filed away and they started to turn themselves into a class act. They were also given much more time in the studio to get the sounds just right, rather than having to rush things." He's right, but there's more to *RTL* than simple improved production and performance. This album took thrash metal's existing standards and raised them to the level of excellence at which established metal acts such as Iron Maiden were working. Suddenly, thrash metal was no longer the province of punkish club-level acts with small budgets and aspirations (and a proportion of the original thrash metal fanbase has been in mourning ever since).

Many of today's established metal writers and performers had their first taste of thrash when they heard *Ride The Lightning*. Martin Popoff remembers: "OK, without a doubt, my fondest memory is getting home from Spokane, Washington and dropping the needle at the beginning of 'Fight Fire With Fire' on *Ride The Lightning*. This literally was the first album since *Sad Wings Of Destiny* where the rulebook had changed. It was a whole new ball game, a whole new level. This was a new kind of heaviness; it craps all over everything off of *Kill 'Em All*; the soft, billowy but explosive production was amazing, the speed was superhuman, the stops, the starts . . . that album, we just played into the ground." Jeff Becerra of Possessed reports: "I remember hearing *Ride The Lightning* for the first time on KUSF radio at about 2am and freak-ing out thinking, this is the greatest song ever!"

James Hetfield told *Thrasher* that the experience of recording *Kill 'Em All* had lent the band a new resolve when they went to Copen-hagen: "When we went in to record *Ride The Lightning* we said, fuck that, we're going to do it ourselves . . . We had a budget to stick to. It was fairly big but not enough to where we could go to the studio we wanted and get the producer we wanted. So we just said, we practically did the last album ourselves so let's just go with the best studio and get the best in-house engineer."

So why is it so good? Popoff is right when he points to the 'soft' production, which Rasmussen has made sound massively more professional than the scratchy, treble-heavy production of *KEA*. But the true quality lies in the twists and turns of the songwriting, the epic, crushing atmospheres of the songs, and the way that nothing at all about this album is lightweight or predictable. Even the cover art, an electric chair floating amid a storm, is intimidating, and the back cover band photo, a shot of Metallica in a gloomy industrial lot, is much more convincing than the teenage gurning of the *KEA* picture. Photographer Ross Halfin, who began working with the band later in 1984, took that shot and recalls: "I went to San Francisco to shoot the rear sleeve of *Ride The Lightning*, the one where they're in an alleyway. It's an industrial area, it's been raining. I did that and started to have a relationship with them from then on."

The shock for those used to the over-the-top macho-isms of *Kill 'Em All* came with the introduction of the first song on *RTL*, 'Fight Fire With Fire'. It starts out with an ominous acoustic figure (a first for Metallica, but not the last), before dropping into a brutally fast riff leading into a full-band gallop. James' lyrics in this song are sneered between gritted teeth rather than wailed or barked, as beforehand. The song deals with the threat of nuclear war (a theme that would obsess many thrash metal acts which would follow in Metallica's footsteps), and remains one of the fastest they have ever written.

'Ride The Lightning', which emerges with a wail of duelling guitars from the enormous nuclear explosion which ends 'Fight Fire With Fire', is a paranoid, spiralling stream of consciousness from the brain of a person condemned to die in the electric chair. An intense, mid-tempo grind, its primary characteristic is tension: the chords rise sporadically as Hetfield tells his grim narrative. It's also notable for a powerful, layered lead guitar section in which Hammett excels, dropping fusillades of reverbed notes into an extended instrumental section.

On the other hand, 'For Whom The Bell Tolls' (misprinted on some pressings as 'For Whom The Bells Toll') is a simple, superbly effective heavy metal song, with not a hint of thrash about it. The tolling knell which starts it and Cliff's exquisitely distorted bass solo, which signals its beginning, are both masterstrokes, and Metallica have rarely equalled it as a straight fists–aloft composition. The remarkable 'Fade To Black' follows, an acoustic ballad which heralded a new, more cerebral Metallica. Inspired (as rumour had it) by the equipment theft of early 1984, it seems to deal with the theme of suicide and descends into a much heavier closing section, thus establishing a pattern of songwriting which Metallica would adhere to for at least one song on each of the next three albums.

'Trapped Under Ice' returns to a much faster format, with its choppy riff and Lars' rapid snare pattern the very essence of the thrash style. But it returns to standard tempos and wanders in and out of mood in a very progressive style, as does 'Escape', which follows it. "Life's for my own, to live my own way" goes the ethereal chorus at its end, marking another slightly melancholy concept which, again, would never have appeared on earlier work.

But the best song on *Ride The Lightning*, to these ears at least, is 'Creeping Death' – an absolute masterpiece based on a slippery, unforgettable riff and a collection of vocal and guitar harmonies in its chorus which belie the song's status as a moshpit anthem. With a grandiose, sweeping beginning and end and Hetfield's epic lyrical themes of ancient Egyptian pharoahs and biblical plagues, this song manages to be both dramatic and atmospheric at the same time. The whole band are on peak form here: Hetfield's vocal ferocity is at its best on the first word of each line, which he practically screams; Burton throws in tiny fills here and there (a classic comes at the very beginning, just before the guitars join in with James' introductory riff); Hammett's solo is astounding, with a double-tapped section at its end to rival anything he has done before or since; and Ulrich provides solid, machine-like support.

The album closes with the mighty 'The Call Of Ktulu' (printed on some pressings, incredibly, as 'The Cat Of Ktulu'), the instrumental epic which Metallica had tried out so many months before. Something of an underrated classic, this song was generally regarded as a fine way to end the album but didn't resurface as a live standard until 1999.

As soon as the album was out, Metallica had a tour to begin. This is the usual routine, of course: release an album, then take it on the road. But in this case there was some business to sort out. The band had decided

132

that their relationship with Megaforce would have to come to an end at some point: if *RTL* was as big as they hoped it would be, Jon Zazula would have neither the time nor the funds to accommodate their progress, as manager or record company boss. As it happened, Megaforce had organised a showcase of the acts on its roster at Roseland in New York for August 3. Metallica, alongside Raven and Anthrax, were scheduled to perform in front of the industry's finest and, after a secret gig on July 20 at San Francisco's Mabuhay Gardens at which they billed themselves the Four Horsemen, Metallica came back to New York.

The show was packed with industry notables. By the summer of 1984 'thrash metal' had become something of a buzz-phrase on the lips of A&R departments nationwide. Even the bigger record labels were starting to wake up to its potential and were sending out feelers to shows just like this one in search of new acts to sign. Present at the Megaforce showcase were Cliff Burnstein, the co-founder of a management company called Q-Prime which had made its name handling the affairs of the successful British metal act Def Leppard, and A&R director of Elektra Records Michael Alago. Both men were impressed by Metallica's powerful performance, which included *Kill 'Em All* songs such as 'Phantom Lord' and 'The Four Horsemen' as well as newer material such as 'Creeping Death' and 'For Whom The Bell Tolls' (which made its debut live appearance at this show).

Negotiations commenced between Burnstein, his partner Peter Mensch and Metallica, who met on August 1, and shortly afterwards between Q-Prime and Elektra. In a remarkably short space of time Metallica signed contracts with Q-Prime and then with Elektra, a move which put them in a completely different, far more favourable, situation. Jon Zazula, although he was a seasoned manager and a hardworking record company chief who had taken more than his fair share of chances on Metallica, simply lacked the resources to take the band further. The move made sense all round, although to this day Zazula is reflective, perhaps even a little sad, that the professional relationship came to an end.

As he says now: "We were like father and son. The relationship was very close. That's why it was very heartbreaking when the parting came, right when *Ride* was out. I would have loved to keep them, but you know, it was very hard in those days to compete with the managers of Def Leppard." He adds that although Megaforce went on to much greater things, Metallica could not have been expected to know this at that early stage: "They didn't know that we were going to have a parallel successful destiny as well as them, and basically they went for the insurance. I guess that was a smart business move." Furthermore, he seems resigned to the fact that sooner or later they would have switched labels, simply because Megaforce had primed them for such a move: "I think it would have happened either way, because Elektra Records had approached me and said that the job we had done was a million-dollar-plus job. No one had broken a band like this in the States for a long time. We had really broken the band by the time they were handed over on a silver platter."

Financially, Zazula profited from the band's departure. Although he had never made back the money he invested in *Kill 'Em All* despite its respectable sales figures ("We got up into the 17,000 area, up to 35,000 eventually"), the deal he signed with Elektra and Q-Prime helped his company stay afloat. "I was actually in quite a debt. A huge debt. A terrible position, that came at the time Elektra finally signed them. So at the time, my debt was taken care of," he recalls. Not that he himself profited immediately: "The money I got from them I put into Anthrax and Raven, so it wasn't like we got to see it," he chuckles. However, Zazula has every right to be contented. His label went on to sell over 37 million records from acts like Anthrax and Raven as well as SOD, Frehley's Comet, King's X, Testament and Over Kill. In later years, Lars Ulrich referred to Jon and Marsha Zazula in an MTV interview as the "godparents" of heavy metal: praise indeed.

Kirk and James told *Thrasher* two years later about the change in record label and management, recalling a lot of interest from other labels, not just Elektra. Kirk explained: "We looked at each [offer] individually and it seemed from what we saw that Elektra was better. Even though other offers were financially better, Elektra had a reputation of giving complete artistic freedom to their acts. They had acts in the past, like The Doors, the Stooges . . . it was a pretty liberal label. They had a reputation for trying out new things that were pretty experimental at the time."

James continued: "Right then there were [a lot of] bands being signed, snatched up on major labels. All the major labels were saying, 'Oh, metal's like the new thing, get in on the money right now.' They're still doing it. Elektra only had Mötley Crüe and Dokken and all these other labels had many more. We'd be, say, third on the list of so-called metal bands with Elektra, so we'd get at least some support. Instead of signing with Atlantic where there were ten metal bands . . . There wasn't a clutter of metal on that label, so we figured we'd do something to get some support." Kirk added that, not for the last time in Metallica's career, they had received some criticism for 'selling out' by signing with a major company, but that "It didn't affect us at all. We basically didn't give a fuck. We were going to stick to our guns."

One of Elektra's first actions under the new Metallica contract was to reissue *Ride The Lightning* in November 1984. Although the album was the same as the previous version, the promotion that accompanied it was much more thorough, centring on the release of an EP, or more precisely a 12″ single. The song they chose to release was the outstanding *RTL* track 'Creeping Death', housed in a green and grey sleeve depicting a weird bridge and skull design that comes across today as a blend of the amateurish and the entertaining. The choice of B-side was key and, interestingly, Metallica chose to back up the song not with another *RTL* track but with two classic NWOBHM covers, Diamond Head's 'Am I Evil?' and Blitzkrieg's 'Blitzkrieg'. Diamond Head singer Sean Harris remembers receiving an unexpected phone call one day in the summer of 1984: "Metallica had to contact me for the rights to use the lyrics to 'Am I Evil?' – me personally. I had a phone call from Peter Mensch. It was just basically, 'We'd like to record these songs.' And I was like, 'Well, I can't see the point, but yes you're welcome to!' I'm glad I did now!"

Many Metallica fans were also glad that Harris gave his permission for Hetfield and co. to use his band's best-known song: it went on to become a high point of their set and even stalwart Head followers tend to admit that Metallica's incredibly precise version of the song surpassed the original. This was most evident in the song's second half – a fast, powerful blaze through a stunning solo which Kirk Hammett more or less duplicated from Brian Tatler's excellent original. 'Am I Evil?' was the first step on a trail of covers which Metallica would record across the years. 'Blitzkrieg', a less spectacular but more raw and punkish song than the Diamond Head composition, is simply a showcase for James' clean, accurate riffing, and a chance for Hammett to show that he could play economical as well as fancy – the song's final solo is a single-string droned line of simple, and effective, brilliance. The song ends with a messy clash of instruments, a belch and laughter from Hetfield, perhaps in an effort to demonstrate that Metallica were still as much about good-time debauchery as virtuosity. The two songs were sometimes referred to by the band as 'Garage Days Revisited', a reference to their old rehearsal space and often later confused with the *Garage Days Re-Revisited* EP which would appear in 1987.

Ride The Lightning, backed with the *Creeping Death* EP, spread like wildfire through Europe and America (it actually made Number 100 on the *Billboard* chart, although it had received virtually no exposure on radio) and Metallica prepared to take it on the road with their first major tour, the Bang The Head That Doesn't Bang tour (named after the famous Rich Burch quote on the rear sleeve of *Kill 'Em All*), for which they would be supported by NWOBHM stalwarts Tank. In the tradition which would later see Metallica tour to greater and further extents than almost any band had dared to do before, the European trek would be followed up by an even longer jaunt through America – a sign of the dedication which the Q-Prime and Elektra-backed band were investing in their music.

The European tour began on November 16, 1984, in Rouen, France, and went on to Poperinge in Belgium before returning south for shows in Paris, Lyon, Marseilles, Toulouse, Bordeaux, Montpellier and Nice. Concerts in Milan, Venice and Zürich followed before the bandwagon entered Germany for concerts in Mainz, Nuremberg, Mannheim, Sindelfingen and Cologne. Next came Amsterdam in Holland, Osnabruck and Hamburg in Germany once more before a triumphant hometown show for Lars in the Danish capital of Copenhagen and then Swedish, Finnish and London concerts: at the last of these Bernie Torme was the first support act.

After a Christmas break back home in the Bay Area and Los Angeles, Metallica embarked on a US jaunt, firstly co-headlining with WASP and then as headliners. Armored Saint were the support act. The scheduled opening night – on January 9 in Boston – was cancelled at the last minute, so the tour officially started the following evening in Scotia, New York, before moving west and north. Concerts in Hartford, Philadelphia, Baltimore, Montreal, Ottawa, Toronto and Buffalo were next, before the band returned to New York for shows in Elmhurst and Brooklyn. But the agenda, it seemed, was to take *Ride The Lightning* to America's masses whether they wanted it or not. Metallica stormed through Columbus, Cincinnati, Indianapolis, Detroit, Madison, Minneapolis, Cleveland, Milwaukee, Chicago and Green Bay, Wisconsin, before two Iowa shows in Cedar Rapids and Burlington.

The heartlands of the country were next, as the tour ploughed on to St. Louis, Kansas City, Wichita, Tulsa and settled briefly in Texas, where the band had a rapidly growing fanbase. Crowds were at their liveliest in Austin, Corpus Christi, San Antonio (where three shows were necessary to satisfy the local metal population), Pasadena, Dallas, Houston and El Paso.

Moving westwards through Albuquerque, Colorado Springs, Denver, Phoenix and San Diego, the end was in sight by March 1985 after shows in Hollywood and Palo Alto as well as two in San Francisco. Seattle and Vancouver followed before the long tour came to rest in Portland, where Metallica performed the song 'The Money Will Roll Right In' by Fang, accompanied by Armored Saint.

Saint singer John Bush has fond memories of this enormous tour, which did much to bring his band as well as Metallica to the awareness of the American public: "We toured with Metallica on the *RTL* tour, when we had *March Of The Saint* out. It was a really new, fresh, incredible time for that kind of music." He recognises that his band wasn't quite in the same style as the headliners, but that the package worked well nonetheless: "Armored Saint was never a thrash band in the traditional sense, but we were heavy and powerful. We had big hair but we were way heavier than any hair-metal band, so we were in a kind of limbo. Later on that worked against us because we didn't know where to fit in."

The huge effort which Metallica had put in across the previous five months had taken its toll, and from May to July 1985 they spent their time recuperating and working on songs for a third album. Recording sessions for the next LP were scheduled to begin in September; the pace of the band's career was clearly not about to let up. However, the four musicians were clearly up to the task ahead of them, as evidenced by their appearance at the famous British metal festival Monsters Of Rock (not to be confused with the later, Van Halen-led tour of the same name in 1988) at Castle Donington on August 17, in front of a crowd of 70,000 fans. After rehearsing a set in Birmingham four days earlier, Metallica appeared onstage between two glam-metal acts, Ratt and Bon Jovi. This highly inappropriate placing escaped neither the band nor their fans, and was highlighted when Hetfield uttered the immortal (and much-quoted) words at the start of the set: "If you came here to see spandex, eye make-up, and the words 'Oh baby' in every fuckin' song, this ain't the fuckin' band!"

Even the huge Donington show was eclipsed two weeks later when Metallica played in Oakland, California, at the Day On The Green festival before 90,000 people. A remarkable gig featuring the now-established setlist plus 'Am I Evil?', which had become a staple of the show on the previous tours, this concert was captured on video and would appear a couple of years later. The day after the show Lars flew to Copenhagen, where he began recording drums for the next album, a move that reflects the relentless enthusiasm for work that he and his band were feeling at the time. This period in Metallica's career was, perhaps, the one which is most characterised by a relentless urge to create.

One person who had got to know Metallica well by this time was the British photographer Ross Halfin, who began working with them at the tail-end of the *Ride The Lightning* tour. Already a veteran of photo shoots with Iron Maiden and Def Leppard, Halfin recalls how he first came into contact with Metallica: "I used to shoot Queensryche, and I was going to shoot them in Seattle when Peter Mensch called me up and said, 'I've just signed this new band and I want you to shoot them.' So I went to shoot them in San Francisco for the cover of *Kerrang!* and had no idea what to do with them, so we painted Lars silver . . ." The resulting picture was a strange image: it depicts the sunglasses-wearing drummer sprayed a silvery pink and looking decidedly uncomfortable. Halfin goes on: "It was embarrassing, it was stupid. It was a crap photo session . . . so that's really how I first met them, and it sort of went on from there. I got on with Lars really well."

Ross recalls those early days with great clarity, and states that as the relationship grew, Metallica were always professional subjects: "They were great for pictures, they would turn up and get on and do it. It would always be in the afternoon because Lars wouldn't get up, but once he got up he was very focused. Great to work with. When he decided he was gonna do it, he was great. Cannot knock him on that at all." Did they suggest ideas for photo shoots? "No, I mainly did. We'd get up and do photo sessions and then get pissed in the evenings. We went to the Algarve and did the shots with all the rocks, then in

Australia holding up a tyre, then up on a glacier in Alaska . . ."

However, Halfin remembers that they initially impressed him less in musical terms: "I remember thinking, this band are terrible, they can't even play. I thought they were appalling . . . in hindsight, of course, that's when they were good. Because they were so basic. They were very amateurish, which was part of their charm."

Their enthusiasm to get on and do the job was evident in the final show they performed before re-entering the studio for the third album. This landmark event took place on September 14, 1985 at the Loreley Metal Hammer Fest in Germany, a massive festival at which Hetfield's practised spiel with the crowd was extremely well received. Venom were also playing at Loreley and to this day guitarist Jeff Dunn recalls with respect Metallica's incredible performance: "The first time I knew Metallica were gonna be huge was at the Loreley Festival. We were headlining and they were on just beneath us. I remember being back-stage and hearing them playing 'Seek And Destroy' and the whole audience singing it. Then James shouting, 'What the fuck was that!' And then the whole place going mad. James had that rapport with the audience, they were his that night. It was at that point I can honestly say that Metallica were starting to overtake us, that was the European gig where they definitely made their mark."

Not only had Metallica's live performance begun to excel, leaving Halfin's earliest impressions behind, but the band were developing their reputation for serious partying on the road. It was about this time that they adopted the nickname Alcoholica, a sobriquet placed on them by a fan whose T-shirt (a version of the cover of *Kill 'Em All* with a bottle spilling vodka instead of a hammer and blood) had appealed to the band's baser instincts.

And yet Metallica's talents as creators of dramatic, moving music were developing too. When recording finally began, it was immedi-ately obvious that their summer 1985 songwriting sessions were bearing fruit. And to an almost unprecedented degree: the songs which they were writing were destined not just to bring them to the next level of success. They would change the face of metal itself.

12

The Truth About *Master Of Puppets*

**Myth 5: With *Master Of Puppets*, Metallica made the finest
thrash metal album of all time.**

Master Of Puppets is one of the most accomplished metal albums ever
made. In the specific field of thrash metal, it may well be *the* best. Ask
any fan of Eighties thrash to list their favourite records and the chances
are very high that it will appear in their Top Three.

And yet the circumstances of its creation were unusual, to say the
least. For starters, the deal which decided who would finance its
recording was unorthodox: Metallica had agreed that Elektra would
distribute their work in North America, but their European distributor,
Music For Nations, needed to be repaid for its earlier funding of *Ride
The Lightning* when Metallica's then-American label Megaforce had
run out of money. As MFN founder Martin Hooker recalls: "As the
band had done a deal with Elektra to cover North America, we agreed
to give them *Ride The Lightning* for no charge and in return Elektra paid
all the recording costs for *Master Of Puppets*. Oh for a deal like that
now!" A good deal, indeed: the recording of *Puppets* took a gruelling
three months, with spiralling studio and related costs, while *RTL* had
been completed in a matter of weeks. Little wonder Hooker was
pleased.

A second uncertainty – initially at least – was the choice of producer.
Although it was *Ride The Lightning*'s Flemming Rasmussen who was
ultimately chosen to record the album, there seems to have been some
other options in the band's collective mind: the affable Rasmussen confirms that Lars originally considered other studios than Sweet Silence:
"I got credited as producer, because I said I wasn't gonna go over [to

140

America] unless I got points on the album. In the end Lars decided that he'd rather do it in Copenhagen and the boys just went, 'Fine'. Basically they were happiest recording *MOP* where they'd done *RTL*, perhaps because they'd got the whole management/label deal on *RTL*. So they didn't wanna do something totally new at that point." Ulrich also told fan club members in April 1996 that he was "definitely interested in Martin Birch in the early years when he was making all those Iron Maiden records, but the relationship with Flemming Rasmussen was too strong to break."

The decision to use Sweet Silence, even though it was Rasmussen's own territory, was also one that took a while to reach. As Flemming explains, the choice of studio was one that weighed heavily on the band: "Lars contacted me in the spring and said that they were in the middle of writing songs and that they were gonna start checking out studios. So I went over to LA for a week or ten days and me, Lars and James checked out a lot of studios. The room we used to record the drums on *Ride The Lightning* was this huge empty warehouse which we had at the back of the studios, with practically nothing in it, so there was a lot of reverb and ambient sound in there, and they wanted a room like that to do *Master Of Puppets* as well. We went studio-shopping for a long time, but at that time most studios in the States were really sound-isolated, with no reverb, and a totally close kind of feel. That noise-gated kind of snare they used to go for in the mid-Eighties. An Earth Wind & Fire kind of thing, a country sound!"

Ultimately, however, the Rasmussen/Sweet Silence combination proved to be the one that Metallica went for, and recording commenced in September 1985. Unbelievably for a band which had recorded two albums without much financial backing, Metallica didn't emerge from the final sessions until December 27, with Ulrich even returning to the studio briefly after that date. Rasmussen: "Actually I was in the studio with Lars on December 30, he had to fly out and do tom-fills. And he had to fly home because they were doing a gig in San Francisco on New Year's Eve!"

Why did Metallica take so long to record *Master Of Puppets*, then? The answer seems to be that they had at last become songwriting and recording experts: after almost five years as a band, and with two albums behind them, they had finally learned to create multi-layered songs with depth and character – and they had developed a

141

perfectionist sense which they applied with stubborn tenacity to the recording (and associated activities such as mixing and mastering) of their work. As Rasmussen explains, it seems that Metallica had become very driven about moving themselves to the next rung of the ladder: "It took forever, man, because ambition levels had risen so high, we used about three or four months without even mixing it." Ah – ambition: not a word that would have been used among Metallica's fanbase before this point: after all, they were known as a light-hearted, debauched musical force as well as a powerful one. But no: this had changed a little since the success of *Ride The Lightning*. Now an aware band as well as a focused one, Metallica seem to have understood that nothing less than utter commitment would do at this stage.

Some of this impression may stem from the fearsome, almost machine-like precision which the very first seconds of *Master Of Puppets* impress on the listener. The first song is the immortal 'Battery' which, like the opener of *Ride The Lightning* – 'Fight Fire With Fire' – opens with a layered set of acoustic guitars. But where those guitars on 'Fight Fire' are politely low in the mix, their counterparts on 'Battery' are deep, bass-heavy tones, and in a slow, deliberate way, filled with malice. They grow almost imperceptibly until there are half a dozen of them, addressing a melodic but patient riff which worms its way into the skull – before one of the most awe-inspiring moments in the entire Metallica canon: an enormous wall of guitars leaping from the speakers like some vengeful army, repeating the riff which the acoustic instruments had introduced with massive force. This is the clarion call of *Master Of Puppets*; an intense blast of horrifying, triumphant, beautiful noise worth all the clichés in the book: 'slamming', 'bursting', 'crushing' – these terms could have been invented for this moment.

"The idea to make the intro to 'Battery' so big evolved in the studio," says Rasmussen. It seems that the dozens and dozens of guitar tracks which make this riff such a bludgeoning monster were simply added at the time to see how far they could go: "There are tons of guitars on there, we just kept tracking!" he laughs. And all this is just the introduction . . .

'Battery' moves swiftly from its huge entrance into a snaky, speedy solo riff from Hetfield, joined rapidly a heartbeat-thudding second later by Burton and Ulrich, before settling into a perfect, mid-tempo thrash rhythm which has a slightly eerie, off-beat edge that keeps the listener's attention focused. It's this weird, not-quite-normal aura pervading the riff and the doomy, slightly distant nature of the production which makes the song so memorable: the immediate impression is that Metallica have moved worlds away from the fast-but-simple strumming of 'Fight Fire With Fire', and universes away from anything on *Kill 'Em All*, which now sounds like a demo made by teenagers in comparison. And then there's James' voice, deeper and darker than it was on *Ride*, and with a richer, more profound – even *trained* – tone which can only have come about through those extended tours. He isn't screaming, as he did on *KEA*; he isn't barking or hoarse, as he was on *RTL*; he is *intoning* the words with a subtle virulence that was almost entirely missing beforehand. All the more remarkably, since his lyrics are focused on what seems like simple violence: he talks of "hypnotising power, crushing all that cower . . . smashing through the boundaries . . . bounding out aggression" and a classically metallic set of intimidating expressions.

The song's mid-section sees Metallica strip down to a simple, brutal riff, behind which Lars plays snare both on- and off-beat to vary the atmosphere: Kirk's sublime solo, which covers both slower and faster riffs, is a perfect synergy with his wah pedal and is jaw-droppingly precise, as are the factory-like grooves coming from James and Cliff. When 'Battery' comes to a close, it grinds to a halt with a split-second of silence before the next track comes in. But this next song, 'Master Of Puppets' itself, begins, as 'Battery' virtually does, with a single, stamped beat: a heart-stopping lunge which almost leads the listener to conclude that it is just a continuation of 'Battery'. However, the title track is a full-formed beast of its own, with a lyrical stance quite unprecedented in Metallica's history.

'Master Of Puppets' is an anti-drug song. Famously, James referred to 'chop[ping] your breakfast on a mirror', an obvious reference to cocaine. As he told *Thrasher* just after the album appeared, " 'Master Of Puppets' deals pretty much with drugs. How things get switched around: instead of you controlling what you're taking and doing, it's drugs controlling you. Like, I went to a party here in SF, there were all these freaks shooting up."

Musically the song is a masterpiece, although it's based on several relatively simple riffs and an E to F-sharp chord change that was effective, but hardly original. Where many fans differ is in their liking or otherwise for its central section, a slow, cleanly picked part over which Hammett repeats a melodic, multi-tracked lead line and an almost wistful minor-key improvisation. Some hardcore fans dislike it for its mellowness; others love it for its total break from the atmosphere of the other sections of the song. It's worth noting here that for some years James and Kirk would attempt to reproduce this section live, with both men playing the harmonies in unison, but they almost always sounded slightly out of key with each other.

After 'Master Of Puppets' slides to a halt with an echoing hail of evil laughter, created to emulate the puppet-masters of its title, a truly weird song begins. This is 'The Thing That Should Not Be', heaviest song on this album or on any that Metallica had produced to date. It's very, very powerful, based on a slow, lurching, almost slimy riff that resembles some huge, wounded beast dragging itself along the sea bed, and boasts lyrics to match. It's a brilliant, inspired piece of composition. Hetfield's lyrics, a sinister barrage of references to the 'great old one lurking beneath the sea', hint back towards the Lovecraftian mysteries of *Ride The Lightning*'s 'The Call Of Ktulu', its own title referring to the mythical, tentacle-faced monster Chthulu.

The next song, 'Welcome Home (Sanitarium)' is less otherworldly than 'The Thing', but is even darker, as it's a narrative from a suicidal inmate of a mental institution. The theme of suicide had been broached in Hetfield's lyrics in 'Fade To Black' and would later resurface in the war epic 'One' in 1988. The idea of escaping existential horrors through voluntarily ending one's own life is clearly one that had intrigued James over the years and nowhere is it more explicit than here, where he muses "Kill is such a friendly word . . . got some death to do." Musically, it's unforgettable, beginning with a cleanly picked combination of single strings and harmonics and developing into an eerie, reverbed structure on which Burton and Hammett both excel. There's a fast, powerful middle section which develops into a long multi-layered solo section, making the song one of Metallica's most popular live choices.

But for this writer at least, the best song on *Master Of Puppets* is 'Disposable Heroes', a blisteringly fast, dexterously performed epic in which James addresses the horrors of war for the first time, albeit without the pain and sensitivity which would later characterise 'One'. The story of the plight of a 21-year-old soldier forced to fight in what seems like a World War One-style trench environment (from Hetfield's gritted sneers of "Back to the front!"), the lyrics consist of the evil glee of his masters (those puppeteers again) who revel in his helplessness with phrases such as "You coward, you servant, you blind man" and "You will die when I say you must die". The soldier himself looks around in terror at his circumstances, saying, "Bodies fill the fields I see, hungry heroes end" and most memorably, "Barking of machine gun fire, does nothing to me now/ Sounding of the clock that ticks, get used to it somehow".

It's powerful stuff, and a wake-up call of some strength: the fact that Metallica can address real-life themes such as drugs, mental illness and military callousness (as well as imaginary undersea creatures) says much about how their outlook had broadened. But this change was happening right across the thrash metal scene: the band Nuclear Assault, whose lyrical themes revolved around the idea of society's destruction in World War Three and the death of the planet through environmental abuse, released their debut album, *Game Over*, in 1986. German thrashers Kreator also addressed the idea of nuclear war in a flexidisc-only track, 'After The Attack', shortly after. And even Metallica's closest rivals in the thrash arena, Slayer, were on the way to abandoning their specialist subject, the devil, although they were still mostly sticking to satanic themes at this stage. Thanks to general developments such as these – the reflection of the growing maturity and sophistication of thrash metal songwriters as the genre came of age – albums such as *Master Of Puppets* were beginning to appear, fuelling debate over serious, 'real' subjects. As Slayer frontman Tom Araya says, "People find solace in good songs, wherever that song may take them. Society is a tough place to be. We no longer have a free society. Social commentary is a common theme we all share. There's always something to say, because there's always a critic."

And the criticism continues on 'Leper Messiah', a twisted, skewed beast of a song based on a decidedly malicious set of riffs with a powerful mid-section. This time it's TV evangelists who come into Hetfield's sights: his message is encapsulated in the line "Send me money, send me green/ Heaven you will meet/ Make a contribution and you'll get a better seat". As a lyricist, James is at a new peak with this song; seeking to invoke the theme of sickness and decay, he uses phrases such as "rotting your brain", "infection is the game", "stinking drunk with power" and "spreading his disease", which add a livid, almost tangibly decrepit aura of corruption to the song. If 'Battery' or 'Disposable Heroes' is the musical peak of this record, 'Leper Messiah' is where it excels most in terms of lyrics. This song caused a little controversy when Dave Mustaine made a public claim that it was based on an old song he had authored called 'The Hills Ran Red'. Metallica dismissed the claim, stating that the song was based on an old riff but not one of Mustaine's – all of which added some fuel to the tales of inter-band rivalry which occasionally cropped up in the metal press.

Just as James' lyrics had started to expand and take in more ambitious subjects, the band were beginning to stretch their wings in composition terms, too. Cliff Burton was now showing the world what he could do as a composer rather than just a performer, bringing his considerable talents to bear on the next song, 'Orion', an instrumental composed of several cohesive but differing sections. The intro is a layered sheet of bass notes, heavily processed and sounding almost orchestral: it also fades in, a highly effective device which adds to its mesmeric quality. It was sections such as this which made the recording sessions so lengthy: as Flemming Rasmussen recalls, "I fiddled around a lot with some AMS Harmonizer stuff for the intro to 'Orion'. That stuff took a while to record, and took longer and longer as the album went on."

Fascinating as the intro is, it's a later section of the song in which Burton truly displays his skills. After a mid-tempo, almost thoughtful riff leads through some dexterous interplay between Hammett and Hetfield, the song cruises to a halt, and there is a moment's pause while the sound decays. And then, very subtly, a semi-classical, semi-bluesy bass guitar figure emerges, low in the mix but perfectly audible none-theless. Some harmonics from Hammett follow before a beautiful, slow, arcing lead guitar pattern takes off, all winged harmonies and diving finishes. It's awe-inspiring, and Cliff was behind it all, as the band later revealed. His classical training, which had given him a pro-found awareness of harmony structure, enabled him to compose this part of the song and embellish it with an overdriven solo of his own that complements Hammett's perfectly.

Let us remember, however, that *MOP* stands up as a thrash metal album – and, I repeat, among the very best of the genre – and therefore that sheer speed is an important factor. And so it's appropriate that the final track on *Puppets* is breathtakingly rapid; the classic 'Damage, Inc.', a song on which Hetfield's wrath is aimed at no discernable subject in particular, being as it is a series of threats and/or general rants about power, violence and vengeance. With non-specific couplets such as "Blood follows blood and we make sure/ Life ain't for you and we're the cure" and "Inbred, our bodies work as one/ Bloody, but never cry submission" James appears to be setting out the manifesto of some group of thugs hellbent on destruction, with the most evident pointer to this coming from the line "Know just how to get just what we want/ Tear it from your soul in nightly hunt". And there's the infamous "Fuck it all and fucking no regrets" line, which led Metallica to place a sticker on the cover of some versions of the album proclaiming sarcastically that "The only track you probably won't want to play is 'Damage, Inc.' due to the multiple use of the infamous 'F' word. Otherwise, there aren't any 'shits', 'fucks', 'pisses', 'cunts', 'motherfuckers', or 'cocksuckers' anywhere on this record". Despite this rather naïve piece of propaganda, the song is as brutally memorable as anything Metallica have ever written, and it remains a near-perfect way to end an album. It also boasts a Burton-penned intro which, like its equivalent on 'Orion', fades in as a series of bass chords which producer Rasmussen recorded and reversed to create a weird, tension-building effect.

And so *Master Of Puppets* was recorded and mixed by the end of 1985. Its overall sound was more distant than that of *Ride The Lightning* (as Flemming remarks: "I didn't mix *Puppets* so I wouldn't know why it was so different from *Ride*. I think there's some freshness on *Ride* which has probably got lost on *Puppets*"), but simultaneously it is more composed. The interlocking guitars which made, say, 'Battery' so intense were much heavier than anything which had appeared on a previous album and, as we've seen, the fact that Burton's more progressive tendencies had been allowed to come through in the songwriting gave the record a more accomplished, thoughtful air than earlier Metallica records. The progression in the songwriting is the key aspect which most fans noticed first (Rasmussen again: "I think some of the songs on *Master Of Puppets* are absolutely brilliant. Although 'Fight Fire With Fire' and 'Creeping Death' on *Ride The Lightning* are two of my favourite Metallica songs, I think the songwriting has improved on *Puppets*") and is a theme which would continue with subsequent albums, all of which – until the mid-Nineties at least – sound markedly different from each other. With *MOP*, it felt as if Metallica had grown up at last, even though all the band-members were still in their early twenties. It's an enormous achievement.

Master Of Puppets is also notable for the influence it played on the metal scene as a whole, even if some fans initially found it hard to accept its more sophisticated content. As Thomas Fischer of Celtic Frost recalls, "I was mainly exposed to *Ride The Lightning* and *Master Of Puppets* through my songwriting partner and bassist, Martin Eric Ain, who played that music to me very enthusiastically. I perceived that Metallica's sound had become much bigger and more powerful, but I found it extremely hard to overcome my own personal enthusiasm for their first album and to be sufficiently open for their subsequent work. Having experienced the rise of the new modern heavy music and the inception of the American metal wave with Metallica as one of its main exponents, *Kill 'Em All* had etched itself into my mind as a very special event which was nearly impossible to top, in spite of Metallica's very obvious fantastic development." However, once Fischer and his contemporaries had become accustomed to the progressive edge of the music, the album's scope and depth impressed almost everyone who heard it and it began to be entrenched in the metal-buying community's psyche as *the* thrash album of 1986.

Or was it? Great as *Master Of Puppets* was and is, another record appeared the same year which to this day is the only album within the thrash genre which approaches *Puppets'* godlike status. Also a work stuffed with aggression, technical dexterity and innovation, Slayer's phenomenal *Reign In Blood* helped to redefine the scene with its simple, far-better-and-faster-than-anything-else excellence. A shocking, energising record which squeezes in ten fully formed songs into just 28 minutes – such is the band's focus on brain-frying speed – the album was briefly controversial due to the subject matter of the opening track, 'Angel Of Death', which detailed with painful accuracy the atrocities committed by Auschwitz scientist Dr. Josef Mengele. But it's *Reign's* agonising velocity and power which has made it a classic, not its now rather mundane devilry-and-murder lyrics.

Arguments rage to this day over which of the two records is the best thrash album ever made, although some experts offer one of a very short list of alternatives such as Testament's *The Legacy*, Exodus' *Bonded By Blood*, Dark Angel's *Darkness Descends*, Kreator's *Pleasure To Kill*,

Anthrax's *Among The Living*, Megadeth's *Rust In Peace* or, indeed, Metallica and Slayer's own second albums, *Ride The Lightning* and *Hell Awaits*. But usually it's the *MOP* versus *RIB* pairing which is the talk of the newsgroups and the fanclubs, and to this day – despite the late-Nineties rise of a superb neo-thrash metal scene with remarkable albums from the Haunted, Carnal Forge, Hypnosia, Corporation 187, Imagika and others – neither has been surpassed, least of all by their own creators. And the race for the top spot has always been close: for example, in a 2003 poll dedicated specifically to thrash metal in the UK's *Terrorizer* magazine, *Reign* came in at No. 1, a hair's-breadth ahead of *Puppets* at No. 2.

In fact, the status of both albums demands that both need to be stripped down and analysed factor by factor. To begin with, if untrammelled velocities are the key point, then *RIB* wins hands down. Track three, 'Necrophobic', has been timed at an astonishing 248bpm, while all the other nine songs are based on a standard, rapid thrash rhythm (or contain a section which is so based). *Puppets*, on the other hand, contains only two truly fast songs, 'Disposable Heroes' and 'Damage, Inc.'. 'Battery', the title track, 'Leper Messiah' and 'Welcome Home (Sanitarium') have rapid sections, it's true, but overall Metallica had slowed down since *RTL* and speed for its own sake was no longer their top priority.

Sheer heaviness – the use of slow, downtuned, deliberately 'dark' and crunchy riffing – is an area which is difficult to quantify. Both are fearsomely heavy, but *Puppets* just takes it thanks to the numbingly weighty 'The Thing That Should Not Be'. The term 'heavy' in this context also refers to the crushing, intimidating or downright frightening atmosphere of the music, and this important point was an issue on the thrash scene right from the beginning.

Drummer Gene Hoglan recalls that in the early days Slayer blew Metallica away when it came to heaviness: "I was searching for the heaviest stuff I could find in LA. At the time there was Motörhead, Metallica and Dark Angel, who were my old buddies from high school. I thought Metallica were all right, but they could have just been heavier. Everybody else was like, 'Oh my God, it's so intense' – and I was like, 'Yes, it's wicked, it's awesome' . . . but I'd seen Dark Angel and Slayer. When I saw Slayer I was like, 'This is it! Finally!'" As he reports, even the musicians themselves could occasionally be prone to worrying about where their band stood in the overall heaviness stakes: "I used to soundcheck the drums for Slayer on the Haunting The West Coast tour, and all they played at soundcheck was Dark Angel songs. I remember Slayer guitarist Jeff Hanneman saying to me *(adopts worried tone)*, 'Dude, Dark Angel, I saw 'em back in LA, they're faster than us, they're better than us, they're heavier than us.' And I was like, 'Dude, you're in *Slayer*! What are you worrying about Dark Angel for?' "

Speed and heaviness aside, there is the issue of technical skill, and on that note it is *Puppets* which scores most highly. Not, it should be noted, because the Slayer musicians couldn't compete when it came to musical dexterity – drummer Dave Lombardo was and remains light-years ahead of Lars, who has always been a competent rather than scintillating sticksman – but few musicians could play with James Hetfield's startling precision or match up to Cliff Burton's staggering musical awareness.

The levels of complexity which Metallica introduced on *Master Of Puppets* (and which they would take further on their next album, leading to a logical ceiling at which they had to re-evaluate themselves) were a great impact on progressive metal (or prog-metal) acts such as Dream Theater, whose playing ability would later leave even performers such as Cliff behind. The Canadian guitarist and singer Devin Townsend, whose band Strapping Young Lad would also take a prominent place in the prog-metal movement, told me that *Puppets* had left an indelible mark on him: "It was the melodies. I think the new Strapping Young Lad record is like *Master Of Puppets* to a certain degree." He explained that in his mind he allocates colours to albums, adding that: "*Puppets* had a red vibe to it – fire, hell, war, anger, chaos."

Perhaps it's best simply to declare the competition for the all-time top thrash album spot a draw. Play *Puppets* and *Reign* back to back and you'll soon see why they complement each other – the former with its breathtaking innovation and atmospheres, the latter for its venomous, bloody aggression – and why it's so hard to place one above the other. For the purposes of Metallica's story, it's enough to confirm that with their third album they produced a monster: a record which would expand their fanbase, cement their place in metal and ensure their place in musical history.

In this case, the myth is true.

13

1986

Metallica saw out 1985 with a December 29 show at the Sacramento Memorial Auditorium, at which they opened for Y&T, and a New Year's Eve concert at the Civic Center in San Francisco, alongside Metal Church, Exodus and Megadeth (the first time the two bands had shared a stage). At the latter show Metallica debuted 'Master Of Puppets' and 'Disposable Heroes', completing the latter moments before the countdown for the new year.

By this stage the band had come to value highly the work of photographer Ross Halfin. As he remembers: "They used to pursue me and ring me up whenever they could. I got on with them, I was the only one who shot them." And the attraction worked both ways, it seems: the photographer, whose tolerance for poseurs and fakers is legendarily low, remembers an early show at which they totally outstripped the headliners: "It was Adam Bomb, them, and Armored Saint at the Palladium – and Armored Saint, who were in their home town, couldn't follow them. Everyone was leaving, they went down really well. It was very much them against the world." At that particular concert, Metallica's prankster tendency came to the fore: "I always remember that Cliff Burton was absolutely terrified before that gig, because for a wind-up they got me to tell him that I'd phoned Geezer Butler and he was in the audience watching him. He was really worried!"

In January 1986 *Master Of Puppets* was mixed in Los Angeles by Michael Wagener, and a European press tour was organised. Lars Ulrich elected to conduct interviews on his home continent while the other three remained in the Bay Area – an early sign, perhaps, of the radically differing personalities of the Metallica musicians. Halfin says of Lars that, "It was his vision in the end which drove it. You have to say that without Lars taking over, they never would have got to where

151

they've got to." Journalist Martin Popoff also reports that Lars was "very energetic, moving from point to point, although it seems that he never really did get a good grasp on the English language, which is odd. I guess it's a mixture of California Valley girl talk and his Danish origins and a very active mind."

James, on the other hand, is a very different character to the 'very metal' guy who appears on stage. "James is actually very quiet. His stage persona is very much modelled on Ted Nugent without the excess," says Halfin, while, "Kirk Hammett is just glad to be there. He's quite funny." Halfin also drops the revelation that: "I think up until 1988, Kirk was always worried that they were going to replace him with Dave Mustaine! It was always a bit of a thing. It was never spoken, but it was definitely there." As for Burton, Halfin knew him little but respected him fully: "Cliff was the one I knew the least, and probably the one I was most friendly with. He very much did his own thing." The band would split into two camps, says Ross: "Cliff and Kirk would always share a room, and so would Lars and James. They were the two camps, that was how it went."

While Lars was abroad building up press expectations about the imminent new album, James and Cliff formed a joke band called Spastik Children alongside vocalist Fred Cotton and guitarist Jack McDaniel. Hetfield played drums in the impromptu quartet, which performed a January 31 show at Ruthie's Inn in San Francisco and later SF gigs in February and March. Journalist and Metallica associate Harald Oimoen later explained to the fanclub that "Spastik Children was James and Cliff's side band that they did whenever they were off tour and they were bored. I asked Cliff what the deal with Spastik Children was, and he said that it was just an excuse to go out and drink a few . . . have a good time and not care what it sounds like or anything. I happened to be at one of their practices and Fred Cotton, the singer . . . just started singing stuff about me, like Harald you're a dick, Harald you're an ass, Harald you're a fag, all this crap."

The band was an outlet for the most basic instincts of James and Cliff, it appears, and was focused on one simple activity: getting drunk and singing stupid, improvised songs for fun. As Oimoen continued: "This became 'The Ballad Of Harald O' . . . I'd get up on stage all drunk and dance and sing and just get really stupid on stage. Spastik Children was a stupid thing, it was meant to be stupid. That's what's so great about it

. . . people would go expecting to see some kind of thing like Metallica and they would just go up there and play this awful noise, just like the worst punk rock . . . you couldn't even classify it as rock, just noise."

Unfortunately, Metallica's home-town profile was getting too big for their ridiculous side-project and audiences began arriving with the expectation of a serious show: "Word got out that it was the Metallica guys," recalls Oimoen, "and little by little the gigs started getting more and more crowded . . . all these people would wear their Metallica shirts, and they were thinking there was going to be something musical like Metallica, and then they would go out there and play this awful spewage noise." It got to the point where the band refused to publicise it, it appears: "I asked Cliff about it and I go, 'Is it cool to mention Spastik Children in this interview I did?' And he said, 'Fuck that! If I do then everyone's going to ask me about it all the time, every interview I do they are going to say, what's this Spastik Children thing?' He's all, 'Fuck that! It's just a fun local thing to do.'" The band had also prac-tised at the so-called Metallica Mansion, the house the musicians occu-pied on Carlson Boulevard in the suburb of El Cerrito: "It wasn't really a mansion," sniggered Harald, "and in the backyard they had the jam room where lots of crazy stuff happened. Spastik Children practised there . . . whenever it rained they would have to play on these milk crates elevated off the ground so they wouldn't get electrocuted and stuff. Yeah, it was great."

After Spastik Children had made their initial, and thankfully short-lived, foray into the live arena and Lars had returned from Europe, he and James took a brief holiday in the Bahamas before the release of *Master Of Puppets*. Q-Prime had landed Metallica a slot supporting Ozzy Osbourne for some months in 1986 and they knew that the pres-sure would be intense: the ex-Black Sabbath frontman was riding a wave of popularity at the time, and the exposure to more mainstream metal audiences than the thrash crowds to which they were accus-tomed meant that Metallica's music would penetrate further than ever before.

On February 21 *Master Of Puppets* was released, peaking at number 29 on the US album chart the following month. *Kill 'Em All* was also reissued, although it climbed only as high as 155. The ground had been well prepared – in Europe thanks to Lars' recent round of interviews and the ceaseless backup of Music For Nations (Martin Hooker recalls:

"By the time the third album was released, we'd given the band gold albums in the UK and monster sales all over Europe"), and America was ready to be conquered by the Ozzy tour. But more than this, by 1986 the extreme metal scene had opened up much more than it had been in the earlier days, with press, fans and promoters all more willing to accept and publicise faster, harsher and more lyrically intimidating metal than had previously been the norm. As Possessed frontman Jeff Becerra explains, "The venues were much, much bigger: bands like Slayer and Metallica became gods in their own right. European tours became much more accessible and paved the way for us."

Perhaps this change in the wider awareness had come about because younger audiences had become more and more used to the idea of heaviness in music. What had once been seen as the ultimate in riffery was now regarded more as radio-friendly rock, with classic bands such as Deep Purple and the NWOBHM stalwarts that followed them superseded by the new wave. The world was becoming addicted to heaviness, in a sense, and barriers were falling away daily. As Silenoz of Norwegian black metal band Dimmu Borgir explains: "Def Leppard was considered heavy, then Slayer and Metallica came along. It was like a different world, so to speak. There were a lot of great bands in this genre coming out in the Eighties. People can say whatever they want but I believe that decade was pure metal, extreme or not, and we will never see anything like it ever again. It doesn't mean that I think metal is dead these days – far from it – but the feeling, the atmosphere, all of the things that involved metal in the Eighties was unique."

It was an exciting time to be into thrash metal. As Silenoz adds, the acts that were active at this time or shortly after were a veritable who's-who of thrash: "The bands that had an immense impact on me were Dark Angel, Kreator, Destruction, Sodom, Agent Steel, Tankard, Sepultura, Anthrax, Nuclear Assault, Death Angel, Megadeth, Possessed, Testament, Forbidden, Exodus, Sabbat, Exciter, Onslaught . . . I can go on all night!"

The extreme metal scene was also starting to fragment into other subdivisions than the established thrash and the less commercially successful (but more sinister) black metal genre. As Quorthon of Bathory does elsewhere, Jeff Becerra recalls inventing the term 'death metal' in time to use it as a title of one of the songs on Possessed's 1984 debut album, *Seven Churches*: "Everyone was jockeying for position for their own 'metal' term . . . to tell you the truth I wrote the song 'Death Metal' in an English class when I was supposed to be doing a test. Needless to say I flunked the test, but I invented the term death metal." Although *Seven Churches* itself was more a thrash record than true death metal, the seed had been sown and shortly after the appearance of *Master Of Puppets*, a Florida band called Death began demoing material which would qualify as the first true DM on a debut album in 1987 called *Scream Bloody Gore*. Characterised by low, brutal riffing, intense speeds and the bellowed, primal vocals of singer Chuck Schuldiner, Death's music became massively influential and the death metal movement expanded rapidly.

The story of Metallica and thrash metal developed in parallel with DM, rather than crossing over into it or absorbing it: even today, the death and thrash metal scenes are distinct entities, with only one or two bands such as early Sepultura and now The Haunted hovering near the boundaries.

As thrash flourished, black metal fermented bleakly underground and death metal was born, another offshoot appeared: the punk/metal crossover scene. An obvious legacy of the times when the punk and metal audiences would meet at shows by mutually acceptable bands such as Slayer, the genre brought together the speed and precision of thrash and the rawness and discontent of punk. DRI were one of the movement's bigger bands, as were the NY band Ludichrist, whose frontman Dave Miranda sees his band as crossing into both genres without sticking too firmly to either one: "When I first joined Ludichrist, which was clearly a thrash metal type band at one point, I had never previously heard the term 'thrash metal'. Prior to that I considered Ludichrist more of a hardcore band, even though we were playing more rock/metal type of things mixed in with hardcore. Ludichrist sort of just smoothly evolved from hardcore to thrash, I'm not sure why or how . . . I guess we were influenced by the bands around us such as Agnostic Front and Crumbsuckers. All these bands evolved into a more metal or 'thrashy' mode at around the same time in the mid to late Eighties. I don't remember it being a conscious effort, it just happened. I don't remember too much separation between metal and hardcore: of course you had some real serious punk hardcore kids who hated metal, but other than that, it seemed that most metal and hardcore people just blended together, and the music blended together too."

This, then, was the environment into which *Master Of Puppets* was born: a far more conducive atmosphere to the development of thrash and extreme metal in general than in earlier times. However, although thrash audiences had taken Metallica to their bosoms years before, it remained to be seen whether their fast, uncompromising riffing would be accepted with Ozzy Osbourne's crowds. Metallica knew that nothing could be taken for granted on this tour and rehearsed a tight, gripping set which mirrored the *MOP* album by starting with 'Battery' and 'Master Of Puppets' and ending with 'Damage, Inc.', but also included plenty of singalong stuff which the Ozzy crowd would enjoy ('Seek And Destroy', 'For Whom The Bell Tolls', 'Am I Evil?' 'Creeping Death') and more subtle material such as 'Welcome Home (Sanitarium)'. The set rarely deviated from these songs over the three-month jaunt, which took in over 50 shows between March 27 and June 17, 1986.

It was immediately obvious that Metallica had found their niche on the tour when crowds reacted with enormous enthusiasm for both the new and old material in the set. The tour swept through Kansas, Oklahoma, Missouri, Michigan, Illinois, Wisconsin, Indiana, Ohio, Pennsylvania, New York, Maryland, New Jersey, Rhode Island, Con- necticut, Massachusetts, North Carolina, Tennessee, Louisiana, Texas, New Mexico, Colorado, Utah, Arizona, Iowa, Minnesota, Nebraska, California and Nevada, winding up in San Francisco. Metallica had become fairly road-hardened by now and were learning the value of taking their music to the people, wherever they might be – a lesson they would continue to apply to incredible effect a few years further down the line. A clue to their endurance skills came when they met Thomas Fischer in LA that summer: despite the slog they had just been through, the Celtic Frost frontman found them in great spirits: "I first met somebody from Metallica in person in Los Angeles, in the summer of 1986, when we were playing our first US tour and went to a club on an off-day. Lars was there and waved us over to sit with him at his table, and it was an extremely nice and friendly experience which I never forgot."

And yet the touring wasn't done yet, not by a long chalk. More Ozzy-led American shows were planned, as well as a European jaunt for later in the summer and autumn; James and Cliff even squeezed in a Spastik Children show at Ruthie's Inn on June 21. But then it was back to the grind of taking *Puppets* to the country, with shows in June and July criss-crossing the American interior. A concert in Washington was followed by a brief festival stopover in Europe (Wvaskyla in Finland and the Roskilde Festival in Denmark) and then further appearances in Wisconsin, Illinois, Indiana, Ohio and Michigan. At the last of these, a July 26 show in Evansville, Indiana's Mesker Theater, a minor upset occurred when James managed to break his wrist while skateboarding before the show. The gig was cancelled and the errant frontman was obliged to wear his arm in plaster until September, an inconvenience which was soon remedied when the band asked Metal Church guitarist and then-Metallica roadie John Marshall to step in on rhythm guitar for the live dates.

Marshall recalls the stand-in duties with good humour today, remembering that for those first shows, he preferred to stand offstage, virtually unseen: "The first six gigs I played in '86 were opening for Ozzy, and I stood off to the side of the stage where the audience couldn't see me. James would introduce me after about two songs or so. The rest of the gigs that year were in Europe and the UK. I was sort of off to the side where the audience could see me, but kind of in the background. After a few gigs Cliff would motion for me to stand more on stage, and eventually I was onstage every night. I remember the crowd reaction usually being positive. After all, it was still Metallica, just with one more guy onstage!"

Was it tough matching up to James' guitar skills? "Well, the hard part was trying to match the vibe and intensity of his guitar playing. I knew how to play the riffs and song arrangements OK, but getting the feel right was difficult. It was also hard because the rest of the band follows his voice and guitar onstage. I wasn't used to that type of situation. I think I was more worried about what the rest of the band thought, than what the audience thought . . . The first time I played I literally had to learn the songs overnight, so I didn't have much time to think about it. I remember feeling really excited, a little stunned that they had actually asked me, and a little nervous."

Marshall had gelled with the band immediately, with only one show being cancelled, and Metallica continued onward, winding up their US tour with shows in Tennessee, West Virginia and Maryland. Despite his broken wrist, when the tour wrapped up Hetfield still managed to participate in a Spastik Children show on August 29 at the Rock in San

Francisco. Once again, the pace was not allowed to let up for more than a couple of weeks, possibly due to Ulrich's self-confessed tendency to be bad at doing nothing. The band were scheduled to fly to Europe, where one of the most famous shows of their career, a concert with Anthrax in support at London's Hammersmith Odeon, would take place on September 21. As Anthrax guitarist Scott Ian recalls, "We really felt that we were part of something; the crowds were crazy and we really felt as if there was something happening. The energy was palpable."

The ten-show UK tour, with Anthrax on board, did much to advance both bands' cause in the UK. *Master Of Puppets* had received rave reviews in the British press, and Anthrax's own new album, the powerfully speedy *Among The Living*, was the best work they had ever done. The shows in Cardiff, Bradford, Edinburgh, Dublin, Belfast, Manchester, Sheffield, Newcastle, Birmingham and London were all chock-full of energy, and to this day those who were there will recall them as the moment when the thrash metal wave revealed its true strength in Britain.

The September 20 concert at Birmingham's Odeon featured as a surprise guest local resident Brian Tatler of Diamond Head, with whom the band performed 'Am I Evil?' "We did the introduction," recalls the quietly spoken Brummie, "and then Kirk looked over at me and I did the widdly-widdly bit! I thought he was going to do it, and I hadn't played it for a while . . . anyway, I did that and we did the song. We didn't do the solo, they went straight into 'Damage, Inc.', but I'd run off by then."

After bidding farewell to Anthrax, Metallica boarded the ferry for Sweden, where the next leg of the European tour was scheduled to begin. *Master Of Puppets* had sold well in Europe and the band were looking forward to taking the music on the road there. James' wrist had almost healed and he was itching to get out of plaster and back onto rhythm guitar. Never the most natural of stage-singers with only a microphone to occupy him, Hetfield had acquitted himself well in his singer-only role, but it was obvious to all that he would be happier once he strapped on one of his much-loved white Gibson Explorers again.

A show in Lund, Sweden, was followed by another in Oslo, Norway. After this concert Metallica asked John Marshall to stay on as roadie while James resumed guitar playing, presumably with the proviso that if Hetfield's wrist had not healed enough to allow him to play, he could take it up again. However, the next show, at Stockholm's Solnahallen venue, went superbly, with James' riffing abilities clearly back to full strength and the band in general on great form. Cliff in particular was playing at near-genius levels, and on top of his usual bass solo, he added a version of 'The Star Spangled Banner' which had the crowd open-mouthed in amazement.

After the show, the Metallica party, in two tour buses, set off for Lars' hometown of Copenhagen. The drive from Stockholm to Copenhagen is lengthy, and the drivers were keen to get started. The route they were scheduled to take would involve using several minor roads, in fairly mountainous countryside. It was a dark night, and the forecast was for low temperatures. Nightfall came and the buses rolled on into the darkness. There was a 45 minute gap between the first, carrying the band and crew, and the second, which held the equipment.

The tragedy of that journey is best told by someone who was actually there.

At about 6.30am on the morning of Saturday, September 27, roadie John Marshall was asleep in his bunk on the first tour bus. "We were all asleep," he begins. "The band was on the bus, as well as the backline crew, and the tour manager. It was a two-lane road, and pretty cold outside." At the time the bus was travelling along the E4, which passes between the Swedish towns of Ljungby and Värnamo. To be exact, the bus was not far from a road restaurant called Gyllene Rasten, about two miles north of Ljungby.

Marshall continues: "Apparently the bus drifted off to the right side of the road, and the driver steered left to correct. As he did this, the back end of the bus spun out to the right. While this was happening, I remember waking up, being bounced out of the bunk because the tyres were 'chattering' as the bus skidded."

After a long skid, reportedly lasting up to 20 seconds, the bus came to a halt, but not upright. Marshall: "By the time it stopped, the bus was on the right side of the road, facing the other direction. As it slid into the right shoulder of the road, it caught the gravel and tipped onto its right side. When the bus tipped, the two rows of bunks collapsed together, trapping guys underneath."

Imagine the moment. The scene in the bus was utter pandemonium. It was pitch dark. The occupants had been asleep for several hours and, having been woken suddenly by loud noises and the shuddering of the coach, were confused. Then the bus fell onto its right side, leaving the interior impossible to navigate in the dark. Bunks had fallen together, their occupants trapped beneath.

Marshall recalls that after a few seconds, he made it out of the bus. "I remember crawling out of the door, which was now facing upwards (it was a UK coach, with its entry on the left side) and jumping to the ground. I remember sitting out on the ground, waiting for help, just stunned at being awakened this way, and trying to take it all in. Bobby Schneider, the tour manager, was still inside the bus, helping to get the guys out."

After a minute or two the bus was empty. Kirk and James emerged, shaking, with minor flesh wounds. Lars had broken a toe and was limping. Marshall, his fellow guitar roadie Aidan Mullen, Metallica's drum technician Flemming Larsen, tour manager Bobby Schneider and the bus driver, who had a foot injury, all climbed or were helped from the bus and sat, in deep shock, to wait for help to arrive.

Stepping back from the overturned bus, James heard his friends shouting, and pointing to the bottom edge of the tour bus which was resting on the road. He went closer, still in shock, to see what was going on.

Two legs protruded from under the bus, and had been covered with a blanket by one of the shaking, numb men nearby. They belonged to Cliff Burton. He was dead.

John Marshall and others were taken to the hospital in Ljungby by one of seven ambulances which arrived during the next hour. "Kirk, Bobby and I were in the first ambulance back to the hospital. It was at the hospital that Bobby told me that Cliff was gone," he recalls sadly.

There was no such calm reflection for James Hetfield – or not yet, anyway. As he said in 1993: "I saw the bus lying right on him. I saw his legs sticking out. I freaked. The bus driver, I recall, was trying to yank the blanket out from under him to use for other people. I just went,

'Don't fucking do that!' I already wanted to kill the guy. I don't know if he was drunk or if he hit some ice. All I knew was, he was driving and Cliff wasn't alive any more."

James was in a state of shock, dressed only in the underwear he had been sleeping in, and his rage against the driver was building rapidly. The driver told him that there had been black ice on the road, which had caused him to lose control. However, Hetfield later said in an interview that he had smelled alcohol on the driver's breath (although this was taken no further, which might imply some uncertainty on James' part) and that he then walked up and down the road looking for black ice. The bus' trajectory had been at least 60 feet long, and he travelled all of it, cursing and crying, searching for the reason why his friend had been killed. He found no black ice.

In the end a paramedic came and James, along with the others, was taken to hospital.

A little later a crane was summoned to the scene and the bus was slowly lifted from Cliff. Although no formal conclusion was drawn for some days as to the manner of his death, it was clear from the outset that as the bus jolted to a halt, Cliff had been thrown from his bunk through the adjacent window. The bus then fell on him, with the probable outcome being that he was killed instantly. It emerged later that Kirk and Cliff had argued over who should sleep in which bunk, drawing cards to make a decision: Cliff had drawn the card which gave him the window-side bunk.

When the Swedish police arrived on the scene a few minutes later, they arrested the driver as a matter of routine. Burton's body was removed and the scene was thoroughly examined for forensic evidence. Cliff's passport, number E 159240, was cancelled and mailed to his parents.

14

The Truth About Cliff's Death

Myth 6: The Ljungby coach crash was caused by black ice.
**Myth 7: If Cliff had lived, Metallica's future path would
have been different.**

As with the coach crash itself, the only way to be completely certain
about what happened next is to ask someone who was there. My
research took me to the Ljungby tourist office, the library and the local
newspaper, *Smålänningen*, and one day I found myself talking to
Lennart Wennberg, a 58-year-old photographer who runs a photo
studio in central Ljungby and specialises in advertising and portrait
photography. He also does a certain amount of freelance work for
newspapers: in September 1986, almost 17 years before our interview,
he was working for the newspaper *Expressen*.

The interview went as follows, and is reproduced here in question
and answer format for the sake of clarity.

*On the morning of September 27, 1986, how did you hear that there had
been a coach crash near Ljungby?*
Expressen phoned me. I was at home.

What time of day was it when you heard of the crash?
Around 7.30am I went there by car.

What was the first thing you saw when you arrived?
The bus, a break-down lorry, and there were also people around
the scene of the accident.

How many people were there?
There were about 10 people there; group members plus rescue

personnel and people from the break-down lorry. It was quiet, there was a certain tension in the air.

Where was the bus?
The bus had overturned, but when I arrived the salvage team had put the bus back up again so that it was on its wheels. The bus was by the side of the road.

What were the musicians doing?
The group members (the musicians and their manager) had been taken from the scene to Ljungby hospital. The driver wasn't there, as far as I could tell – but I may be wrong, since I didn't know who he was.

How long were you there and how many pictures did you take?
I was at the scene of the accident for maybe half an hour. I took about 20 pictures of the location of the bus: from the back, from the front and from the side. I can't recall speaking to anyone. The police didn't mind me taking pictures, but there was someone in the band's entourage who felt I should stop taking pictures.

Did you see Cliff Burton's body?
No, it had been removed from the scene.

Did you see any ice on the road?
It was said that this may have been a cause of the accident. Personally, I consider that out of the question. The road was dry. I believe the temperature had probably been around zero degrees Celsius during the night, but slippery? No.

Can you describe the driver?
I saw him a couple of days later in central Ljungby. He may have been around 50, well-built, normal height.

In fact, the driver's identity has never been revealed. He endured a series of interviews with the local police, but was ultimately released without charge. Wennberg confirms that the band themselves remained in the town for a short period after the crash, having taken photographs of them as they entered the courtroom where the investigation was taking place a few days later: "I was never in the courtroom and I am doubtful as to whether the members remained in Ljungby longer than until Sunday morning. But I did take pictures of the members and the manager when they arrived by police car from the hospital and entered the Hotel Terraza in Ljungby (about 10 metres from car to hotel entrance). The manager came down to me and the *Expressen* reporter in the hotel lounge to do an interview. But after a few minutes he got a phone call and never came back."

On the night of the accident a few local Metallica fans got wind that it had happened. According to the musician, Mortiis: "The accident was very close to where I lived for five years. The friends I had in Sweden were older than me, and they went to all the hospitals where they thought he might be. They went to all the local hospitals, but I think he was taken to a big specialist unit in Gothenburg or somewhere."

The local newspaper, *Smålänningen*, gave me permission to reproduce in this book translations of certain articles which it featured on the incident at the time. On the Monday morning after the crash, the front page bore the headline *Rock Star Killed*, and began its report with the words: "The European tour of the American hard rock group Metallica ended in tragedy in a fatal accident in Dörarp on the E4 road on Saturday morning." Significantly, the story went on to state: "The driver thought that an ice spot was the reason why the bus slid off the road. But there were no ice spots on the road. 'For that reason the investigation continues,' said detective inspector Arne Pettersson in Ljungby. The driver has denied that he fell asleep while driving. 'The accident's course of events, and the tracks at the accident location, are exactly like the pattern of asleep-at-the-wheel accidents,' said the police."

The supposition appears to have been raised that either black ice caused the bus to skid, or that the driver fell asleep at the wheel. Hetfield himself alleged that the driver had been drinking. Lennart Wennberg denies categorically that there was ice on the road. However, the report goes on to state that, "The driver said under oath that he had slept during the day and was thoroughly rested. This was confirmed by the driver of the other bus."

The newspaper report continues: "The accident happened some minutes before seven o'clock on Saturday morning. On a minor left curve not far way from the Gyllene Rasten restaurant in Dörarp, the bus suddenly went off the road surface and went into a ditch. The driver managed to drive the bus up onto the road again, but a skid developed. The bus turned over and was lying on the wrong side of the

road. Cliff Burton was thrown out through a window and was probably crushed under the bus. 'We never saw what happened: all of us
were sleeping,' said the group members to the police."

Revealing that by coincidence a doctor passed the scene of the accident in her car and was able to give some first aid to the injured, the
report goes on to say: "The driver said that he suddenly realised that the
bus was sliding off the road. When the bus came up on the road again, a
new skid developed and the bus turned over. 'He said that the accident
had been caused by an ice spot, but nobody else at the accident could
see any ice spots,' said the police."

The following day, Tuesday, September 30, *Smålänningen* followed
up on the story, reporting that "The driver of the tour bus . . . is now
free from arrest. He is forbidden to travel and must contact the police
once a week until the investigation is over. The driver was arrested
after the accident, suspected of being careless in traffic and causing
another person's death. He said that the bus drove off the way because
there was ice on the road. But the technical investigation from the
police said that the road was totally free from ice at the time of the accident. The driver is suspected of having fallen asleep at the steering
wheel. The group was on its way to a concert in Copenhagen: that
concert, and the European tour, has been cancelled."

The following day the paper stated that the driver was staying in a
local hotel while the case developed, and that a technical investigation
of the bus would take place that day. On October 6 the report revealed
that, "There were no technical faults on the bus of the American rock
group Metallica. This was established by the National Road Safety
Office in a quick investigation." Nine days later, it reported that the
public prosecutor had lifted the travel ban on the bus driver, who
would be allowed to return home while the case was being decided.

Other newspapers told a similar story. *Expressen* reported that on the
night of the accident, the band-members had watched a movie on
video until about 2am and the bus had continued through the night
apart from a half-hour break in the town of Ödeshög. It described the
actual accident as follows: "The driver stated that he suddenly noticed
that the bus was sliding off the road. He tried to steer it back up on the
road again, but failed. It was only after yet another attempt that he got
the bus back on the road, but then the devastating skid occurred, which
made the bus overturn."

Tour manager Bobby Schneider was quoted in *Expressen* in a second article based on an interview he gave shortly after arriving at the hospital in Ljungby. With a dislocated shoulder and displaying classic shock symptoms such as shaking and confusion, he repeated the phrase, "I just can't believe it," several times before explaining, "We were asleep when the crash happened . . . when I managed to get out of the bus I saw Cliff lying there in the grass. He must have died immediately, because he went right through the window. It all went so quickly that he couldn't have felt anything, and that's a kind of comfort . . . None of the guys in the band is able to play now. We just want to get back home as quickly as possible and make sure that Cliff gets a decent funeral." The writer also added that Peter Mensch had arrived quickly after the accident and was talking to the musicians, while the Danish promoter of the Copenhagen show, Erik Thomsen, had also come to the hotel. Mensch had arranged for Lars to be picked up by his parents, who were presumably in Denmark at the time and could come down to southern Sweden to fetch him.

The three surviving members of Metallica stayed in a hotel in Ljungby that night. James drank copiously and, in an alcoholic frenzy, smashed two windows and screamed in rage and sadness. Kirk and John Marshall were shaken up so badly by the whole incident that they left a light on in their room.

The Swedish authorities conducted an autopsy before flying Cliff's body back to the United States. The examining official, a Dr. Anders Ottoson, attested that the cause of death was "compressio thoracis cum contusio pulm", or fatal chest compression with lung damage. His funeral took place on October 7, 1986 at the Chapel Of The Valley in his hometown of Castro Valley, California, and his ashes were scattered at the Maxwell Ranch. His friend Dave Donato, with whom he and Jim Martin had jammed until a mere five or six years before, reported: "We stood in a large circle with Cliff's ashes in the centre. Each of us walked into the centre and took a handful of him and said what we had to say . . . then he was cast onto the earth, in a place he loved very much." At the end of the service, 'Orion' was played, the piece which he had written and which had helped to make *Master Of Puppets* so powerful.

There were many tributes to Cliff. *Kerrang!* contained a black double-page spread from Jon and Marsha Zazula with the words "The Ultimate Musician, The Ultimate Headbanger, The Ultimate Loss, A Friend Forever", and another page from Music for Nations which simply stated 'Cliff Burton 1962–1986'.

Cliff's friends and colleagues were stunned by the news of his death. His friend Jim Martin recalls: "I think his mother told me. I was home at the time, in between tours. My heart sank. He was part of the think-tank, he, Donato and I. We lost a partner. The Swedes had to autopsy him and the customs paperwork involved in shipping human remains must be very complex and plentiful, because it took about six weeks for them to return his remains Stateside. I travelled home in between tour dates to attend his funeral. It was a pretty rough time, especially for his folks."

Dave Mustaine, whose band, Megadeth, was beginning to make waves in the metal arena, had developed a heroin addiction and took the news badly. Talking to *Metal Sludge*, he explained that the news led him to write a song, 'In My Darkest Hour': "Maria Ferraro [who] worked for Megaforce . . . called me the day that Cliff had died or somewhere close to it. No one else from Metallica or their management did. I went straight to the dope man, got some shit and started singing and crying and writing this song. Although the lyrics have nothing to do with him, his untimely passing gave me this melody that lives in the hearts of metalheads around the world."

Jon Zazula was grief stricken. At the time Metallica's tourmates were Anthrax, who he was managing: "I had just left Metallica, two days before. My partner at the time was Tony Incigeri, and he was still out on the road. I was in San Francisco and had just come off the Anthrax/ Metallica tour to see a new band called Testament for the first time. At three o'clock in the morning Tony called Marsha and I in our hotel room in SF and told us that there had been a terrible accident and Cliff was dead. It was devastating. When they were at the house, Cliff used to read fairy-tale stories to my daughter Ricky. He was the sweetest thing."

Ross Halfin was shocked, too: "The weird thing is, I was about to go out with them. I shot them rehearsing beforehand and I was meant to join them on tour later. Strangely enough, I was playing 'Battery' in the car, and then it came on the radio that he'd died. It was a weird thing. That was how I found out."

Metallica's fellow musicians were devastated. His mellow personality had made him a popular tourmate and, of course, his musical skills were admired by many other players. Jeff Dunn of Venom says: "It was a tragedy. We were really, really shocked, we thought, fuckin' hell, what's gonna happen to the band? Because Cliff was such an integral part of that band. I think he was a very underestimated bass player as well."

Jeff Becerra of Possessed was especially saddened, having been such a huge fan of the band: "I remember every one of my friends were walking around in a daze. It was like when 9/11 happened or something. Some of the girls were crying and everyone just couldn't believe that Cliff had died. I felt like I lost one of my biggest influences. It was a truly sad day."

Producer Flemming Rasmussen, who more than anyone else outside the band had witnessed Cliff's remarkable playing at close hand, is sombre to this day about the incident: "You know on 'For Whom The Bell Tolls' there's that line, 'Take a look at the sky just before you die', and then Cliff got killed? That rang a bell when I heard it . . . My mum woke me up when she heard it, I was sleeping real late, I'd probably been in the studio all night. She woke me up at about seven in the morning and told me that somebody in Metallica died in a bus crash, and that the gig in Copenhagen was cancelled. I think she didn't want to be the one to break the news. It was on the news in Denmark. I called everybody I knew who could tell me what had happened. Then they said it again on the news later." John Bush of Anthrax and Armored Saint reflects: "It was a tragic, mind-boggling way to die. Who knows what would have happened with Metallica?"

What would have happened with Metallica if Cliff hadn't died was a question which fans and non-fans alike have considered ever since that tragic night.

In 1992, Lars himself explained at some length (as is his wont) that Burton's musical awareness had a profound impact on his and James' songwriting: "Cliff was responsible for a lot of the things that happened between *Kill 'Em All* and *Ride The Lightning*. [He] really exposed me and James to a whole new musical horizon of harmonies and melodies, just a whole new kind of thing, and obviously that's something that greatly influenced our songwriting abilities on *Master Of Puppets* . . . the whole way that me and James write songs together, I mean, that was shaped when Cliff was in the band, and was very much shaped around Cliff's musical input; the way he really taught us about harmonies and melodies and that kind of stuff. I mean, I don't want to sound corny, but his vibe is always with us, and he was certainly a big part of the whole way that we got our chops together in the early days, about our attitudes and our musical vibe and our everything. He was a great part of the way Metallica has turned out, even after he is no longer with us." James continued on the theme of Burton's musical education being an influence when he told *Aardschok* that "Cliff brought certain melodies into our music, which he had learned at school during his classical training. He knew how certain harmonies function."

But it wasn't just his knowledge which directed Metallica's path. His innate intelligence and charisma seem to have played a part too, as John Bush explains: "Cliff was a great guy, he was a very down-to-earth, humble dude. He was a pretty bright guy and had a knack for interesting statements and comments, things that the average person probably wouldn't say, so you could tell he was pretty well read. He was a very important part of Metallica even though Lars and James have always been the guys at the forefront. He had a lot to do with that band's sound and attitude. He was awesome."

This was reflected in Cliff's popularity with Metallica's fanbase, who responded to the news of his death with thousands of letters to his parents, Ray and Jan Burton. The couple talked about the fans' reaction in an interview the following year. His mother said, "Here, a year later, I'm still getting letters! That's real love and affection, and that's really helped us through this last year. I can't begin to express how much that has meant to us. I've written them, they've written back to me, and we've got a little correspondence going. It's a healing process, that love is being returned and sent."

Ray added: "I felt that he was an extraordinary young man, and the fact that he was my son made it all the more satisfying to me. He set his goals and made the choices of how to obtain those goals, and he did it. He felt that with Metallica there was a possibility of success. He stated that, 'Every once in a while we may fall on our face, but we insist on doing what we wanna do.' We was not I. It was always *we*. He always took the other three fellows' points of view. I felt it was a very empathetic organisation. He certainly had some bad times, especially on that first tour when they went back East . . . but it didn't stop him, even when everything was stolen except three guitars. He still stayed in there and persisted. I can only admire and love the kid, along with Kirk, James and Lars. They were a marvellous team. He was doing something he definitely enjoyed and got that fulfilment from his job. It's just too bad that his part of it was terminated. Many of the letters have said that his memory will live on."

With Cliff's death Metallica lost an integral part of the drive to succeed. James and Lars had to take more responsibility for the musical direction of the band. Kirk continued to play a more peripheral role in the songwriting, preferring to restrict his composition to the solos which he added to the songs.

But the 'progressive' edge of Metallica, which we may define as the more technical, complex or musicianly element of the songs, was gone after Cliff died – at least for a time, until his work on the following album was released and the songwriting he had completed before his death was revealed. The direction which Metallica would take as the decade came to a close would be radically different.

Had Cliff lived, he would almost certainly have honed his phenomenal dexterity further and composed more and more complex bass parts and guitar riffs, perhaps until the point where his work fell into the prog-metal genre. That's one prediction. Another, however, is that he would have tired of noodling away and stripped down his playing to basic, hardcore levels: a route which Martin Hooker of Music For Nations foresees would have been a delight for him. As desert-rock bands specialising in Black Sabbath- and Deep Purple-influenced space jams such as Unida and Queens Of The Stone Age rose to prominence in the late Nineties, Cliff might well have chosen to go with them. "If Cliff was alive today he'd be playing in a band like Electric Wizard," says Hooker. "Stoner rock could have been invented for him!"

Either way, his influence would have remained strong on Metallica. A metalhead to the core, the softer direction which they would ultimately take a decade after his death might not have been to his taste. Their later work might have been harder, faster, more complex or more melodic: these are fair predictions to make given his enormous talents, the nature of his musical tastes and the influence which he wielded on Lars and James.

★   ★   ★

An epilogue to the Cliff story comes from writer Garry Sharpe-Young, who interviewed Burton at the Birmingham Odeon on September 20, just a week before the coach crash. "I had arranged to interview Lars," reports Sharpe-Young. "He was late and I was just hanging around at the backstage door waiting, when Cliff popped his head out to find someone from the crew. I asked him if Lars was around and he offered to do the interview instead. What was really funny was that Cliff looked exactly like every picture you ever saw of him, with those bell-bottoms and that Misfits T-shirt."

Intrigued by the affable bassist, Garry settled into the interview. "We talked about bands back in the US, mainly because I was trying to save my 'real' questions for Lars! We did the interview in the same room as I had done a ton of other band talks before. Cliff found it funny that every backstage area in the British venues was painted in prison colours." The interview complete, writer and musician shook hands and parted ways, Burton returning to the dressing-room before taking the stage where he would be joined by Diamond Head's Brian Tatler.

A week later, Sharpe-Young heard the news of Cliff's death: "I had not actually written the interview up at the point when I learned he had been killed. I was writing for two mags at the time, *Metal Forces* in the UK and *Aardschok America* in the US. Bernard Doe at *Metal Forces* thought it would be disrespectful to print the interview, but the Americans wanted it bad. Then I started getting calls from agencies and other magazines. That's when I learned it was, from what I was being told, Cliff's last interview . . ."

Since then, the fact that Garry had conducted Cliff's last-ever interview has not escaped wider notice: "I've had three labels want to put it out on an interview disc over the years, one only recently. I never let the interview out. I think I'll hang onto it," he says now.

Sharpe-Young concludes by saying, "Funnily enough Cliff and I also talked theoretically about what Metallica would do if one of the band was killed: we were actually talking about Led Zeppelin and John Bonham. What we were actually discussing was the hypothesis of Lars meeting his maker . . ."

Burton's response? "Cliff said they would have a big drunken party in his honour, and then get in a new drummer. Fast."

15

1986–1988

Brian Slagel remembers the events of October 1986 as if they were yesterday: "What happened was, about three or four weeks after the accident I got a call from Lars, who said, 'Well, we need a new bass player.'" He adds: "So I said, I think I got the guy for you . . ."

Metallica returned from Europe a shadow of their former selves. After Cliff's funeral the three men were left to stare at each other, wondering what to do next. Their grief was profound: perhaps more so than they realised. Certainly, their decision to recruit another bassist within weeks of their return allowed them no time for that grief to be addressed.

But at the time it must have seemed like the right thing to do. In an interview he gave four months later, Kirk explained: "Right after the accident happened, we individually decided that the best way to get rid of all our frustrations would be to hit the road and get all the anxiety and frustrations out on stage, where they should go. They should go toward a positive thing like that. We were very traumatised, and felt a lot of emotional distress over the situation . . . The worst thing we could do is just sit in our room and sulk over the matter and wallow in our pity. The more you think about it, the deeper you sink. We each thought individually, we have to keep on going, we have to work because it wouldn't be fair to Cliff to just stop. Also if he were alive for some reason or another and like, y'know, he couldn't play bass, he wouldn't tell us to stop. That's the way he would've felt. He would've wanted us to go on."

Four years later, James would tell MTV a similar story: "The last thing Cliff would've wanted us to do was quit. He'd be the first one to kick us in the ass and make us wake up."

It was true, of course – but what the musicians failed to realise (although at the age of 23 and 24, such lack of vision is understandable) was that by internalising the pain and shock they were experiencing, they were storing up problems for themselves in years to come; problems which would have to be faced sooner or later.

All that was far from their minds, however, as Slagel recommended a suitable candidate to replace Cliff. His choice was an old friend of Metallica: Joey Vera, bass player with Armored Saint, whose singer John Bush had once been a target for recruitment himself. "The first and most obvious choice for them was Joey Vera, that was what I said," remembers Brian. "They were all good friends and everything, and he was their first pick as well – but he turned it down because at that time Armored Saint was not that far behind Metallica."

Like Bush before him, Joey couldn't bear to leave his bandmates, and as Slagel says, the Saint were still in with a good chance at the time of hitting the big time under their own steam. "Joey had grown up with all those guys in that band, they were like his brothers," adds Slagel. "And he felt at the time that it was a great opportunity, but that he wanted to play out the Armored Saint thing. Once he said no, I said, 'I think I got the guy for you. We have a band called Flotsam And Jetsam on our label – and the bass player is absolutely amazing.'"

Life had moved forward slowly but steadily for Jason Newsted, the farm boy from Michigan. His band, Dogz, whose line-up comprised singer Erik A.K. Knutson, Kevin Horton and Mark Vasquez on guitar, Jason on bass and backing vocals and Kelly Smith on drums, had changed its name to the more intriguing Flotsam And Jetsam in 1984 and dumped the two axemen in favour of Michael Gilbert and Ed Carlson. After scoring a track on Slagel's *Metal Massacre VII*, F&J signed to the expanding Metal Blade label (which, like its counterpart Megaforce on the East Coast, had gone from strength to strength in Metallica's wake) and released a stunning thrash metal album called *Doomsday For The Deceiver* in 1986. The album was famously so popular at *Kerrang!* magazine that the reviewer awarded it six out of a maximum five points, a move which guaranteed it instant success.

Slagel's recommendation was enough for Lars and James to add Jason's name to the list of 40 or so players who had been invited to jam with them in separate auditions back in San Francisco. "Lars said, 'OK, cool, send me some stuff,' " says Brian, who obliged by sending Ulrich examples of Newsted's best work. By now a solid, inventive player, Jason would have more than enough talent to impress Lars, thought Brian. He was right: the drummer approved and asked that Newsted come up to SF.

"Apparently a couple of other people Lars spoke to had thought of Flotsam And Jetsam and told him, 'Yeah, that guy's really good,' " confirms Slagel. "So we arranged for Jason to fly up to SF to audition. I called Jason and said, 'I don't want to get you too excited . . . what would you think about possibly auditioning for the Metallica gig?' " Brian laughs as he remembers: "He was freaking out, saying, 'Are you kidding me? They're like my favourite band of all time!' I think he was more nervous than anything else – like, really? This is really happening? And I was like, yeah! You should definitely do it. It was hard because Flotsam And Jetsam was his band. But then again Metallica was his favourite band, so it didn't take too much arm-twisting to get him to go up there."

Several players auditioned to fill the Metallica slot, including Les Claypool of Primus, Laaz Rockit's Willy Lange and Watchtower bassist Doug Keyser. Many others tried their luck: Hetfield recalled later that one of them, an unknown, had brought a friend, who stayed outside the door and attempted to record his bass-playing chum's audition.

On October 28, 1986, a month and a day after Cliff had met his end on the dark Swedish highway all those thousands of miles away, Jason Newsted arrived at Metallica's rehearsal room, bass in hand. He had spent the previous two days learning every song in their back catalogue, and once he had plugged in and tuned up, and James had asked him which song he wanted to play, his answer was "Any one you like: I know them all!"

It was probably this commitment which attracted Metallica to the gaunt, wiry country boy with the fast fingers: the fact that he had striven so hard to master all the band's songs must have been an early indicator that he meant business. As Jason told me in 2002, when he approached a band, he gave it total concentration: in Flotsam And Jetsam he had fulfilled a multitude of roles, including marketing, promoting and booking the band as well as composing and bass playing duties. "Every waking moment I was tape-trading, international communications – which in those days meant putting all the parcel post

Photographer Ross Halfin's first photo shoot with Metallica in 1984 saw a wiser and more experienced band moving onward and upward. *Ride The Lightning,* released that year, was a startling leap forward in subtlety and precision. *(Ross Halfin)*

Fooling around backstage on the neverending tours kept the band sane.
James and Kirk backstage *(Ross Halfin)*

Lars photographed covered in paint for the cover of
Kerrang! by Ross Halfin, who muses: "It was
embarrassing, it was stupid. It was a crap photo
session". *(Ross Halfin)*

Nicknamed Alcoholica in the mid-Eighties due to their
endless partying, Metallica did their best to live up to
their name. It was funny at the time, but less so a few
years down the line. *(Pete Cronin)*

The incomparable Cliff Burton: a much-loved man and a much-worshipped bass player. *(LFI)*

The scene of the coach crash on 27 September 1986 which claimed Cliff's life.

Cliff's successor, Jason Newsted: a man with big shoes to fill.
"There were so many emotions following Cliff's passing," he said. *(Ross Halfin)*

Metallica in Japan, where they toured immediately after Jason joined them, despite still being in shock after losing Burton: "We were very traumatised, and felt a lot of emotional distress over the situation," recalled Hammett some years later. *(Ross Halfin)*

As Metallica's profile grew, so did the venues they played: luckily, Kirk knew how to hold the attention of an entire stadium of fans with his unearthly guitar solos. *(Ross Halfin)*

The mile high club: James and Lars aboard a private jet - a long way from the tour buses which had been their primary mode of transport for so many years. *(Ross Halfin)*

Lars in his element: pounding the skins in front of thousands of rabid fans. But are those spandex trousers he's wearing? *(Ross Halfin)*

The Four Horsemen in the late Eighties, heading steadily up the metal highway.
A switch to the mainstream could never happen. Or could it? *(Ross Halfin)*

The talented, troubled Mr. Hetfield: the voice of the biggest metal band in the world. *(Ross Halfin)*

together, and all the airmail crap, no internet thing where you push one button and a million people got it – it was the real deal!"

This drive to succeed must also have impressed Lars, James and Kirk. Jason is a likeable, relaxed guy, but his determination to make things work comes through very clearly and he will talk at great length (almost as great, in fact, as the permanently loquacious Ulrich). Writer and Hades guitarist Dan Lorenzo laughs: "Man that guy can talk! We argued about Dave Mustaine. Jason told me he thought Megadeth were a watered-down Metallica. I told him he was wrong!" Journalist Martin Popoff adds: "Jason is a gas. He's a very energetic, interesting, smart guy, a very precise, colourful and aggressive speaker. He loves music passionately and has the art of it all placed on a pedestal where it should be." Hirax frontman Katon DePena explains that Newsted's attitude to Metallica was a new perspective for them: "Jason is a really good guy. I think because he got in the band late, and he came from Flotsam And Jetsam, that he really understood the Metallica fans – because he was one. I don't think he ever forgot it. He is probably the most level-headed guy to ever be in Metallica."

Finally, Jason's abilities as a player are beyond criticism. From the moment he joined Metallica, observers compared his style and overall competence with that of Cliff. His technical skills were advanced, of course, or he wouldn't have been considered: but Jason possessed something more, an unquantifiable extra aspect which enabled his rock-solid playing to gel with and complement the razor-sharp riffing of Hetfield. As John Bush of Anthrax says: "Jason came in there and did amazing things. Those were tough shoes to fill and he filled them very well."

And so, with all these qualities in place, it's no surprise that after a second audition and a drinking session at Tommy's Joint, a San Francisco bar which Metallica had frequented for some years, Jason was invited to join the band. As legend has it, Hetfield, Ulrich and Hammett found a reason to visit the bathroom at the same moment, conferred and made the offer on their return. Metallica was a foursome again.

While Jason was immensely excited by this turn of events, he neverthe-less had the disagreeable task of informing his long-time colleagues in Flotsam And Jetsam that he would be leaving their ranks. There was some bitterness about this, apparently: Newsted explained a little later to the press that he had once attached to the wall of the F&J rehearsal room a list of golden rules to do with being in their group – along the lines of 'Be punctual', 'Be imaginative' and so on. One of his bandmates walked up to the list after Newsted had imparted his news and wrote on it 'Join another band'.

However, once this sticky moment had passed and Jason had played his last Flotsam show on October 31, 1986, things began to move fast. Almost freakishly fast, in fact. Jason had just one week to rehearse to everyone's satisfaction before the first gig Metallica played with him on November 8 at the Country Club in Reseda, California, as support for Metal Church. This was a secret gig in that the new line-up's appearance had not been widely publicised, and featured a full 13-song set from Metallica, including material from all three albums and a solo spot from Kirk. A second show the following night was shorter and took place at Jezebel's in Anaheim. Both band and audiences at both concerts were delighted with Jason's performance and his energetic stage moves which, as a new member, he kept fairly restricted at this stage. He later recalled that his philosophy at this point was not to attempt to replace Burton, but to simply discover what he could bring to Metallica by being himself and himself alone: an honest approach which the other musicians must have appreciated.

A five-date mini-tour of Japan followed from November 15 to November 20, with three concerts in Tokyo plus one each in Nagoya and Osaka. The set now included a bass solo immediately after 'Ride The Lightning', a brave move considering that Metallica could not yet have known how Newsted would be received. However, the crowds loved him and the band as a whole and the tour proved to be a perfect welcoming experience for Jason.

Perfect, that is, except for one initially amusing but later rather bizarre fact. James, Lars and Kirk used the tour as an excuse for a barrage of pranks, humiliations and practical jokes which they fired at Jason, perhaps masking an uneasiness, or even a degree of resentment, at the way that recent events had treated them. Photographer Ross Halfin was there on the Japanese tour, taking some memorable shots of the band with fans and on the road, and witnessed this 'hazing' at first hand: "We'd all pick on him," he recalls in disbelief, 17 years later. "We'd all get a cab and make him get a cab on his own. We'd sign all the room bills to his room. This was before they had money . . . They used to really, really pick on him. It started off as a joke and then it got really beyond a joke. One of the first ones was that they'd all slept with me and that I was gay, and that he should too if he wanted to stay in the band. And he was actually worried about it for a while. I'm serious!"

As Jason later told *Playboy*: "One time, it's four in the morning, they're hammered and knocking on my hotel door when we were in New York. 'Get up, fucker! It's time to drink, pussy!' You know? 'You're in Metallica now! You better open that fucking door!' They kept pounding. Kaboom! The door frame shreds, and the door comes flying in. And they go, 'You should have answered the door, bitch!' They grab the mattress and flip it over with me on it. They put the chairs, the desk, the TV stand – everything in the room – on top of the mattress. They threw my clothes, my cassette tapes, my shoes out the window. Shaving cream all over the mirrors, toothpaste everywhere. Just devastation. They go running out the door, 'Welcome to the band, dude!' "

Jason knew what was happening, though, telling *Rolling Stone*: "It was a test all the time – wind-ups from everyone to see if I could cut it. Everybody would go down to the bar to have sushi and sake for days and charge it to my room. We'd go to take pictures at the temples, and they'd all get in one taxi and make me ride by myself. This went on for a year. If I was going to buckle, they had to know. I took it and that was that."

So why did the band feel that Newsted, who they clearly respected as a player and a colleague, had to endure this round of torture, good-natured as it may have been? Halfin: "I think it was because he wasn't sure. He came over very arrogant when he joined, but I don't think he was arrogant – he just didn't know. Looking back on it now, he didn't know how to act, didn't know what to do. He really did pass an initiation ceremony big-time with them."

It was not until 2002 that Jason offered his own opinion on his initiation. His theory was the other members of Metallica needed an outlet for their feelings about Cliff, who had been taken so suddenly and shockingly from them, and that he was the obvious scapegoat. Talking to *Classic Rock*, he explained: "There were so many emotions following Cliff's passing. There are three or four stages of grieving but they probably didn't even start acceptance until I'd been there for five years. Metallica have a really dry, sarcastic humour, and they do say that ten per cent of sarcasm is truth. Suddenly I was the guy standing in that space; maybe it was their way of venting? They've all since admitted that and apologised for it."

Perhaps more worryingly, Ross Halfin believes that Lars had a problem with Jason on that first tour which ran deeper than a merely surface-level degree of mockery. "I know for a fact," says Ross now, "that after he'd been in the band a month, he did the Japanese tour we did, that was his first tour. And Lars wanted to fire him. He wanted to replace him. But Peter Mensch said to him, 'You've made your choice, now live with it.'" Halfin knows of no specific reason for Lars' attitude: "He just didn't get on with him as a person. It wasn't because of Jason's playing skills, it was purely because he didn't get on with his personality. He came on tour and he didn't know if was going to keep his job."

Clearly there were issues at large among the Metallica camp, and given the trauma of the last few months plus the on-the-road pressures they were undergoing, there is little wonder. But there was no time to stop and reflect on this, as a medium-sized tour was beckoning which would keep them occupied (and in each other's close proximity) until mid-February, 1988. Perhaps this lack of time to address their underlying sadness was the reason that so little real healing took place in the minds of Lars, James and Kirk for so long.

A week after returning from Japan, on November 28, the tour – this time of the US East Coast and Canada – kicked off in Poughkeepsie, New York, after which the band played packed-out dates in New Jersey, Hartford, New York, Quebec, Ontario, Winnipeg, Saskatchewan, Alberta, Vancouver, Washington and Oregon before a couple of weeks holiday at Christmas. A January 2 show in San Francisco topped off the US tour for the moment, but the ride wasn't close to finishing yet: the band were due to fly to Europe, still with Metal Church in support, for an extended jaunt which would include shows in the East (remember, this was still a long, long way from the freeing influence of glasnost) for the first time. First on the schedule, appropriately, was Copenhagen which had missed out on a Metallica appearance due to Cliff's death just the day before the concert. The bands then moved on to Sweden, Germany, France, Spain, France and Germany again, Switzerland, France yet again and then Holland, where they played at in Zwolle on February 8. On this final date they played with Swiss legends Celtic Frost, as frontman Thomas Fischer remembers: "We played on the same bill with Metallica only once, in February 1987, on the Aardschok Festival in Zwolle in the Netherlands. We were in the midst of the recording sessions for our *Into The Pandemonium* album." This would be the only occasion on which these two great bands would share a stage – a dream date for many metal fans.

Kirk Hammett was interviewed at the festival and talked at length about the band's decision to continue playing and touring so soon after Burton's death. Explaining that Burton would have wanted them to go on ("If we had hung it up, Cliff would've been so pissed off") and that the rationale for doing so was nothing less than a duty to the late bass player, he also talked a little about the emotions which had threatened to overcome them: "Right after the accident happened, we individually decided that the best way to get rid of all our frustrations would be to hit the road and get all the anxiety and frustrations out on stage, where they should go. They should go toward a positive thing like that. We were very traumatised, and felt a lot of emotional distress over the situation . . . The worst thing we could do is just sit in our room and sulk over the matter and wallow in our pity. The more you think about it, the deeper you sink."

This openness reveals something about the personality of Hammett, who has always been the dark horse of Metallica, neither a frontperson nor a spokesman but who stands slightly to one side, bringing his talent to the band but rarely his voice. In fact, Hammett had been developing quietly as the band expanded: the previous year he had produced a seminal demo, *Kill As One*, by the thrash metal band Death Angel, and had spent four years honing his guitar skills with occasional lessons from guitar god Joe Satriani, as he later explained: "Joe was a big influence back then, but not so much these days. He showed me how to use modes, and he showed me a lot of theory – like what chords to play over what scales, and vice versa. I learned a lot of finger exercises, as well. I had lessons from 1983 until '87, on and off, maybe four lessons a year, sometimes. I never had enough time because I was always touring. And then when he hit big with *Surfing With The Alien* he didn't have time either. In fact, I think I was probably his last student."

Looking at Metallica's schedule at this time in 1987, it's apparent why Kirk ran out of time to study with anyone: the tour continued through

Poland and concluded once more in Sweden, but the decision had been taken that some recording would be done before the summer and arrangements were made for this to take place back home in San Francisco. The idea was to lay down some tracks which would allow Jason to showcase his bass skills and perhaps release them in time for festival dates which Metallica had been booked to play in the summer.

But before this could happen, there was a somewhat surprising departure for Metallica with the release in April, 1987 of a video. And this from the band which had always sworn it would never make a video, as this would represent a sell-out to the MTV mentality. However, the package, entitled *Cliff 'Em All*, sidestepped the issue in two ways: firstly, it was far from a glossy, made-for-TV production. *CEA* is a grainy, shaky, cobbled-together excuse for a video that is resolutely amateurish and absolutely essential viewing for any Metallica fan, or indeed any fan of early to mid-Eighties metal. Compiled from bootleg footage recorded by fans, personal film belonging to the band and photos sourced from various locations, the film pays homage to Burton's remarkable talent and unique personality and even in the era of DVD remains gloriously watchable. The scene in which Cliff good-humouredly enjoys a joint, as well as those onstage moments in which he displays his fearsome simultaneous soloing and headbanging approach are utterly memorable.

Within two months of its release, *Cliff 'Em All* was certified both gold and platinum. James' handwritten notes on the back of the sleeve made it clear what it was supposed to say: "Well, we finally went and did what we always talked about not doing, releasing a vid!! Before you throw up in disgust, let us (except K---) tell you the idea behind this. First of all, this is not your typical piece of shit home video done with high-tech 10 camera production and sound, it's a compilation of bootleg footage shot by sneaky Metallifux, stuff shot for TV that was never used, but were held onto, home footage, personal fotos & us drunk. But most important, it's really a look back at the 3½ years that Cliff was with us and includes his best bass solos and the home footage & pix that we feel best capture his unique personality & style. The quality in some places ain't that happening, but the feeling is there and that's what matters!!!"

Secondly, no one complained because *Cliff 'Em All* is an emotional piece of work with a very serious purpose behind its deliberately lo-fi qualities and ham-fisted production. It is a fine tribute to a much-missed musician, and no one – not even the most rabid, no-sell-out underground metaller – could mistake its message. To this day, it's as integral a part of Metallica's history as *Master Of Puppets*.

Before the summer festivals, the band rehearsed new material at a professional practice facility in Marin County. However, they famously disliked its plush interior and didn't really settle into the rehearsals. As an alternative, the foursome (led by Jason, who had some previous experience as a carpenter and interior decorator) opted to customise Lars' garage, making it as near to a rehearsal and recording studio as possible. It's interesting to note that despite the professional surroundings which they had now come to regard as normal (although none of them had yet become wealthy enough to expect to live in luxury), the environs of a home-made studio still suited them better even though it was pretty spartan: some of the carpets which Newsted had attached to the walls to form soundproofing and deaden the acoustics were less than clean, and the place soon began to smell fairly badly.

More inconvenience soon came their way on March 23 when James managed to break his arm again in another skateboarding fall, this time more seriously. The band had been scheduled to appear on NBC-TV's *Saturday Night Live* but had to withdraw, and rehearsals of new material had to be put on hold. Hetfield was forced to take a break of several weeks to allow his wrist to heal, and the band spent the time finishing off the garage and discussing what to do next. Help with the garage insulation came from none other than Lars' old friend John Kornarens, who came up from LA as a favour.

A decision was duly made, and in June the band began rehearsing songs for an EP to be released in time for the summer. They recorded vintage rock and metal covers which summed up fairly succinctly the range of influences which had made Metallica the band they were. First and most obviously, there was a Diamond Head song, 'Helpless', followed by 'The Small Hours', a track composed by the NWOBHM band Holocaust. Killing Joke's 'The Wait' was next, before Budgie's 'Crash Course In Brain Surgery', and the EP was scheduled to end with a bang with a back-to-back rendition of two Misfits songs, 'Last Caress' and 'Green Hell'. Recording sessions for the EP, appropriately titled

The $5.98 EP and with the tag line *Garage Days Re-Revisited*, began on July 8.

The EP was released on August 21, 1987, and was instantly popular, helped along by three festival shows at which Metallica performed in front of over 200,000 people. A 'secret' warm-up gig for the first festival, the renowned Donington festival at which Metallica had last appeared in 1985, took place at the 100 Club in London, where the band performed as Damage, Inc. A huge number of fans arrived, all probably alerted because the name they chose was hardly difficult to see through. Most were turned away at the door, as the club is relatively small.

This was not a problem at the enormous Donington festival the following day. Just as they had two years previously, Metallica shared the stage with Bon Jovi, who were riding an enormous wave of success thanks to a series of radio-friendly singles which the British and European rock-buying public had taken to its bosom. Now with fixtures at the less extreme end of the glam-metal wave, Bon Jovi had managed to woo mainstream pop audiences while retaining some sort of rock credibility. This reflected the two-tiered nature of the metal scene in the mid to late Eighties, with the more clean-cut end of metal soaring above (in commercial terms, anyway) the thrash metal wave beneath them. The following year's Donington would feature Megadeth and Guns N'Roses on stage together, another bill that mixed hair-metal and thrash in the hope of appealing to fans across the spectrum.

Just as Bon Jovi had their own product to promote, Metallica were pushing the *Garage Days* EP, but as it was a truly excellent piece of work, audiences needed little persuading. It had been recorded at the A&M and Conway studios in LA, after Metallica manager Peter Mensch managed to persuade veteran rocker Ted Nugent, who was recording there at the time, that his band urgently needed six days of studio time. Nugent made a space in his schedule and was thanked for his efforts on the back of the sleeve, which also bore James' scrawl as follows: "After coming off the 'Puppets' tour in Feb. 87, we needed a place to jam and ended up in a fancy, so-called "real" rehearsal studio. IT HELLA SUCKED! So in May, after a BREAK in the action, we decided to return to the old reliable, ever-comfortable & smelly garage; Super-duty soundproofed by us, (except K---), under the direction of building master J. Newkid. To break it in, we started bashing out some old ~~tunes we dig~~ favorites of ours in true Metallikatz fashion, and after a bit, we thought it would be good fun to record and release them. So in early July, we flipped down to L.A. and did it in six days (about the same time it took to load in the gear on the last album). Like the first 'Garage Days Revisited', these are cover tunes and you shouldn't take all this too seriously, CAUSE WE DON'T!! ENJOY!!" Note James' sly reference to his broken arm, the reference to Newsted as 'Newkid' and the dig at Kirk, who had (perhaps wisely) stayed away while the hard work of soundproofing Lars' garage was going on.

Ironically, Metallica would become known in later years as a band that placed maximum focus on the importance of the production on their records – and yet this EP, which was recorded in such a short time (and which also bore the disclaimer 'Not very produced by Metallica') boasted one of the best overall sounds they would ever achieve. The guitars are fast, thick and clear; Jason's bass is stomach-jarringly powerful, with just the right amount of overdrive to make it sweet; Lars' kit sounds as if it's in the same room as the listener; and James' vocals are sublime, all barked, precise invocations and grunts. A few deliberate twitches and fret-buzzes were left on the record, along with the sound of the amps and pedals being manipulated, some shouted instructions and laughter from the band. It's all highly atmospheric, and quite brilliant.

The opening track, 'Helpless', is utterly gripping. Opening with some aimless humming, probably from James, the song features a dexterous drum pattern and slides into a heavy, mid-tempo riff which accelerates to blinding speed in the chorus. Each stroke of Hetfield's pick is cleanly reproduced, leading the listener to wonder how he would perform under the much cleaner environs of a real album. Holocaust's 'The Small Hours' is, alongside 'The Thing That Should Not Be', perhaps the heaviest thing that Metallica have ever done: a sickly, picked pattern creeps into a brutally weighty riff which is so far superior to the British band's original version that they're almost two different songs. It also has a fast section in which Hammett displays both amazing nimbleness and a breathtaking melodic awareness.

'The Wait' is the odd track out here, but is worthy of investigation, specifically by British audiences, who missed out on it because it was omitted from UK versions of the EP so that the record could qualify for chart inclusion (four tracks was the maximum number which could be included). It's a darker song than the others here, with a trance-like central riff, a weirdly echoed solo and processed, watery vocals which generate an aura of eerie instability. 'Crash Course In Brain Surgery' is another excellent song, with a stop–start riff and a descending scale in the chorus which echoed that of 'Sanitarium', recorded two years before. And as for the 'Last Caress' and 'Green Hell' medley, this was easily the most memorable track on the EP, simply for the deliberately moronic, punkish lyrics ("I got something to say . . . I raped your mother today" and so on), and the extremely fast, drone-like riffing of the latter, which sees James spitting out the minimal, abstract lyrics against a virulent blast of thrash beats.

The inclusion of songs by a punk act – The Misfits – wasn't so unusual, given the band's background, as they explained to *Thrasher*. "Cliff turned us on to them," said James. "All of his friends were into them and he taped some stuff from his friends." Kirk added: "It just grew on us and we started listening to it a lot. I like The Misfits. I liked the songs and then I saw pictures of them and went, wow, this is cool. The imagery that they used was like some of the stuff I've seen in old horror comics."

The EP ends with a few seconds of the intro to Iron Maiden's 'Run To The Hills', albeit a warped, twisted take on it, with the riffs all out of tune: a deliberate joke at Maiden's expense. The record as a whole is a remarkable piece of work, and one which went down a storm at all three August festivals where Metallica played. The Donington crowd saw a set which began with three *Ride The Lightning* songs ('Creeping Death', 'For Whom The Bell Tolls' and 'Fade To Black') and included the 'Run To The Hills' moment as well as 'Last Caress', which would be a live staple for years to come. The August 29 concert at the Messegelände in Nuremberg, Germany, saw Metallica play a shorter set before headliners Deep Purple which included killer renditions of 'Whiplash', 'Master Of Puppets' and 'Last Caress' again, while the following day's set at the FCP Stadion in Pforzheim (again with Purple) was shorter still, although the closer, 'Battery', gave the headliners an intimidating closing song to beat.

After the dying chords of their set in Pforzheim, Metallica left the stage and flew home, the year's activity completed and nothing more scheduled in the public eye for some months. Time was spent writing a new set of material for a fourth studio album. The *Garage Days* EP was a stop-gap release which the fans had appreciated, not least for the opportunity to sample newcomer Jason's bass skills on vinyl, but the band's forward momentum had slipped a little on the album front – it had now been almost two years since they had been recording *Puppets* – and the time was ripe to create new music. So they retreated to San Francisco, not to be seen as a band again until 1988.

By the end of 1987, music fans were beginning to use the term 'the Big Four Of Thrash Metal'. *Master Of Puppets* (which only finally slipped from the US album charts in August, having spent a phenomenal 72 weeks there) had brought Metallica to this level, while Slayer's equally breathtaking *Reign In Blood*, also released in 1986, had guaranteed them inclusion. Anthrax's excellent third album *Among The Living* and Megadeth's *Peace Sells . . . But Who's Buying?* were both released in 1987 and saw those bands gain sufficient exposure to warrant membership of this select group.

The latter had risen a long way in a short time due to the powerful playing and composing of Dave Mustaine, but their new-found success had not made him any happier with his ex-bandmates in Metallica, as he revealed in an interview that year: "I really don't want to start anything with them, I don't think there's any way to win that one for me. If I say nice things about them, I'm lying. If I say bad things, it looks like I'm trying to generate some sort of publicity. So what I've done is try to avoid the subject as much as possible – which isn't easy. When I'm asked about their album, I tell everyone that I really like it, that it's a great album. But if they ask me about them personally, that's another matter. They're dicks who really don't know as much as they think they do. You've got to remember, they gave it to me pretty bad when I left the group. It's one thing to part ways and just bury the hatchet, but they were trying to bury it in my head . . . The good part is that now I have the chance to make them eat their words. I feel sorry for them because of what they've had to go through recently, but that really doesn't change my feelings."

Most fans and musicians were happy with the Big Four label, although one or two of Metallica's big-selling contemporaries were less contented. Eric Peterson of Testament, whose band came the closest of all other thrash acts to rivalling the Big Four's sales figures, told me:

"It's weird how they say the Big Four, because they left out Exodus and Testament. We weren't chumps, we sold millions of records too. We definitely made our mark. It's bullshit, because it made us the underdogs, which is bull." The element of us-and-them which the term implied is not to his taste, either: "When our first record came out in 1987, a lot of reviewers were saying that this is the record that Metallica should have made. We were honoured by that but kind of pissed off at the same time. Those were our heroes and our friends, and all of a sudden we're competition to them? We didn't like that, it pushed our friendship away from them."

Another seminal metal record which had appeared in 1987 – in fact, shortly before the *Garage Days* EP – was Guns N'Roses' debut album, the still-essential *Appetite For Destruction*. Veering from drunken, ranting songs such as 'You're Crazy' and 'Nightrain' to sublimely mellow elegies such as 'Sweet Child O' Mine' and 'Think About You' and all points in between, *Appetite* was a breath of fresh air to main-stream metal, which had suffered for some time from the under-performance of the initially promising Mötley Crüe and the MTV-friendly blandness of Bon Jovi and Europe. GNR had a very saleable set-up, with the unpredictable frontman W. Axl Rose and his lead-guitar cohort Slash a perfect echo of Plant and Page of Led Zeppelin and Steven Tyler and Joe Perry of Aerosmith, but they also played with superb panache, composing songs which were unforgettably sleazy, and gave great interviews.

Their album sounded great, too, with a bass-heavy production to die for, and Metallica were watching closely as this pack of layabout, drunken junkies rose to the top of the rock tree. *Appetite* had been produced by Mike Clink, and Lars and James decided to procure his services on the next Metallica album. Rarely had such a crossover between the worlds of glam and thrash metal taken place, but then both acts were all about rule-breaking (or at least their public profile suggested this) and if no precedent existed, then one would be created if necessary, it seemed.

Clink wasn't the band's first choice, however. Initially Lars had called Flemming Rasmussen and asked him to produce a third Metallica record. In the event Rasmussen had other commitments in January 1988. Flemming apologised but was surprised to receive a phone call from Ulrich shortly afterward. Things had not, it seemed, gone to plan, as he says: "Lars phoned me up at the end of January, and they were on hold, they hadn't done any recordings at all. It didn't work so they called me in. They couldn't get the sounds they wanted, so Lars asked me when I could be there. So I pushed my sessions neck to neck and two weeks later I flew out. Mike got sacked the day before I came."

Although Rasmussen doesn't know precisely what went wrong with the Clink* sessions, he does know that on his arrival he stripped down the recording set-up and started again from scratch: "I tore everything down and put it up again and completely bypassed the desk they were using and used some old shit they had sitting in the back of their studio. Then I fiddled around with some mikes and shit and we got it." Perhaps, he thinks, Clink and Metallica had just come from too disparate backgrounds: "I knew the sound these guys wanted and Mike had done more rock stuff: always in the back of his mind he was still going for that kind of sound."

The sessions restarted on January 19. This time around, the band were in the One On One studio in Los Angeles (there would be no European jaunts on this occasion) for almost five months. They didn't emerge, in fact, until early May, when the job of mixing still had to be completed. Meanwhile, in January *Kill 'Em All* was reissued again in the USA, this time with 'Am I Evil?' and 'Blitzkrieg' as bonus tracks.

The name of the new album? Apocalyptically, and revealingly, the new record would be called . . . *And Justice For All*.

---

* I contacted Clink with an interview request during research for this book, but received no response.

16

1988–1991

Before the album could be released, it had to be mixed to the increasingly demanding standards of Hetfield and Ulrich. However, there was one small problem: from May 1988 Metallica were booked to play on a genuinely huge rolling tour, confusingly named the Monsters Of Rock tour (like the European festival) and headlined by the enormously successful Van Halen. Metallica would play in the centre of the bill, after Led Zeppelin clones Kingdom Come and hair-metallists Dokken and before the still-huge Scorpions and Eddie Van Halen's crew.

As James told *Rolling Stone*: "That whole Monsters Of Rock tour was a big fog for me. Those were my Jägermeister days. It was bad coming back to some of those towns later, because there were a lot of dads and moms and husbands and boyfriends looking for me. Not good. People were hating me, and I didn't know why. That's when I realised Jägermeister is not the great elixir of life I thought it was. It was OK to feel drunk and fucked-up back then."

After two now *de rigueur* secret gigs before the tour (for which Metallica named themselves Frayed Ends, a reference to one of the songs on the forthcoming album), which took place on May 23 and 24 at the Troubadour in LA, the enormous touring package started its run. A new song had been debuted at the secret shows, the slightly eerie, distant-sounding 'Harvester Of Sorrow', which crowds liked but which, with its picked, sinister intro and relentless, slow to mid-tempo riffing, took a little time to get used to.

Opening in Wisconsin and, after a week's break, moving to Florida, the tour was a lumbering beast as befitted its enormous size, and this allowed James and Lars to drive between shows to Bearsville Studios in Woodstock, New York, where album mixing was taking place under the supervision of Steve Thompson and Michael Barbiero. June shows in Washington, Philadelphia, Massachusetts, Michigan, Pennsylvania and New York state meant that the band were never too far away from Bearsville to miss out on the sessions and the album was completed and ready for release by the end of the month. However, the constant travelling was stressful for both, which may or may not have been reflected in the final sound of the album, which was not due for release until September.

The Monsters Of Rock package moved at a sloth-like pace through Ohio, Maine, New Jersey and then down to Texas after another week of rest. Indiana, Tennessee, Missouri, Minnesota and then San Francisco's Candlestick Park were next: the show remained on the West Coast for a while, taking in Seattle and Denver before the end of June, where it finally rolled to a halt. Most critics regarded Metallica and Kingdom Come as the victors, if any one band had to be selected as the best: fired with enthusiasm as the new album drew near, Hetfield and Co. had put on a blistering performance night after night and the fans were primed for the new material to appear.

Lars loved the tour, telling *Rolling Stone*: "It was fucking great. It was '88, right before . . . *And Justice For All* came out. We were at the bottom, sandwiched between Kingdom Come and Dokken. Basically, at that time, we used to start drinking when we woke up. We'd get the gig over by three o'clock, and then we'd have eight or nine hours to drink. It was awesome. This was our first exposure to big crowds, like, 50,000 people every day. Well, we were just drunk basically all the time. Girls knew we were part of the tour and wanted to fuck us, but at the same time we could blend in with the crowd. There's a point where you end up sitting in your dressing-room because there's 14 layers of security. Back then it was like, who gives a shit? Let's have another rum and Coke and go back in the audience and see what's happening. There are pictures of us at the top of Tampa Stadium with our pants off, flashing everybody. It's four o'clock in the afternoon and we're already drunk off our asses. The not-giving-a-fuck meter was peaking."

. . . *And Justice For All* was finally released on September 5, 1988, just after its predecessor, *Master Of Puppets*, was officially certified platinum, commemorating sales of over one million units in the US. Even on the day it was born, *Justice* had much to live up to.

Musically and lyrically, *Justice* was a triumph, and remains one of

Metallica's finest albums to this day. Like all classics, it took some getting used to. Whereas the killer hooks of *Kill 'Em All* and *Ride The Lightning* had stuck in the ear from first listen, and the enormous, brooding power of *Master Of Puppets* had bludgeoned the listener into instant submission, *Justice* was a subtler, more insidious record that repaid only those who gave it serious concentration. Although its most contentious point was its overall sound (a point to which we will return in detail), the subject matter which Hetfield chose to address marked it out as a new step for Metallica. Like many a rocker before him, James had developed resentment towards the establishment, and was now in a position to express his anger with a deft mixture of venom and lyrical elegance.

The album starts with the superb 'Blackened', a more refined equivalent of *Puppets* opener 'Battery'. Like the latter, the song begins with a memorable intro before turning on a dime and slipping into a feverishly quick (but not pure thrash) riff: the sound of that whispering, multi-layered intro of wailing, sinister guitars fading in from the ether is unforgettable. Also like 'Battery', Hetfield's main riff is a slippery creation, with a tail that makes it slightly unpredictable (and which makes its time signature a little hard to nail down). James' theme is the death of Planet Earth – the first time he had addressed the subject in any depth. "Population laid to waste . . . see our mother put to death; see our mother die!" he wails.

The title track, as with *Ride* and *Puppets* the second song on the album, is a long, complex, successfully progressive metal composition based on a strange drum pattern from Lars and a martial, almost minimal riff allied to it. Its intro, a gentle acoustic strum, stops and starts once in a manner surely designed to make the unprepared listener snigger, but after a while its classical structure becomes clear and the song unfolds. At around nine minutes in length, '. . . And Justice For All' can sometimes feel more like a string of connected song sections than a single, cohesive piece (especially as the main riff comes sneaking back in on several occasions, as if to remind you that the wheel is still turning), but it works effectively, even if you might not want to hear it too many times in a row.

The third song, 'Eye Of The Beholder', is the weakest song on the album. Based on a staccato, mid-tempo E/G/F-sharp progression which mirrors that of the much more nimble 'Disposable Heroes', it's dark and atmospheric but not brilliant. The same cannot be said, however, of 'One', the song which is remembered most from this album and which marked a step forward for Metallica in many ways. After 'Fade To Black' on *Ride The Lightning* and 'Sanitarium' on *Master Of Puppets*, some sharp-witted critics asked Metallica which song on *Justice* would be the token ballad; laughing, Lars told them that it would be 'One', although his was the last laugh.

'One' does start with a cleanly picked, melodic section, with Kirk's keening, non-overdriven solo almost a poetic moment. James' narrative, the sad words of a wartime casualty who has lost his limbs in an explosion, is suitably bleak ("Tied to machines that make me be . . . cut this life off from me") and leads into a brief but heavier chorus section which becomes progressively weightier as the song moves forward. And when the song finally takes off, it does so with – at last – the furious power fans witnessed on *Puppets* songs such as 'Damage, Inc.'; a very accurate, sixteenths-based motif intersperses some fantastic soloing from both guitarists, stretching across an extended closing section which is near-apocalyptic by its end. The song is simply awe-inspiring.

After this (on the next record, for those who purchased the double vinyl LP), the album slows down a little, with 'Shortest Straw' another competent but forgettable song like 'Eye Of The Beholder' leading into the superior 'Harvester Of Sorrow', which audiences on the Monsters Of Rock tour had now been hearing for some weeks. 'Harvester' also became the first single from *Justice* and was backed by super-tight versions of Budgie's 'Breadfan' and Diamond Head's 'The Prince': both were played at such velocity and with such incredible precision that one or two writers actually asked Lars and James if the master tapes had been speeded up after recording.

'Harvester' is a slow song by Metallica standards, and is based on an almost catchy main riff which is extended in the song's central section into a fiendishly difficult showcase of the precision of the bandmembers, specifically James. When the song resumes after this complex segment, it does so on an off-beat that still throws the listener every time. This progressive edge continues on 'Frayed Ends Of Sanity', with its unexpected time change between the verse and the bridge.

'To Live Is To Die' is a mostly instrumental song, apart from some lines which James speaks and which had been written by Cliff Burton before his death: "When a man lies he murders some part of the world/

These are the pale deaths which men miscall their lives/All this I cannot bear to witness any longer/ Cannot the kingdom of salvation take me home?" Eerily prophetic perhaps, and certainly appropriate in the context of the song, which is a long, complex, multi-sectioned composition a little like 'Orion', a little like 'The Call Of Ktulu' and more developed than either.

Finally, Metallica spit out a 'Damage, Inc.'-like slab of high-speed fury to close the album, with 'Dyer's Eve', fast enough to qualify as the sole pure thrash metal composition on . . . *And Justice For All*, thanks to Lars' very speedy snare work and the frantic, muted power of the main riff, which comes in and out with satisfying unpredictability. Lyrically, the song is a rant from James to his parents ("I've outgrown that fucking lullaby!"), the first appearance of such a self-confession. His resentment is clear ("Do as I say, not as I do") and forms the basis for later, more focused songs such as 'Holier Than Thou', which were still a world away.

James' genuinely angry lyrics, which seemed to be based on his own troubled emotions, were extended on *Justice* from his own background to social ills in general. 'Blackened' dealt with the decay of the planet; the title song with government and other corrupt entities; 'One' with warfare and its consequences; and the other songs, to a lesser or greater degree, with the generally dismal state of the world. As we saw with *Puppets*, this refocusing of attention was slowly taking place throughout the thrash metal scene, with contemporaries such as Slayer beginning to deviate from the standard satanic fare to a more topical stance. (Slayer singer Tom Araya summed it up neatly when he gave me his view on society: "People are gonna keep on killing people – they're just gonna be more creative about it . . . Something very catastrophic is going to have to happen to wake people up and say, 'What the fuck are we doing?' ") But Metallica stood out from their colleagues on this issue, with Hetfield's anti-social vitriol appearing some time before the rest of the Big Four looked in that direction.

The record was certainly powerful. There were few negative points made about the music or lyrics of *Justice*. Which would mean that it's mostly perfect, right?

Wrong. The point that fans still make today, almost 15 years after it was released, is that it sounds strange. Very strange. As producer Flemming Rasmussen reflects now: "The sound was totally dry, totally in-your-face, and no reverb. Thin and hard and loud. It's unbelievably dry." To put it bluntly, it's ice-cold, with the guitars and bass drum offering a powerful mid-tempo tapestry, but there's no bass guitar, other than the occasionally audible plectrum click in less busy parts and a few ethereal rumbles behind the picked parts of 'One'. This was all the more surprising given that the *Garage Days* EP had featured a full-throated, brash bass presence from Jason Newsted which drove the songs forcefully along and which competed with Hetfield's always-enormous guitar presence. Why would he be reduced to nothing on the subsequent album, his first 'real' recording with his new band?

Not by accident, it seems. Rasmussen says: "They absolutely loved it when we had done it . . . but then about two or three months later, they realised, hmm, this might have been a bit over the top." The producer himself didn't mix the album – that was the job of professional mix team Steve Thompson and Michael Barbiero – but he knows how his recordings hung together on completion: "That album sounds almost 99 per cent the way they wanted it to be, but in retrospect we should have done it differently. I would have done it more like *Ride The Lightning*."

Ross Halfin tells the same tale. He explains: "I ended up liking Jason a lot. It was very much those three and him. On the *Justice* album there's no bass on it. This is a true story: there was one notch and Lars went, 'That's one notch too much,' and pressed it to zero when they were mixing it." In other words, Lars deliberately mixed Jason out of the album.

Why would Ulrich do such a thing? In 2001, well over a decade after this development, Jason explained exactly what happened on this album – and it's a revealing, not to say somewhat depressing, story.

"All the recording I'd done up until that point, including the *Garage Days* EP, was done in a couple of days," he says. "So I'm still just right in that pocket, and that's how I knew to record, right? That's what I knew. So I went in on *Justice*, and obviously there's still weird feelings going on. It was the first time we'd been in the studio for a real Metallica album, and Cliff's not there."

The Mike Clink versus Flemming Rasmussen changeover had made things a little confused, it seems, especially as the recording of Jason's bass parts fell squarely between the two men: "They're juggling producers. There's no order. And no authority to say, we need this producer doing this, at this time, to record that, to make that happen. Even though we had the money. Even though we had the support of the label. Even though we had a nice studio. And all that kinda thing. None of that was in order . . . I stepped in with an assistant engineer and I had my same gear that I would just play on the stage. There was no time taken about 'you place this microphone here, and this one will sound better than that, should we mix it with the DI, should we use this bass instead of that bass, should we get that tonality, should you use a pick, should you use your fingers? Any of the things that I know now, that make a really good bass sound. You plug in, you play the song. I could play 'em standing on my head with my eyes closed, any of those songs. I rehearsed those up the *ass*. Right?"

Newsted was on his own during recording, as he explains: "So I go in and I knock 'em out. Basically, doubling James' guitar parts. Because that's the kind of bass player I was then. Lars and James weren't around to say, 'You should try that there instead of that there.' Or a real producer or a manager, or anybody saying, 'That's OK.' I'd go in and record three or four songs in a day or an afternoon. I'd just sit there and knock it out. And there'd be mistakes and whatever. I'd just play it and that would be that. And, 'OK, you did good – bye!' "

Would he record this way today? "Usually nowadays I'd take one day per song. That's what I do on albums. So I allow myself to get in early, to get the sound you want, you go and you record all day to get that fit, that's what I allow myself. Now some guys take a lot longer, some guys take less time. But back then, I didn't even know anything about that shit. Just played it and that was that, right?"

On top of this was the bizarre scenario in which Metallica were performing on the Van Halen tour while mixing was going on. This contributed to the confusion, as Jason explains: "So then we get the offer to go on Monsters Of Rock in the summer, OK? And by the time they've bopped Mike Clink out of the producer's seat, and there's a void, and then Flemming comes in, my stuff's already on tape and put in the back and forgotten. We get to the mixing stage and no one is chosen for the mix. Still no order in that either. We go on this tour with Van Halen and Scorpions – the guys who *invented* partying, and all that shit . . . that was the first taste for us of dipping your foot in the actual scene of rock'n'roll, you know. So we're doing a few shows a week with those guys on that special festival – and on the days that we aren't, James and

Lars are flying to Bearsville, New York, to mix it with these two other cats [Thompson and Barbiero], right, that I never met in my life, and I had no idea at all."

The crunch is coming. With all this going on, it seems that Lars, James, or perhaps Lars *and* James, developed a single-minded attitude about the bass parts and did indeed order them turned down: "So they're partying, travelling back and forth, getting no sleep, going there early with kind of an attitude about the bass – *(whispers under his breath)* it's not Cliff, and yadda yadda – and they go in and tell the dudes, get the bass just where you can hear it, and then take it down a half a DB. Then turn all the frequency up on the guitars, and all that stuff. And then try to make the bass drum to fill in all the space so it can be all per-cussive and all that kind of thing. And that is why it is."

But Jason isn't bitter, although he was hurt at the time: "I've learned a lot from that. I was so in the dirt, I was so disappointed when I heard the final mix, I basically blocked it out, like people do with shit. We were firing on all cylinders, and shit was happening. I was just rolling with it and going forward. What was I gonna do, say we gotta go remix it, when we were down to the last minutes with people saying, we gotta say when, we gotta say when? And all that bullshit."

In fact, he learned from the experience, gained in confidence and knows now what Lars and James would say about the whole bass issue if we asked them about it today: "Now, if you were to ask them, now that they have time and they're fathers, you know, life, maturity . . . they would go, fuck. Whoops! They would say it right to your face."

He's right. In 2000 Kirk said to Twec.com that "I wish that we would have recorded . . . *And Justice For All* better. At the time it seemed like an interesting concept. But that album just doesn't sound good to me nowadays. I love the songs, but the way it sounds is funky. Funky as in bad, not funky as in groovy." Ross Halfin says simply: "I think to this day Lars is embarrassed by the record because there is no bass on it."

Flemming Rasmussen, a very relaxed individual, attributes the lack of bass on *Justice* to several factors: "Lars and James being the only band-members present in the mix room would probably account for that. Drums up, and guitars up. And Jason was brand new, so for most of his bass parts he's playing the guitar line in unison, so he's basically just a part of the guitar sound. The fact that there was so much bass on the *Garage Days* EP was because they didn't multi-layer all the guitar parts, which leaves room for the bass. In order for it to sound bigger you have to hear all the instruments. But again, I didn't mix that. The mix guy was hired when I was flown in. At the time I liked it, I could see where they were going. I kinda missed the bass in a lot of the songs. Maybe they just forgot to worry about the bass. I think it's a great album. It's extremely tight, it took days and days to get it that tight. I did tons of editing on it, just to get the drum parts to be 100 per cent. They're perfectionists, but then so am I when it's necessary."

All this work paid off for all those involved, it appears. Flemming became a known metal producer, going on to work with Morbid Angel among others ("In international terms it's been difficult to come out of just being known as the guy who produced Metallica, but not domestically. It hasn't been that bad. I got a Grammy in 1992 for a Danish band called Black Sun," he explains), while the cover art for the album, which had been created by a writer and artist called Brian Schroeder (aka Pushead) gave this whole era of Metallica's career an identity. And, in true Metallica fashion, the enormous Damaged Justice tour which followed made them very well known indeed, taking the band to almost all corners of the globe and bringing their patented brand of mayhem to the masses with an apparently unstoppable force.

Famously, the crumbling statue of Lady Justice which adorned the sleeve of *AJFA* was replicated for the Damaged Justice stage set: the huge, 20-foot-high statue was designed to fall to pieces during the show, a move which emulated the onstage excesses of other rock acts (Dio's dragon; Motörhead's bomber plane; Parliament's 'mothership') but with no theatrical stupidity, only simplicity. Crowds loved the concept and the tour, which commenced on September 11, 1988, was a legendary jaunt. Initially Metallica were supported by Danzig, on whose songs 'Twist Of Cain', 'Possession' and 'Am I Demon?' James performed backing vocals.

The tour began in Hungary and moved rapidly through Italy, Switzerland, Spain, France and the UK and Ireland (no fewer than 14 dates, one of which the author, at the time a callow 17-year-old, is proud to have attended). At this point the support slot was taken by Queensryche, whose proto-prog-metal complemented the advanced nature of the new Metallica material perfectly. Moving on through Denmark, Finland, Sweden, Norway, Germany, Belgium, France and

Germany again, and Holland, the European tour wound up on November 5 and after ten days' rest and recuperation, resumed in North America. This time Ohio, Illinois, Wisconsin, Indiana, Michigan, Missouri, Oklahoma, New Mexico, Arizona and California were the first states to feel the Metallica whiplash as autumn became winter. Dates in Utah and Colorado were completed by December 18, when the tour took time off for Christmas.

Or almost took time off, that is. In early December Metallica took the (for them, at least) unprecedented step of filming a professional video, to accompany the single 'One', which itself had been remixed down to a more palatable length for TV. The response from some fans was uncertain: hadn't Metallica always said that videos were a waste of money, and that to make one would be to sell out? In fact, no: although the 'One' clip was functional rather than scintillating (it oscillated between the band headbanging earnestly in a rehearsal room and shots of a limbless man taken from the movie *Johnny Got His Gun*), it was made to serve a purpose – to give the music TV channels something to play alongside the song – rather than to glamorise or lionise the band themselves.

After a genuine break, the Damaged Justice tour rolled on into 1989. After a Spastik Children show in Oakland, the 'real' band rehearsed in Tennessee before heading on to Alabama, Louisiana, Texas, Oklahoma, Arkansas, Florida, Georgia and North Carolina. On February 22 a milestone event took place: Metallica were nominated for a Grammy, with the ceremony due to take place at the Shrine Auditorium in LA. In a first for a thrash metal act, the band were asked to perform at the show, and chose to play 'One' there, a move which astounded both their hardcore fans (who had not expected such a thing to occur in their lifetimes) and non-metal fans (for whom the blast of power at the end of the song was equally unexpected). On the night, however, Metallica's nomination (in the Best Heavy Metal category) went, thanks to the ridiculous decision of the Grammy committee, to folk-rockers Jethro Tull. This was a sure sign of the confusion which categories such as heavy metal and hard rock were causing certain members of the industry, and a decision which seems almost unbelievable from this many years' distance. Not that Hetfield and Co. seemed to mind: they simply added a sticker marked 'Grammy Award Losers' to some pressings of the *Justice* album.

And so the tour rolled on, with its next targets North Carolina, Georgia, New Jersey, Pennsylvania, New York, Maryland, Virginia, Massachusetts, Connecticut, Rhode Island, Maine and then Canada (Nova Scotia, Ontario, Quebec). By now it was April, and the Queensryche support slot ended after final shows in Michigan, Ohio, Illinois, Wisconsin and Minnesota. On April 21 Metallica bid farewell to their long-time tour-mates and rested for a couple of days before taking the longest flight of all: to New Zealand, which would mark the start of the biggest and most exhausting leg of the Justice tour yet. Support on the ensuing shows would be provided by The Cult.

Concerts in New Zealand, Australia, Japan, Hawaii and Alaska saw Metallica play their clean, economical metal to audiences of all stripes, before they resumed the well-trodden path through British Columbia, Alberta, Saskatchewan, Manitoba, North Dakota, Minnesota, Iowa, South Dakota, Nebraska, North Dakota, Kansas, Illinois, Wisconsin, Indiana, Kentucky, Michigan, Ohio, West Virginia, Pennsylvania, New York, New Hampshire, Connecticut, New Jersey, Massachusetts, Vermont and Maryland. At the last of these shows, on July 28 in Londover, Jason gave an interview to two reporters from the MetalWorx radio station. Asked if he had felt that any expectations had to be met when he joined Metallica, he answered: "Well, naturally somebody had to be able to be strong enough to take on what was about to happen. Not just somebody that could play but somebody that also was able to take it mentally as far as taking Cliff's place, living up to all the people in the family and all the crew people and all. There was 40 or 45 people tried out and they wanted to find someone that could take it in all aspects, you know."

On the *Garage Days* EP he said: "We just started messing with a bunch of cover songs, and they were pretty cool, and we hadn't had a producer out for a while, so we just said, you know, fuck, this sounds pretty cool, why don't we just do it and put it out? In one day, I did all tracks in four hours or something. I just blew 'em out. Just for silliness, and that's pretty much how it came out too, and you could tell it was done just to be silly," before addressing the subject of *Justice*, which he explained had been mostly composed before his recruitment. He wanted to write more, however: "We get all our tapes together and whoever comes up with the coolest shit, that's obviously the stuff we're going to use, whatever is the most appealing stuff . . . James comes up with some pretty sick shit you know, and so does Kirk, so it's just a matter [of writing] cooler stuff than them." Revealingly, Jason also explained that his favourite Metallica song is Cliff's showpiece, 'Orion': "I can't play it worth shit. The lead bass line in that, and I've heard it 700 thousand times, every time I hear it, it still gives me huge goose bumps."

The Damaged Justice tour still wasn't over, but the end was now in sight, and with it the cessation of activities for 1989. Three months of touring through Pennsylvania, Virginia, Delaware (the last of these a fan club members-only show, a first for Metallica), Tennessee, Ohio, South Carolina, Georgia, Mississipi, Texas, Colorado, Washington, Oregon, Idaho, Montana, Wyoming, Utah, Nevada, Arizona and California proved to be the necessary dose of metal for the USA, and after September and October dates in Brazil the rolling machine finally, *finally* ground to a halt.

The dust settled, and there was an eerie silence from Metallica. Where the air had been filled with enormous power chords, James Hetfield's primal roar and the raging percussion of the ever-enthusiastic Ulrich, now there came no sound at all. Metallica, it seemed, were finally having a rest.

The stillness continued for some months. The Damaged Justice tour, which had evolved into a Frankenstein's monster of some serious power, had drained all the personnel involved, like some freakish, metallic bloodsucker: and now, it seemed, was the time to recuperate.

Nothing was heard from any member of Metallica until January 1990, when it was suddenly announced that the band would be recording a cover song for a compilation album celebrating Elektra Records' fortieth anniversary. The concept was simple: the label's artists would record a song by another label artist. Metallica chose to record a version of Queen's 'Stone Cold Crazy', a precise, knowingly over-the-top composition on whose original version singer Freddie Mercury had excelled, with theatrics in line with his usual act and muscular riffing from guitarist Brian May. The song seemed perfect for Metallica.

And yet their version is strangely lifeless. The stop-on-a-dime riffs, the powerhouse drumming and even Mercury's camp squeals were reproduced dully, almost crankily, by Metallica. This failure to match up was a first for them. Was something wrong with them? Had the previous year's tour taken too much of their energy? Whatever the truth, 'Stone Cold Crazy' is just that: stone cold.

Other than a Spastik Children show on January 8, and an appearance at the Grammys the following month, in which Metallica won an award for 'One' (and thanked Jethro Tull "for not releasing anything this year"), the first few months of the Nineties continued to be quiet. A sense that a chapter had finished, while another was waiting to begin, was definitely in the air: many metal fans were enjoying the music of bands other than Metallica while they waited for their heroes to regroup after the excesses of Justice. Some, in particular, were focusing their attention towards Seattle, where a new rock movement was growing. If you listened carefully, the sound coming from the city could almost be taken as a mixture of classic metal riffs, punk aggression and production, and pop choruses.

But in May 1990, stirrings of activity could be detected in the Metallica camp. On May 19 a box set called *The Good, The Bad & The Live* was released in the UK, containing two previously released 12″ singles together with live songs. It climbed to an unspectacular number 56 but alerted the British fanbase that Metallica activity was growing. A series of festival appearances was also announced, and on May 11 they performed a secret gig as 'Vertigo', supporting Metal Church at London's Marquee, followed by shows in Holland, Germany, France and the UK, supported by Warrior Soul. Two stadium shows with Aerosmith followed: on June 29 in Toronto and the following night at the Silver Stadium in New York.

Something had rejuvenated the Metallica musicians, it seemed: perhaps some musical discovery, or a renewed enthusiasm. Lars even assembled a moderately well-received metal compilation album called *NWOBHM Revisited*, which featured songs by Diamond Head and Iron Maiden and was issued in time to celebrate a decade since the movement's peak.

But 1990 was largely a quiet year for Metallica, even if a hum of concentration could be detected around the band as summer became autumn. In October, they vanished for good into the studio, where they intended to put together a new album. Apart from a November 9 appearance at a Hollywood Palladium party to celebrate the launch of *Rip* magazine, at which Lars, James and Kirk jammed with Axl Rose, Slash and Duff McKagan of Guns N'Roses and Sebastian Bach of Skid Row (under the collective name Gak), that was all the world would hear of Metallica for several months.

Once locked in the studio, Metallica gave few signals to the world of what was happening inside. But rumours began to fly. Some said that the new album would be a departure for them like no record they had made before. What form this music might take was unknown, but the anticipation began to build. And this time, it seemed, the music which Metallica were making might even overpower its creators.

17

The Truth About The Black Album

Myth 8: *Metallica* **is variously Metallica's best, worst, best-sounding, best-produced, sell-out, breakthrough or definitive album.**
Myth 9: The album changed the face of metal.
Myth 10: The album is massively overrated.

Metallica's self-titled album of 1991 attracted enormous amounts of attention, with both positive and negative reviews flying around for years after its appearance. The album turned Metallica into bona fide rock stars and alerted millions of hitherto uncommitted people to the existence of music called 'heavy metal'. So many people who love Metallica (the band) think *Metallica* (the album) is either excellent or terrible, which makes it hard to discuss rationally.

Let's take facts before opinions. *Metallica*, the 12-song album which was recorded and mixed between October 6, 1990 and June 16, 1991, emerged on August 12, 1991 with a plain black sleeve, other than the slightly lighter-coloured details of the band's logo and a coiled snake. It was referred to as the Black Album almost immediately: Lars hinted initially that within the band the record might be labelled 'the snake album', although this apparently did not come to pass. The album credits stated that recording had taken place at One On One Recording Studios in North Hollywood, LA, with the production "by Bob Rock with Hetfield & Ulrich" and the actual recording executed by Randy Staub and his assistant Mike Tacci.

The choice of Bob Rock as producer was immediately controversial. Rock, a veteran who had produced mainstream (or at least, defiantly non-extreme) albums by The Cult, Aerosmith and Mötley Crüe – and in doing so had become known for the crisp, bass-heavy sound he specialised in – was hardly a thrash metal producer. . . . *And Justice For All* had been a progressive album, for sure, but it contained sufficient elements of thrash for Metallica still to claim a place at the mellower end of extreme metal. The news that Rock had been selected to produce a Metallica record was a shock for their older fans.

It emerged that Metallica had in fact been cautious about their choice of producer. Flemming Rasmussen, who had so memorably produced their last three albums – and who had saved . . . *And Justice For All* from the Mike Clink fiasco – was asked to remain on standby at the start of the Black Album sessions, just in case the Rock set-up didn't pay off. "They actually paid me to take a month's vacation at the start of the Black Album, in case it didn't work out with Bob Rock," remarks Rasmussen. "We'd done that with *Justice* and they didn't want to end up in a situation like they had before, where they were stuck and couldn't go any further. I was on vacation in Denmark, it was cool. But that album went on for a year and a half . . . I think I would have killed them by the end of that time!"

However, the Rock and Metallica partnership seemed to be workable (although the producer had surprised Lars at an early meeting by observing that the band had never managed to capture their live energy on record – a remark that evidently struck the drummer as a little presumptuous) and sessions commmenced. And continued. And kept going . . . in fact, the nine-month-long recording and mixing of the album was another head-scratching aspect of its creation. How could a single album take so long to complete?

The germ of an answer lies in an interview which Metallica had given to *Thrasher* back in 1987, after the *Puppets* sessions. Asked why their recording sessions took so long, Hammett responded: "You have to live with it, and that's brutal. If you make mistakes in the studio and it goes to vinyl, you have to live with that mistake for the next year and a half to two years. We just don't want to do that." James clarified: "It wasn't that we were making mistakes and shit in the studio, it was getting sounds together. Lars was being way too fucking picky. Like, the snare would always be going out of tune, this much out of tune, 'OK hold on,' so he'd bang for another hour tuning the snare and then go in and bash." However, James may have been a little uncharitable to Lars in saying this: he himself was a meticulous perfectionist, adding layers of guitar to various tracks with famously time-consuming accuracy: "I did most of the songs with three rhythm tracks," he explained, "one on each side and one down the middle."

This obsessive approach, mostly the province of Lars and James (Jason was at this stage a fast worker – remember the speed of his tracking on *Justice*? – and Kirk, while interested in detail, was recording only solos, after all), was the primary reason for the length of the sessions. Ulrich in particular would record like a man possessed, coming into the studio in the late afternoon and continuing to work into the early hours of the morning. This drive continued into the mixing stage: reportedly, the album was completely remixed no fewer than three times. In fact, after so long in the studio, the final mix was only completed just before the deadline for mastering and pressing arrived. Rock recalled later that when he, James and Lars finally finished their work, they went to a bar to celebrate but were too dog-tired to do more than simply drink in silence.

After all this work, what had they achieved? Let's examine *Metallica*, track by track.

The first track, 'Enter Sandman', would be voted the Best Heavy Metal Song Of All Time in a *Kerrang!* readers' poll. Opening with a sinister, picked intro rather like that of 'Harvester Of Sorrow' (it's interesting to note that all Metallica's albums, up to and including this one, begin either with a clean intro such as this or a fade-in), the song soon resolves to a simple, Hammett-penned riff of superb immediacy and simplicity. It's this riff which makes the song, along with the cyclical chorus and the bludgeoning, E and F pattern that underpins the verses.

James sings of childhood nightmares and horror – "Never mind that noise you heard/ It's just the beast under your bed/ In your closet, in your head" – with a satisfyingly dark, gleeful tone. In the middle section, Kirk's wah-laden solo prefaces a spoken-word section in which James intones a 'Now I lay me down to sleep' prayer, which is repeated by a child's voice: a new departure for Metallica but one which helped propel the song, which was released as a single two days before the album appeared, to number 5 in the UK – a previously unimaginable feat. 'Enter Sandman' is catchy, energetic, deftly constructed with a deliberate less-is-more ethos and heavy enough to keep most old-school fans satisfied. However, it is also relatively slow, and was the first blow to the hopes of Metallica's thrash-based fans that *Metallica* might be a fast album. However you take your helping of 'Sandman', you have to admit that it's memorable.

The next song, 'Sad But True', was less palatable to the masses and a slight breath of air for established fans, who realised (perhaps with a slightly sinking feeling at this stage) that if Metallica were no longer interested in being speedy, they were still very much into being heavy. James downtuned significantly, allowing Rock to take his riffs and layer them to the point of crushing weightiness. But the groove of the riff, which made the choruses' opening lines of "I'm your dream, make you real" or "I'm your dream, mind astray" stick so firmly in the listeners' consciousnesses, was a factor the song has in common with 'Enter Sandman': this knack which Metallica had evolved of creating hooks to be remembered, despite the power of the songs that surrounded them, was the first, and most obvious, reason why the album was so popular.

'Holier Than Thou', on the other hand, was destined never to be a radio single, although (like Moby's *Play*, released eight years later) at some point or other every song on this album was played on main-stream radio stations at some point or other. Built around an urgent, driving riff and showcasing the first real lyrical venom of the album, the first lines "No more! The crap rolls out your mouth again" are barked by Hetfield with obvious passion and appear to be aimed at the religious do-gooders reflected in the title, which itself is sung with an extended howl from James. A slightly odd song because of this un-expected melody, it found favour with newer fans simply because it veers close to the hard-to-pinpoint line between rock and metal, despite the fact that it's faster than the two songs which precede it.

'The Unforgiven' was a complete surprise to many fans. It's an impassioned, heartfelt radio ballad with an effective pop awareness that is too sugary for many metallers' tastes but which the new fans who flocked to Metallica's side on the album's release loved. Here, for the first time, James showcased a much softer, crooned singing style which divided the band's fanbase: the thrash fans had problems accepting this departure, but others enjoyed it and regarded the new step as a success-ful experiment. His older style prevailed in the verses, however, with the new method being confined, more or less, to the lines "What I've felt/ What I've known/ Never shined through in what I've shown". Other lyrics such as "New blood joins this earth/ And quickly he's

205

subdued/ Through constant pained disgrace/ The young boy learns their rules" would appear to be aimed at the childhood traumas James had hinted at as far back as 'Dyer's Eve' and on this album's 'Holier Than Thou', although this has never been confirmed. Either way, a self-absorbed, almost confessional theme was starting to emerge in Hetfield's writing – and in fact the next two songs on *Metallica* also refer to the self.

'Wherever I May Roam' has an almost epic feel to it, although musically it isn't particularly grandiose or overblown: Hetfield sings of 'the road' becoming his bride, and that the narrative concerns a "rover, wanderer, nomad, vagabond" whose burden is one of constant travel. It's a concept song rather than one aimed at the fanbase with a hook to offer, and its title and theme would be utilised in the names of the long tours which followed.

However, 'Don't Tread On Me' is much more direct and focused: its message, rather like that of Jimi Hendrix's version of 'The Star Spangled Banner', has been debated endlessly, largely because some listeners viewed it as a patriotic song and others believed it to be quite the opposite. Its title is the motto of an American fighting force, the Minutemen of Culpeper County, Virginia, who use it on a white flag bearing an image of a rattlesnake and the slogan 'Liberty Or Death'. Some of James' lyrics would certainly seem to indicate some pro-American sentiment ("Liberty or death, what we so proudly hail/ Once you provoke her, rattling of her tail") and echo the Minutemen's famous policy of neither initiating violence nor backing down once it has begun ("Never begins it, never, but once engaged/ Never surrenders, showing the fangs of rage"). 'Don't Tread On Me' was the first significantly political (and politicised) song which James had written, and notable for its reversal of polarity when compared with the strongly anti-establishment sentiments of songs such as '. . . And Justice For All'.

Musically, the song is based on a chromatic progression, and contains one of *Metallica*'s few complex sections when Hammett's solo cuts in. Until this point the album has been simple and direct, with few of the intricacies that had typified the previous three records: this song contains a reminder, perhaps, that we are dealing with a phenomenally talented set of songwriters. The moderately speedy (but not thrash) riff which introduces 'Through The Never' reinforces this point: that Metallica could play fast and complex if they wanted to, but chose not to do so for most of this record. A relatively short song at just over four minutes, 'Through The Never' reverts to this moderately gripping riff periodically and is by far the most 'traditional' Metallica song here, although as the whole record is a departure in itself from their old style, the term is strictly relative.

Like 'Fade To Black', 'Sanitarium' and 'One' before it, 'Nothing Else Matters' is this album's token ballad, although 'The Unforgiven' could count as one also. A slow, picked love song of unabashed honesty and vulnerability, it split the fans' opinions more radically than any other tune here. This is because for the first time ever, Metallica resort to orchestral backing. Previously the province of dinosaur rock acts with overblown ambitions, the pairing of orchestra and rock band is one which must be handled with subtlety and humility if an air of ostentation is to be avoided – but in this case the strings, arranged by veteran classical conductor and producer Michael Kamen, do not intrude on the song, which builds to a climax dominated more by James (who, in a rare move, took the guitar solo slot from Kirk) rather than the accompaniment itself.

Some Metallica fans genuinely hated 'Nothing Else Matters' and continue to regard it to this day as the start of a slippery slope for a band that had previously been so proud of its status at the forefront of heavy, confrontational, fast music. It was certainly a surprise, not least when it became known that newly-wed couples were asking for the song to be performed at their wedding celebrations. Metallica, leaders of the Big Four Of Thrash Metal – wedding-night favourites?

Love it or loathe it, 'Nothing Else Matters' irrevocably altered the texture of the album which maintains its fog of introspection with a darker, more thoughtful atmosphere than the crisp 'Enter Sandman' and the bright-as-day vitriol of 'Don't Tread On Me'. 'Of Wolf And Man' is a reflection on seeing through the eyes of a werewolf, with James enunciating observations such as "Bright is the moon high in starlight/ Chill in the air cold as steel tonight": perhaps one of the first reflections of Hetfield's growing interest in hunting, but with a supernatural touch worthy of the oldest-school Metallica lyric. 'The God That Failed' returns to the theme of corrupt or unreliable faith and its associated agonies, with James' grim observation that "Broken is the promise, betrayal/ The healing hand held back by the deepened nail." Neither song is musically remarkable within the album itself, standing rather as the trademark-bearers of *Metallica*; the songs by which the album can be recognised, rather than compositions which call for attention among the 11 others here.

'My Friend Of Misery' is more individual, with Jason Newsted's chorded bass guitar intro segueing into a layered, considered riff that carries a notable degree of lyrical venom. Hetfield appears to be addressing some unidentified figure who insists that gloom and depression are to be valued rather than avoided. It emerged some years later that Jason's intro was several minutes long and that he had hoped it would stay that way but this was not to be, although he retained it for his solo spot in the subsequent live shows. Finally, 'The Struggle Within', which clocks in at an almost single-friendly four minutes, closes *Metallica* with a final gritted-teeth wail from James of "What the hell/ What is it you think you're gonna find?"

So what conclusion should we reach about this album of contradictions? After all, this was a record of definite heaviness ('Sad But True', 'Through The Never') and slick, bantamweight balladry ('The Unforgiven', 'Nothing Else Matters'); an album of lyrical fortitude ('Don't Tread On Me') and introspection ('Of Wolf And Man'), and while still recognisably Metallica, a whole new direction for this most individual of bands.

Perhaps the simple truth is this: *Metallica*, while it contained its uncompromising moments, was a good, well-crafted heavy rock record rather than a metal record. It sounded clean, cared-for and thought-out: radio and TV loved it, fans worshipped it, even non-metal fans turned towards it, thanks to its sound. Bob Rock had certainly earned his fee, bringing a sigh of relief to fans of Newsted with its bass-to-the-fore production. Lars explained it in a way that even vindicated Jason's endurance of the *AJFA* issue: "With Jason I guess we misfired on *Justice*, but this time around I didn't want to make the same mistake again, so very early on we steered the bass more towards the drum kit and away from the guitar a little." He added that he and James had never really known how to place bass before: "I guess the bass guitar has always been this weird instrument in the band, it's always been overlooked because [Cliff] was always off on Planet 9. I mean, there were always times when me and James would try and get Cliff to adapt his bass playing a little differently, but Cliff was Cliff and he just did it in his own way and that was that."

Flemming Rasmussen says of *Metallica*: "It *is* a good album. The big difference on *Metallica* is that James is actually singing, and he'd never done that before, and also the songs were just one riff instead of about 25 riffs in seven-minute songs." Respected metal producer Andy Sneap comments: "I thought the Black Album was great. I think they needed to mature as a band after . . . *And Justice For All*. I actually think Bob Rock was one of the best things that happened to them. Everything that Bob Rock does, the vocals are – rightly – the main focus. When 'Sad But True' kicks in in a nightclub it still sounds amazing. It has the snare drum from hell!"

Journalist Borivoj Krgin recalls: "I heard this album a few weeks before it came out at the offices of Elektra Records in New York, and I was very impressed by it. At first, it was weird hearing Metallica playing songs that were arranged in a more traditional way (verse, chorus, verse, chorus, lead, etc.) but the strength of the material once again shone through. The production was by far the best they'd ever had up until that point – all credit to Bob Rock – and there were plenty of classic cuts on there, including 'Sad But True', 'Wherever I May Roam', 'Unforgiven' and 'Nothing Else Matters'. I suppose 'Enter Sandman' was as well, but I became sick of this song after hearing it for the millionth time. Again, it was the right record at the right time, and once again, Metallica were ahead of everyone else when they decided to streamline their sound and make it easier to digest by the masses. I remember other bands – particularly Testament – struggling to make the same change in their sound after the Black Album was released, but they didn't have the same songwriting skills as Metallica, obviously, to pull it off, and ultimately Testament's strength lay in the more aggressive, heavier material."

But fans will never agree about the Black Album. It's just such a huge presence that fans and non-fans alike will continue to talk about it for decades, and when people exchange opinions, sparks fly. This is how its legacy will remain alive. And it continues to raise so many issues, even among those who don't understand why it is so loved and hated: for example, Diamond Head guitarist Brian Tatler was one of the select few who heard demos of the new material before the album's release – and his reaction was cautious rather than committed: "In 1990 I stopped over at Lars' house in LA and he introduced me to Bob Rock. He also played me some demos of the songs, 'Sad But True' and so on.

At the time it was just James singing 'wah-wah-wah' on each track, just drums and guitar. And I was wondering how this was going to sell!"

Writer Martin Popoff shares this lack of enthusiasm: "I didn't like the Black Album at all. I thought that was where they screwed up. It's just boring and slow. It's not innovative, it's not recorded all that well, for all that painstaking crap they went through with Bob Rock. It's just there. It's a competent recording and nothing more. It's not brave, interesting, or different. It doesn't even sound very, very produced . . . The best song on it was the advance single, 'Enter Sandman', so you could imagine my let-down when I got to hear the whole album."

Music fans are notoriously guilty of over-intellectualising their music, too. Perhaps *Metallica* should be regarded simply as a piece of music, not a high art statement. Deep Purple's Ian Gillan once told me that some songs simply don't require analysing: "We were on stage performing 'Black Night' last year, and Roger Glover said to me, 'What the fuck is that song actually about?' I suppose it must have meant something profound at the time. But a lot of songs are misunderstood." It's the same for Metallica and every other band, too. After all, this is the band that specialised in keeping things simple, even when they developed those initial ideas to more complex levels. Seasoned musicians respect this less-is-more approach, as Cult guitarist Billy Duffy says: "I took a perverse pride from writing as many Top 20 singles as I did using the same three chords. Metallica did it and AC/DC did it too."

Other musicians watched and learned from what happened to Metallica in the wake of the Black Album, some with disapproval (Phil Fasciana of Malevolent Creation: "They had a loyal following for a long time, but when they released *Metallica* they just blew up into mainstream music and became more acceptable to everyone. I personally gave up on them after that album. They are merely a rock band now") but others with slightly grudging respect. (Jeff Waters of Annihilator: "You gotta respect what they did from the Black Album onwards; great business moves and an emphasis on a killer live show and selling lots of CDs. And writing more sellable/commercial songs. It sounds like Bob Rock showed them the way and they followed brilliantly!")

The other point which must be remembered in any analysis of *Metallica* is its timing. It appeared just as the tides in mainstream music were turning, especially in metal. At this exact point, the summer of 1991, thrash metal was an ailing movement, with only Slayer of the Big Four staying true to their speed roots. Also, a new breed of metal fan had begun to appear in recent months, not reared on a diet of boastful Deep Purple-like rock, or even the gleefully malignant likes of Venom (whose sense of humour runs deep in their music) but on wilfully miserable, pessimistic music such as doom and death metal. Jonas Renkse, of the experimental Swedish death metallers Katatonia, is one such, whose current music reflects this. Yes, he listened to Metallica and the Big Four, but his roots were darker and more gothic: "I listened mainly to Paradise Lost, which I liked because it was gloomy. I was a big goth when I was younger, with the black hair and so on." People like Renkse would grow up to be fans of Nineties-style 'new' metal, with his roots in traditional thrash, as he recalls: "When I was about 13, the first time I heard thrash was when a friend of mine had a tape of *Reign In Blood*, which we thought was a joke because it was so hard. But as time went on I borrowed it more and more and then I started to feel like a pervert because I liked it so much."

However, many of the old guard respected Metallica's new direction. Celtic Frost's Thomas Gabriel Fischer observes: "Metallica made it so big because their music was perhaps the ideal development of heavy rock for the Eighties and early Nineties. They were also an extremely professional band, and I mean that as an unreserved compliment. Their music was tough, precise, and rigorous, and James was a perfect front man for it. He was a star, but he still could be perceived as one of the crowd." Whiplash drummer Tony Scaglione adds: "The thing that I always respected about Metallica is that they tried something different with each of their albums and allowed their sound to mature. This is a major point of dissatisfaction with many of Metallica's older fans, but I feel it is their strong point."

Metallica knew, it seems, that some of their older fans were feeling deprived of the adrenaline burst of speed which they had pioneered. Newsted told the press, with a degree of wisdom beyond his years, that: "I can appreciate the people who want us only to go fast. If you dig those bands, please buy their records and see their shows so we can keep it alive – but don't disrespect the people who paved the way and broke down the doors for so many of the groups you enjoy now. One of the bands that played a big part in that was Metallica. We're the guys

211

that wrote 'Damage, Inc.', 'Fight Fire With Fire', 'Whiplash' . . . you name it, we helped invent it. And we can still play it better than anyone. I'll go up against any death metal band – pound for pound, hour for hour, we'll crush 'em. I have great respect for them, but those are the facts."

But there's one more factor in the *Metallica* puzzle which makes it important, and that is the simple fact that its release, while a landmark event which made an enormous impact, was not the most significant event of 1991 in rock terms. On September 24 – only 43 days after the Black Album landed squarely on the charts – a Seattle trio named Nirvana released their second album, *Nevermind*. And while *Metallica* announced that heavy metal was now due to come of age, *Nevermind* trumped it by insisting that the death-knell for metal was about to be rung at any moment.

"Grunge," sighs The Cult's Billy Duffy. "It was a bit like a plague, wasn't it? A lot of bands got wiped out. Good thing too. It's like there was rock'n'roll, teddy boys, then mod, then psych. It's natural." Natural selection, it seemed, applied to metal too: by the Nineties, hair-metal in particular had proliferated to the point of saturation, with the movement refusing to mature with its fanbase. Quite simply, grunge killed them off, like a dose of musical bleach (pun intended) injected into the clogged-up drains of rock. And it wasn't just Nirvana and their big-league contemporaries Pearl Jam, Soundgarden and Alice In Chains which slew the metal beast: 1991 was an incredibly fertile year for rock and its associated genres, with landmark releases from the Red Hot Chili Peppers (their own 'Black Album', *Blood Sugar Sex Magik*, saw them go stratospheric in its wake), Guns N'Roses (whose *Use Your Illusion* albums, released simultaneously, saw them fly above the hair-metal cull with ease), U2 and Primal Scream. Meanwhile, key albums from the KLF, De La Soul, Public Enemy, Blur, Cypress Hill and Mercury Rev kept the flag flying for the hip-hop and indie scenes as well as the nascent dance movement.

As Kirk Hammett rather snootily pointed out some years later, "When we were making *Metallica*, nobody even knew who the fuck Kurt Cobain was," but that situation changed rapidly. Only the strongest metal bands survived the grunge wave, which, as Slipknot drummer Joey Jordison says, had a negative effect on the scene: "When that whole scene came in, it was supposed to make music more open-minded, but it made it more closed-minded than ever. I really think it did. I can't stand Pearl Jam – I've never been a fan of them – and Alice In Chains was always a metal band in hiding, with a grunge umbrella."

Labels or not, the more intelligent metal acts knew the game was up as a portion of their fanbase 'went grunge'. Bobby Ellsworth of Over Kill says that the only thing which kept his band going was sheer perseverance: "We were dead in 1991, we knew that. Someone said, 'Metal's dead and so are fuckin' Over Kill!' But out of ignorance or determination I kept us going. Grunge came in and deposed so many of the bands that were here, which was a thriving scene, but we looked at that as an opportunity." He explains how the change had to come, in any case: "Change is necessary to cleanse the scene. What happens with any scene is that there is a handful of bands in a genre or subgenre, and later there comes an over-saturation of bands. The record companies are the perpetrators because they wanna get in. In our movement, metal, there were so many bands who came on and wanted to be Def Leppard that the scene had to be cleansed."

Metallica's return to the simple heaviness of traditional metal, but housed in digestible, not over-complex songs, enabled them to escape the killing field of grunge and keep them afloat: and not merely afloat, but standing head and shoulders above every other metal act apart from the obvious untouchables, Guns N'Roses and Iron Maiden. Even stalwarts such as Judas Priest and Motörhead went through a lean period in the early Nineties, while other giant acts such as Bon Jovi survived by moving into rock territory. This simplicity, it emerged, had come through in the production of *Metallica*, with Kirk – the one Metallica member whose style was supremely technical in an old-style metal sense – taking giant strides into the new decade: "Guitar players in the Nineties seem to be reacting against the technique-oriented Eighties," he told *Guitar World*. "Basically I just had to say, screw everyone around me, from now on I'm just gonna play what I think is important to me and our music. So I gave the big finger to all the current trends for technical wizardry, and just went off and did what I felt was best for the songs." Hammett had also diversified a little, guesting with funk-metallers Primus on December 11, 1990 at a Portland show where he played on 'Tommy The Cat' and a cover of 'Master Of Puppets'.

So, to bust those myths: is *Metallica* Metallica's best album? As I see it, not at all: the first four are better by a long way. But apart from *Kill 'Em All*, which spawned a million imitators, it's certainly their most influential, even taking into account the mighty *Master Of Puppets*.

Does *Metallica* boast the finest sound the band have ever achieved? Again – and despite the gargantuan effort which they and producer Bob Rock put into it – I'd say no. *Ride* and *Puppets* are cleaner, smoother and subtler. Even the *Garage Days* EP is more atmospheric. *Metallica* simply sounds professional.

Did *Metallica* change the face of metal? Undoubtedly – *but in context*. Grunge was metal's Grim Reaper: the Black Album simply showed metal fans (and metal bands) how to survive its appearance.

Did *Metallica* bring metal to the masses? Yes; but what is more, it attracted the masses to metal. Its power should not be underestimated. Even today, some of those songs are unforgettable.

Is *Metallica* overrated? By many, yes. But its place in history is assured – and whether or not 20 million record buyers can be wrong is something that you, not me, will have to decide for yourself.

The first six months of 1991 were quiet, but busy, for Metallica and their crew. A super-tour the likes of which had not been seen for some years was being organised in the backroom of Metallica's offices, and the recording and mixing of the album was still to be completed. The band surfaced once in February, when they were awarded a Best Metal Performance Grammy for their version of 'Stone Cold Crazy', but otherwise they were out of the public eye until July, when announcements of a new single and album were made to the press.

On July 30 the video clip of 'Enter Sandman' was premiered. Directed by Bon Jovi videographer Wayne Isham (who had won an MTV Video Vanguard Award for his work with the New Jersey quintet), the video was dark, disturbing and bleak, depicting the song (and the band) as a nightmare experienced by a young boy, who finds himself at the end of the dream running away from a mysterious juggernaut which is pursuing him. Two days later the first show of the enormous Wherever I May Roam Tour took place at the Phoenix Theater in Petaluma, California. Of the 13-song set of Metallica standards, only 'Enter Sandman' (the opener – a wise choice given that it was about to be released as a single) and 'Sad But True' appeared from the new album. After a second night at Petaluma, the band flew to Europe for a series of dates. An August 10 show took place at the Gentofte Stadium on Copenhagen – 'Enter Sandman' was released the same day – and was the last concert before the release of *Metallica* two days later.

The hysteria which surrounded the release of the album was unprecedented, at least in heavy metal terms. Many retailers opened their doors at one minute past midnight on August 12, with crowds of metal fans surging in to buy the album. Unbelievably for a band whose first video had received only borderline attention three years before, *Metallica* shifted 600,000 units in the first week in the USA alone. It debuted at number one on the *Billboard* Pop Album Chart and stayed there for a month.

No doubt delighted with this news but perhaps slightly unnerved by the behemoth which they had created, Metallica moved on to Poland for a Katowice concert on August 13, before performing at Castle Donington alongside Mötley Crüe, AC/DC and Queensryche on the 17th. The tour then moved onto Hungary, Germany, Switzerland, Belgium, Holland, Austria, Italy, France and Spain before a show on September 28 which would certainly be Metallica's most important to date: a slot at the Tushino Air Field in Moscow. An incredible 500,000 fans attended the show, which was part of the Monsters Of Rock tour and also featured AC/DC and Pantera. Legend has it that the Russian prime minister Mikhail Gorbachev personally invited the band to play at the free concert, which took place at a disused military airfield, converted to a performing arena in the wake of the recent collapse of the former Soviet Union. The show was a success but was marred by the violence of the Russian police, whose strategy for controlling the virtually unpoliceable crowd appeared to be based on chasing drunken youths and beating them when they caught them. During the show Lars caught his finger between the snare drum rim and one of his sticks and bled profusely.

After three weeks' rest, Metallica embarked on the next leg of the tour, incorporating a diamond-shaped section of the stage set, the 'Snake Pit', in which a privileged set of fans (competition winners and so on) could witness the band at extremely close quarters. By now the route across America and back was well established: as the tour took in the Day On The Green show in Oakland on October 12 and concerts in Illinois, Wisconsin, Michigan, Iowa and Minnesota, audience enthusiasm grew perceptibly and the second single, 'The Unforgiven' was issued on November 9. The Metallica virus had spread to Canada, too, and the band hammered it home with a brief tour through Ontario and Quebec before heading down through Pennsylvania, Indiana, Missouri, Nebraska, Ohio, New York and Massachusetts. A final jaunt to Japan for a New Year's Eve show at the famed Tokyo Dome rounded off a spectacular year for Metallica.

1992 would be no less busy, as the Wherever I May Roam Tour stretched as far as any reasonable schedules would allow. It would take time – huge swathes of time, it seemed – before the noise being made by the Black Album, the most popular metal album of the year, would finally abate. And then, of course, Metallica would have to decide what to do next . . .

18

1992–1995

The next four years in Metallica's history will take up no more than this chapter, which may seem strange since the single year 1982 stretched across no fewer than four. By the early Nineties Metallica had not only evolved into a fearsomely professional touring and recording machine, despite their enormously committed drinking habits, but they now had both the budget to take a truly gigantic show on the road, and armies of fans who wanted to see them live. Having embarked on the enormous tour to support the Black Album, Metallica found it logical to stay on it until its wheels stopped turning of their own accord.

January and February saw them heave their gargantuan equipment to shows in Nevada, California, Texas, Louisiana, Arkansas, Oklahoma, Tennessee, Colorado, Utah and Nevada before the Grammy awards at New York City's Radio City, where they accepted their third award, this time for 'Enter Sandman', which had been deemed Best Metal Performance. The following day the video for 'Nothing Else Matters' was premiered: an in-studio rehearsal video, it was directed by Adam Dubin and contained footage which was slated to appear in a later documentary on the band. Other than not-particularly-memorable scenes of Jason playing pool, studio crew loading gear and the band generally fooling around, the clip was useful primarily as a look behind the scenes rather than providing any artistic concept.

Shows in Maine, New York, Rhode Island, Ohio, Illinois, Tennessee, Indiana, Virginia, Florida, Alabama, Kentucky, North Carolina, West Virginia, Georgia, Maryland, New Jersey, Pennsylvania, Ontario and Connecticut took the band as far as mid-April, when they flew to London for an appearance at the Freddie Mercury Tribute Concert at Wembley Stadium. The Queen singer had died from AIDS on November 24, 1991, and several prestigious acts had lined up to perform in his honour, with Metallica no doubt invited because of their recently successful rendition of 'Stone Cold Crazy'. A Metallica single, 'Live At Wembley Stadium London April 20th 1992', appeared a few days later and contained live versions of 'Enter Sandman', 'Sad But True' and 'Nothing Else Matters', with all proceeds from its sales and the gig itself donated to Mercury's AIDS fund. 'Stone Cold Crazy' itself was played by a supergroup consisting of James, Black Sabbath guitarist Tony Iommi and the remaining Queen members (guitarist Brian May, bassist John Deacon and drummer Roger Taylor) – one of the standout moments of the entire concert.

'Nothing Else Matters' was released on May 2, 1992, and included a famous live version of 'Harvester Of Sorrow' in which the band forgot to include the entire second chorus. The single received immediate heavy airplay (those deftly arranged Michael Kamen strings must have hit middle America right where it counted) and boosted by this, the tour moved ever onwards. Going via Washington, Idaho, California, South and North Dakota, Manitoba, Saskatchewan, Alberta, British Columbia, Alaska, Oregon, Utah, Wyoming, Montana, Arizona, Louisiana, Mississippi, Missouri, Ohio, Michigan, Wisconsin, New York and Pennsylvania once again, this leg of the tour finally wound up on July 5 – although there were no plans to take a break. After two weeks off, a truly monster tour co-headlining with Guns N'Roses, who were by then Metallica's only serious metal rival in commercial terms, was set to begin. The openers were scheduled to be Faith No More, three of whose members – guitarist Jim Martin, bassist Bill Gould and drummer Mike 'Puffy' Bordin – had links with Metallica going back as far as Cliff Burton's schooldays.

GNR had become huge stars on the strength of two double albums, *Use Your Illusion I* and *II*, which were released simultaneously on September 17, 1991. Stuffed with hooky, melodic singles and helped along by the constant mouthing-off of singer Axl Rose, the records provided sufficient commercial impetus for the co-headlining tour to make a lot of sense, even if Metallica's Black Album had sold in greater quantities. Much of the fanbase of the two acts listened to both bands, and had been doing so since Guns N'Roses' seminal debut album, *Appetite For Destruction*, had been released a year after *Master Of Puppets*. As Jan Transit of the experimental Norwegian black metal band . . . In The Woods recalls, all brands of metal fan understood the first GNR record:

"The first rock'n'roll experience that really blew me away was the debut album of Guns N'Roses. Their attitude left me with an acceptable standard of how to take care of things."

The four-month tour, which began on July 17 at the RFK Stadium in Washington, was initially pleasant all round, with the two headliners respecting each other's talents and Faith No More, the funk-metal clowns, doing a great job of preparing the crowd for the two metal colossi that followed. However, things began to deteriorate for unspecified reasons but which can (allegedly, m'lud) be traced to GNR singer Axl Rose's 'fragile' attitude to performing, which often saw him threaten not to play. Faith No More bassist Bill Gould sighs as he recalls the truth of playing on that tour: "You know what it was like? That was like working a shitty job. Axl had an army of lawyers and nobody was gonna do any direct confrontation with anybody else." Was the problem that Axl was being a diva about things? "There was a little bit of that, for sure, but when you get into the big stadium rock shows, there's a lot of organisation and a lot of people get in the way between the artist and the audience. There's security issues, there's all the shit . . . nothing really happens except this low level of unrest and grumbling."

And yet Gould knows how implausible this is: "On paper, this tour looked like the greatest opportunity in the world, to play in front of millions of people. But actually, it dragged on for like four or five months, and it was tough on our heads because we had been playing clubs before that. It was like working for a big corporation." Maybe the bands were so big at this stage that clashes were inevitable? "Exactly. It comes with the territory, or at least it makes it worse, because it becomes impersonal no matter how you slice it." Guitarist Jim Martin is less direct but equally negative, describing the tour as a "huge and ponderous nightmare".

The nightmare reached its logical conclusion at an August 8 show in the Olympic Stadium in Montreal, when Metallica were playing before Guns N'Roses. During the song 'Fade To Black', James stepped into the wrong area of the stage and was partly enveloped in flame as a pyrotechnic firework exploded beneath him. Avoiding death by a matter of inches, the frontman suffered second and third degree burns to his left arm and hand that left his skin, as Newsted later described it, literally bubbling and coming away. The show was stopped, James was taken to the local emergency room (a process which took some time, he later recalled, even though he was suffering from intense shock and agonising pain) and the crowd waited to hear from Guns N'Roses. To add to the drama, Axl Rose then told the promoter that his throat was suffering from overuse and that Guns N'Roses would not be able to perform. The announcement was made that the concert would be finishing early – but the fans rioted, causing thousands of dollars of damage to the venue.

The tour was halted while Hetfield was treated, but he pulled through rapidly and, just as in 1986 when he had broken his wrist skateboarding, he decided to perform on vocals only while his burns healed. Also as in '86, it was roadie John Marshall who took his place on rhythm guitar. On August 25 the tour resumed, and continued through Arizona, New Mexico, Louisiana, Georgia, Florida, Texas, South Carolina, Massachusetts, Ontario, Minnesota, Missouri, Colorado, California and Washington, winding up on October 6 at Seattle's Kingdome. The headliners walked off the tour with no love lost between them.

After Hetfield's injuries had healed sufficiently for him to reclaim his guitar, the band travelled to Europe, where the Black Album was still selling in enormous quantities over a year after its release. Late October saw Metallica perform in Belgium and two shows at the Wembley Arena again, the second of which was notable for the appearance of vocalist Animal of the Anti-Nowhere League, whose signature song 'So What?' had been covered by Metallica. Interest in vintage punk was shown by several of the larger metal bands – Slayer would release an album of punk covers called *Undisputed Attitude* three years later – and this, it seems, was Metallica's acknowledgement of the debt they owed to this harshest, most ground-breaking of musical genres. 'So What?' is an obscenity-ridden blast through meaningless sexual boasts ("I've fucked a sheep, and I've fucked a goat" runs one memorable line) and Metallica reproduced it faithfully, although they added a guitar solo where the original, rather cack-handed version had a simple, lumbering riff. James also replaced two instances of the line "you boring little cunt" with "you boring little fuck", perhaps to make the song more palatable to American audiences.

More UK concerts at the end of October '92 and the beginning of November went smoothly, with the 'Wherever I May Roam' single released on October 31 and a concert at the Birmingham NEC on November 5 made unforgettable by the surprise appearance of the four members of Diamond Head. The slightly bizarre sight of all eight musicians jamming on 'Am I Evil?' and 'Helpless' came off successfully, and the performance was kept for posterity in a later fanclub-only release.

In the same month, two long-form videos were released. A far cry from the home-video rawness of *Cliff 'Em All* or the slightly naïve conceptualising of 'One', *A Year And A Half In The Life Of Metallica Parts 1 & 2* contained all of the studio footage which fans had glimpsed in the 'Nothing Else Matters' video clip and provided a long, detailed look into the workings of the band and Bob Rock. The first movie focused on the recording sessions which had produced the Black Album, with the tension between the producer and band-members (and the hilarity of the moments in between) fully obvious. The second film was composed of footage from the early dates of the Wherever I May Roam Tour, which, tellingly, was still a long way from being finished even when the videos were released.

1992 was brought to a close with more stadium shows in Holland, France, Spain, Italy, Switzerland, Austria, Germany, Denmark, Sweden, Norway and Finland, and the release of the 'Sad But True' single. A month of rest at home was much needed, and the band and tour crew parted ways until mid-January, 1993. Although the Wherever I May Roam tour had offically come to a close (the next leg was labelled the Nowhere Else To Roam jaunt, with typical Metallica humour), the reality of it appeared to be that the band were resolved to spend the best part of three years on the road, even if the odd break now and then made it seem as if separate tours were taking place.

Before the tour started, Elektra's marketing department suggested to Metallica that in view of the enormous wave of Metallica-related activity which was engulfing the world at the time, a 'Metallistore' event would be a good idea. In due course, a location was found in Manhattan and on January 21, 1993, the four musicians spent the day there, meeting fans and selling Metallica albums and merchandise. A special Metallica cassette was manufactured for the event, consisting of a medley of songs recorded at the Tushino airfield in the summer of 1991. James created the cover, a 'scary guy' picture resembling a bloody skull and crossbones which would appear in one form or another on many items in the future.

But the never-ending tour was beckoning again, and the next six months saw one gigantic trek through North America and other continents, firstly taking in Minnesota, Ohio, Pennsylvania, Iowa, Wisconsin, Tennessee, Kentucky, South Carolina, New Brunswick, Nova Scotia, Quebec – where James' now-healed arm must have throbbed a little – and Florida. Mexico was next, with five dates, and then Hawaii (two dates), Japan (six dates), a show in New Zealand, nine in Australia, two in Indonesia, one each in Singapore, Thailand and the Philippines, two in Brazil, one in Chile and two in Argentina.

The world couldn't get enough of Metallica in 1993 – so much so that when the band returned from the Far East and South America, they simply decided to play more shows in countries where they had already performed. Metallica completed May with shows in Germany, the Czech Republic, Denmark, Sweden and Finland, before a landmark UK show on June 5 at the Milton Keynes Bowl with none other than Megadeth in support. Also on the bill that day was Diamond Head, who recorded their 40-minute set and released it as the *Live Evil* album. Sean Harris recalls: "They're wonderful guys. James frightens you a bit – I think he's meant to! But they were quite nice to us."

Much was made by Dave Mustaine and the press of the fact that the feud between the two bands was now offically over, with Mustaine commenting onstage: "The ten years of bullshit is over between Metallica and Megadeth!" He later explained: "I figure that Metallica are such an integral part of me – what they do, how they think – because of how we all started, these three minds. Maybe I'm flattering myself by drawing the comparison, but I think there are a lot of similarities that people deny. The mannerisms that James and I have onstage, some are identical. A lot of the things Lars says are things I used to say. In those days I used to handle all the interviews. When I watch them, it's like I see a part of me, and I'm so happy for them . . . I talk to Lars all the time." He added, more sombrely: "For whatever reason, James and I haven't really sat down and ironed out the past. I was so hurt by getting fired with no warning that I had a lot of resentment. I was very jealous as I watched my baby go away from me. I watched their success for so long, and for the longest time I was so bitter. But then I realised that I still get royalties from the songs I wrote, and people still make the connection between us."

The Metallica and Megadeth saga was a long, strange ride for Dave Mustaine. After he had overcome his addictions, he found God and appeared to settle down into the role of family man. For a time he was quoted, rather pompously, as having said: "I keep comparing Megadeth to Metallica. I realised that often people hate the things which they really love. I loved to play with Metallica. When they kicked me out I lost something which I loved and I started to hate them. Now every morning I fall to my knees and thank God for being able to finally see this truth." He also claimed that the inter-band arguing was less venomous than was often supposed: "A lot of that was just me getting frustrated and putting it all out at the one time. It was blown way out of proportion. At interviews, the guy would ask a question that he knew would get an answer that would make it look like I was angry with Metallica, and I hated that. A lot of it was one magazine that wouldn't give up the issue until I went out of my way to resolve the situation. Now Lars Ulrich and I are good friends and we drink together. It's great that we can be friends now because when I was in Metallica, we argued a lot and that led to me drinking excessively, which made the situation worse. That's in the past now and I want to look towards good things in the future."

What was also notable about the Milton Keynes show was the poor quality of Megadeth's sound, which had evidently not been honed sufficiently by the technicians – or had perhaps even been tampered with. Mustaine might have been expected to fly into a fury about this. However, when I met Dave in 1999 he was a reasonable, self-deprecating guy who passed this off as sheer bad luck: "We had a volume clamp, which most support acts have. I don't think that Lars or James would have sent the message out to fuck with us, but you know, people do strange things. There were so many people who were part of the Metallica–Megadeth war that personalised it. The feud had been over for years."

And so Mustaine appeared to reach peace at last. Meanwhile, another ex-member enjoyed a brief sojourn in the spotlight a little later. In early summer the first Metallica biography appeared, a book called *Metallica Unbound*, written by former fan-club manager KJ Doughton. The story of the band's early years, this breathless but useful book did a competent job of introducing fans to Metallica, although it was hampered by its slender size. In a notable interview on the radio station KNAC, none other than Rob McGovney resurfaced from the obscurity in which he had remained since being ejected from the band in 1982 with several acerbic comments on *Unbound*: "It should be called *Untrue!*" he remarked. The show contained an interesting fan segment in which listeners could phone in and ask the bassist questions: one such was his niece, who expressed some annoyance over Ron's ill-treatment (as she perceived it).

Meanwhile, the Metallica tour continued to eat up the months of 1993, careering through Slovakia, Hungary, Holland, France, Portugal, Spain, Switzerland, Italy, Turkey, Austria, Greece, Israel and Belgium – many of which they had played in before, some which they had not. In either case the stadium crowds were rabid in their appreciation: the band had somehow, improbably, become bona fide rock stars, with their demonic creation, the Black Album, devouring all in its path. In July the tour finally rolled to an end, with the members and crew dispersing to their families for a well-earned rest.

Kirk and Jason plunged into their time off, but James and Lars felt at something of a loose end after the hubbub of the touring had died down. Eyeing the enormous number of live recordings which the tour had provided, the pair decided that the time was right for Metallica's first live album: the perfect way to present the audiences with a genuine tour souvenir, to clean out their stores and to get some Metallica product on the market again, over two years since the last album had been released.

The result took some time to appear, and much work went into it. On November 29, 1993, a miniature Metallica flight case containing three CDs, three VHS video cassettes, an extensive booklet and some items of memorabilia including a replica backstage pass and a stencil was released under the charming (and very metallic) title of *Live Shit: Binge And Purge*. The audio content was a single concert recorded in Mexico City in February 1993, while the two shows on video were taken from San Diego in January 1991 and Seattle in August 1989. A comprehensive package for anyone interested in the touring persona of the pre- and post-*Metallica* foursome, *Live Shit* was an instant success and went on to sell over 600,000 copies – even despite its hefty price tag of $85, which drew some criticism.

James countered this with the reasonable point that: "If we put these things out separately over the years, it would cost the same amount of money, maybe more. It seems that other bands put crap out because 'wow we need money' or something, and this is absolutely not that! It's chock full of various stuff, more than enough, more-than-enough. There's stuff in the book we shouldn't even be showing people, some of the faxes and stuff. It is way over the top and yeah, I think it's great. Nothing's really stood out like this does, as far as live albums or videos are concerned." Lars added: "What we're doing is saying, here it is, take it or leave it. And the reason it costs $89.95 is not so we and Elektra can walk away with big fat bank accounts, it's basically to cover the fucking costs of about two and a half million bucks. Our management did a survey and discovered that this is the most expensive packaging anybody has ever put together. You've got everything in there, nine hours of music, a 72-page book, backstage passes, stencil, keys to our houses . . . so fuck, take it or leave it!"

The drummer explained that it had been necessary to issue such a large package (rather than, say, a single-CD live album) because a certain amount of psychological cleansing needed to take place: "I think it's turned into a great way of getting the last three and a half years out of our systems. Now the slate really is completely clean. We wrote the album, made the album, toured the album and here's the documentation of the album's music on the road. Now we can take our nine months or whatever off and start with a clean slate. Everything about this tour is gone. It will enable us to completely let go of everything from the last few years, and when we begin to approach the next album we can do so without any lingering, left-over baggage."

The timing was also right: Lars reasoned that Metallica would be out of the public eye for a while (although at the time, he didn't realise how long a break it would eventually become) and that the live collection would satisfy fans' needs in the meantime: "It's our first attempt at a live package, and it's definitely the right time in our career to do this. It's also the right time for us to take a step away from everything for however long. And it's the perfect way to leave our hardcore fans with something to listen to while we're away."

Although Metallica chose not to promote the album with a full interview schedule, reasoning that the concept of a live collection should be self-explanatory, one telling statement made by James has

225

some resonance to this day: "I wanted to hang onto [the Seattle audio tapes] for a long time, because it was the only properly shot old shit we had. It had a lot of stuff that we – myself anyway – didn't really wanna get rid of right now. We'd always talked of it being something that would come out ten years down the line, like, wow, here's some vintage crap that's never been seen and, wow, it's on proper film, that sort of thing. But as we started watching it, we found that it was pretty all right stuff, and we agreed to just get it all out now so it doesn't look really out of place later." With ironic prescience, he concluded: "If we'd held on, it could've been a situation where we're rockin' along and this thing comes out ten years later, people see it and start saying, 'Hey . . . they used to be good!' Hahaha."

Indeed.

May 1994.

Having taken six months off after the release of *Live Shit*, Metallica decided to plough through another tour for a few months, until the point later in the year when recording sessions for a new album were due to commence. The Shit Hits The Sheds 1994: Binging And Purging Across The USA tour commenced on May 28 in Buffalo, where two 'rehearsal' shows slipped the band back into touring mode. From that point on they played with Danzig in support in New York, New Jersey, Quebec, Ontario, Pennsylvania, Vermont, New Hampshire, Ohio, Michigan (at a June 22 show in Detroit, Glenn Danzig and Chuck Biscuits from Danzig guested on 'Last Caress'), Iowa, Wisconsin, Missouri, Indiana and Illinois, where a Chicago show saw Danzig reappear on the Misfits song 'London Dungeon', and Suicidal Tendencies played along with 'So What?' The Suicidals included among their ranks the bassist Rob Trujillo, a fearsomely nimble player with whom the band struck up a lasting friendship.

Concerts in British Columbia, Washington, Oregon, California, Arizona, Utah, Nevada, New Mexico, Colorado, Texas, Oklahoma, Kansas, New York, North Carolina, Tennessee and Florida followed. At the August 21 show at the Bicentennial Park in Miami, Rob Halford of Judas Priest joined the band for a rendition of Priest's classic 'Rapid Fire' – a mutual honour which saw old and new meet: or were Metallica, slowly but surely, joining the old guard alongside Halford?

In October 1994 Metallica entered a rehearsal studio to begin work on new material. In the same month, the Epic subsidiary Immortal released the self-titled debut album of a band named Korn. Jumpy, paranoid and edgy, the album sold enormously despite being neither innovative nor consistently good, and the media began to employ a buzz-phrase to describe the hip-hop-inflected music it contained: 'new metal', a slightly vague term which made more sense a little later when the 'new' was shortened to 'nu'.

That's 'new' as opposed to 'old', of course.

In February 1995, Metallica joined producer Bob Rock and engineer Randy Staub to begin recording their sixth studio record at the Plant Studios in Sausalito, California. The studios were situated relatively close to their homes, which made for a different atmosphere to previous recordings: the band's enthusiasm was running high and the months in the rehearsal room had generated more songs than they needed. The question of what to do with so much material was one which they pondered long and hard before reaching a decision.

1995 was to be a year out of the public eye other than for a short sequence of big-profile events. August 23 saw the band emerge blinking into the sunlight for a short Escape From The Studio tour, which commenced with a fanclub-only show at the London Astoria. Two new songs, entitled '2 x 4' and 'Devil's Dance', were played for the first time. A week later Metallica took the unusual step of performing the so-called 'Coldest Show On Earth' in Tuktoyaktuk in the Yukon in Canada, a concert sponsored by Molson Breweries and performed for 500 contest winners who were flown in by charter plane. The arena, a tent in the shape of a clover leaf, was warmed by fuel-burning heaters and was dubbed the Molson Ice Party.

On December 14, after more studio sessions, Metallica made an unforgettable appearance at the Whisky A Go-Go in honour of the 50th birthday of Motörhead singer Lemmy. Performing 'Overkill', 'Damage Case', 'Stone Dead Forever', 'Too Late Too Late', 'The Chase Is Better Than The Catch', 'We Are The Road Crew' and a jam based on 'Overkill', while dressed as Lemmy (in black wigs and white cowboy boots), Metallica's performance was blisteringly powerful. I asked Lemmy in 2001 if he had enjoyed Metallica's versions of his songs. His reply was typically acidic: "Yeah, they're all right. I think 'Too Late Too Late' was the best one. It was funny hearing Jimmy imitating my voice, because they obviously didn't get it. They obviously think that shouting's all it is, and it's not. It's just my voice."

From Lemmy, that's a compliment – a commodity which might be in short supply before long. Metallica were on the point of splitting their fanbase more radically than they had ever done before.

19

1996–1997

The silence remained unbroken for the wider Metallica fanbase until the summer of 1996, although Lars did reveal one or two details of the new album to fans in April – such as the fact that some of the lyrics were a little more introspective than had previously been the norm. One of the events which had influenced this was the death of James' father, Virgil, who had succumbed to cancer early in the year.

James would later talk to the band's fanclub magazine *So What!*, edited by veteran British journalist Steffan Chirazi, at length about his father, explaining: "My hero has got to be my dad . . . Only later on did I realise how much he influenced me and was such a vibe in my life. I didn't really realise how much he had been a part of my life, and influenced me growing up, until later on. And when we finally got back together, I saw we pretty much liked the same stuff and got along really good after all the B.S. that happened in our family life . . . While he was sick I realised how strong he was and got a lot closer to him which was great, because a lot of people don't get to do that. Sometimes people just go, people leave us without warning. There was at least a little warning with him, and I got to get a little closer and even closer at the end."

He also talked a little about the troubles of his upbringing: "I did have a pretty huge problem with the religion growing up, Christian Science, pretty strict rules that I'd had in my youth and growing up, not fully understanding the religion. I just knew that there were rules around it, which was pretty frustrating. That's the kind of religion that you can really get into after you've lived a bit . . . as a kid it didn't make sense to me, and I battled it quite a bit through my teens and twenties, and it kind of messed with my head. But later on when my dad was a bit sick, I kind of realised how much it played a part in his life and how pretty magical and powerful it was in his mind. Through talking with my sister we really both agreed that he was probably the most powerful man we'd ever known."

Hetfield revealed elsewhere that two new songs, 'Poor Bleeding Me' and 'Until It Sleeps', were about his father's illness. Virgil's fight with cancer and subsequent death had clearly forced James to think deeply about his childhood, perhaps opening up mental debates which had long lain dormant – and while Metallica's lyrical themes had become ever more introspective and sophisticated as the years had gone by, now it seemed that the note of wrath which had filled anti-religious songs such as 'The God That Failed' and childhood-rebellion anthems like 'Dyer's Eve' would be replaced with a more thoughtful, less enraged tone. Were Metallica about to grow up at last?

In May 1996 it was announced that the new album, entitled *Load*, would be released on June 3. The news caused a flurry of excitement among fans, non-fans and media alike: many of the questions they asked were the obvious ones, such as: would *Load* sell more than the Black Album? Would it contain the usual ballad? Would it be heavier? And would Metallica tour for three years again? However, more cautious listeners wondered if Metallica, who had ruled the hard rock world so forcefully from 1991 to 1993 in the wake of their last album, could still cut it in the new era. And a whole new era it certainly was: grunge had died with Kurt Cobain in 1994, Britpop bands like Oasis, Blur and Pulp were infusing pop music with an infectious retro groove which was already starting to outstay its welcome – and as for thrash metal? Dead and gone, with the sole exception of the indefatigable Slayer: black and death metal were the dominant forms of extreme music in the mid-Nineties, with At The Gates, Morbid Angel, Cradle Of Filth and Dimmu Borgir the biggest bands from the genres.

Undeterred, Metallica embarked on a May press tour to promote the album. Perhaps understandably, the first shock reported by the media was that all four men were now sporting short hair. It didn't take long for questions about this to become irksome (James was reported in one interview as giving "short shrift" to a journalist who mentioned his new look), but that didn't stop the debate, especially when press shots for the album, which had been taken by fashion photographer extraordinaire Anton Corbijn, showed the foursome in various non-metallic guises. Kirk appeared in a Thirties-style pimp suit and fedora, with a very Nineties spike pierced through his bottom lip and the words 'Made In SF 11.18.62' tattooed around his navel; James sported braces, pinstripe trousers and hair dyed black; Jason wore glasses, sneakers and a short, curly haircut that made him look like an accountant; and perhaps most surprisingly, Lars had daubed his eyes with make-up and wore his hair fairly long at the back and floppy at the front – a cross between Hugh Grant and a mullet. Little wonder that fans were flabbergasted.

On May 20, 'Until It Sleeps' was released as a single. It was immediately apparent that it wasn't only Metallica's image which had changed: far from opening with a flurry of riffs or a picked intro like all the singles which had preceded it in Metallica's career, it was Newsted's slightly chorused, fretless bass atop a positively quiet drum pattern which began the song. A staccato, stamping riff does come in and form the bulk of the song, but it's James' melodic, repeated, sung (not growled or barked) chorus and Kirk's pedal steel guitar which characterise the song. In brief, it's a rock song, and a fairly inoffensive one at that, with country and western touches which are completely at odds with Metallica's earlier work. Odder still was the fact that dance guru Moby had been asked to provide a beats-heavy remix of the song for club crowds – as the metal/electronica crossover had rarely worked (although Fear Factory and Atari Teenage Riot had pulled it off semi-successfully), old-school thrash fans closed their eyes and prayed.

Sonically, however, there's nothing wrong with the song: fans who had feared the return of a 'bass-less' album along the lines of *Justice* breathed a sigh of relief. Producer Bob Rock had done a powerful job on the new material. However, many others read the advance reviews of the album with horror (*Q* magazine described *Load* as "Metallica's pop album", for instance), and after buying their copy, sat down to listen to it with some trepidation.

A week after a listening party was held on the second day of the Dynamo Festival in Eindhoven, Holland, at which *Load* was played through the PA for 60,000 audience members, the album received a worldwide release. Housed in a sleeve depicting a gooey red and white montage of liquids (actually a piece of art called 'Blood And Semen' by the controversial artist Andres Serrano, consisting of bovine blood and the artist's own ejaculate), the record also contained a range of band portraits by Corbijn and set a record on its release as the longest CD ever, with 14 tracks clocking in at 79 minutes.

Industry pundits as well as fans and reviewers had much to say about *Load*. The managing director of the band's UK parent label Mercury, Howard Berman, was quoted as saying: "The last album was such a huge phenomenon that it would be naïve to assume that we could surpass it" – wise words indeed. Metallica's co-manager Peter Mensch was reported in the same feature as responding to the question of whether *Load* could outsell *Metallica* with the words: "Can it be as big? Fucked if I know! . . . One believes it can't be repeated, but I don't know. We can maybe sell as many records in Europe but the US is tougher because things change a lot quicker here."

Things might have changed in the US, but the five years since the release of *Metallica* had brought much change to the band too, judging by *Load*. Its first song, 'Ain't My Bitch', is the track most similar to any-thing on that previous album, with a driving riff and a focused adher-ence to Lars' simple, powerful drum rhythm that is almost reminiscent of a medium-weight Black Album song such as 'Enter Sandman' or 'Holier Than Thou'. In fact, *Load*'s sole example of a near-thrash, sixteenths-based riff comes in increments of a bar in each chorus of 'Ain't My Bitch'. Otherwise, the song is country-influenced rock, with a memorable descending sequence and a crisp, heavy tone.

Unfortunately, this opening promise doesn't continue. '2 x 4' is a plodding, repetitive, dull song based on a redneck, stop-start riff which would never have made it through the band's editing process in the Eighties. A slightly creepy atmosphere is created by James' subtly intoned hiss of the word 'retribution', but – for the first time in Metallica's entire canon before this album – it's possible to be bored by the song's main riff. And to many fans' (and as is probably obvious by now, my own) disgust, this lack of innovation continues into the next song, 'The House That Jack Built', which is more of the same scratchy, ho-hum growling, at least until a chorus with an almost hummable melody.

Load isn't doing well, and 'Until It Sleeps', which seemed harmless rather than scintillating on its release as a single, seems positively excel-lent after the two songs which precede it. Fortunately, the next track, 'King Nothing', keeps up this strange, not-great-but-good-by-*Load*-standards quality level, with a nifty riff from Jason opening up the vague intro and leading into a passable, anthemic song with a steadily increasing tension courtesy of Hetfield's monotonous riffing and his gleefully dark question of "Where's your crown, King Nothing?"

At least 'Hero Of The Day', a fairly obvious single, isn't pretentious about what it is and what it wants to be. A simple, melodic lament along themes of estranged youth and – perhaps – mother-and-child themes, the song intersperses clean, picked verses with heavier lines and a satisfyingly weighty outro. However, as *Load* progresses on to 'Bleeding Me', a slow, almost languid slice of angst, it's clear that there will be little of the apocalyptic rage that made *Master Of Puppets* so exciting or even the simple energy that infused *Kill 'Em All*. Introspection, it seems, is the primary colour of this album. 'Bleeding Me' is perhaps the epitome of this new direction, with James complaining vaguely that he is "Caught under wheels roll/ I take the leech/ I'm bleeding me" and "This thorn in my side is from the tree I've planted". The song is redeemed a little by a killer solo from Kirk, but on the whole it's just too limp to take seriously. And at the halfway point of the album, things aren't looking good for *Load*.

'Cure' keeps standards disappointingly low. One of the dullest songs Metallica have ever written (and remember, back in 1996 the impact that this made on the old-school thrash fans listening to this in the hope that Metallica would have regained their old venom after the Black Album was profound), it's a singalong trip to nowhere based on a fairly tedious, bluesy riff. Irksomely, 'Poor Twisted Me' (another 'me' title: what was James trying to say?) is even worse, a clutch of reverbed, empty riffs and spaces leading into a messy spiral of notes. The touches of Southern rock which pop up from time to time are just unnecessary.

More blues-based chart-rock it maybe, but at least 'Wasting My Hate' has a healthily upbeat tempo. By this stage, thrash metal fans were probably trying to salvage whatever shred of respectability they could from *Load*, and perhaps this song offers a helping hand: while it's a fraction as heavy or innovative as any Metallica song pre-1990, at least there appears to be some energy behind it. However, this doesn't last and 'Mama Said', the most reviled song on *Load*, is next.

'Mama Said' isn't great (put simply, it's a country and western ballad that had many listeners gagging) but, like 'Hero Of The Day' before it, it's an honest bid for radio and MTV acceptability, and competently done in those terms. Although the thought of Metallica producing a C&W song was and remains difficult to swallow, it's less nauseating than the mid-tempo blues workouts such as 'King Nothing' and 'Cure' which masquerade as heavy songs. Had Metallica forgotten what 'heavy' meant? Had they decided to ignore the blistering speed and vitriol of – say – 'Disposable Heroes'? Hello? Was anybody listening?

Three songs of almost painful mediocrity wind the album up. 'Thorn Within' starts boringly, continues in the same vein with an achingly dull riff based on a pointless shuffle of notes and sinks into a sea of dullness. 'Ronnie' is just dreadful, a plodding sequence of empty picking which even today I can't bear to hear in full. Yet another tortured-childhood epic ("Small town boy/ Big time frown/ Never talks/ Never plays" growls James), the song had more astute listeners praying that Hetfield would get some counselling, overcome his demons and stop plaguing us with sob-stories about his upbringing.

Harsh? Perhaps. But listening to this stuff, whether in 1996 or seven years later, takes some patience – and we still have 'The Outlaw Torn' to go, which lasts a soul-sapping nine minutes and never progresses in that time beyond a mid-tempo, dark, unspecific rant ("Outlaw of torn/ Outlaw of torn/ And I'm torn" wails Hetfield, meaninglessly).

The conclusion? *Load* is a massive step down in songwriting and concept from any music, even the weakest, most cynically radio-friendly Black Album track that Metallica had done previously. Not that Metallica themselves agreed with this, of course. James, giving press interviews in Australia, had much to say about his group's enormous swing in direction: for starters, it seems, he had discovered some new music. "I had never discovered The Who until just a little while ago and I'm really into that, and then there is the country stuff. I've gotten more into poet musicians like Tom Waits, Leonard Cohen and even Nick Cave. That darker, kind of twisted stuff that is kind of cool." As for the fate of *Load*, he mused: "I really hope that they [the fans] can understand what we are up to. I hope that they can follow through with us. The fans are hopefully going to be honest and truthful in what they say, as we are in our music. Obviously, Metallica is a very personal band for some people and people like us for different reasons, which is great. There are the fans who like us for our speedy stuff, there are fans who like us for our deeper, more melodic stuff and there are fans who like us for our long hair."

Note the reference to speed: James obviously knew perfectly well that some elements of Metallica's fanbase would be disappointed at the slower, more lightweight material. He also talked about the involvement of Bob Rock once again, explaining that the stresses which had arisen between band and producer during the recording of the Black Album had been resolved over the years: "Well, we figured we got to know Bob really well on the last recording. We didn't really make him completely insane, so we had to come back and finish the job. He had a couple of brain cells left that we had to tweak. I think after the Black Album, we told each other that we were never going to work together again. But time heals all, and we never really could see this record with someone else. It was always him, we knew he'd be back. This time there was no intimidation factor and there was no 'you can't tell me what to do' bullshit. All that petty crap was out of the way, it was more like a friendly set of ears in the studio . . . Bob tends to help us dig deeper. We tell him what we're after and he tries to help us achieve that."

Although I've damned *Load* with my review, at the time no one knew if it would be embraced by the public and that a few years down the line people would be comparing it negatively with its predecessors, and the usual live and promotional frenzy was poised to take place. Two 'Truckload' shows, during which the band performed from the back of a flatbed lorry, took place on San Jose on June 4, followed up by three concerts on June 9, 10 and 11. Respect is due to Metallica for embracing the new internet technology at around the time of the launch of *Load* (a move made ironic in the light of the industry-shaking struggle which would commence four years later): not only was their fan club, Metclub, based round a website with member-only content years before many other bands came online, they also performed a webcast gig in the early days of the medium. The June 11 show, which took place at Slim's club in San Francisco, was distributed live online, one of the first to be so broadcast.

Metallica's music also appeared in soundtrack form at this time, accompanying a documentary entitled *Paradise Lost: The Child Murders At Robin Hood Hills*, made by film-makers Joe Berlinger and Bruce Sinofsky. The movie, which followed the fate of three Arkansas teenagers who were jailed for murder of three children, presented the argument that the decision might have been influenced by the fact that the three suspects wore black and listened to Metallica – an ironic twist, given the family-friendly face of the 'new' Hetfield, Ulrich and Co.

The songs used were 'Sanitarium', 'The Call Of Ktulu' and 'Orion'. The band struck up a friendship with the two documentary-makers which appears to have lasted: at the time of writing, a Metallica movie created by the pair is said to be in production.

After two more fanclub-only shows on June 23 and 24 in Ontario and Washington, Metallica embarked on the 1996 Lollapalooza tour, a surprise move which reinforced for many fans the idea that they had evolved from a heavy metal act to an alternative rock band. "The organisers thought it had all become a bit stale and predictable and they thought it was time to take a sharp turn," said Ulrich at the time. "They always wanted to be less alternative, more a gathering of groups from different musical backgrounds." It emerged that Metallica had also been offered the chance to select some of the other acts on the bill, with Lars rooting for two British bands, Oasis (who were reaching their commercial peak at the time with a series of huge singles from their *What's The Story, Morning Glory* album) and the more obscure and funkier Black Grape, led by ex-Happy Mondays frontman Shaun Ryder. Of these unlikely choices, Lars explained: "Underneath [Oasis'] well-crafted pop songs was a rock band with tons of attitude, a group who want to kick everyone's ass. But 'Wonderwall' broke and suddenly became the biggest thing on the planet and that was it. I also love Black Grape. Their record is my favourite from the past year."

The Lollapalooza tour kicked off in Kansas City on June 27, 1996, and featured Soundgarden, The Ramones, Rancid and others on the bill. Rolling through Iowa, Illinois, Indiana, Ohio, Ontario, Quebec, Vermont, New York, West Virginia, Florida, North Carolina, Tennessee, Louisiana, Texas, Arizona, Washington and California, and winding up in early August, the tour attracted all manner of rock fans, and provided many with their first taste of the new, softer Metallica – although the set-list always featured one or two old reliables from the *Puppets* and Black Album era.

With no time to lose (as Jason Newsted put it, "We wanted to take the music to a new generation of Metallica fans") the European 'Poor Touring Me' tour began. Designed to bring the *Load* message to Europe as efficiently as possible, shows swept through Austria, Poland, the Czech Republic, Germany, Belgium, France, Spain and Portugal. On September 23 a live video was recorded for 'Hero Of The Day', which would be released as a single a little later. The song already had a studio-shot concept promo (a series of bleak scenes involving a weak-looking, gloomy teenager), but the live Barcelona footage was used to promote the single on various TV shows including the UK's *Top Of The Pops*. The recording itself was difficult: a metronome was used to guide the band along with the song (which would be broadcast in its studio version over the live footage, so the two versions had to match exactly) and sounded through the PA, to the confusion of the audience. Metallica needed three takes to nail the song, and Ulrich asked the crowd to be louder for each take, with the result that the final version was accompanied by a baying audience – perhaps inappropriately given that the song is one of the more downbeat of their catalogue.

The song was released on September 28, after the band had performed two shows in Italy, and peaked at number 17 in the UK. Moving from Italy through France, England, Ireland, Scotland, Wales, Germany, Switzerland and Holland, Metallica also took time to perform on the British TV show *Later With Jools Holland* on November 13. They played a brief set of 'Wasting My Hate', a solo acoustic version of 'Mama Said' from Hetfield and 'King Nothing', which was later available on the *Later, Louder* DVD released in 2003. The following night Metallica appeared at the European MTV Awards, also in London, where they ran through a quick and chaotic medley of 'Last Caress' and the ever-popular 'So What?' Unusually, they told a reporter that they liked the work of ex-NWA rapper Dr. Dre and were interested in working with him: Dre later responded, "Well I don't wanna work with them!"

The same month a feature appeared in *The Guitar Magazine* in which James spoke at length about *Load* and its aftermath. It emerged that Kirk had also contributed to the rhythm guitar tracks on the album, a total departure from previous records, on which James played them all himself. As he told reporter Douglas Noble: "Getting Kirk to play along with me and have the parts complement each other was an even bigger challenge than me trying to double it and get it tighter than a gnat's ass, like we did before. And it's obviously affected the sound – it's broadened it and made it deeper, instead of being a one-dimensional sound. Most of the time my rhythm parts are mixed on the left and Kirk's are on the right so you can hear who's doing what – which is cool." However, Hetfield didn't explain why the renowned heaviness of Metallica's earlier work had been replaced by bluesy, lightweight rock playing . . . although he did elaborate a little on the simpler, more organic song structures which his band had been creating since the Black Album: "Sure, the arrangements are simpler. It's a reaction to *. . . And Justice For All*, which was really, really anal. Every little bit was worked out. The arrangement was so orchestrated that it got really stiff, and when we were on tour it got really boring. So we knew we had to move on and the Black Album was pretty much the opposite. I think *Load* is even more simplistic, in a way. First we chose riffs that were great, and Lars and I would go jam on them. Then, instead of trying to force one riff with another riff, it was like, 'Let's jam on it,' and we'd see what came out of that. 'Does it have to be another riff? Maybe an open chord bit would sound better?' It was more of a feel thing when we were writing this stuff. So the songs kinda started writing themselves, in a way, which was a little more fun than just trying to stick a bunch of riffs together."

Metallica's songwriting process was a little looser and more relaxed, it appeared: "I think, when we took a break between the albums, we grew up on our own and came back with a little more respect for each other," said James. "Lars and I were clamped down pretty hard on a lot of the stuff in the past and we could see the other guys were a little unhappy. Everyone's gotta be happy so you've gotta give and take sometimes, and it's working out really good." Asked about the implications of joining the renownedly alternative Lollapalooza tour, he added with a frown: "People forget that when we started we were pretty fucking alternative, man, and we haven't changed to fit in with anything . . . We did Lollapalooza because we wanted to and it was cool. It was as simple as that. We got to see a few great bands and make some new friends. We played in front of some people who came to see us and some people who wouldn't normally listen to us."

Concerts in Sweden and Finland took Metallica up to the release of 'Mama Said', which appeared on November 18 and featured a promo video of James strumming a guitar in the back of a taxi, cowboy hat and boots in place and the very picture of the modern country star. The song went to number 19 in Britain and was similarly successful worldwide. For two shows over two nights, Metallica's support act was Apocalyptica, an unlikely but interesting choice of opener: the Finnish band is a cello-only outfit which plays covers of Metallica songs in a classical style, with greater success than might be imagined.

Moving on through Sweden, Norway and Denmark and back to the USA in time for the end of the year, Metallica rounded off a successful (but controversial) 'comeback' year with six Californian concerts. The final show, on New Year's Eve, took place at the SJ Arena in San Jose and featured an appropriate jam on Iron Maiden's 'Two Minutes To Midnight' at 11.58pm (Metallica had been including snippets of other metal songs in their set for some time, including the intro of Slayer's 'Raining Blood').

The first five months of 1997 were practically solid touring for Metallica. With Corrosion Of Conformity (one of James' favourite bands) in support, they took *Load* through the established routes which, by now, they knew so well: Utah, Arizona, New Mexico, Nevada, Colorado, Iowa, Minnesota and Kansas all hosted the Metallica experience. In an interview with *Metal Edge* magazine, Lars insisted that the band were having the time of their lives despite the hard work they were putting in: "We're in better shape than we've ever been in before. We're definitely having our fun, but overall we're probably partying less than we did when we played in America before. I'm in much better shape than I was in '92. I'm running, doing my five or six miles. Aerobically and physically I'm in much better shape than I've ever been in before. I can feel that it's not much of a struggle. I can remember nights on the '92 tour where I'd struggle to get through the last hour but I don't feel that any more."

This tour was notable for an onstage trick Metallica performed to shock the audience: towards the end of the show, James would pretend to be injured by a rogue pyrotechnic and vanish from sight. A stuntman dressed as one of Metallica's crew would appear, covered in flames, and roll in apparent agony on stage while a flock of paramedics attended him. Lars explained that many audience members failed to see the joke: "I gotta tell you, even with press and the internet I'm pretty amazed . . . the other day we were signing autographs and these girls said, 'Tell your pyro guys we hope they're OK.' About 75 per cent of the people I talked to believed it's real. They're saying, 'I can't believe you kept playing with a guy running around on stage on fire' . . . It's one of the guys on the pyro crew. He sets himself on fire every night."

While James soaked up country music and mellowed out, Lars discovered the joys of a steady relationship (he had been married once before, to Debbie Ulrich, although little is known about her or their life together). His girlfriend, Skylar Satinstein, was a medical student who he had recently met. He explained, "I feel for the first time in my life the relationship I'm in is on a par with the band in terms of importance. I've never had a relationship like that, the band was always more important. I find that I really value spending time away from it now. I was the guy who had the reputation of dealing with Metallica 24 hours a day, and getting all manic about it. It's not like that as much any more." Lars had met Skylar in a New York bar and been impressed when she didn't know who he was: "What's so cool about the last ten or eleven months together for us is that she doesn't give two shits about all of this. She respects it and appreciates it, but it's not what brought us together and it's not a big part of our life together . . . We spend every given moment that we can together but I'm out here travelling now. When we have ten days off I'll be in New York with her, she comes out on weekends when I'm on tour and she has a month off here and there." Wedding plans were on the cards. Lars proposed to Skylar (who had been close to the actor Matt Damon when she first met Ulrich. Damon had allegedly referred to Lars as a "fucking stupid rock star", although he later apologised for this) with a bouquet of 255 roses – one for each of the 254 days they had known each other, plus one for the future. No wonder he was in good spirits.

A further sign of Metallica's growth came when Lars explained that his band dabbled in recreational drugs on occasion. James had mentioned the subject in a *Kerrang!* interview and Lars expanded on it as follows: "We've always on a very recreational level [used] drugs at specific times. It's been the same for the last 15 years. Nobody goes overboard. We'd basically lie about it to the press whenever anyone asked us about it, and there came a point in the last year where we stopped lying about it if people asked. Everybody apart from James dabbles a little bit on a recreational level . . . It's possible to dabble in something without it having become something that takes over your life, whatever it is – alcohol, drugs, anything. It doesn't have relevance in our daily lives and isn't anything to worry about, because if there's anyone who's at the top of the game in terms of doing what we're doing and being professional about it, it's us. What other people think makes no difference to me. What I do on a day off is my business, end of story." Drug references had been few and far between before this point, although evidence was there if one cared to look (Jason told me about 'piles of powder' on the Monsters Of Rock tour of 1988; Kirk later referred to his and Jason's love of a mutual joint; Lars admitted occasional use of cocaine in the late Nineties), but now that social attitudes were changing a little – the 'just say no' generation of the Eighties had matured much by the mid-Nineties – the subject was less taboo.

One pointer to the future came when Lars referred to unspecified 'friction' which the band and Jason had had during the recording of *Load*. However, this appeared to have died down by this stage: "We're a lot more respectful," said Lars. "We have some fun with each other but the most important thing for us is to go on stage and play good and connect and do our thing, and right now we're doing that, probably the best we've ever done. That makes everyone get along really well and respect each other really well, and we can have fun with other side things and poke fun at each other."

It later emerged, however, that on the Lollapalooza tour Newsted was travelling separately from the rest of the band: a sign of trouble ahead, perhaps?

If the Lollapalooza tour had been tiring and the subsequent months in early 1997 exhausting, the rest of the first half of 1997 was remorseless. In February, March, April and May, Metallica criss-crossed the USA and Canada several times (a notable stage appearance from Ted Nugent in Detroit saw the two acts perform a rendition of the loinclothed huntsman's 'Stranglehold' together). However, Metallica were clearly enjoying the experience: perhaps Lars' insistence that his band get physically fit was paying off, or maybe the fact that he and Skylar got married on January 26 had filled him with renewed vigour. The couple tied the knot at a small ceremony in Las Vegas, having cannily prepared for any rush of sightseeing fans by spreading a crafty rumour that the event had been cancelled. James was Lars' best man, a fact acknowledged by Ulrich the following night at the American Music Awards. Metallica performed 'King Nothing' and accepted an award for Best Metal/Hard Rock Album: in his speech Lars said, "I would like to thank this man, James Hetfield, for putting on his best suit and being my best man at my wedding last night."

After the tour finally rolled to a halt in May, Metallica had a couple of months off before the summer festival season and, it was announced, the release of a new studio album. James used some of this time to get married himself: on August 17, he and his girlfriend Francesca Tomasi became husband and wife. The couple had known each other for some years, Francesca having begun her association with Metallica as a member of the security crew before becoming part of the wardrobe team. As the story goes, Hetfield proposed to her in a restaurant after trying unsuccessfully to place the ring on the table without her noticing. The only way he could think of was to tell her she had spinach in her teeth, which prompted her to visit the bathroom. On her return, the ring was in place and the question was popped.

A week later, the band played at three European festivals in Belgium, Germany and the UK. Firm announcements had now been made that a new album would be appearing in November. The content of the album would be more tracks from the *Load* sessions, making the new record a kind of Part 2 to the previous year's release. In October Metallica announced that they would be promoting the release with a free show, somewhere in the States, on Veterans' Day, November 11 – but that the fans could suggest which venue would be best. Giving the fans a toll-free 800 phone number and an email address for suggestions, Metallica sat back and waited for a response. Over 120,000 fans called the number.

Meanwhile, a film entitled *Spawn* was making a modest return at US box offices: the story of a cartoon-strip hero obliged to fight the forces of hell, it was a darkly entertaining tale and featured on its soundtrack a song called 'Satan', co-composed by Kirk Hammett and the British dance act Orbital. The song is unremarkable other than for the fact that it shows a certain open-mindedness on Kirk's part: the idea of partnership with a purely electronic act was progressive, even if the results were unspectacular.

In October Metallica performed two acoustic-only sets at the annual Bridge School Benefit Shows at Shoreline Amphitheater, San Francisco. This yearly event, organised by Neil Young, raises funds for the Bridge School for disabled children, and has become a regular feature of the rock calendar. At the first concert Metallica played an hour of songs, including a new track called 'Low Man's Lyric' and a rendition of the Lynyrd Skynyrd song 'Tuesday's Gone' alongside Jerry Cantrell from Alice In Chains. Also on the bill were Kacy Crowley, The Blues Travelers, Lou Reed, The Smashing Pumpkins, Alanis Morissette, The Dave Matthews Band and Neil Young himself.

On October 22 a new Metallica single appeared entitled 'The Memory Remains', which featured guest vocals by Marianne Faithfull, the husky voiced former lover of Mick Jagger and arguably the first ever Rock Chick. It was accompanied by a spectacular video – easily Metallica's best yet. It was superb, revolving (literally) around the idea that the band were standing on a platform which was spinning around in a large room. In fact, a room was created in a giant box, which itself spun around the band's platform to give the impression that they were flying around in a circle and defying gravity. It's a gripping spectacle, with plenty of dark elements: the room is decorated like a gothic, Victorian parlour, and Hetfield sneers into the camera with tangible venom. The video was shot at the Van Nuys airport in LA and cost more than $400,000.

Unfortunately the song itself, 'The Memory Remains', is just awful. Based on a slow, boring, resolutely un-powerful riff, it lumbers along incessantly, constantly trying to clamber out of the swamp onto a more enlightening level, but failing. Even Faithfull's deliberately witch-like, croaked chorus of "Na na na-na" is incongruous rather than chilling. It was a massive disappointment for anyone who was hoping that the new material might be better than that of *Load*. Of Faithfull's involvement, Lars told MTV: "We sat there and we wrote this song, and it started dawning on us that maybe having a character on the song would be a good thing, having a voice or character, somebody playing part of the scenario that was being created for the song. And we had a very, very short list of people, Joni Mitchell . . . there was basically nobody, and every time we said we need someone charismatic, someone who is weathered in every possible way . . . so I called her up on the phone and said, it would mean a lot to us if you would sing on our record, and she did. Me and James jumped into an airplane and flew over to Dublin, and I had the tape under my arm . . . we hung out all day and drank wine and exchanged stories, and she sang on our record and that was it."

Despite the mediocrity of the results, nothing, it seemed, could affect the commercial status of Metallica and the single jumped to number 13 in Britain, helped along Stateside by the enormous free show which the band finally performed on November 11 as scheduled. The venue chosen was the parking lot of Philadelphia's CoreStates Arena, but the road to the show had not been smooth: many local government officials had been opposed to the idea from its inception, with one city councilman, James Kenney, telling the local press: "On the face of it, I think it would be a big mistake. Once again, you're going to have problems with crowds in a residential area. You'll have noise and traffic congestion . . . If the heavy-metal rock group wants to hold a concert here, why not hold it inside the CoreStates Spectrum?" He added with commendable subtlety: "And if you're putting all these Beavis and Butt-heads in the parking lot, where are you going to park the cars?" Neighbours of the parking lot also mounted a protest, but permission was ultimately granted and Hetfield told the press in a statement that: "We asked our fans to find us a place to play, and they came through. And now on November 11 we're going to blow them away. There's no better place to play millions of decibels than the Hard-CoreStates arena."

The show, dubbed the "Million Decibel March", was a success, with the set a well-judged mixture of old songs ('Helpless', 'The Four Horsemen', 'The Thing That Should Not Be', 'Am I Evil?', 'Master Of Puppets', 'No Remorse'), recent covers ('Stone Cold Crazy', 'Tuesday's Gone'), Black Album and *Load* reliables ('Of Wolf And Man', 'King Nothing') and two new songs, the dismal, unaccountably popular 'The Memory Remains' and a much better, faster new song, 'Fuel'. The set finished with a blast through 'Damage, Inc.'. The *Philadelphia Inquirer* said about the show: "It was part burlesque show, part rugby match, and hearing-loss loud. The band was profane on stage and charming before the show. Police pronounced the fans better behaved than a Philadelphia Eagles crowd. And neighbors who feared the worst from the self-styled Loudest Band in the World complained more about the sound from the news choppers circling overhead."

On November 13 Metallica performed a free concert in London, selecting (with a very late-Nineties perversity) a dance venue, the Ministry Of Sound. Lars said, with typical assurance: "I've never heard of the Ministry Of Sound but I'm sure Metallica playing there will make it a hit!" Four days later, the new album – *Reload* – was released. MTV asked Metallica to explain their motives behind releasing another record so soon after the last one, and Lars answered: "People ask me,

'How does it tie in, is it Part Two of *Load*?' It's nothing more, nothing less. It's not the scraps, it's not all the B material. It's the other 13 songs. *Load* was supposed to be a double album and it still is. The two records just came out a year apart." James explained that the second set of songs needed some studio work but that the band wanted to get on the road before they could be finished – hence the year's delay between the two albums: "We liked the songs and we wanted to get back into the studio after a little less of a tour. A lot of them needed a little work. We re-recorded at least one of the songs because it wasn't the right feel. 'Low Man's Lyric' is the one. It's got a more broken-down feel to it, and the kind of homeless feel to it, which is pretty cool."

Asked how fans were reacting to the newer style of music, he added: "There's a little more opinionated responses on these last couple of records, I think. It's not like, 'It's OK,' it's 'I hate it,' or 'I love it,' you know? Which is how I think it should be. We're not meant to be background music while you're driving. You either live Metallica or you don't want to live Metallica. And I think at the end of the day, it's us pleasing ourselves. We're selfish bastards, and have been since day one, and that's how we've stayed pure and how we've kind of lasted all this time."

If purity is what Lars was after, Metallica certainly achieved it with *Reload*. Pure mediocrity, that is. The album is even worse than *Load*. It has one decent song, 'Fuel', which starts the record: a powerful, staccato statement of intent with a neatly executed gasoline/blood metaphor, and admirable in its economy and precision. But it's all downhill from there. We've already discussed the interminable 'The Memory Remains', and 'Devil's Dance' isn't much better, a plodalong tale of boredom with James attempting and failing to replicate the creepy child's-nightmare vibe he perfected on 'Enter Sandman'.

'The Unforgiven II' is well constructed, at least, as was its predecessor: opening with an almost old-school metal-style dual lead riff, the softer sections of this ballad-like song are satisfying enough – even if Lars' clod-hopping snare-bashing spoils the song's texture utterly. Rimshots would have sufficed, but Ulrich has never been renowned for his subtlety, and the song's riffier sections are nothing new.

The next chunk of the album is all downhill. 'Better Than You' and 'Slither' are just terrible, permeated by a dull, repetitive riff in the former and a nauseatingly cheery, upbeat motif in the latter. Both settle into turgid, overly 'rock' mode very soon after an intro – and on the latter, Hetfield's vocal is even reminiscent of mid-Eighties blues-rock. 'Carpe Diem Baby', one of the least attractive titles in Metallica's canon, has absolutely nothing to recommend it other than a slightly doomy bridge which brings some welcome atmospherics to an otherwise mundane song. 'Bad Seed' is staccato riffing of the least impressive order and is helped out only by an inspired solo from Kirk. 'Where The Wild Things Are' is seven minutes of moderately interesting, dark chords – see, they can still do it when they can drag themselves away from the turgid, mid-tempo grind – but it inevitably outstays its welcome.

Unfortunately, the remainder of the record is a parade of unrelenting grimness. Thrash fans will understand how depressing it is to write the following words: 'Prince Charming' is just unnecessary, punchy, stop-start riffing along the lines of a faster 'The Memory Remains'; 'Attitude' is a kind of sub-Kiss, sub-Aerosmith, sub-everything attempt at horrible FM rock; and 'Fixxxer' is another pointlessly long album closer, all undefined riffs strung together and far too much wah pedal from Kirk and/or James. Along with 'Fuel', the only other song on *Reload* worth your time is 'Low Man's Lyric', which – if you can get past the fact that, just as with 'Mama Said', you're listening to Metallica playing a roots ballad – is perfectly serviceable, with a pleasant hurdy-gurdy and violin. James' self-consciously 'sensitive' singing lets the song down a little, but bear with it and it's not bad at all.

But if 'not bad' is the conclusion about a song which is the second best track on a Metallica album, you know you have a problem. Even the worst song on *Ride The Lightning* ('Escape', perhaps) or *Master Of Puppets* (possibly 'Leper Messiah') are several times better than 'Fuel', *Reload*'s 'high point'. And *Load* was only slightly better, after all.

How on earth had Metallica come to release two such albums? Had their songwriting ability deserted them entirely since the intensely rewarding thrash metal days, or even since the populist but acceptable Black Album? What had gone wrong?

20

The Truth About *Load* And *Reload*

Myth 11: *Load* and *Reload* were the innovative sound of Metallica growing up and stretching out.

After winding up 1997 with a slot on *Top Of The Pops*, another show at the Ministry Of Sound, a stab at 'The Memory Remains' on the TV show *du jour*, Chris Evans' *TFI Friday*, a set for Virgin Radio, and promo concerts in Germany, Sweden, Denmark and France, Metallica returned to the USA for a December 6 appearance on NBC's *Saturday Night Live*, the *Billboard* Music Awards in Las Vegas and an acoustic set on San Jose radio. Not until this point would they have had an opportunity to sift through the reviews of *Reload*.

It's amusing to speculate what they must have read and how they reacted. Reviews of *Load* and *Reload* (which the band treated as two halves of the same album, so we will do likewise) basically fell into two camps, just as James had suggested when he declared that people either loved or hated the new direction. Fans of brutal, fast metal disliked them and found them boring and weak (in case you hadn't realised already, I'm one of those). Conversely, there was a whole demographic of music fans who enjoyed both records immensely. The latter group can be summed up as (a) mostly younger than the first group; (b) more open-minded; (c) less experienced in metal; and (d) more enamoured of Metallica and the notion that 'their' band could do very little wrong – and if they did make a false move, it was acceptable because they were just trying out new ideas or growing older and more experienced as people.

Let's be positive and look at the good things about the *Loads* and what they reveal about their creators. Firstly, there is one simple, and eternal, truism to which rock music conforms: all artists grow older, and in doing so, usually become more contented with their lot. With contentment comes a lessening of the desire – or need – to innovate (because there is less desire to change the way things are) and to express anger (because there is less anger to express). With less anger comes emotions which are expressed as calmer, quieter: less dramatic feelings such as sadness, curiosity, love, anxiety, fear and so on. These make less of a noise than anger – and if this occurs in the case of heavy metal, which itself is the music of anger, the results must by definition be less powerful.

Lemmy once told me that "The great thing about Motörhead is that we never lost our hunger – a great asset for any band"; an admission, perhaps, that Motörhead never reached anything like the global popularity level of Metallica, which at the same time kept them from mellowing out. By the time that *Reload* was released, the four members of Metallica (and specifically the main songwriting team of Lars Ulrich and James Hetfield) were in their mid-thirties, with almost two decades of playing aggressive music under their belts, wives and girlfriends to soothe their tempers, a loyal fanbase who loved their work, enormous personal wealth and teams of assistants to pander to their whims. Who wouldn't be content in this situation? And so the mellowing-out of the *Loads* is just part of life, you might conclude: 'Mama Said' and 'The Unforgiven II' are the inevitably relaxed results of being mature, and more interested in expressing positive than negative emotions.

Secondly, the business of creating new songs and albums, over and over again, must inevitably become stale after decades of the studio-tour-studio-tour routine. In Metallica's case, where each album progressively represented a longer and harder commitment to perfection, the urge to do something different must have become irresistible. For instance, James always exercised an iron control over the rhythm guitar tracks on Metallica songs: with the *Load*s he allowed Kirk to come in and help out, which led to a looser, less 'metal' and more 'rock' vibe. This new sound is a direct result of Hetfield getting older and more relaxed and the band's desire to move forward.

Dave Mustaine explained that he and his band Megadeth went through a similar process. When I asked if he was still interested in playing thrash metal, he said: "We can still do it, but we were more into it when we were young and getting laid. Then all we wanted to do was get the songs over with as quickly as possible. As we matured I think the whole ritual became more important. You know, I'm not gonna say that I have to put 'Bolero' on and light candles and drink wine, but to me the craft of making a song is much more important nowadays. We wanna write a song which is timely as well as timeless." It seems that age brings a depth of skill that youth cannot simulate: "I think it takes a really developed songwriter to make heavy melodic music. Anybody can write heavy music, and anybody can write melodic music, but to do the two is really hard, and it's even harder to write something that's your own."

Much of this maturity comes through experience, and Metallica had plenty of that. Just a single six-month world tour is a gruelling journey stuffed with eye-opening experiences – but to go through it a dozen or more times must be a learning curve like no other. Add to this the wealth of personal trauma which anyone goes through in their life – for example, Lars, Jason and Kirk all endured divorces in their twenties – and it's little wonder that once they had achieved a measure of personal contentment, they stepped off the gas.

What's more, there is the argument that with the *Loads*, Metallica demonstrated not sterility but progression. As producer Andy Sneap said, "They've done their own thing. If they'd done a Slayer and done the same thing constantly, I think we'd all be saying, they've run out of ideas. They're getting older, and I'm sure their bank balances aren't hurting." It's true that (as far as we know) Metallica have always done what they think is right, rather than bowing to managerial or record company pressures – and for this they deserve a measure of respect. After all, what's wrong with pushing out the boundaries and trying new things? Life is about progression and change: stagnancy means death.

Another point in Metallica's favour is that the *Load* and *Reload* era may simply be a glitch. In two decades' time, music fans may refer to Metallica's 'mid-period' career of the *Loads* as simply a time when they lost their way for a little while, before returning to form. Look at the careers of long-serving artists such as Neil Young, Bob Dylan, James Taylor, Joni Mitchell, Elton John and the Rolling Stones, for example. For them, a two-album slump is a mere blip on the radar of their 30- or 40-year career. Can we not forgive Metallica for two lame years?

Yet another argument in defence of the *Loads* is that times have changed. Truly wrathful music is different in the 21st century to the beast it was when Metallica ruled the roost. In 1986 they, Slayer, Anthrax and Megadeth made the most evil, angry, fast and uncompromising music available anywhere on earth. But even a couple of years later, harsher and heavier bands than the thrash metal titans of the day were emerging in the death metal field: by the early Nineties Death, Morbid Angel, Deicide, Cannibal Corpse and a whole range of vitriolic acts had taken over the reins of brutality, even if their sales figures never even approached those of the Big Four of Thrash, especially those of Metallica, in their heyday. By the late Nineties and the turn of the century, these were being superseded by even heavier, faster, sickeningly powerful acts such as Nile, Hate Eternal, Mortician and the Berzerker, whose gut-churning, massively downtuned riffing and insanely fast blastbeats made even Metallica's heavier songs ('The Thing That Should Not Be' is an example) sound lightweight. How, then, should we expect *Load* and *Reload* – written, performed and toured by affluent, comfortable men in their thirties – to compete in the heaviness stakes?

And this isn't even taking in the black metal and grindcore movements, whose phenomenal musical power and often horrifying lyrical stance is worlds away from the pleasant blues-rock of the *Loads*. The Norwegian musician Samoth (Thomas Haugen), the ex-Emperor and current Zyklon guitarist, remembers a time when Metallica fitted into this pantheon of metallic horror – and his memory of the way that 'heavy' music progressed and became more extreme is an exact illustration of this: "At some point somebody gave me a copy of Mayhem's *Deathcrush* mini-album on tape and that was by far the most intense, sick shit I ever heard. Previous to that I had become more interested in thrash and speed metal and was a big fan of bands such as Metallica, Testament, Slayer, Megadeth, etc. I kept opening my eyes to the worldwide underground network and soon discovered more brutal bands like Morbid Angel, Death, Obituary, Cryptic Slaughter, Sepultura and so on. I also became very interested in black metal . . . I was already familiar with bands such as Bathory, Venom, Celtic Frost and Possessed of course, but at that point things started to happen in Norway and there was a new movement on the rise."

Finally, there is the often-made point that between the 27 songs shared between *Load* and *Reload*, there was one pretty good album's worth of material. Metallica's error, you might say, was simply that they were too loose when it came to editing, and that one record composed of the best 13 or 14 songs from the *Load* sessions would have been perfectly acceptable. As Andy Sneap concludes: "I think they could have got one good album out of the two *Load* and *Reload* albums. It was just spread a bit thin."

So much for the pro-*Loads* arguments.

For every single one of these points there is a persuasive counter-argument. Yes, all artists do get older (unless they die or retire early) and most of them become more contented, which means that their music is less aggressive. But this is neither here nor there. What the music fans want is what they like, not what they don't like – and if the quality is not there, he or she will not simply shrug it off and accept that their favourite band is older and calmer these days. Not at £16 per CD, anyway.

Yes, for many artists the business of creating new songs and albums, over and over again, must inevitably become stale. But so what? Recording a song isn't like working in a coalmine. Tuning a guitar isn't like digging a hole in the road. If the recording process is boring, either change it or do another job. If the slog of recording and then touring is getting you down, perhaps it's time for a performing artist to consider a career change?

Yes, maturity brings wisdom, and wisdom leads to calm, which doesn't sit well with heavy metal. But that's no excuse for dull, un-imaginative songs like 'Ronnie', 'Attitude', 'Fixxxer' and 'The Memory Remains'. You can be calm and innovative at the same time (look at Miles Davis, for example).

Yes, it's possible to view the slowing-down and mellowing-out that typified Metallica's songwriting between the Eighties and the Nineties as artistic progression. But if progression is defined as a move from one plane to another higher, better or more interesting one, so be it – but that's hardly what happened with the *Loads*. The difference between the Eighties albums and the Black Album is that the group became efficient, clever and honest. The difference between the Black Album and the *Loads* (which even together sold millions of units fewer than their earth-shaking predecessor) is that Metallica slowed down, drifted aimlessly in search of a direction and ultimately released two records' worth of vague, undefined songs. That isn't progression.

Yes, the *Loads* era of 1996–1998 may be just a glitch in what could go on to be a long and distinguished career: in 2003 Kirk Hammett told *Classic Rock* magazine that he thought his band had "ten good years" left in them. If this proves accurate and they retire from active service in 2013, they will have been a performing unit for 32 years, out of which two or three boring years is no great shakes, it's true. But the next studio album after *Reload*, of which there will be much, much more later, was a massive disappointment. Also, in the 22 years of Metallica's existence to 2003, they produced seven original studio (i.e. not live, not covers-based) albums: the fact that two of that seven are of a dismally low standard is difficult to explain away.

Yes, times have changed, and heaviness has been redefined since Metallica's thrash heyday so many times that they hardly appear heavy at all nowadays. But who asked them to play super, super-heavy? No one! They could have played at a level of speed which didn't approach the standards of the vanguard of extreme metal – but still been heavy enough to satisfy their fans. There is a middle way: nobody expects a blur of white noise. But their fans did expect some energy – not lily-livered blues-wailing like 'Ronnie'.

Finally, the idea that between the 27 songs shared between *Load* and *Reload*, there was one very good album's worth of material just isn't true. Is there one truly excellent, life-changing, barrier-breaking song on either *Load* or *Reload*, which might match up to – say – 'Master Of Puppets' or 'One'? No. Are there any moderately good songs on the albums? Yes: I'd say 'Fuel', 'Hero Of The Day' and 'Ain't My Bitch' are worth a listen (although I'm being generous here). But the rest are mediocre or worse – and three good songs do not an album make.

So why did this happen? What's the reason behind this terrible, unexpected fall from grace? Maybe they just got too successful: perhaps the Black Album hindered Metallica as much as helped them forward. As Ian Gillan said (but not about Metallica, or anyone else for that matter): "It can happen that you get a little complacent and you forget why it was you started out in the first place. When you're successful you forget to set yourself the required challenges." Or maybe Metallica just made their changes too fast. As Dave Mustaine told me: "Without directing this conversation towards anybody in particular, if the public has something that they like and it changes radically, it's a little hard to take. You have to round the edges off slowly."

Perhaps the million-dollar question should be, did Metallica sell out? To answer this we need to agree what 'selling out' actually means. Selling out is when an artist deliberately changes his or her work in order to generate more money or approval, or when they go against their own principles for monetary reward. To me, Metallica never did this, not least because the *Loads* albums cannot have generated the kind of income they enjoyed from their three previous albums. They released two poor albums, it's true, but as far as anyone knows, they did it because they thought it was the right thing to do, not because they planned to earn money or prestige from doing so. A central theme I wish to emphasise in this book is that Metallica simply lost their touch, not that they sold out.

The truth is that Metallica are a metal band who tried to embrace other styles of music (certainly alternative rock, maybe blues, perhaps pop) but, in doing so, lost their grip of what they do best: heavy metal with power, aggression and skill. They stretched themselves too far, and lost credibility as a result. Remember Lars' sudden love of Oasis and Black Grape? This change in perspective is, perhaps more than any other, indicative of the changes which had transformed Metallica by the mid-Nineties. Lars, once the unswerving disciple of Diamond Head, Venom and Motörhead and lover of the NWOBHM, was now expressing his admiration for pop-rock acts who were topping the charts. Add to this Hetfield's softer compositions ('Mama Said' was a direct inspiration from his country and western idol, Waylon Jennings) and the broader palette of sounds on *Load* and *Reload* and the net result is a band which had diversified, expanded its horizons and tried to push out its self-imposed boundaries. And lost its way in doing so.

Still not sure what really happened with the *Loads*? Then read this and think. The one overriding fact is that these two albums simply aren't very good. They have their moments, but mostly they're boring, and in parts they're terrible. No matter whether Metallica got old, tired, bored or just curious about other music, the result is that these records are Not Very Good. No more, no less than that. Asked what he thought of *Load*, Kerry King of Slayer told *Kerrang!* in July 1996 that: "The new record is so lame, and I'm not just saying that because of the way they look now. I don't care what they look like. I just hate the

253

record because it has no attitude, no fire, no nothing. It sucks." He was right.

As was journalist Borivoj Krgin: "*Load* was one of the most dis-appointing metal albums ever released, in my opinion. After seemingly doing everything right for over a decade, Metallica, for the first time, did everything wrong, and the songwriting was just weak and was lacking the fire and the excitement of their earlier material. I didn't give a shit about the hair aspect – which is something they got a lot of flak for – I simply thought the songs were inferior to anything the band had done prior to that album, and everything about it seemed watered down. *Reload* was more of the same, and I can't say it was a huge dis-appointment, since we basically knew exactly what to expect at that point."

If you find it strange that I've spent two-thirds of a book heaping praise on Metallica and the last two chapters damning them, you'll know how I – and thousands of other genuine lovers of their music – felt on hearing these albums for the first time. I was shocked, and to a degree I still am.

21

1998–1999

1998 started with more diverse activities for Metallica: at the end of January Kirk married his girlfriend Lani Gruttadauro in Hawaii, with an informal, flower-strewn ceremony. Lars chose to add to his ever-expanding interests by founding a record label, which he called the Music Company and co-managed with a former Metallica tour accountant, Tim Duffy. After striking a distribution deal with Metallica's own record company, Elektra, the Music Company began signing bands which Ulrich had come across and liked, including the Vancouver ska-punk act DDT, the Austin, Texas-based rockers Goudie, the Georgian alternative metallers the Brand New Immortals, and – the best-known Music Company signing to date – the California band Systematic, whose line-up includes ex-Slayer drummer Paul Bostaph. Ulrich divided the rest of his time between preparations for the forthcoming *Reload* tour and visiting his parents: his mother Lone Ulrich was seriously ill with cancer. Sadly, she died on March 22, the night after Metallica played a rehearsal show in San Francisco for MTV.

Boosted by the popularity of the 'Unforgiven II' single, which was released on March 3 and reached number 15 in the UK, the Poor Re-Touring Me '98 Tour took off in earnest in Australia on April 2 and was an instant sell-out, with the hordes of Antipodean Metallica fans delighted to see their idols back, despite the flaws of *Reload*. Ten Australian dates, two in New Zealand, two more in Korea and then a string of eight Japanese dates saw the Metallica message hammered home by the end of May, in time for James to fly home for the birth of his first child, a daughter named Cali Tee Hetfield, who arrived on June 11, 1998.

However, the pace of touring didn't let up and within two weeks of his daughter's arrival Hetfield was obliged to hit the road again for an extended US tour. By the end of June Metallica had played dates in Florida, Georgia, North Carolina and Virginia; July saw them take in Maryland, Ontario, Ohio, Illinois, Michigan, New York, New Jersey, Massachusetts, Connecticut, Pennsylvania, Tennessee, Indiana, Wisconsin, Missouri, Kansas and Texas. 'Fuel' appeared as a single on July 4 (and made it as far as number 31 in Britain), and a month later, Lars too became a father, with his son Myles Ulrich born in New York City on August 5. Both these events gave the August dates in Texas and California renewed vigour.

On September 5, after concerts in Sacramento, Portland and Vancouver, Jason sustained minor head injuries when an unidentified member of the audience threw a glass bottle at the stage. He left for medical attention but returned to finish the set, with James commenting acidly after the show: "We're here to give it all we've got, but I don't understand why we have to watch out for shit thrown at us during the show. I hope they find that fucker who did it." The tour wound up on September 13 after final concerts in Utah, Colorado, Arizona, Nevada and a final night in San Diego.

The day after the tour ended, Metallica surprised many by going straight into the studio to record an entirely new album. Not, however, an album consisting of new material: a record composed entirely of covers, and due to appear later in the year. Little was revealed about its content until an October 18 show at the Playboy Mansion in Los Angeles, at which they performed a 45-minute set including two new cover versions: a take on The Misfits' 'Die Die My Darling' (not particularly surprising: after all, The Misfits' 'Last Caress' had been a staple of Metallica's live set for several years) and a cover of 'Turn The Page' by MOR stalwart Bob Seger (a much more unusual choice). The latter was intended for a single release and a video clip was made for it on October 21. Directed by Swedish director Jonas Akerlund (who also filmed Madonna's award-winning 'Ray Of Light' video and The Prodigy's controversial 'Smack My Bitch Up'), the shoot was held at Raleigh Studios in Los Angeles. The results were subtler and more moving than the technicolour, abrasive edges of either of those well-known promo videos: the video depicted a single mother, eking out an existence as a stripper and prostitute while trying to look after her child in motel rooms.

A series of club shows was set up to promote the new album, which was to be titled *Garage Inc.*, but before this could happen a lawsuit had to be settled. It had come to the attention of Metallica's management that the Amazon.com website was offering for sale a CD titled *Bay Area Thrashers: The Early Days* as a UK import. The 30-minute album purported to be a live recording from 1981 made by the Mustaine/ McGovney line-up, but was in fact revealed to be the contents of the following year's *No Life 'Til Leather* demo spruced up with some crowd noise and some dialogue by Hetfield taken from the *Cliff 'Em All* video. The item swiftly vanished from Amazon's website and remains sought after for those who collect Metallica bootlegs: the band had clearly become aware that bootlegs existed and were prepared to take steps against those who sold them.

With the case underway, Metallica performed their small-venue concerts to promote *Garage Inc.* and took the novel decision to ask a Metallica tribute band called Battery to support them. The shows featured Metallica playing covers and Battery Metallica originals, and were fanclub-only affairs in Ontario, Chicago, Detroit, Philadelphia and New York, the perfect live tryout for the 'new' material. After a November 22 video shoot for one of the songs, Thin Lizzy's 'Whiskey In The Jar', the new album appeared in the form of *Garage Inc.* two days later.

A double-CD set, *Garage Inc.* was split into one disc of new recordings and a second containing the covers which Metallica had recorded to date. The aim had clearly been to demonstrate the breadth of Metallica's influences, as there were some unexpected choices on there: also for the first time came a detailed explanatory sleevenote text, written by journalist David Fricke, which cast some light on the stories behind the choice of songs. Add to this images of early tickets, diary entries and other memorabilia, reproduced images from the *Garage Days Re-Revisited* EP and two photo spreads depicting Metallica as a bunch of oil-smeared mechanics and the 'Metallicats', a white-tuxedoed covers band, and *Garage Inc.* felt like a fairly complete package for a covers album. But was the music any good?

'Free Speech For The Dumb', the 1982 song by British punk band Discharge, was a promising start. After the unnecessary noodling and vague textures of the *Loads*, this minimalist, simple grind, consisting of one repeated bellow of "Free speech for the dumb − free fuckin' speech!", a harsh, grating riff of near-perfect economy and a deliberately anarchic solo from Hammett, sounded completely fresh. The booklet text confirmed that it was Cliff Burton who had introduced Metallica to the joys of Discharge, whose infectious, simple hooks and choruses were soon part and parcel of the band's on-the-road listening.

Diamond Head's 'It's Electric' is less successful, its winding, sub-Purple riff nothing Metallica hadn't performed a hundred times before and the whole, back-to-1980 up-tempo texture seemed less impressive than the other DH songs which Metallica had adopted. Similarly, Black Sabbath's 'Sabbra Cadabra' from 1973 was competent rather than eye-opening; perhaps the homogenous production, which doesn't really allow any individual instrument to stand out, lets it down. 'Turn The Page', by Bob Seger, is much better; behind a sensitive reading of a subtle song, Metallica's dense arrangement makes the original, rather bland composition into a darker, more palatable brew. The Misfits' 'Die Die My Darling' is pretty entertaining too, with Hetfield's snarl of "Just shut your pretty mouth!" suitably venomous. Like 'Free Speech For The Dumb', this is a song which Metallica simply couldn't get wrong, as are the other Misfits tunes which they have covered over the years.

Nick Cave's 'Loverman' is a weird one. Metallica's version isn't entirely successful – it's overblown, lacks the subtlety of the original, and goes on too long for even the most patient listener – but the fact that the band even attempted to emulate the dark, dark sounds of Australia's most cerebral songwriter deserves respect. Metallica's homage to vintage black metal, 'Mercyful Fate' (a medley of the Danish band's 'Satan's Fall', 'Curse Of The Pharoahs', 'A Corpse Without Soul', 'Into The Coven' and 'Evil') is another no-brainer: the songs, segued together perfectly, reach the same polite levels of aggression as the originals and, while the result isn't particularly enthralling (a take on Venom's 'Black Metal' or Bathory's 'Possessed' would have been much more exciting, for example), it's acceptable.

Blue Oyster Cult's 'Astronomy' isn't great, unfortunately. A blues-rock workout of unavoidable tedium, it never really takes off apart from some crisp lead work from Hammett. The background atmospherics work well, but listeners had had more than enough of that with *Reload*. Much better is Metallica's take on Thin Lizzy's 'Whiskey In The Jar' – or, to be exact, Lizzy's arrangement of the traditional Irish folk tune, which had been a hit for the band in 1972. While the original lacked bass (Lizzy frontman Phil Lynott lent his vocals only to the keen, acoustic tune), Metallica's driving, gripping take was catchy enough to be memorable but hard enough for credibility. Amazingly, James pulled off lines like "Whack for my daddy-o" with aplomb, although many critics disliked the song. When it later appeared as a single, the CD artwork was a collage of negative reviews from magazines.

Lynyrd Skynyrd's 'Tuesday's Gone', the first record which James Hetfield bought as a child, was next, and seems to go on forever. But at least it has depth, perhaps due to the calibre of special guests which appear on it: the recording was made in December 1997 at the studios of KSJO FM in San Jose, with Alice In Chains drummer and guitarist Sean Kinney and Jerry Cantrell, harmonica player John Popper (Blues Traveller), bassist extraordinaire Les Claypool of Primus on banjo, plus guitarists Pepper Keenan (Corrosion of Conformity), Jim Martin (ex-Faith No More), and Gary Rossington (an original member of Lynyrd Skynyrd). Perhaps it's the vanity project of a bunch of rockers wanting to display their softer side, but it works, not least in the choruses, which are both evocative and subtle.

Subtlety is not the name of the game on Discharge's 'The More I See', however; another, short, nasty song based around one riff and one line. Like the song which opens the disc and 'Whiskey In The Jar', it's one of the album's true highlights.

Old-school fans probably already had the second CD, a simple 16-song collection divided into the *Garage Days Re-Revisited* EP (which allowed UK fans the chance to hear Metallica's take on Killing Joke's 'The Wait', which had been omitted from the original vinyl to allow it singles-chart status); *Garage Days Revisited '84* ('Am I Evil?' and 'Blitzkrieg' – the 'Creeping Death' B-sides); *B-Sides & One-Offs '88–'91* (the 'Harvester Of Sorrow' B-sides plus 'So What?', 'Stone Cold Crazy' and a version of Sweet Savage's 'Killing Time' which Metallica had recorded as a B-side to the UK single 'The Unforgiven') and *Motörheadache '95* – the four songs which had been performed at Lemmy's 50th birthday party.

The second disc was much better than the first, and this was the verdict of most reviewers. Perhaps the older songs seemed to have more power than the newer, more considered material ('Helpless', a phenomenally tight, fast track, is a prime example, as is 'Breadfan'); maybe the rawer production of the older songs made them sound more exciting; possibly nostalgia was playing a part. Either way, the album sold respectably if not hugely, keeping Metallica's name in the musical bloodstream and causing some debate about their past and future.

Some of the artists which Metallica had covered were intrigued by what they heard. King Diamond, singer of Mercyful Fate, told me that Lars had phoned him before the recording and told him that Metallica had recorded an album of covers. On hearing the Mercyful Fate medley, Diamond was so stunned that all he could say was "What the fuck have you guys been doing?" Diamond Head singer Sean Harris had known for a long time about Metallica's interest in his band, of course, and remarked: "We didn't make much money out of their versions until the *Garage Inc.* album. I never heard their covers until 20 years later, they sent us the *Creeping Death* EP with 'Am I Evil?' on it. We just thought they weren't as good as ours! They were just becoming the beast that they are now. Even at the beginning you could tell they had their own way of doing things. Don't forget, we were young then, we thought we were gonna be the biggest band in the world too." Guitarist Brian Tatler adds: "They never expected to be as big as they are, they just wanted to be in a band that was a bit like Diamond Head and Motörhead."

Whatever their attitude towards Metallica covering their songs, there can be no question that many of those bands covered benefited enormously from the situation, in particular Diamond Head, for whom mechanical royalties must have accumulated in significant quantities since Metallica first released the *Creeping Death* EP in 1984. In some cases, the honour (and, it can safely be assumed, the financial boost) received by a band lucky enough to be covered by the world's biggest metal band even secured a return from the grave. The Anti-Nowhere League, for example, reformed briefly in the wake of 1991's Metallicised version of 'So What?' Mercyful Fate also enjoyed a period in the spotlight after the widespread approval bestowed on *Garage Inc*'s 'Mercyful Fate Medley' (the nearest Hetfield and crew had been to playing black metal since *Kill 'Em All*).

On November 6, 1998, Kirk underwent an emergency appendectomy in London, but was sufficiently recovered after a few days' bed-rest to continue with promo duties. Metallica finished off the year with two mid-November shows at the Aragon Ballroom in Chicago and the 19th & State Theater in Detroit. While the material went down well, rumours had it that another ambitious recording project was in the works and that *Garage Inc.* would soon be followed up by more product. This turned out to be the release of the *Cunning Stunts* (ho ho, James) live video and DVD, a bog-standard concert video which, however, was one of the very first music-based releases designed specifically for the DVD format.

Eyebrows went up as the industry trade publication *Pollstar* estimated that Metallica had made 32 million dollars for the year 1998 – a far cry from the $16 which Lars had entered into the *Garage Inc.* sleevenotes as the band's pay for their first gig back in 1982.

1999 got underway rapidly, with 'Whiskey In The Jar' released on three different CD formats (it reached number 29 in Britain) and the news the following month that the song 'Better Than You' from *Reload* had been awarded a Grammy for Best Metal Performance. More prestigiously (and reasonably), Metallica were invited to attend a ceremony on March 16 at which the Recording Industry Association of America would present a Diamond Award to the band for 10 million sales of *Metallica*, released almost eight years previously. At the show, which was held at New York City's Roseland Ballroom, other Diamond Awards went to The Eagles and AC/DC, and became the first such presentations. It says something for the giddying spiral which Metallica's commercial fortunes had performed in the Nineties that they should be present at a celebration of such enormous popularity. In his acceptance speech, James Hetfield thanked Bob Rock "for making the big noises extra big". The accolades continued: San Francisco mayor Willie Brown paid tribute to his city's heaviest sons by naming April 7 'Metallica Day' and the band were also inducted into *BAM* magazine's Walk Of Fame.

At about this time James told the press that they planned to headline the forthcoming Woodstock '99 shows in the US and Europe, which were being held to celebrate the third decade since the original New York State event (Metallica had also guested at the 1994 Woodstock show). He added that the project on which they were working at the time was a symphonic recording, with the central concept being that Metallica would record an album with a full orchestra.

That's right – an orchestra. Not content with surprising long-time fans with two dismal albums and just about everybody else with a covers album, Metallica were now planning to tread the route followed by rock dinosaurs since time immemorial (remember 1970's cumbersomely titled *Concerto For Group And Orchestra*, performed by Deep Purple and the Royal Philharmonic Orchestra? No? Well, Metallica clearly hadn't) and take the classical route. Plans were afoot, it was revealed, for 'Nothing Else Matters' strings arranger and conductor extraordinaire Michael Kamen to arrange and conduct the orchestration provided by the San Francisco Symphony Orchestra at two concerts in April, which would be recorded for a live album and DVD release later in the year.

Before this could happen, however, there was the next leg of the Poor Re-Touring Me Tour to complete, this time with Monster Magnet in support. A couple of weeks after Kirk performed a show in San Fran with a band called Swarm who were friends of his, the tour swung into action and three shows were played in Hawaii and Alaska. April 21 and 22 – the dates scheduled for the so-called 'Symphonica' dates – came up quickly, and the band were evidently feeling some nerves about the shows, scheduled to be held at the Berkeley Community Theater. James told the press that Michael Kamen, whose work with Aerosmith, Bob Dylan, David Bowie and Eric Clapton was well known, was "kind of the bridge between two worlds". Kamen himself explained: "Let Metallica be Metallica. Let the San Francisco Symphony be the San Francisco Symphony . . . We have more things in common than things that are different, although the differences are spectacular." Jason Newsted added: "We know they can play, and they know we can play. It's just a matter of figuring out the volume of each other."

The concerts were duly performed and recorded, but little feedback would be heard until the results were released later in the year. In the interim there was the small matter of a world tour to complete. Metallica played the first show in Mexico City where, on April 30, Pantera singer Phil Anselmo joined the band onstage for a rendition of 'Creeping Death'. Supported by Monster Magnet, Sepultura and Marilyn Manson, the band continued through South America, playing in Columbia, Venezuela, Brazil, Chile and Argentina before hitting Europe for the festival season. Support acts for the cross-Atlantic jaunt included Monster Magnet again, Mercyful Fate (a nice touch) and Apocalyptica, all of whom went down a storm at Rock Im Park in

Germany and the Dynamo Open Air Festival in Holland. At the latter festival Metallica brought a group of metal musicians, including Evan Seinfeld of Biohazard and Scott Ian of Anthrax, on stage to sing the middle section of 'Creeping Death'.

The tour rolled on, taking in the Czech Republic, Germany, Sweden, Norway, Poland, Hungary and Italy, where – at Milan's Gods Of Metal Festival on June 5 – old-school followers were delighted to see King Diamond and Hank Sherman of Mercyful Fate accompany Metallica on the medley of their songs which had appeared on *Garage Inc.* More concerts in Slovenia, Romania, Bulgaria, Greece and Turkey were followed by a swift return to the States for the KROQ Event at Irvine Meadows in Irvine, California. Concerts in Switzerland, Germany, Ukraine, Estonia, Denmark, Finland and Belgium ensued, before a memorable show at Dublin's Point venue on July 5 saw Thin Lizzy guitarist Eric Bell appear on stage for a version of 'Whiskey In The Jar'.

More and more live concerts followed. July was spent in France, the UK, Spain, Portugal and Israel before the Woodstock show took place on July 24 at Griffiss Air Base in New York. The three-day event saw dozens of acts perform, notable among which were Metallica and Limp Bizkit. The latter were a rapidly rising force in the 'nu-metal' genre, mixing rap and rock to no great innovation or dexterity but enormous commercial success. However, Woodstock '99 has since been pretty much dismissed as an organisational failure and a depressing indictment of the state of modern youth, thanks to a riot which broke out, temporary buildings being set on fire and the reported rape of a female audience-member. Various eyewitness reports confirm that the show became a spectacle of looting and destruction at some point on the Saturday night after Metallica's set, although contradictory estimates of the actual extent of the violence mean that no one is sure to this day how many of the reported incidents actually took place. What is certain, however, is that the festival's expressed intention – to celebrate the thirtieth anniversary of the original Woodstock with three days of love and peace – was way out of kilter with the actual desires of a portion of the audience. It'll be interesting to see if a Woodstock '09 is suggested on its fortieth anniversary.

Metallica's set was one of the fullest in recent months, with a blast through several of the *Garage Inc.* tracks (including 'So What?', 'Turn

The Page', 'Die Die My Darling' and 'Sabbra Cadabra') reminding the nu-metal generation of older times, plus their own, now-classic material such as 'For Whom The Bell Tolls', 'Battery', 'Enter Sandman', 'Seek And Destroy' and 'Creeping Death'. *Load* and *Reload* yielded 'Fuel', 'King Nothing', 'Bleeding Me' and 'Fixxxer', which many of the crowd relished – perhaps a more telling indictment of the youth of today.

As publicity for the *Garage Inc.* album and the forthcoming orchestral collaboration – which, it was revealed, would be neatly titled *S&M* after its protagonists, the San Francisco Symphony Orchestra and Metallica – began to overlap, the 'Die Die My Darling' single was released on June 14, backed with live tracks recorded at the Roseland Ballroom in New York in November 1998. While the single performed respectably in most territories, it hardly set the charts afire and it was generally concluded that the world could have lived without it. Speculation that Metallica were over-exposing themselves a little peaked when it was announced in September that 'Fuel' would be used on the soundtrack for Hotwheels Turbo, a Playstation car-racing game. Metallica for pre-teens? Now, it seemed, a reality.

Some of the critics' post-*Load*-era Metallica-weariness subsided on the release on November 23, 1999 of *S&M*, a lavishly assembled double album, video and DVD of the April concerts in San Francisco. Metallica promoted the release by reprising the shows in Berlin's Velodrom venue and New York's Madison Square Garden, the former accompanied by the Babelsberger Film Orchester and the latter with the New York Symphony Orchestra. Around this time a flurry of reissue activity saw the *Cliff 'Em All* and *A Year And A Half In The Life Of Metallica* videos released on the then-relatively new DVD format. Faced with such a barrage of product, some observers amplified their 'over-exposure' remarks, while others simply accepted that the band had now become a brand with unrivalled commercial presence.

Luckily, the *S&M* package is a worthy item. Yes, the concept may be overblown and even a little dated, but the music stands on its own merits and, aside from a few blunders in choice of material, it's mostly worth your time. Whether or not fans' devotion to Metallica extended to listening to two hours of previously available material, however, was debatable.

It starts well. The atmospherics of 'The Ecstasy Of Gold', Metallica's intro tune for some years before this, are perfect, even if the Ennio Morricone soundtrack vibes may strike you as a little self-indulgent for a so-called metal band. Either way, the orchestra sounds fantastic – a far cry from the often-subdued taped introduction that audiences are used to. The first full song, the rarely heard 'Call Of Ktulu', which closed 1984's *Ride The Lightning* so memorably, is also a marvellous re-creation, with James' deftly picked intro disguising the nerves he confessed to feeling on the accompanying DVD. The song is a good choice to use at this stage: as an instrumental it lets the listener focus on Michael Kamen's massively dramatic orchestration and the interplay between the two musical groups. Amazingly, both Kirk and Jason can be clearly heard under the swathes of strings and brass that underpin Hetfield's staccato riffs, while Lars' percussion – which he attacks with his usual enthusiasm – is never too intrusive. One slightly sour note comes from the early lead guitar parts, which sound a little out of tune: but as a whole this is a great start.

'Master Of Puppets' doesn't match up to 'Ktulu', unfortunately: a denser, much faster song, the orchestra can't keep up with the riffs (and wisely, Kamen hasn't attempted to do any such thing) but the dashes of strings and stabs which accompany the harder sections of this, one of Metallica's most loved songs, don't add much to the experience. However, where the pairing does work is in the song's extended middle section, in which the orchestra creates a mellow wash for Kirk's fantastic soloing to shine.

'Of Wolf And Man' is a little better, with Kamen's almost horror-movie soundtrack-style orchestration creating a backdrop for Hetfield's none-more-basic, stabbed introduction. It's at moments such as this, when the San Francisco Symphony complements and enhances Metallica's songs, that the album works. In this instance, however, the song itself isn't particularly memorable (although a Hetfield-led bit of audience participation adds some vigour to the otherwise fairly humdrum riffing), but it's a sign, perhaps, that more and better moments are to come. "We got any wolves out there?" shouts James, to a rapturous response from the half-classical, half-metal crowd.

Intentionally or otherwise, the orchestra prefaces the next song, the *Master Of Puppets* highlight 'The Thing That Should Not Be', with a couple of repetitions of the riff underpinning Black Sabbath's classic 'Black Sabbath' – based itself on the sinister tritone (or *diabolus in musica*) which so spooked religious authorities in medieval times. But it's just an interesting moment rather than a full-on tribute, it seems, and the song lurches into motion a few seconds later. This one works extremely well, too, with that fearsomely heavy riff echoed in the strings section, the demonic reverb added to James' vocals bringing an epic feel to the performance (the fact that the singer messes up a line and breaks into laughter at one point doesn't detract from this) and the relentless coda, supported by subtle brass tones, leading into a dramatic, extended ending and a spacey solo section from Hammett.

'Fuel' and 'The Memory Remains', unfortunately, are inessential: the former is strong enough to stand on its merits and doesn't really benefit from the extra backing, while the latter is – to me at least – so dull that nothing can make it better. At least the audience like both songs, with a high point of the DVD being the intro of 'The Memory Remains': as James intones the introductory lines, the camera focuses in on a middle-aged, evening-suited front-row occupant who calls out the lyrics with evident delight.

One of the two new songs on *S&M*, 'No Leaf Clover' is a surprisingly memorable contender for song of the album. Perhaps because of its simplicity (it's based on a simple refrain of "And it comes to be/ That the soothing light at the end of your tunnel/ Is just a freight train coming your way"), and the very poppy hook at end of the song (for the first time in his career, James hits a falsetto on the repeated line "And it comes to be"), the song stands out from much of Metallica's late-Nineties material. 'Hero Of The Day', too, is another successful blend of Metallica's power-ballad clean-dirty-clean-dirty template, with the song's basic structure interesting enough to stand repetition without the need for too much additional instrumentation.

The first disc takes a dip with 'Devil's Dance', which is as ploddingly uneventful as the original *Reload* version, but the *S&M* take on 'Bleeding Me' is far superior to the better-known recording, simply because the strings add a much-needed richness to the song. It's still far too long – its nine minutes could easily have been reduced to five and nobody would have complained – but it's a genuine relief to hear that the song has been redeemed a little by Kamen's intervention. In fact, perhaps he should have been approached to work on the original? The concert's first half ends with James' call of "Thank you friends . . . we shall return." It's been a mixed bag, but there have already been enough highlights to make *S&M* better than either of the *Loads*.

The second disc commences with a strangely polite version of 'Nothing Else Matters', the song which – in theory at least – should have been the most successful on the record. Conversely, James sings the lyrics in a weird, almost wah-wah-like manner. The tempo seems a little too fast, the bass and drums are much lower in the mix than the original, which kept the song anchored well away from slush territory, and there are too many cheesy extra orchestral parts. Both band and orchestra sound bored, even a little embarrassed, by the arrangement. The song just doesn't work, which is still hard to understand. Revealingly, the usually quite boring 'Until It Sleeps' is much better: perhaps the orchestral parts need to be offset with some riffing in order for the concept to work? This counterbalance certainly makes the song more interesting.

Refreshingly, 'For Whom The Bell Tolls' is much, much better than either of its predecessors. It's annoying that Jason's bass intro is so low in the mix, but the way the strings and guitars mesh on the first riff is enough to interest any fan of the song, and the track as a whole pulls off the trick with aplomb. The spaces between the bars – in the verse, Metallica hit one extended chord for each line – allow the orchestra to expand without becoming intrusive, making it ever clearer that for the whole collaboration idea to function, both parties need to give each other space to work.

The up-down-up quality levels of *S&M* continue with the album's other new song, 'Human', which doesn't match up to 'No Leaf Clover' in any way. Granted, it has a grinding central riff which shows initial promise, but the strangely Oriental orchestral touches are gratuitous rather than complementary and the song staggers from start to finish rather than building any atmosphere. However, Metallica know the value of a crowd-pleaser and have inserted 'Wherever I May Roam' immediately after 'Human', and a good thing too: although the song's pseudo-sitar intro is bland, the dark, 'Thing That Should Not Be'-like tension which fills it is welcome. Does the orchestra add much to the song? Not significantly, but '. . . Roam' isn't a flop like, say, the contemporaneous 'Nothing Else Matters'.

'The Outlaw Torn' is the last *S&M* song which really doesn't work, as Metallica end the show with four classics immediately after it. Another Hetfield-on-the-road epic from the mid-Nineties, 'Outlaw' is just boring, the bane of so many of Metallica's latter-day introspective songs. Its sole positive aspect is that the band are brave enough to strip it down in several places to just James' voice, bass and drums, with the huge musical ensemble merely throwing in an occasional flourish. This song, along with the others from the *Loads* and the Black Album, feels as if the orchestral extras were added without much real vision by Kamen: as if he knew that the songs really didn't require much input from him, meaning that the parts he did eventually contribute sound optional rather than essential.

'Sad But True' should sound enormous. Instead, it sounds pedestrian: its central riff should crush everything in sight, but given that this is a collaborative performance by dozens of musicians, perhaps the mixing team couldn't give the guitars the huge space they need. Fortunately neither point is true of 'One', which occupies a more light-weight set of frequencies and has the all-important clean-picked section for the strings to come through. Once again, the initial tempo feels too fast – perhaps due to the onstage adrenaline? – but after the song is established, its opening section works just fine. However, as 'One' 's apocalyptic finale approaches, the listener wonders exactly how Kamen is planning to orchestrate it: after all, the sixteenth-based riffs cannot, surely, be replicated by an orchestra? The conductor's answer, it seems, was simply to ignore what the band is doing and chuck a load of exaggerated strings-based meandering over the top. The results aren't great: where the San Francisco Symphony Orchestra has always sounded dignified beforehand, it just sounds uncertain now, and the fact that Metallica themselves are necessarily lower in the mix doesn't make them sound too good either. Let's call 'One' an experiment that didn't work.

'Enter Sandman' is better, as its slower, subtler build of tension gives Kamen the time to develop orchestral backing which supports rather than simply embellishes what Metallica are doing. But the song is what it is: as the 'new' Metallica's best-known song, 'Sandman' will always sound the same, wherever and whenever it is performed.

It's a pleasure to note that *S&M* ends on a high note, and for the first time on the record it must have been difficult for even longtime fans to identify the final song from its opening notes. The acoustic intro of 'Battery', always a beautifully chilling moment in any Metallica show, is extended here into a series of strings-led musings which lead into

James' crunchy riff with great expertise. It's also satisfying to hear that the band rip through the song with absolute conviction: "How does it feel to be alive?" howls Hetfield just before Kirk's solo and the semi-thrash backbeat laid down by Lars, supported by the rock-solid playing of Newsted, makes the song a clear highlight of the whole affair. An extended ending sees Hammett tear up his fretboard, the orchestra manage to sound almost discordant, there's a final scream from James – and it's over.

Writer Bernard Doe recalls: "I spoke to Lars Ulrich backstage after a show in Stockholm in 1993 and we were talking about the success of the Black Album and where the band went from there, and Lars said then that he thought that the band had possibly reached their peak and wasn't too worried if the next album didn't match that success in terms of sales. He cited Deep Purple as a band, past their peak, that just carried on releasing the occasional album and touring every few years, and seemed content if Metallica's future would carry on along those lines. Well, I guess *S&M* was Metallica's answer to Deep Purple's 1969 *Concerto For Group And Orchestra* album."

As Metallica albums go, relatively little promotion surrounded *S&M*: perhaps Metallica felt that, as with *Garage Inc.*, the album's title (which, it was revealed, was almost going to be *Symphonica* at one point) would explain itself. One interview that did occur, however, was with the Israeli newspaper *Yediot Aharonot* and came from Kirk Hammett, rarely the mouthpiece of Metallica. The guitarist revealed his love for jazz artists like Miles Davis, John Coltrane and Dave Brubeck, world music from artists like Buena Vista Social Club from Cuba, and classical works by Wagner ("He was the heavy metal of the 19th century") and Schubert. As for *S&M*, Kirk explained that the concept had arisen "because it's a new challenge for us. It breaks the continuity of recording, performing, recording. It's new. The option to record with a symphonic orchestra, it's a great thing. It is in fact not the first time it's been done, the connection between rock and a symphony orchestra, but when Deep Purple did it, it was different. Because we take old and known songs, and put them up with the orchestra. They did new things, that weren't necessarily received well." How did he regard *S&M*? "It is sophisticated, complex, without compromise," he answered.

"It's a challenge. No one expected this from us, and we're taking a risk. That in itself is a statement of some kind."

Lars also told MTV: "You know, the thing about the symphony stuff . . . part of what makes it really cool is the fact that it's not something that ends up being sort of overkill. I don't want to go on tour with this record for 100 dates. It's a great thing to be able to come back to and do once in a while in special situations, you know, 'It's 2002 and we're down in Australia for two weeks, let's go play one with the Sydney Symphony Orchestra,' that type of thing. But to go out and sort of tour it? No, I think that would take away from the specialty vibe of the whole thing."

Asked how the *S&M* shows were different from a normal Metallica concert, Ulrich mused: "It's a lot more intense. Nobody probably wants to hear this, but when you're playing your eighth show in Germany in ten days, sometimes the mind can wander a little. The two shows in Berkeley with the San Francisco Orchestra . . . that was about as focused as I've ever been onstage, in terms of wanting to hold down our part of it and not screw up and not let the team down. I guess it's one thing, letting a team of four down. Another is letting a team of 108 down . . . That's what I remember about the two shows: a complete inner focus and really just dealing with my aspect of it and not wondering about the lights or the pretty girl in row three, and really just holding down my end of it more so than ever. That's the ugly truth."

Lars also revealed that rather than choose singles to be released from the album, Metallica had taken the innovative decision to hand over four videos to MTV and five songs to radio for the broadcasters to play at will: "Here's five songs, radio can play whichever one, and here's four different videos to you guys . . . Basically it's our refusal to be the ones to decide on something specific. Let somebody else do it."

The fanbase was keen, it seemed, and sales of the album were encouraging. Metallica finished off 1999 with a pre-millennial mini-tour called M2K with Kid Rock and Sevendust in support, playing in Nevada and Florida before a New Year's Eve extravaganza in Detroit called the Whiplash Bash. A co-headlining effort with Ted Nugent (which in retrospect seems a little odd, as Metallica's commercial status was way above that of Nugent's), the show had been long in the planning, with the whole event tinged with the millennial fever of late 1999.

Back in black in the Nineties: Metallica poised to invade the world of commercial music with their fifth album, the enormously successful *Metallica*. *(Ross Halfin)*

If you want blood, we got it: Lars with evidence of an injured finger after the 1991 Tushino Airfield show in Moscow which saw riots and police beatings. All in a day's work... *(Ross Halfin)*

James Hetfield meets his public in the moshpit. *(Ross Halfin)*

A break in the action while assembling the *Live Shit: Binge And Purge* box set in 1993... *(Ross Halfin)*

... which had been recorded complete with 'live atmosphere' courtesy of the world's metal followers. Note the 'Snake Pit' behind Hetfield, containing a handful of privileged fans. *(Ross Halfin)*

Jason, sporting a sweaty Afro, and Kirk, lip newly pierced, at Donington in 1995. *(LFI)*

When heavy metal met alternative rock: the newly short-haired James Hetfield rubs shoulders with Smashing Pumpkin Billy Corgan and Hole singer Courtney Love at the MTV Awards in 1996. *(LFI)*

Lars and James with Marianne Faithfull, who sang
on 1997's 'The Memory Remains' single: a
disappointment for old-school Metallica fans.
(Tony Smith)

Relax, ladies, he's married: eyeliner, a fluffy haircut
and a lip spike complete Kirk's transformation from
denim-clad headbanger to fetish-club reject.
(Ross Halfin)

The pre-millennial Metallica: having survived the slings and arrows of outrageous fortune, they could
hardly have foreseen that the greatest challenges of their career lay just ahead. *(Fryderyk Gabowicz)*

And Justice For All: well, in theory at least. When Metallica took on Napster in 2000, they may have been fighting for their rights — but they also alienated thousands of their most loyal fans. *(Corbis)*

Heroes of the day: Metallica, with Newsted's replacement Robert Trujillo second left, step up for their moment in the sun at the *MTV Icon* show dedicated to them in May 2003. *(LFI)*

The formidable Robert Trujillo. "Metallica's music can be pretty fast and ferocious," he observes. "They're pissed off, man. They scare me up there." Can he take his new band back to the critical heights they once scaled? *(LFI)*

All within their hands: Metallica in 2004, older, happier, more sober and - it is to be hoped - wiser.
Will they return to 'kill us all' once again? *(Mick Hutson)*

The gig was an almighty success, with a full set of Metallica songs including old and new material leading up to a pre-midnight 'Enter Sandman'. When the moment came, the band tore through a version of Kiss' 'Detroit Rock City' with Sevendust, Nugent and Kid Rock, before finishing off the show with a jam on Black Sabbath's 'Supernaut' and 'Jump In The Fire' and finally, 'Phantom Lord'. The new century had arrived, and had been greeted by two of Metallica's oldest songs . . .

An omen? Who knew. And in fact Lars announced to the press that his band would be taking some time off after January 2000: "January 9 in an unnamed city in the Midwest of the US will be the last Metallica commitment for a long time," he said. "I think it's been six years since we were staring at a schedule that was blank. We put out four records in four years now, and we always have something in front of us, and this is the first time that we don't have anything in front of us. That is both exciting and frightening." He went on: "A couple of months ago, I was really excited about it. Now I'm starting to get very scared about it, because what's gonna go through your mind that morning? Who am I going to call and bother? It's going to be very interesting to see, so maybe I'll find some new hobby. Start painting? Who knows? Waking up without something to do will be pretty frightening." However, Lars added that in fact he had his record label, the Music Company, to run, and so he would have plenty to do.

If only Lars had known that, in fact, the year 2000 would be the most controversial year for Metallica yet, he might not have expressed his worries so casually. The claws of controversy, which his band had managed to avoid for so long, were about to close in and catch hold. And this time, Metallica wouldn't come out of it with their credibility intact.

22

2000–2001

The M2K mini-tour rolled through Cleveland (where, on New Year's Day 2000, James started the show by calling, "Hey, I'd just like to say thanks to you all for being Metallica's first gig of the millennium!"), Milwaukee, Chicago and Minneapolis. At the penultimate show, on January 9, Kid Rock joined Metallica onstage for the chorus of 'Turn The Page', and the following night a huge jam on 'For Whom The Bell Tolls' was performed by Rock, Joe C of Rock's band and Clint Lowery of Sevendust. So far, so spectacular, so normal.

After the dust on the M2K tour settled, Metallica completed the recording of 'I Disappear', a song destined for the soundtrack of the forthcoming *Mission: Impossible 2*. Not a remarkable event, it might seem (other than the fact that it was the first song which the band had recorded to order in this way), but the inoffensive, staccato track would become the cause of a much, much bigger phenomenon.

Three days later, a few eyebrows elevated among Metallica's fanbase: it was reported that on January 14 the band filed a lawsuit against Victoria's Secret, the lingerie company, citing trademark infringement, false designation of origin, unfair competition, and dilution. Part of the lawsuit text read: "Victoria's Secret manufactures and sells lip pencils bearing the mark Metallica. The packaging for Victoria's Secret's Metallica lip pencils also bear the mark Metallica. These lip pencils continue to be sold by Victoria's Secret throughout the United States." The band and/or their legal representatives were clearly not about to allow anyone to take liberties with their name which, of course, represented their brand – a logical step. However, a more trivial case was taken less seriously: a furniture maker called Kim Hodges received a certified letter from Metallica's lawyer asking him to change the name of his business. Hodges told the press that he would not fight the case in court and that he was "somewhat amused" that Metallica would threaten a "piddling" furniture company. However, Jill Pietrini, a lawyer for the band, was quoted as saying: "When we find out about things like this, we actively protect the band's trademark rights. It's not like we're trying to protect a name commonly used, like United. It's a unique name."

So, to recap: Metallica recorded a song for a movie, delivered it and forgot about it. Meanwhile, their legal representatives were busy protecting their clients' trademark. The two events did not appear to have anything in common, not immediately anyway. But it would soon become clear that they would combine with far-reaching consequences.

Picking up a Grammy on February 23 for 'Whiskey In The Jar' for Best Hard Rock Performance and releasing 'No Leaf Clover' a month later on three different formats, Metallica approached the early months of 2000 in relaxed mood. Having released four albums in four years, the time was perhaps ripe to take things easy and have some fun. Clearly the band were on good form at this point: King Diamond recalls Kirk Hammett approaching him at a backstage party at around this time, and saying: "Man, you have no idea what it meant to me to be playing on the same stage as you." (Diamond's response: "Surely it's the other way round?") All seemed well in Metallica's world.

Until, that is, news came through in late March that bootlegged versions of 'I Disappear' had found their way into the public domain: some radio stations were even playing the songs, even though the soundtrack to *Mission: Impossible 2* was not scheduled for official release until April 19. Now, Metallica had been bootlegged before (James told *Thrasher* as far back as 1986 that: "I get pissed off once in a while listening to bootleggers out there. I almost fucking slammed one of them, then I realised, shit, I might get arrested and then I can't play the show!"), and in ever greater quantities since their Nineties success – but there were two different factors about this particular rip-off which were unusual. Firstly, the song which was appearing on the radio was one of no fewer than six early versions of 'I Disappear', rather than the later, finished song which Metallica had perfected for the soundtrack. Where had the early work-in-progress come from? Secondly, the medium of distribution for the bootlegged song was not tapes or even CDs, the common currency of the bootleg market: it was the internet, which had expanded geometrically since the mid-Nineties, when millions of users (mostly young, and many of them music fans) had discovered the joys of the online community and the freedom, entertainment and information that the web held.

One of the most enticing aspects of the internet was and remains the way that files could be copied and exchanged across a phone line: the nature of digital information is such that repeated copying is possible and, in the case of music, copying can take place without obvious deterioration in quality, the bugbear of analogue copying media such as cassettes and vinyl. The virtual legions had begun file-sharing in earnest by the time that Metallica noticed that 'I Disappear' had made an unauthorised appearance; and one of the most popular tools (although certainly not the only one) used to exchange music files, usually compressed into a manageable file called an MP3, was a program produced by a company called Napster.

Napster's concept was simple and effective. Users could visit the company's website, download and install a free program on their computer, register some details and begin searching for MP3s. The program itself resembled an internet browser and comprised a search facility and a results page: the user would enter the name of a song (or a band whose songs were desired) and then view a list of results. If the right song came up, the user could choose to download a copy of it to their own hard drive, where it could be played, copied to a disc or emailed to a friend. Clearly the implications for music distribution were far-reaching – because all this cost nothing, as the music was made available by users, who copied (or 'ripped') songs from CDs and made them visible to other users, who could then download them.

Metallica moved fast. On April 13 the band filed suit against four parties: Napster itself and three American universities whose computer networks permitted the use of Napster's program. The suit charged Napster, the University of Southern California, Yale University and Indiana University with copyright infringement, unlawful use of a digital audio interface device, and violations of the Racketeering Influenced & Corrupt Organizations Act. The actual wording read that Napster: "encourages and enables visitors to its website to unlawfully exchange with others copyrighted songs and sound recordings without the knowledge or permission of Metallica". Letters to educational institutions asking them to restrict students' access to Napster also went out to Columbia, Harvard and Stanford Universities, the University of Virginia, Boston University, the Georgia Institute of Technology, the Massachusetts Institute of Technology, Princeton University, the University of Michigan at Ann Arbor, the University of California at Berkeley and the University of California at Los Angeles. Within a couple of days the legal representatives of the hip-hop artist Dr. Dre had also joined the fray.

Six days later the first results appeared when Metallica's lawyers announced that Yale University would be dropped from its lawsuit. A Yale spokesman said: "Last Friday, we began to block Napster around the clock in response to the lawsuit and until we can clarify the legal issues surrounding Napster." A Metallica statement read: "We appreciate the prompt and responsible reaction by Yale University in dealing with the gross violations of copyright laws and the protection of intellectual property."

Relatively few of Metallica's fans had heard of the Napster case by this stage, but the issue moved to a different level after an online webchat on ArtistDirect.com between band and fans on May 2. Before the chat took place, Metallica made another official statement along the lines of: "Metallica is suing Napster because we felt that someone had to address this important artistic issue, and we have always been known for taking a leadership role in the fight for artists' rights. We were the first band to sue our record company, Time Warner, for the right to control our future. Rather than allowing the record company or any other corporation to own our recordings and compositions, we chose to fight for (and eventually win) control of our music. This issue is no different. Why is it all of a sudden OK to get music for free? Why should music be free, when it costs artists money to record and produce it?"

After this statement was distributed, one or two fans came to the webchat with a grudge. The ever-reasonable Newsted tried to defuse tension by pointing out that the idea behind the lawsuit was "to spearhead some kind of activity within the powers that be – the government – to lay down the laws with the computer, to exercise some kind of control and govern the companies like Napster that steal outright from artists", but when Hetfield said, "Metallica has always felt fans are family," a fan retorted with the words, "Your family just got a lot smaller."

Perhaps the core of the whole issue was revealed at this early stage when Lars decided to play hardball. James had remained reasonable, explaining, "There has to be some laws and guidelines to go by before it gets too out of hand and sucks the life out of musicians who will stop making music," and making the reasonable point that Napster, far from being an underdog company deserving of sympathy, was "a big machine . . . The person who invented Napster is an employee of the big machine as we speak." However, Ulrich may have put his foot in it when he said, "The goal is clear and simple. Put Napster out of business," and then, "For the doubters out there, Metallica will carry on for the next 20 years . . . whether you're around for the ride or not, that's your problem, not ours."

What to conclude from the early salvos of the file-trading battle? As photographer Ross Halfin says, "Lars had a point. But the thing is, if it had been 1986, they would have been all for Napster. They would have been copying everything for themselves. So you gotta look at it like that. And he's done himself a lot of damage with it. It's the arrogance of it, really." Perhaps this: that while Metallica were right to protect their work from exploitation, they should have approached the issue more sensitively.

The arrogance to which Halfin refers blew up in Lars' face after the next step in the Napster case. An announcement came that Metallica would personally deliver to the Napster company headquarters in San Mateo, California, a list of over 300,000 users of the program who were alleged to have exchanged Metallica recordings online. The document, which ran to 60,000 pages, would be accompanied by a request that the users be removed from Napster's system as punishment for violating the band's copyrights.

This, more than any other move by either side in the whole debate, caused the most ill-feeling among the band's fans. Why would Metallica deliver their own fans up for punishment? After all, only those who enjoyed Metallica's music would download their songs, they reasoned – and therefore were fans. The dismay many listeners felt was compounded by the news on May 11 that another MP3 site called MP3.com was backing down from the debate by voluntarily removing all content owned by the so-called 'Big Five' record companies (in the

States, Sony, Warners, Universal, BMG and Capitol) from its central database. While it retained over 400,000 songs from independent artists and smaller labels, no one who used the service much was fooled. Users tend to want popular material, not new and untested music, and by offloading the juicier stuff MP3.com may have saved itself several lawsuits, but it also rendered itself much less attractive to users.

As for the Napster hordes, Lars did deliver the document listing users which he had promised – and the company promptly obeyed his request, banning the 300,000 or so users which Ulrich's list named. However, about 10 per cent of these – around 30,000 users – protested the move, claiming that they had been unfairly punished because they had been mistakenly identified. The claim was easy to file, as Napster had placed a notice on its site informing users how to file a counter-notification if they felt they had been misidentified. This made things difficult for Metallica, as US copyright law states that if the band did not file suit against the individual users within ten days, Napster could reinstate them.

It got more complex still. Metallica's lawyer, Howard King, said that the band would not be suing those 30,000 users as this would be futile and impossible. James Hetfield said at the time that: "We are going after Napster, the main artery. We are not going after individual fans." The Napster founder, 19-year-old computer prodigy Shawn Fanning, said, "The fact that so many people have come forward and disputed Metallica's accusation that they did not break the law demonstrates that this is not a black and white issue." Meanwhile, the debate moved into the public arena when Napster's site was awarded two Webby Awards (the internet version of the Oscars) by a panel of industry greats including film director Francis Ford Coppola, *Simpsons* creator Matt Groening and singer David Bowie.

It was time for Metallica to face their fans, and on May 25, Lars gave an hour-long interview with *Slashdot*, the online magazine. James was otherwise engaged – his second child, Castor Virgil Hetfield, had arrived the previous week – and Ulrich was on his own. Nonetheless, he had plenty of salient points to make, even though his personal popularity appeared to be sliding rapidly downhill.

Lars opened by saying that the Napster issue had been initiated by Metallica themselves: "The record company had nothing to do with it whatsoever . . . we took it upon ourselves, there was never really much in term of support . . . I'm quite stunned at the lack of communication and input from the record company," and went on to explain that he was protecting his work from exploitation, saying: "I don't want to sound too combative here, but you know, when somebody fucks with what we do, we go after them." He knew of the other file-sharing applications which existed – "Are we aware of the Gnutellas and all these other things? Of course we are, but you can only take it one step at a time . . . Right now, you know, we know what is not right for us, which is Napster" – and that internet distribution would probably be a part of his band's future business. "We are not stupid," he added. "Of course we realise the future of getting music from Metallica to the people who are interested in Metallica's music is through the internet. But the question is, on whose conditions, and obviously we want it to be on our conditions."

Interestingly, Lars explained that Napster could simply have requested permission from Metallica to use their material and avoided a lot of legal hassle. "Napster could have so easily avoided this whole thing. It's like, 'OK, we have this service, we would like to know if you are interested in being part of it.' If we'd said yes, then there's no issue, if we'd said no, then this whole thing would have never . . . Are we assholes for wanting to get off this service that I was never asked if I wanted to be part of in the first place?" he asked.

Napster, Lars added, had just secured $15 million in funding from venture capitalists, even though Metallica's action against them was, ironically enough, not about money as its central issue: "Understand one thing: this is not about a lot of money right now, because the money that's being lost right now is really pocket change, OK? It's about the principle of the thing and it's about what could happen if this kind of thing is allowed to exist and run as rampant and out of control for the next five years as it has been for the last six months. Then it can become a money issue. Right now it's not a money issue. I can guarantee you it's costing us tenfold to fight it in lawyers' fees, in lawyers' compensation, than it is for measly little pennies in royalties being lost, that's not what it's about."

The finer points of Lars' stand weren't shared by many of Lars' peers. On the subject of internet piracy, Kiss bassist Gene Simmons is emphatic that money was the key issue, telling the author: "Robbery is robbery, whether it's petty, larceny, or major. People say, 'Why do you guys care if someone downloads your record – you're rich?' Well, it's actually not for anybody else to determine anything that belongs to you. People only understand it in this way. When you, an average person, sign a contract or a cheque, something belongs to you. So why can't I use your signature? Because it's not up to anyone else. If I write a song, that's mine, and I can sign a contract with a record company, but I can control it, decide who gets it and where they get it. If I own a restaurant, I don't want someone stealing a piece of bread and telling me, 'What are you worried about? You've got a restaurant!' Well, it's not up to *you* to tell me whether I'm doing well or not." Asked if taking down the illegal download programs was about the money or the principle, Gene didn't hesitate: "It is about the money. It's bullshit, and people are very unhappy about that. You're not allowed to take a penny from me. It's not permissible."

It seemed that Metallica were very much aware of the bigger issues, and went out of their way to plead the case for smaller acts who might stand or fall depending on their distribution through Napster. "Where it *can* affect people," said Lars, "where it *is* about money, is for the band that sells 600 copies of their CD, OK? If they all of a sudden go from selling 600 copies of their CD down to 50 copies, because the other 550 copies get downloaded for free, that's where it starts affecting real people with real money." As for the bootlegging issue itself, Lars reminded his readers that Metallica themselves had always been pro-bootleg: "First of all, you have to remember that you're talking to somebody who advocates bootlegging, who has always been pro-bootlegging. We have always let fans tape our shows, we've always had a thing for bootlegging live materials, for special appearances, for that type of stuff. Knock yourselves out, bootleg the fuck out of it . . . You know, home taping 10 or 15 years ago really was about, you had vinyl records, and you had the neighbour down the street with you know, his Iron Maiden records, that you wanted to make a tape of so you can play in your car. There is a difference [between that and] going on the internet and getting first generation, perfect digital copies of master recordings from all the world . . . we're talking about a network that includes millions and millions of people, and tens and tens of millions of songs that these millions of people have, they can trade."

Perhaps most tellingly, the issue of Metallica's delivering the hundreds of thousands of user names to Napster was cast in a different light after Ulrich explained his motives for doing it: "This is another misconception in the last couple of weeks, this whole thing about 'Metallica serves Napster with 300,000 names.' You have to remember, they asked for this, OK? That's a point that not a lot of people include. They asked. They said, 'If you can give us the names (ha ha), of people that are doing this (ha ha ha) and we'll take them off (ha ha ha),' like you can't. It was sort of like a dare."

A couple of days later, Kirk Hammett told the press: "We're about to deliver another bunch of names to them." This time, another 332,000 names were emailed to Napster with much less publicity than before. "The 332,293 distinct users represent 2.2 million copyright violations," said Gayle Fine, a spokeswoman for Q-Prime. When asked why there was no press conference for the delivery of the second set of names, Fine responded, "Because we're just trying to get the job done."

Lars finished the *Slashdot* interview with some salient points. Explaining that his band was acting out of sensible business motives – "We treat the business with the respect that it deserves, because if you do not respect the business side of it, you can get fucked . . . the music world is littered with the careers of people who did not pay enough attention to the business side of what they were doing and ended up getting majorly fucked" – he added that despite the potential for internet distribution, the music business would always need record labels: "Record companies will never be completely extinct, for one reason and one reason only, that there will always be a need to develop younger artists, and record companies will always be able to play a big part in that, because this whole thing about 'I'm a young band, I'm an upstart band, I'm going to put my music on Napster, and then I'm going to become successful?' Fantasy. The only way you will become successful is by having a publicity and promotion campaign behind you that elevates what you're doing above what your competition is doing."

Lars reinforced this with some statistics: "When we monitored Napster for 48 hours three weekends ago, we came up with 1.4 million downloads of Metallica music, there was one, one downloading – one! – of an unsigned artist the whole time. You can sit there and talk about how this is great for up-and-coming artists or for unsigned bands, but a big counter-argument that nobody gets is, me and you could form a band together, and we could like, make a demo and then we could put it up on Napster. Who is going to give a fuck?"

Ulrich estimated that future web distribution for Metallica would be "somewhere between a real possibility and a certainty" and closed by emphasising the difference between home taping and filesharing. "[It's] the size of it and the quality of it. When we go in, and check Napster out, we come up with 1.4 million copyright infringements in 48 hours, this is a different thing than trading cassette tapes with your buddy at school."

Lars may have put his points eloquently. But the tension was still mounting.

Life went on relatively normally for the rest of Metallica despite the storm raging around Napster. James, for instance, found time to jam with Motörhead in San Francisco on May 28, where he called them "the godfathers of heavy metal" and played 'Overkill' with them. On June 3 the band performed 'I Disappear' (which was now out and legal) at the MTV Movie Awards at Sony Studios in Culver City, California, and three weeks later a slot at the opening of the new Experience Music Project museum in Seattle, alongside the Red Hot Chili Peppers, No Doubt, Beck, Dr. Dre, Eminem, and Snoop Dogg among others. Finally, as Metallica readied to embark on a new tour – the Summer Sanitarium tour, which would feature Korn, Kid Rock, Powerman 5000 and System Of A Down in support – James could be heard providing vocals in a song called 'Little Boy, You're Going To Hell' in the *South Park: Bigger, Longer And Uncut* movie.

The tour swung through Massachusetts, North Carolina and Missouri before a July 4 show in Baltimore, Maryland was marked by tragedy: a 21-year-old man fell from the upper balcony of the stadium onto the pavement below, reportedly after losing his balance. Shaken, the bands moved on through Georgia, Kentucky and Texas, before a lesser but still-painful blow hit: James managed to injure some discs in his lower back and couldn't make it to three shows on July 7, 8 and 9. At these concerts a superstar band composed of members of Korn, SOAD and Kid Rock jammed some Metallica songs, although full make-up concerts were performed later.

But the creature which Metallica had created would not lie down, and the Napster case continued to occupy much of the band's time. On July 11 Lars was called to give testimony on the case to the Committee on the United States Senate Judiciary, and delivered a lengthy speech which began: "My name is Lars Ulrich. I was born in Denmark. In 1980, as a teenager, my parents and I came to America. I started a band named Metallica in 1981 with my best friend James Hetfield. By 1983 we had released our first record, and by 1985 we were no longer living below the poverty line. Since then, we've been very fortunate to achieve a great level of success in the music business throughout the world. It's the classic American dream come true."

After running through the sequence of events from the discovery that radio stations were playing a work-in-progress version of 'I Disappear' right up to the current state of play with Napster, Lars spoke in some detail about the issues that the whole debate raised. Choice was the primary issue at stake, it seemed: "Just like a carpenter who crafts a table gets to decide whether to keep it, sell it or give it away, shouldn't we have the same options? My band authored the music which is Napster's lifeblood. We should decide what happens to it, not Napster – a company with no rights in our recordings, which never invested a penny in Metallica's music or had anything to do with its creation. The choice has been taken away from us." He added a careful caveat: "Make no mistake, Metallica is not anti-technology. When we made our first album, the majority of sales were in the vinyl record format. By the late Eighties, cassette sales accounted for over 50 per cent of the market. Now, the compact disc dominates. If the next format is a form of digital downloading from the internet with distribution and manu-facturing savings passed on to the American consumer, then, of course, we will embrace that format too. But how can we embrace a new format and sell our music for a fair price when someone, with a few lines of code, and no investment costs, creative input or marketing expenses, simply gives it away? How does this square with the level playing field of the capitalist system?"

Crucially, Ulrich noted that the Napster program itself does not permit users to exploit it without permission: "To underscore what I've spoken about today, I'd like to read from the Terms Of Use section of the Napster internet web site. When you use Napster you are basically agreeing to a contract that includes the following terms: 'This web site or any portion of this web site may not be reproduced, dupli-cated, copied, sold, resold, or otherwise exploited for any commercial purpose that is not expressly permitted by Napster'." This last argument is convincing, revealing a depth of cunning in the drummer which might be startling to some. Of course Napster does not permit its products to be exploited – very few programs do – but it takes a keen intelligence to notice this and use it as a legal weapon.

Meanwhile, the tour continued with July dates in Colorado, California, Arizona, New Jersey and Illinois. At the show on July 12, James returned from his back injury with the warning to the crowd that "If you see me on the ground, it ain't because I'm doing my Angus Young impression!" The final show of the Summer Sanitarium tour took place in Phoenix and saw Kid Rock onstage once again for 'Turn The Page' and System Of A Down jamming on 'Enter Sandman'. The following night Lars and Kirk played with Rock on the *Tonight Show With Jay Leno* on 'American Badass', a recent Kid Rock single which had been based on the main riff of 'Sad But True' and had been an enormous hit.

After six make-up shows from August 2 to 9, at which Metallica returned to perform at the arenas which had missed James' presence the first time, the band announced that there would be no touring for a while and that they were planning to start recording a brand-new album – the first new material (apart from 'I Disappear') for three years. However, before the band could take real time off, Lars gave his most revealing interview yet on the Napster case to Steffan Chirazi, editor of the Metallica fan-club magazine *So What*. Ulrich explained that at this stage the job in hand was not to fight Napster itself – "The Napster thing is increasingly more of a sidebar that is ultimately out of our hands, because it's being played out in the courts of California" – but to make people understand what the root cause of all the legal heartache actually was: "What has been taking up my time, and what I think is really much more valuable right now, is public education: getting people to really understand what this is about." Asked by Chirazi if he was finding it easy to get this point across, the drummer responded: "Well, I sort of have this quiet peace with the fact that anybody who doesn't really get it, or is vehemently opposed to what we're saying, doesn't know the information or doesn't really understand the issue, so it comes out of ignorance more than anything. I don't really feel that it's an issue; you cannot really oppose the fact that whoever creates something should have the right to decide what happens to it. It's not an argument."

Interestingly, Lars revealed that in 1994 Metallica had wanted to purchase ownership of their own back catalogue so much that they sued their own record company, Elektra. "In 1994, when we sued our record company, we were basically wanting ownership of the songs that we wrote. We felt that by us not owning what we created, the possibilities for our songs to be used for something other than what we wanted later on was there. One of the clearer things that sparked it off, was when some of The Beatles' songs were made available for Nike commercials in the early Nineties, outside of their willingness because somebody else owned them. So we felt that we didn't want to see 'Leper Messiah' end up as background music in a toothpaste commercial, unless it was something that we wanted and the choice came from us. So now we retain the rights to any master recordings we have ever made, master recordings basically being any songs that we have written and that have appeared on our studio albums."

Lars observed that the whole case had been a learning curve for him, too: "I've done thousands of interviews, and I feel that the music media, the *Rolling Stones* of the world, has been very, very biased against us. The hard thing about this issue is that it's not an issue that you can really explain in what's called a soundbite, in one or two sentences. So it has been very frustrating doing 30–45 minute interviews with periodicals and so on, and then seeing one sentence being used, or taken out of context or something like that." With a touch of humility, he added: "Certainly in the beginning of this process I said some things that were out of line . . . I did an interview with the BBC where I said some things about 'Yes we will go after the fans directly' or something like that . . . this has been a learning process for me also." However, some aggression was clearly still there: ruminating on the fate of the 'next Napster' – i.e. the other file-trading applications which existed – he growled: "Everything we hear from our technical advisors on a daily basis is that these fucking internet anarchists sit there and go, 'Well they will never be able to stop Freenet [or] Gnutella because there's no central server.' Yeah, you want to fucking watch? You want to fucking watch us stop it? You want to fucking see in three months how we can fucking blow your measly little company apart? No problem." Ouch . . .

And so 2000, the most controversial year which Metallica had ever endured, wound down. The band spent a couple of days in late

September recording a documentary on the Black Album for the excellent *Classic Albums* DVD series; Kirk Hammett took part in a November 5 protest march in San Francisco about the high rental costs of rehearsal studios; James sang with The Misfits at a November 17 show at the Maritime Hall in San Francisco; the band performed in front of fans in the car park at the VH1 Music Awards ceremony on November 30, bagging a gong for Best Stage Spectacle; and Lars participated in a December 14 tennis tournament, the Grand Slam Jam Tennis Shoot-out, in which he partnered John McEnroe against tennis player Jim Courier and R.E.M. bassist Mike Mills. After the match Ulrich jammed alongside a pickup band comprising McEnroe (guitar/vocals), Mills (keyboards) and Courier (guitar) on a handful of rock classics.

However, all this off-time fun didn't mean that business was being forgotten, and the year ended with another lawsuit from Metallica's legal team – this time against the perfume manufacturer Guerlain and the American department stores Neiman-Marcus and Bergdorf Goodman. The cause of the suit was a vanilla-scented perfume sold by the stores and made by Guerlain, called – yes, you guessed it – Metallica. The suit stated in part that "Defendants' use in commerce of the mark Metallica for perfume has caused confusion and is likely to continue to cause confusion, deception, and mistake in the minds of the public . . ." Yes, that's right: the idea was that fans might confuse Metallica (the world's state-of-the-art heavy metal band) with Metallica (the perfume), or, heaven forbid, that the world's state-of-the-art heavy metal band was branching out into the perfume business.

As if the Napster business wasn't enough to try them, on January 17, 2001, Jason Newsted, Metallica's bass player of 15 years standing, quit. Permanently.

Jason was resigned but happy, at least when the author talked to him soon after the announcement. Having had some time to think over his decision, which had rocked Metallica's fanbase and left the once-indomitable band reeling, Newsted now had some valuable insights to offer on the workings of the collective Metallica mentality – and explanations that only he could offer as to why he took the decision to leave the band he had loved for so long.

In the official statement he made when he left Metallica, he said that one of the reasons was that he was in danger of damaging his physical health.

Could he be more specific?

"Well, there's a lot of truth to the physical thing as far as the damage that I'd done to my neck and my spine and stuff."

Just from moshing too hard?

"Yeah. Repetitive motion over the years. Like whiplash . . . 'Whip-lash', haha! No, but the doctors kept telling me that I kept giving myself whiplash over and over and I would never let it heal, it just kept going back."

But more than that, I presume he'd just had enough of being in Metallica?

There's a touch of genuine regret: "Dude, I wanted to stay. It was such a big part of me, I always put it first."

So he wanted to stay, but he left because it was physically damaging?

Now he's more reflective. "No . . . that was one of many reasons. I wasn't confident that I could be the '110% dude' performer that people know me as, and I need to have that. And now that I've had a year to think about it, I think that . . . James, where he was in his head space, you know, at that time, with his personal life and different things."

Jason won't elaborate on James' problems, and I don't ask him to. He continued: "The way that he came at it, and all that kind of thing – I understand why. He was having trouble and yet he's always been the protector of the name. He's always been the protector of the integrity of Metallica. That's why Metallica's what it is, one of the main reasons Metallica is what it is. And between Lars' perseverance and James' fuckin' integrity, that's fuckin' *it* right there, man. And I realise that now. He was protecting the whole thing, right? But you know when you squeeze too hard sometimes, you know that deal?"

Jason laughed, a little sadly. "That's kinda what happened. Exactly what he *didn't* want to happen, exactly what he was fighting for the whole time, he actually drove away, or something. So, I came to realise that after a bit, but also I know that it had to happen – it was *meant* to happen – the opportunity that they have now to kick ass and really go for it, man, take the bull by the horns, the next era of Metallica . . . like, they're in their third decade now and they keep showing people how it's done. And it's a great time to do it – metal's coming back, and who's better to show people how to do it? Some of the stuff I've heard so far – he's got a lot of stuff to write about. He's got a lot to play about."

Newsted exhaled. "And that's what it came down to. It was a mixture of all those things. And there's a certain freedom now that's incredible, man."

How long was he unhappy for?

"Well, when you're within something like that – like a job or something – when you're in close quarters with people – egos and spoiled fuckers with money and all that . . . I think I was always cool with it because there was more good than bad. I really, *really* liked meeting people and getting off on that energy. That's my favourite part of it and probably what I miss the most."

He always looked like he was having a good time, I remind him.

"That's the thing. I was, but it just came to a point where . . . I think it was only about four months, probably, that I was really just, shit, man, I really can't be here any more."

Halfway through the interview, I was a little perplexed. Jason was telling me why he left, but he wasn't really giving me any clear information. He was keen to talk about his new band, Echobrain – which was on the point of releasing a competent pop-rock album – but not to expand on the inner conflict in Metallica. All that would emerge later.

Elsewhere, Jason spoke to the press at length about his possible replacement in Metallica. He had recommended Joey Vera of Armored Saint and Fates Warning, one of the original choices to replace Cliff. Asked what kind of man would be needed to do the job, Newsted answered: "It has to be someone who's seasoned and it has to be somebody, I feel, who's in the circle of the band already and that knows the band already. It has to be someone who's been through a lot of the business already . . . You can't have a 20-year-old guy come in and play with guys that have had the band for 20 years."

He added: "Joey looks young, he's in very good shape, he's very smart, he has great production skills, he's a great player, he has great energy. He almost had the gig before, the last time. He was among the last three guys that were gonna get the gig. They've been friends forever. In this day and age, being a fancy and hungry player doesn't mean shit. You have to be able to be a businessman, you have to be a people person . . . it would be tough for a 22- or 23-year-old kid that never tasted it before to step into something of that magnitude and be comfortable and be able to get the respect from Hetfield."

The line he had used about leaving Metallica for physical reasons was real, as he told *Kerrang!*: "For about 20 years I've played heavy maple basses. When you're thrashing about for two and a half hours a night, five nights a week for 10 or 12 years, that starts to take its toll. I've worn down all the padding between my vertebrae and my neck, so it's just bone on bone at my neck and I have to be very careful with it. I can't fully thrash about like I used to . . . I realised that I was not going to be the performer I wanted to be in Metallica, therefore I had to back off . . . with what was happening then it wasn't possible for me to continue playing without constant pain and it wouldn't have been smart for me to carry on."

And so Jason leaves our story, as suddenly as he entered it.

Apart from Jason's shock announcement, January and February 2001 were moderately relaxing for Metallica, with Lars raising $32,000 for charity on ABC TV's *Who Wants To Be A Millionaire?* and jamming live with Jerry Cantrell; MacFarlane Toys revealing a set of Metallica action figures based on the band's black-clothes-and-long-hair of the . . . *And Justice For All* era; James playing with Corrosion Of Conformity; and the band taking home their sixth Grammy, this time for Best Rock Instrumental Performance for *S&M*'s 'The Call of Ktulu'.

As well as all that, on February 12 the Ninth US Circuit Court of Appeals decided that Napster would have to block users who exchanged copyrighted songs without permission, but could continue operating until a lower court redrafted a previous injunction against the company. Metallica issued an official statement on their website which read: "From day one our fight has always been to protect the rights of artists who choose not to have their music exploited without consent. The court's decision validates this right and confirms that Napster was wrong in taking not only Metallica's music but other artists who do not want to be a part of the Napster system and exploiting it without their approval . . . We have never objected to the technology, the internet or the digital distribution of music. All we have ever asked is that artists be able to control how, when and in what form their creativity is distributed through these channels. This is something that Napster has continually refused to do. Now the court has made that decision for them."

However, their relative peace was shattered when on March 5 an issue of *Playboy* magazine was published containing an extended Metallica interview, which had been conducted with all four members (including Jason) some months before. The results were grim: the interviews, which had been carried out separately, were laid out on the page so as to resemble a group interview – with the members bickering at each other like irritable teenagers. A press release containing the juiciest excerpts from the article raised expectations to the limit, as well as fuelling rumours that the band were about to split – especially plausible in the light of Jason's recent departure. The writer, Ron Tannenbaum, was quoted as saying: "I wasn't surprised that Jason Newsted quit Metallica. Just two months earlier, I'd spent a day with each of the four, and I've never seen a band so quarrelsome and fractious. Each talked about his need for solitude. The most unhappy Metallican was Newsted, whom I met at a Marin County recording studio. Newsted gradually admitted that he felt 'almost stifled' in Metallica. He added, 'I would not leave Metallica for another band. I would do it to live my life, not depart to play in another band.'"

The 9,000-word piece is incredibly revealing, even if the way the questions are placed together makes it seem fairly artificial. Inevitably, Lars discusses Napster, explaining: "What we've accomplished most is to bring an awareness to the American public. It turned into the first big issue of the 21st century . . . Obviously, this has been the fucking wake-up call of the millennium to everybody who has anything to do with intellectual property." James added: "I like playing music because it's a good living and I get satisfaction from it. But I can't feed my family with satisfaction."

More light-hearted were some reminiscences of older, more drunken and innocent times, with Kirk claiming: "We would drink day in and day out and hardly come up for air. People would be dropping like flies all around us, but we had the tolerance built up. Our reputation started to precede us. I can't remember the *Kill 'Em All* tour – we used to start drinking at three or four in the afternoon." However, the guitarist had some tougher memories to share: "I was abused as a child. My dad drank a lot. He beat the shit out of me and my mom quite a bit. I got ahold of a guitar, and from the time I was 15, I rarely left my room. I remember having to pull my dad off my mom when he attacked her one time, during my 16th birthday – he turned on me and started slapping me around. Then my dad just left one day. My mom was struggling to support me and my sister. I've definitely channelled a lot of anger into the music. I was also abused by my neighbour when I was like nine or ten. The guy was a sick fuck. He had sex with my dog, Tippy. I can laugh about it now – hell, I was laughing about it then."

All the members of the band nominated James as Metallica's biggest drinker. He said, "I had to have a bottle of vodka just for fun. I'm surprised I'm still alive," while Jason remarked, "James is the only one that ever drank so much he couldn't show up for a rehearsal or for photos. He is the only one who ever actually poisoned himself." When the theme of therapy came up, James said: "Around the time of *Load*, I felt I wanted to stop drinking. Maybe I'm missing out on something. Everyone else seems so happy all the time. I want to get happy. I'd plan my life around a hangover. The Misfits are playing in town Friday night, so Saturday is hangover day. I lost a lot of days in my life. Going to therapy for a year, I learned a lot about myself. There's a lot of things that scar you when you're growing up, you don't know why. The song 'Bleeding Me' is about that: I was trying to bleed out all the bad, get the evil out. While I was going through therapy, I discovered some ugly stuff in there. A dark spot . . . I took more than a year off from drinking – and the skies didn't part. It was just life, but less fun. The evil didn't come out. I wasn't laughing, wasn't having a good time. I realised, drinking is a part of me. Now I know how far to go . . . I wouldn't say I'm an alcoholic – but then, you know, alcoholics say they're not alcoholics."

As for drugs, Kirk recalled: "Cocaine has definitely been in our lives. You hang out with other musicians, and next thing you know, you have five guys crammed into a bathroom stall. I had a bad coke problem on the . . . *And Justice For All Tour,* but I pulled out of that, because it makes me depressed, basically. I tried smack once. I was so thankful that I hated it."

Lars explained: "I tried acid once; I was shit-fucking scared. The only drug I've ever really engaged in is cocaine. It gave me another couple of hours of drinking. A lot of people use it as a way to get closer to you, and you fall for that. I go through cycles where I say, OK, I'm going to pull away for a while. And then I take six months away."

But the most revealing section of all was the one in which Jason discussed his frustration at not being allowed to release any of the many side projects on which he had been working for some time. James pointed out: "When someone does a side project it takes away from the strength of Metallica. So there is a little ugliness lately. And it shouldn't be discussed in the press," adding: "We're getting really close to some things we shouldn't be talking about." The last remark notwithstanding, James said, "Where would it end? Does he start touring with it? Does he sell T-shirts? Is it his band? That's the part I don't like. It's like cheating on your wife in a way. Married to each other." Asked by the interviewer, "So what is Jason supposed to do during the hiatus?" Hetfield responded, "I don't fucking know. I'm not his travel agent."

Complexities were evident: for example, while Hammett supported Jason ("James demands loyalty and unity, and I respect that, but I don't think he realises the sequence of events he's putting into play . . . I think it's morally wrong to keep someone away from what keeps him happy"), Ulrich would not be drawn into the discussion, citing domestic concerns: "I just can't get caught up in these meltdowns. I've got some issues in my family life, with my wife, that are a little more weighty than, like, whatever James Hetfield and Jason Newsted are bickering over."

Finally, the usually tactful Newsted came out and said: "James is on quite a few records: in the *South Park* movie, when Kenney goes to hell, James is singing, and he's on just about every Corrosion Of Conformity album. That's a shot at him, but I'm going to keep it. I can't play my shit, but he can go play with other people."* It was a bleak picture. However, it should be noted that Lars insisted that the conflict was not damaging: "Ultimately, we have a love and respect for each other that supersedes the bickering. The key thing is, we're fucking still here. And we're the only ones that are still here . . . It's an interesting time to interview the four of us separately. You're hearing people get things off their chest – almost using you as the middleman."

Nonetheless, it was now much clearer why Jason had left the band. A

---

* He had a point. James had played on recordings by Corrosion Of Conformity and Green Jelly, while both he and Kirk have recorded on Primus album tracks.

combination of James' control-freakery and the genuine damage that Newsted had done to his neck meant that the time was right for him to make his exit. Now, at last, he was free to record and release as he pleased: his impressive list of side-projects to date includes Echobrain, membership of the revitalised Voivod, a project with Strapping Young Lad's Devin Townsend and Exodus' Tom Hunting called IR8, another collaboration with Hunting, Sepultura's Andreas Kisser and Machine Head's Rob Flynn entitled Quarteto Da Pingo and other groups called El Rone, Fatso, Groove Stang, Judas, Kopper Biskits, Long Ass Johnny & The Fabulous Y-Tones, Maxwell Ranchouse Bands, Sepultallica, Sexoturica, the Moss Brothers and Voodoo Children. It's just a pity that the dirty laundry behind the split had to be aired so publicly.

Emerging blinking from the aftermath of Jason's departure and the *Playboy* interview, James Hetfield, Lars Ulrich and Kirk Hammett pondered their future. The train of consequences which they had set in motion thundered on around them: Napster was giving its last gasp in the courts; the individual band-members still made the occasional live appearance (Lars came onstage with Godsmack on April 4) and gave the odd interview. "Obviously before we play any shows we're gonna need someone playing bass," James told the press at the ESPN Action Sports & Music Awards. "But we can still write and record and do some things together. We have a total free-form attitude right now, so we could go any which way we want. It's a great place to be."

Perhaps the shock of losing a member had been a little therapeutic. "Right now the three of us are gaining strength – the three of us are getting our shit together and whoever comes into this is gonna have to put up with a lot," Hetfield added. "We're really enjoying each other's company and retouching on things we haven't connected on in a long time. It's a fun and healthy time for us." The band also hinted that new material was on the way, and that a new album might even be released before 2002. "The best thing about where we're at right now is we don't have anything in front of us," Ulrich said. "We for once feel a tremendous amount of freedom to basically do whatever we want and whatever comes to us." As for finding a new bassist, Lars explained: "We put out four records in four years, the last four years of the Nineties, and I don't think anybody's particularly missing Metallica . . .

We want to take our time finding the right person to fill in Jason's spot."

And on April 23, 2001, Metallica entered the studio at last, accompanied by Bob Rock. Would this be the real deal? A genuine chance to record some brand-new songs? And would they be better than the *Loads*? Fans hoped so, and Lars added some spice by saying at metallica.com that "We've got a shitload of sick ideas and it's really cool to get back to being a band again." A little later, he confirmed that the new music contained some "sick, ugly, new fucked-up jams".

And so the shutters came down. As always with Metallica recording sessions, the band retreated into virtual silence for the duration, with only occasional forays into the public spotlight. These came infrequently, firstly when Lars and Skylar announced the birth of their second child, Layne, born on May 6. The following week, Ulrich was so moved by the music at a gig by the Icelandic band Sigur Rós that he wrote them a note saying: "Thank you, thank you, thank you! We are in the studio right now struggling to make some sort of album. I'm going to go back after this completely inspired." A few days later Kirk jammed on a version of 'Until It Sleeps' at Van Halen singer Sammy Hagar's Cabo Wabo Cantina club in Cabo San Lucas, Mexico, and the same week Lars took over the microphone to perform a four-hour DJ set of NWOBHM classics at the KSJO radio station in San Francisco.

The most evident break in recording occurred when the band broke their silence on July 12, 2001, to respond to the news that finally the Napster war was over. Both sides announced the settlement of their legal dispute, which was described in some areas as enabling "the parties to work together to make Napster a positive vehicle for artists and music enthusiasts alike".

It emerged that Napster had developed filters which would permit copyrighted material to be safe from deliberate distribution. Interim CEO of Napster Hank Barry said: "Metallica has taken a courageous stand and a tough and principled approach to the protection of its name and creative output, and that of other artists. They brought to our attention the essential artists' rights issues which we've addressed in our new technology. We respect what they've done and regret any harm which this dispute may have caused them."

You can almost imagine the executive officer's smile starting to crack after the effort of the first few words. He went on: "In a career that dates to 1981, Metallica has been in the forefront of creative, technological and marketing initiatives in the music and video world. It's clear that Metallica's longevity and fan loyalty have been earned by looking forward, not backward." More humble pie eating followed: "We understand that Metallica and, indeed, all artists, must have a voice in this evolution. We are delighted that we now have the opportunity to work with Metallica to develop a new business model that will be responsive to the artistic right to choose for which Metallica so vigorously and admirably fought."

To his credit, Lars added to the wordplay with the carefully chosen sentences: "I think we've resolved this in a way that works for fans, recording artists and songwriters alike . . . We believe that this settlement will create the kind of enhanced protection for artists that we've been seeking from Napster. We await Napster's implementation of a new model which will allow artists to choose how their creative efforts are distributed. It's good that they're going legit." Note that he hinted that the actual implementation of the new software was the key issue.

Yet more earnest nonsense came from Napster founder Shawn Fanning, who did his best to pour oil with the words: "Even when we were at odds with Metallica, we always understood that they had the best interests of artists in mind . . . Metallica brought to the forefront an important artists' rights issue. They have taken a lot of flak for that but have persevered because of their belief that what they're doing is essential to the preservation of their art. Despite the litigation, Metallica's position has been a reflection of their high ideals and their private dealings with Napster have always been gracious. It's time to end the court fight and shake hands. We look forward to gaining Metallica's support and respect as we work to develop Napster into a tool that can be responsive both to artists' needs to communicate their art and the desires of music lovers throughout the world. We're pleased that this chapter is behind us."

But was the chapter really behind them? Not really – Napster ceased trading soon after. Even today, two years later, it is still inactive, with only the occasional mailing-list email indicating signs of life.

As for our heroes, they might have defeated Napster. But Metallica still had the aftermath of that particular issue to deal with among their fanbase – how were they to resolve the irrevocable image which many of their die-hard followers now had of them as aggressively litigious money-grabbers?

294

And more than this, there was evident decay in the band. Jason's departure, the interview in *Playboy* and the fact that no new music had appeared since the *Loads* sessions in 1996 and 1997 were symptoms of a deeper, more frightening malaise.

23

The Truth About Napster

Myth 12: By 2001, Metallica had simply become a bunch of money-obsessed, corporate business operators. With the Napster case they demonstrated that they had completely lost all respect for their fanbase.
Myth 13: The case was much more than Metallica versus Napster: many fundamental issues such as freedom of speech were also called into question.

These were the claims aimed at Metallica as the Napster case raged on. Thousands of former fans were angry and saddened by the speed and commitment of Metallica's pursuit of Napster, and – especially after the poor *Load* and *Reload* albums – abandoned them for other bands.

Unfortunately, it's just not that simple.

Firstly, Metallica's involvement in Napster's troubled, brief existence only began relatively late in the day. Shawn Fanning had begun work on designing his revolutionary program in January 1999, leaving Northeastern University after the first semester of his first year there to work on the software. The service went live in June, almost a year before Metallica stepped in. Napster secured funding in June, hired a professional CEO in August and began exploratory negotiations with record companies in October. The idea – that online distribution of the companies' material by Napster could be a workable business operation – failed to take off and in December the Recording Industry Association of America (RIAA) sued Napster for copyright infringement. The plaintiff requested damages of $100,000 each time a song was copied.

While the suit was in progress, Napster's profile escalated enormously as its reputation spread by word of mouth: in early 2000 several universities were obliged to remove the program from their networks because demand by the student body for its use was too great. In the space of one year, Fanning had created and unleashed that marketing specialist's dream: a product which everybody *had* to have. The Metallica suit came in April, together with Lars' list of over 300,000 names.

The key moment came in May 2000, when venture capitalists invested $15 million in Napster. What made this move so important is that Napster was no longer a backroom operation hosted by the geeky, charismatic Fanning and his friends: it was a full-blooded, well-funded company with a business plan, a developed corporate structure and serious commercial clout. Metallica weren't trying to shut down some kind of not-for-profit collective of students: they were fighting a business player of significant resources. That's the first thing that most people don't understand about Napster.

On June 13, 2000, the RIAA filed a motion for a preliminary injunction to block all major-label music (i.e. songs from the Big Five US labels) from being exchanged through Napster. Two days later Napster hired the renowned lawyer David Boies to fight its case – a move which only a wealthy and experienced company would make. Boies prepared a defence based on four key issues.

The first was that Napster users were not infringing anyone's copyright because (a) non-commercial copying of files to a limited degree is recognised as 'fair use' under US law, and (b) that a key act, the Audio Home Recording Act, says that noncommercial copying by consumers is lawful.

The second was that Napster also allows substantial noninfringing services, such as providing extra 'backup' copies of songs which users already own, distributing non-copyrighted material (i.e. from new and/or unsigned bands) and providing material for sampling purposes (which is often regarded as a fair use). There was a landmark precedent for this: in a 1984 case Sony, the manufacturers of the then-new Betamax video cassette recorder, had been sued by the movie-makers Universal Studios. The Supreme Court said that even though VCRs were mostly used to copy copyrighted materials, there were substantial uses that did not infringe copyrights.

The third was that the brand-new Digital Millennium Copyright Act exempted internet service providers (ISPs) from monitoring all of their users' activities, even if the ISP knew that some of this activity was illegal. Napster therefore had to prove that it was an ISP like AOL or Yahoo.

The fourth was that if copyright holders (in this case the RIAA) use their copyrights for anti-competitive purposes, this constitutes copyright misuse and is not permitted.

However, none of these points convinced the presiding judge in the case, US District Judge Marilyn Patel, who on June 26, 2000 ruled in favour of the RIAA and ordered Napster to stop allowing copyrighted material to be swapped over its network by midnight two days later. In her ruling she found Napster's potential noninfringing uses (i.e. the distribution of unsigned bands, etc.) "minimal", adding: "The substantial or commercially significant use of the service was and continues to be copying popular music, most of which is copyrighted and for which no authorisation has been obtained." She also explained that Napster executives knew a) that copyrighted material was being exchanged by users and b) that such activity might be deemed unlawful: "This evidence includes internal documents authored by Napster executives stating that Napster was making pirated music available, stressing the need to remain ignorant of Napster users' identities and IP addresses since they are exchanging pirated music."

With two days to go to meet the District Court's ruling, the cards seemed to be on the table for Napster. However, it was afforded a last-minute delay by the Ninth US Circuit Court of Appeals, which ruled that the company should be allowed to continue its operations. After more court hearings a verdict was reached as late as February 2001 that Napster must stop trading copyrighted material. By this stage the company had announced plans to work in partnership with the German media company, Bertelsmann, to develop a membership-based system which would guarantee payments to artists (although this never materialised) and added a file filtering system to its program which blocked users from downloading specific music files – that is, copyrighted songs.

The case gradually wound down and ultimately Napster either liquidated or simply fell silent. By this stage a whole raft of file-sharing programs were available (Gnutella and Freenet became popular in 2000, Audiogalaxy was big in 2001 – until it too was shot down by the industry – and currently WinMX and Soulseek are the programs in vogue). Napster itself maintains a shadowy presence behind its website, sending out cryptic animated items from time to time.

The file-sharing community, at the time of writing, is enormous, with thousands or even millions of users exchanging material hourly. Until individual cases are brought against users, this is very likely to continue. Looking back at the Napster case of 2000 and 2001, it seems that the predictions of some of those involved – who said that the technology could not be stopped – have come true, and then some: far from being a music-only phenomenon, movies, programmes and images are also the currency of exchange. Now that broadband internet access is common, more or less any unencrypted digital file can be exchanged, it seems, which raises enormous questions about the livelihoods of copyright holders and the nature of copyright itself.

Lars Ulrich had clearly got himself into a complex situation when he entered the fray, with opinions bombarding him on all sides and, most problematically, a large section of his own fanbase turning on him. Once he was involved he could not (or would not) step down, and issued public statements such as, "If some of our fans do not respect the fact that we want to and have the right to do what we feel is important about what's right for us, then I don't want them to respect us, and I don't respect them." This makes the whole issue, for Metallica at least, one of PR.

Many fans were angered because they thought Metallica were suing Napster simply because they were losing money. This was not the case – as Lars said, "Right now, it's really not about the money . . . The money that's being lost right now in this revenue is pocket change. To me, the core issue is people's perception of the internet, and what their rights are as internet users as it relates to intellectual property." But this message simply didn't come across to everyone, and wasn't helped by statements from James such as "This is a clear case of a middle man cutting us out of rewards we should reap for being a band" and Dr. Dre, who said: "Napster is taking food out of my kids' mouths. I've always dreamed about making a living at something that I love to do. And they're destroying my dream."

It's a fact that fewer of Metallica's fans would have deserted them if the band had made it clearer that the Napster case was not about money. But they didn't, and although Ulrich was often both focused and reasonable ("The ideal situation is clear and simple – to put Napster

299

out of business. The only way we can get our music removed is to shut the whole thing down"), it seems that a large chunk of the fanbase couldn't get over the cashflow issue.

While the message coming from the band seemed mixed and unfocused (Lars focused on the wider issues; James discussed the money issue; and Jason and Kirk issued statements only infrequently), the case was muddied further when other artists pitched in with an opinion. Nikki Sixx of Mötley Crüe commented: "I think Metallica have turned into a bunch of fucking corporate pigs. You sold out to your record company and lawyers with this lawsuit. In fact, you sold out years ago," while Courtney Love, then of Hole, offered the opposite opinion: "I will be the first in line to file a class action suit to protect my copyrights if Napster or even the far more advanced Gnutella doesn't work with us to protect us. I'm on Lars Ulrich's side, in other words." Madonna seemed to be somewhere in the middle: "I like the idea of trading information on the net, but to have a whole album online for free is bullshit. I mean, pay for my record."

Perhaps in an effort to clarify his stance amid all the confusion, Lars appeared on *The Charlie Rose Show* on May 12, 2000 opposite Public Enemy's Chuck D (a supporter of online file-sharing) for a televised debate on the subject. The discussion soon polarised into two, equally understandable viewpoints. Lars made a point of explaining that Metallica's stance was not about money, and certainly not in conflict with his band's support of live audience recordings at their own shows: "We encourage people to tape our music at concerts – we have no particular issues with home taping because you're talking about clear generation loss. But when it is the original master recording of our song available in a perfect digital format, that is a different story."

Chuck D presented a broader argument, which took in the fact that the Napster issue was really about record-company control of artists' lives and that the case was about taking the power back to the people – after all, a network of linked individuals sitting at home computers is more or less the modern definition of an underground resistance. As he said, "It's a parallel world, and a new paradigm is taking shape. You have to adapt to it. This goes beyond Chuck versus Lars. This is about the record industry versus the people. The people have got it on their side, and you've got to adapt."

He also pointed out that Metallica were in a different situation to most other artists, because they owned their own back catalogue, and thus that online trading affected them personally rather than a record company. Asked by the host at what point an artist should want his work taken off the internet, Chuck – who had earlier stated that he regarded the web as a form of radio – explained, with a degree of plausibility, that: "Back in 1967 when FM radio came about, there was this big outcry that the quality of it was going to take away from the artists' sales. When cassette recorders came in, it was 'They're gonna rob us, they're gonna take away from our sales.' And this has proven to be the contrary to what has happened – as a matter of fact, these things have been a turbo boost to the music industry. What is going to take place now, is that the computers have allowed the internet to actually expose music throughout the world."

A key moment came when Charlie Rose pointed out that there was nothing to stop the users whom Napster had banned from using their service at Metallica's request from logging off and re-registering with another user ID. Lars responded: "Let's put out one fire at a time. You can only say that someone can always build another nuclear warhead. Does that mean that you shouldn't go and destroy the ones that exist already? You take it one step at a time." This was crucial because it seemed to demonstrate a we-will-proceed-at-all-costs mentality in Lars (and, by association, Metallica) which focused on the now rather than on the future. He wanted, it appears, to stamp out Napster before taking into account the next file-sharing program. But even Lars knew he was up against a hopeless task, warning: "In a couple of years, there will be software where you can download movies, literature, poetry, the whole nine yards." In 2003, we're almost at that point. The rest is inevitable.

Napster lawyer David Boies told *Wired* magazine a couple of months later that Napster had a central index, or central server, which listed songs available for transfer. This gave people such as Metallica a clearly identifiable target to aim at: a legally significant piece of evidence which showed clearly that copyrighted material was being traded. Other, newer programs such as Freenet had no central index (users searched each other's hard drives rather than a central source), which made them, in theory at least, impossible to sue. If Metallica and/or the RIAA succeeded in shutting down Napster, the only workable alternative would be programs with no central index, which would be bad for both consumers and copyright holders.

"There is a real difference between Gnutella and Freenet on one hand and Napster on the other," explained Boies. "Central-server directories provide something that totally decentralised services do not: a much greater ability for users to make choices and decisions, because of the centralised index. I think the real danger here is that if you shut down a service like Napster, which has the potential to be much more efficient and more protective of copyright holders, you will drive everybody to a less efficient system that is less protective of copyright holders.

"The other possibility," he added, "is to drive the peer-to-peer central index technology offshore, or to Canada. And because it is non-commercial, once they set up in Canada, there isn't anything you can do in the United States. If they were selling subscriptions in the United States, you could stop it. If they were charging people, you could stop it. If they were soliciting people, you could stop it. But the thing about this is, you don't need to solicit people. They'll just dial up that Canadian address all by themselves. There really is nothing you can do to stop it."

In other words, by taking out Napster, Lars was shooting himself in the foot. And that's before you start taking into account the number of pissed-off fans who he and his bandmates really should have treated with a little more sensitivity. One of the things Boies said to *Wired* was that an industry which goes to war with its customers is not one which will prevail. The same can be applied in microcosm to Metallica.

What to conclude about the whole Napster public-relations disaster? Perhaps that, as always, it's a tale of two sides of equal validity. After all, Metallica aren't all about money: their website and fanclub activities lose them a quarter of a million dollars a year, they once explained – and let us not forget the make-up shows they performed at their own expense when James injured his back. These facts were obscured in the media storm which sprang up around them in the Napster case, and were further hidden by high-profile events such as a Limp Bizkit tour sponsored by Napster which took place in July 2000. Bizkit frontman Fred Durst made comments such as "[Napster] is an amazing way to market and promote music . . . the internet is here, and anybody trying to fight that, which would be people who are living by certain standards and practices of the record industry, those are the only people who are scared and threatened."

The other point, of course, is that in going after Napster Metallica were only exercising their right to protect their own property. While copyright laws may function perfectly well when it comes to the distribution and sale of hard objects, they clearly need revising to take into account the internet age, when digital copies can be made instantly, perfectly and untraceably. The authorities who assembled the notoriously complex and arcane copyright laws of the US could never have foreseen the impact of a commodity (digital information) which can be replicated in such a way, combined with a cheap, fast, global distribution mechanism (the internet). So while the laws remain obsolete, Metallica did the right thing by attempting to cover themselves. It's just a shame they did it in such a bullish, disrespectful way.

Another possible conclusion is that it hardly matters what Metallica did or did not do vis-à-vis Napster. The battle in which they briefly joined was only a small stage in a massive conflict which will endure for decades and in doing so may overturn many long-held convictions about the nature of ownership and authorship. As David Boies said, the free speech rights of both consumer and Napster were called into question during the case: might the nature of America's precious First Amendment itself be redefined as the struggle continues into the coming decades? Perhaps: and in that context, the moment of contest between Metallica and Napster seems about as significant as the captain of the Titanic losing his wallet just before the ship went down.

Perhaps copyright law is so complex that no clear message will ever be gained from fighting through it. Musical history is littered with cases of artists, fired by ego, avarice or simple eccentricity, laying claim to something that is theirs (or otherwise) and causing a furore in the process. Metallica's hero King Diamond, for example, was once sued by Kiss' legal team because his stage make-up resembled too closely that of Kiss bassist Gene Simmons. "It was crazy to us," he told me, "because we thought that even a three-year-old could tell the difference between the two. They even sent copies of the copyrights to the make-up! Then of course the press found out what was going on."

Business is business, though, and legal struggles are part of it. Let us resolve the issue, as much as it can be resolved, by invoking a true expert, someone who actually knows what they are talking about. In March 2001, Prometheus Books published *Digital Copyright* by an American law professor called Jessica Litman, who lectures at Wayne State University Law School in Detroit, Michigan. The book provided a much-needed overview of the state of play of American copyright law in the internet age and specifically in the wake of the Digital Millennium Copyright Act of 1998.

Professor Litman, who wrote in *Digital Copyright* that copyright laws today are based on the premise that "neither the creator of a new work of authorship nor the general public ought to be able to appropriate all of the benefits that flow from the creation of a new, original work of authorship", agreed to talk about the Metallica versus Napster case for this book. She has been studying and recording internet copyright cases since the early Nineties, when, as she says, "the copyright community was trying to decide how to deal with digital technology, and I found myself – in essence – doing copyright history in real time, and following the efforts of lobbyists and Congress and the courts to deal with the internet as they were doing it."

How do you think Metallica handled the case?

"Metallica in many ways mismanaged the PR. I think that if Metallica had said, 'We're delighted to have our stuff on Napster but only after it's been released by us on CD' . . . I think that people understand that artists want to have some kind of control over their work. As long as you strike people as reasonable, there's no problem. The problem comes when you say, you can't do any of this. Not even for out-of-print recordings that have never appeared on CD."

Lars, as we have seen, could have trodden more softly when he spoke about the issue: "I think those statements were perceived as unreasonable by American Metallica fans. Being the first people to take things to the level of suing universities and monitoring individual users struck people as an escalation. And there was a lot of sentiment over here about how Metallica had earned a whole lot of money, to the extent that people thought it was all about money – which people resented. A lot of Metallica fans probably won't buy their next album. I know they alienated some of their greatest fans."

Copyright laws need updating, and urgently: "You can't do what I do without being deeply cynical, and while I think that the internet will certainly drive change in copyright law – because the system when you apply it to the internet is deeply broken, if only because there are tens of millions of people breaking the law every day, so when that happens the system is broken – I'm not confident that it will change copyright in good ways, simply because the entrenched interests are entrenched."

But will this ever happen? "There's not enough political will to change [copyright law] in good ways. In this country at least, copyright law is not very good at ensuring that creators get paid. So it's not only a bit of a mess if you're someone trying to make use of copyrighted works without breaking the law, it's also not necessarily great if you're a creator trying to make a living. In the pre-internet era, much of that money really needed to go to people who printed books and pressed CDs and had warehouses and so forth. At the moment that money is still going to the publishers and producers who are using it to pay the lawyers that I train to litigate and lobby. And I'm not sure that's an efficient outcome for anybody."

At one point Napster and Bertelsmann looked set to begin working together. Does Professor Litman think that the partnership would have been viable? "No, because it seemed clear at the time that the other record companies had gotten so angry that they wanted Napster buried with a stake through its heart. Napster had become symbolic to them of everything that seemed to them to be going wrong. The recording industry wasn't willing to settle for a world in which it licensed its content for peer-to-peer file-trading, and indeed it's not yet willing to do that. They viewed it as a huge step to license anything for download at all."

How do the record companies view file-trading now, two years after the case? "They continue to characterise peer-to-peer file-trading in this country as piracy, as theft, as criminal behaviour. It's a huge money-making opportunity, and it would also give people access to recordings that are now out of print and can't be bought in stores, but they're not yet willing to settle for that business model."

One of the most profound themes to emerge from the whole debacle is that this could have been a far more earth-shaking case if Napster had achieved one of its aims, which was to challenge the record companies' actual ownership of the music they distributed. This would have called into question the entire foundation of the entertainment industry, which as we know it in its contracts-based incarnation goes back centuries. Litman explains: "Had Napster not run out of money, first of all it was going to challenge the record companies' ownership of the copyrights. Under US law it's really quite unclear that they own those copyrights. The recording industry has claimed to own those copyrights as something called 'works made for hire' which means that if you're an employee in the US, your employer automatically owns your copyrights."

How could such uncertainty exist, I ask? "Recording artists aren't employees, they're independent contractors, and the rule is that except in particular cases, the independent contractor owns the copyright. Now they can assign it, and many artists presumably did do that, but because of the massive consolidation of the entertainment industry, not all of those contracts are easy to find. One thing that happened in the case was that Napster said, 'The copyright statute says that you need to show a certificate of registration before you can sue me. Indeed, give me a list of works you claim to own.' And the record companies said, 'We can't.'" In this context, Metallica's involvement seems trivial: the case might have uprooted tens, possibly hundreds of years of contractual negotiation, and therefore forced the US legal system to reappraise the very roots on which it is founded.

One of the reasons this didn't happen was the very mundane fact that Napster simply lacked the funds to push it through. "Yes," agrees Litman. "I've seen a number of businesses with compelling legal arguments sued into bankruptcy in the past few years." What this says about the whole structure of law in the West is too much to explore here – but the basic points are, I think, clear to everyone. Might is right, it seems, and in the entertainment industry just as much or more so than everywhere else.

David Boies posited that if you force people to use a decentralised service "you will drive everybody to a less efficient system that is less protective of copyright holders". Does Professor Litman agree with this? "Yes. A decentralised service is less efficient in two ways. Firstly, it's less efficient for users who may have to try several services before they find the recording they're looking for. Secondly, when we're talking about any system which is about funnelling money, the more networks there are, the more people there are to negotiate with and the more things there are to monitor. So while a decentralised service is more protective of privacy, if you're looking for efficiency, the more centralised the service, the more efficient it's going to be."

What is the probable outcome of the whole issue, as she sees it?

"People won't stop peer-to-peer file-trading because it's too useful, so what we need is some kind of creative model which will allow creators to get paid for copyrighted works. I think eventually everyone is going to settle for compulsory licences. I think P2P is just too useful to go away, and it beats the best record store in the world, both in the selection and the instant gratification. I think lots of people will be willing to pay for it, just as they pay their ISPs. I assume that you would pay a fee along with your internet service fee, and it would be like any other levy. I can imagine a blank media levy being added to the cost of CD-Rs and so forth, but I imagine the easiest thing is to stick a levy on top of your internet service, probably limiting it to customers with broadband access, because dial-up customers can't download too much anyway."

Is the recording industry pleased, does Litman think, that a warning has been given? "Oh yes. But the number of people who are engaging in peer-to-peer file-trading seems to go up by the hour. It's a great distribution mechanism and there are opportunities to earn a great deal of money from it, if they could just accept that it's going to exist."

One of the key arguments that record companies use to bring down P2P file-trading is that if they lose revenue from established artists, they will be less willing to invest in riskier new acts and thus there will be less music for everybody. And they have a point. But there's another side which they're missing out on, which is that the web can actually boost music sales because it's another form of exposure for artists. Litman explains: "When the VCR came out in the Eighties, the motion picture industry said, 'If this isn't made illegal, the industry will simply stop making movies because there won't be any incentive to make movies knowing that people can make copies of them.' And of course, 20 years later the industry earns more from the sale of video cassettes than it does from domestic cinema releases. And I think a similar thing could happen, I just think the industry is going to have to be dragged kicking and screaming to it."

In two decades' time, perhaps we will all be looking back on the Napster case and its small role in the wider movement, which is the internet finding its niche in the market as it develops and grows – and laughing at how seriously we took it back in the early years of the 21st century. After all, do we now treat the movie industry's protestations against the early VCRs with any respect?

Metallica lost a lot of fans over Napster. This wasn't helped by the albums they had made in the preceding five years being so dull, of course: many of the fans who bid them farewell with a raised middle finger as Napster bit the dust were probably on their way out anyway. But one thing should be clear. The problem wasn't that Metallica went after Napster. It was the *way they did it*: angry, confrontational and stubborn, just like a corporation. Lars opened his mouth once too often. Too many people loved file-trading. Neither Metallica nor their legal team thought of exploiting, rather than suppressing the technology at this stage – and they were just too damn macho about the whole affair.

The myth which states that Metallica had become corporate scumbags, is just that – a myth. They did the right thing by suing Napster. But the way they did it was all wrong, and made them seem uncaring and greedy.

The myth that the Napster case was a far bigger issue than might seem at first sight is fact. The industry came close to losing its footing in 2001, and is still reeling with the shock. But the day of regulated, legal file-sharing must come, because the mechanism is too useful to be taken away without enormous protest and cost – and anyway, everyone can benefit from it, so why remove it?

As Jessica Litman says, "The industry is winning all the battles – but they're losing the war." It's just a shame that Metallica couldn't have worked this out for themselves.

24

2001–2003

On July 19, 2001, the announcement that James Hetfield had entered a rehabilitation facility "to undergo treatment for alcoholism and other addictions" should have come as no surprise.

"Until then," said the official statement at metallica.com, "we have postponed all current activities, including recording sessions for our new album." This left fans in no doubt how serious James' decision to step outside the band, however temporarily, had been: for Hetfield to take time out from the band which he had made as important as his family was unprecedented.

Rumours began to spread. Everyone knew that James liked a drink; Metallica hadn't been nicknamed 'Alcoholica' for nothing. But the 'other addictions' part of the statement had observers wondering if Hetfield had problems with drugs, too. Fortunately for James, there was a white knight waiting in the wings in the unlikely form of Jason Newsted, who explained to the press: "I think that one thing that really needs to be cleared up, that I'm not sure how it's been misconstrued, is that the other addictions have nothing to do with substances. As long as I have known him, he has never touched anything other than alcohol. I know for a fact that he's never done any kind of amphetamines, cocaine or anything like that in his life ever. I know he's never done LSD or ecstasy or any of that shit ever. Any of that thing that people think has to do with drugs is completely wrong."

As to what the other addictions might be, Newsted was clearly as much in the dark as everyone else, pondering: "I don't know. It had to do with the breaking up of the band, too, and some other personal things. Emotionally, he maybe was really drunk with, I don't know, with sadness, tense things or stress. It kinda caught up with him all at once. But he's not a weak person, as you well know. He's a very strong person. It's just what had to happen for him to keep himself together and for him to be able to go on."

Jason had identified something very clearly with his last sentence, which is that in order for James and his band to bring themselves out of the sea of mediocrity and confusion in which they had been drowning for some time, a creative rebirth would need to take place. Therapy, it seemed, would make an unnatural partner for Hetfield, a man's man with the roar of a bull and the onstage presence of a soldier in battle – but it would be the only way forward.

The source of James' problems may have been his childhood and the Christian Scientist upbringing at which he raged on 'Dyer's Eve' and 'The God That Failed'. Anyone who has seen Hetfield interviewed (the measured tones; the shy, almost reserved manner; the storm clouds which lower on his brow if he is asked a question not to his liking) knows that his emotions are held back, deep inside. All that, it seemed, was about to come out.

It appears that James makes a loyal friend, once you get past those barriers. Katon DePena of Hirax enthuses: "James – great guy! A real person . . . not everybody gets to know the side of James Hetfield that I know. He's a real friend. He once carried me upstairs into his house because I had a sprained ankle from playing a concert the night before with Sacrilege and Possessed. He's the coolest guy in the band." But even the steadiest hand may waver in the insane world of showbiz, as Lemmy of Motörhead told me: "I think a lot of people are very highly strung in rock'n'roll. They tend to react compulsively, rather than think things out. You see, it depends on your personality . . . I'm very Buddha, me, I sit and watch the shit go by. But I'm sure if you looked at the statistics you'd find that there are no more suicides in rock'n'roll than anywhere else. In fact I think you'd find that we're one of the lowest. You just hear about ours more."

As the news about Hetfield going into rehab spread, messages of support began to appear. Ten days into his treatment, James himself passed on a statement to Metallica.com which read: "It took a lot for me to admit to my problems, and it's a great feeling to have the support and comfort for me as a person from all the friends I've made out there. Thanks very much, it means a lot." None other than Dave Mustaine posted at the Metallica site, doubling it up at the Megadeth equivalent so that visitors would know it was him: "My heartfelt best wishes go out to James. I know what he is feeling right now, and I know what people are saying. The people said it about me." He added that one of his dearest wishes would be to perform a show or record an album with James, Lars and his own bass player Dave Ellefson. He had clearly been through some counselling himself in his time, closing his post with the words: "I am sure there are people that come here that aren't even Metallica fans, just to post shit about them. Not me. I am a fan. And although I was really hurt by getting fired, I have always been a fan." He told the press: "Lars, to me, is one of the neatest little dudes I ever met. He's a very, very intelligent man. And I think James is one of the greatest rhythm guitar players and singers that have ever graced the planet. I know that if he and I got together again, people would be so blown away they'd probably have to kill themselves."

In September 2001 a Metallica fan convention took place in San Francisco, with Lars and Kirk jamming on renditions by the tribute band Creeping Death of 'Die Die My Darling', 'No Remorse', 'Helpless', '. . . And Justice For All', 'Ride The Lightning' and 'Am I Evil?'

However, after this all was quiet for a few months, until a December 3 update from James at the Metallica website. The webmaster wrote: "Yes folks, we have word from James, and the news is all good. His recovery has gone exceedingly well, he is back out, about and feeling rather good about life." Hetfield added: "My rough road has become smoother reading the show of support from the friends I've met through Metallica. Thank you. They move me deeply . . . My music and lyrics have always been therapy for me. Without this God-given gift I don't know where I'd be. And now I truly feel the impact and connection it's made with others."

The recovery process was made no doubt both easier and more complex with the arrival of James' third child, Marcella, on January 24, 2002, but other than this the year looked set to be quiet, with Metallica sporadically recording new songs in between James' therapy and the various public events involving the other members. Something of Hetfield's stern, pre-therapy approach was revealed in another interview from Jason, who spoke to *Guitar World* at the beginning of the year. After stressing, "I wish those guys the best, and that needs to be put across . . . I wanted to stay, but I had to go," the bassist recalled the conversation which he and James had had when he asked James' permission to release the Echobrain album back in 2000. "James essentially said that I couldn't do Metallica if I was going to have other bands," Newsted said. "It was like, 'If you do anything else, you're not giving full time to Metallica.' And it was kind of strange, because . . . for shows and rehearsals, I was always the first one in and the last one out. I was into it, man. I really was a 25-hours-a-day-Metallica person. Nothing took priority over Metallica."

The link between Jason's departure, due in part it seems to James' iron-fist methods, and Hetfield's life-changing decision to enter rehab is subtle but significant. "My leaving happened for a reason," said Newsted: perhaps Hetfield knew that his old methods would simply not work in the new incarnation of the band. And there was always the old shock of Cliff's death lurking in the background: as Jason explained: "I don't think that the three of them got to actually finish their grieving process. They never got to mourn Cliff fully, so a lot of things were directed at the guy who was filling his shoes. It was not on purpose. It's just that emotions are heavy; and sometimes uncontrollable." As for his potential replacement in Metallica, Newsted mused: "You're gonna have to be a bad motherfucker first of all, to get past the obvious history; and then to stand in the same room and play with James Hetfield and be good enough, because he's the best rhythm guitar player there is in heavy music, hands down. I would like to see an old friend of the family be able to be the bass player; me, personally, I'd like to see Joey Vera."

On February 19, 2001, apparently out of rehab and back in business, James posted a message in tribute to the late Exodus singer Paul Baloff, who had died suddenly a fortnight before. He wrote: "We in Metallica would like to say that we will all miss Paul for his work, his kindness and for just being there . . . We will all remember Paul. Like he said, 'Heavier than time'. He truly was. Cheers Paul! And I would also like to thank all the people that supported me while I was in rehab, thanx." Kirk also spoke to the media at length about the early days of Exodus, when he, Baloff and the rest of the band had sealed *Bonded By Blood* by literally exchanging blood, tribal-bonding style. Those innocent days must have seemed very far off.

At around this time the band began using the services of a 'performance coach' called Dr. Phil Towle, whose function appears to fall somewhere between that of a group therapist and a life counsellor. His role was not fully revealed until 2003, but according to the film-makers Joe Berlinger and Bruce Sinofsky, who began work on a Metallica documentary at this time, Towle appeared in some of the scenes they had shot since April 2001. As yet undefined, the movie appears to take in scenes from all areas of the Metallica world, including the members' private lives: "We've only shot 30 or 40 per cent of it, so Joe and I would be hard-pressed to define the project because it's constantly changing," said Sinofsky at the time. "We told Cliff Burnstein when he asked what kind of film it's going to be, why don't you ask Lars, James and Kirk what kind of album it's going to be?"

It emerged that the duo had approached Metallica with a film idea in the mid-Nineties: "They weren't ready to be completely open back then," said Sinofsky. "They said when they were ready they'd come to us, and they have. And Joe and I are extremely excited. It's looking very intimate, very personal and I think it will excite the band too. Joe said early on that if we were going to make a film, we wanted to know we were going to get access. If we look at one of our films and realise that other people could've got it, then we've failed."

Of the Jason and rehab episodes, Sinofsky explained: "Joe and I have dealt with some really difficult subject matter. You don't wish bad news on anyone, but it unquestionably makes for drama and you're there to capture it. So the band going through some flux and some growing pains is the kind of material a film-maker prays for. Of course, on a personal level you don't want people to go through their tortures and dealing with their demons, but ultimately for the Metallica fan, they will see things they've never seen before."

In April 2002 James, Lars, and Kirk made an appearance at the recording of MTV's annual *MTV Icon* show, which on this occasion was focusing on Aerosmith. This was the band's first public appearance since James had completed rehab and was held at Sony Picture Studios in Culver City. Each man made a brief speech about Aerosmith, Kirk talking about how much he admired the band and wanted to emulate them as a youth, and Lars recounting the way that singer Steven Tyler had made the last weeks of his friend, Rich Burch (author of the "Bang the head that doesn't bang" quote on the back of the *Kill 'Em All* album sleeve), easier back in 1992, when Burch was dying of AIDS. Finally James said, "This is the first time I have been on a stage since I came out of rehab, so I'm a little nervous. My heart is pounding fast, so let me know if I am talking too fast," before talking about the way Aerosmith had inspired him.

Events were moving rapidly. Megadeth had announced their split in April, with Dave Mustaine citing an injured arm as the cause, and Deth bassist Dave Ellefson (like Mustaine a fantastic player) had been rumoured to be joining Metallica. Jason Newsted told the press: "That would be pretty weird. It would be a good fit but only musician-wise. Dave is one of the best bass players there has ever been in metal, no two ways about it. I still look up to him. And he's a good guy, which is why I wouldn't wish it upon him. He could definitely handle the gig as far as the playing and the interviews and all that, but dealing with the inner workings, I don't know."

More importantly, Jason reported that he had recently met up with James, who had, it seemed, gained a lot from rehab and therapy: "He's a changed man. But it's good," said Newsted. "His eyes are clear. He's always been the most honest person I've ever known, and that's still there and it's still pretty serious business, but we hadn't sat together, just the two of us, without anything else going on, in ten years. So we finally got to sit down for two hours, just hang out for a second, and talk. It was good. We're brothers, man."

The year rolled on, with much Metallica activity but little firm news of new music. James appeared on a Gov't Mule track, 'Drivin' Rain', on a compilation album devoted to racecar driving titled *Crank It Up*. Meanwhile, Lars revealed that he was selling his famed art collection at Christie's: apparently he had begun to visit museums and art galleries during the band's long periods on the road some years earlier, graduating to buying at auction and building a collection of expressionist art based largely on the work of the CoBrA artists (Copenhagen, Brussels, Amsterdam) from the early Fifties and other contemporary artists such as the American graffiti artist Jean-Michel Basquiat. "I felt I could lose myself in art and get away from the music world," he told the press. "It became this great hiding place." As for his motives for selling his collection, which was valued at several million dollars, Ulrich explained: "Right now I am at a crossroads where I want to shed some of the things that I have amassed in my present home, mostly before I was married. I want to start over again."

Other Metallica cameos followed, live onstage with Sammy Hagar & the Waboritas at the Fillmore in San Francisco, and on record for a

Ramones tribute album at the request of Kirk's friend Johnny Ramone. Four Ramones songs were played at a surprise show at Club Kimo's in San Francisco on June 4. Metallica, with Bob Rock on bass, performed as Spun and knocked out versions of 'Commando', 'Today Your Love Tomorrow The World', '53rd And 3rd' and 'Now I Wanna Sniff Some Glue'. "That was our little tribute to the Ramones," said James, before the band went into a classic old-school Metallica set which included a new song, tentatively entitled 'Dead Kennedy Rolls'.

Another live show took place on July 6 at the Target Center, also in San Fran (where the band were now holed up, recording in earnest). This time the show was a party held to celebrate the launch of the new fanclub and gave two club members the chance to jam on bass. This took place on 'Creeping Death' and 'Seek And Destroy', with Rock – who now seemed to have settled in as a temporary fourth member – holding down the bass slot elsewhere.

Ten days later, fans were slightly disconcerted by the release of 'We Did It Again', a single collaboration between Metallica and the hip-hop producer Swizz Beatz, plus the rapping skills of Ja Rule. Swizz Beatz explained to the press: "I knew I wanted to do a rock'n'roll track and I knew I wanted to get the biggest act possible to do it, but I never thought in a million years that I'd be working with Metallica on this. They had two songs already that I really liked. I took those and combined them into one song. Then I called Ja Rule and told him I needed him to be on what could be the biggest song of his career. I told him to guess who he'd be working with on it and he was naming all these people he thought it was and finally, I said, 'It's Metallica,' and he said, 'Hell yeah!' This song is a blessing. When people hear it, they won't believe it!"

Rubbish, as usual with these things. Like Kid Rock's 'American Bad Ass', the song was a moderately hummable tune but not better than that, based on the type of riff from Kirk which fans had been hearing since the Black Album, some barked lines from James, a solid but simple beat from Lars and a ragged, yelled set of raps from Ja Rule. Neither rap–metal nor rap with metal, the song is unfocused and inconsequential, like Lars' claim that "I've never heard anything quite like that. It sits in a different place than anything else I've heard. I've never heard anything that sits right where this sits and that's pretty cool."

Would Metallica apply the ultimate insult and 'go nu-metal' in the

315

wake of 'We Did It Again'? Not to date, anyway – but for a while there it crossed a few listeners' minds that such a musical direction might be in the offing. What's more, it was revealed a little later that Lars would be working with the Wu Tang Clan's RZA on a project for the new Quentin Tarantino movie, *Kill Bill*.

October 2002 marked the last of Metallica's extra-curricular projects before the release of the as-yet-untitled new album. James recorded a song for a tribute album to the late country star Waylon Jennings, a cover of Jennings' 'Don't You Think This Outlaw Bit's Done Got Out Of Hand', from the 1978 album *I've Always Been Crazy*. Hetfield performed guitar, bass, drums and vocals on the track, which was produced by Bob Rock at the Metallica HQ in San Francisco.

"The first time I met Waylon was when a college radio station wanted to get the two outlaws together of certain different styles of music," said James. "They thought it was a good idea if I interviewed him and I guess dad helped me out with a few of the questions. It's funny because my dad wanted me to get a CD signed for him, and then Waylon brought some Metallica stuff to get signed for his son."

October also saw the release of a nine-disc 20th Anniversary box set from Metal Blade Records, the Brian Slagel-run label which had given Metallica their first break and which had become a fully fledged independent label of some power in the intervening decades. There had been two different, pre-*Kill 'Em All* versions of 'Hit The Lights' on the first two pressings of the *Metal Massacre* vinyl album in 1982 and 1983. Subsequently, the CD version of the album had contained the later recording of the song featuring Dave Mustaine, making the first version very rare: Metallica and Slagel decided therefore to put that scarce, Lloyd Grant-featuring version on the box set. Lars explained, "This is the earliest and the rawest version of 'Hit The Lights' that exists – come to think of it, it is the earliest Metallica recording ever released, and it's really fun to be able to share this with you. It's got amazing energy and a kind of youthful innocence that, to my ears, holds up quite well 20 years later." Also revisiting old times was Kirk, who was asked to contribute to a VH-1 *Behind The Music* special on Anthrax. Remembering the infamous Music Building, Hammett said: "Anthrax was really nice and helped us out a lot. They gave us a fridge and a toaster oven."

After all this activity, the first real news about the new, changed Metallica and the music they were making came courtesy of their fanclub magazine, *So What*. At last the truth was out about James' mental state, the status of the three band members plus Bob Rock, the new album, and, possibly, who the new bass player might be. Interviewed by writer Jaan Uhelszki, Lars and Kirk revealed that the recording of the new album had been initially sporadic, with the first sessions delayed until a new studio could be found. Having decided that the old premises they had always used – the Plant – were no longer appropriate, the band had settled on Presidio Studios, a recording and practice venue where some music was laid down as far back as April 2001. After three weeks came James' departure to rehab and the indefinite suspension of Metallica activities.

It had been a grim time for all, it seemed, with only Lars and Kirk remaining on standby while James went through his rehabilitation sessions. But when the band finally began recording on Hetfield's return a year later, changes in the way they composed, recorded and even interacted with each other took place immediately, with profound consequences. For starters, Metallica composed the songs on the spot at Metallica HQ, as Kirk explained: "That's the first time we've used that approach. To create on the spot spontaneously. Usually everyone would want to bring in their musical ideas and then James and Lars would take it from there and turn them into songs. This time everything was created spontaneously on the spot so there is much more of a community effort." Lars added that the new method "felt totally right, because it gave us a chance to start over. Start in a different place."

James added that although spontaneity was a good thing, there were benefits to being on a deadline. The band worked from 11am to 4pm each day, with the members enjoying the creativity of the moment rather than comparing their progress on other days. In the old days, he explained: "We worked without any limits or boundaries. I didn't realise how disturbing it was. Because the days wouldn't end. And you'd wake up the next day kind of whenever, and go in the studio. It was just like one cloud, and I'm really tired of living in a cloud." Every day a morning meeting would lead to some 'stream of consciousness' lyric writing, with all the musicians sitting down together, writing and comparing notes. This, it emerged, had been Bob Rock's idea, as the producer remarked: "I said, 'OK, James, you got ten minutes to write the song.' It was like, I think he wanted to punch me." Rock, as an observer of Metallica's recent traumas but not actually a part of them, knew how to make the 'new' band work efficiently: "I don't think any of this would be possible [without] what these guys have gone through personally . . . Because now they're in a different place than they were before, a different place where they're at personally with each other. When I came into it, and I saw how close they were, and they allowed me to be part of the experience, it just became something very natural . . . the egos kind of went out the door, and I think the whole process has been about that."

The essence of the new Metallica was that the burden and responsibility of lyric writing was now shared by all three musicians, with James allowing Lars and Kirk to come into what had been his private zone, with much more equality existing between the three than had previously been the case. This had also had a refreshing impact on the music, it seemed: as Kirk said, "All of a sudden the journey that we've been on in the last year and a half . . . kind of took us back around a little bit, and into some places that we had been before. And felt, like wait a minute, maybe there is something different, a different angle to tackle that from than before." What he meant, it appeared, was that Metallica had made the move that so many fans had been wanting to see for years. They were hinting that they had gone back to thrash metal. Could this really be the case? The jaded Metallica fan noted this, raised an eyebrow and moved on, sure that this was not meant to be taken seriously.

Strangely, one of the reasons why Jason had left Metallica was because he wanted the territorial aspects of the old group to change – but it was only with the shock of his departure that this could happen. Lars explained: "I've said many times, you know, there is such a great sense of irony in the fact that some of the things that Jason was the most discouraged and annoyed about with Metallica were all the things we've shed . . . he had a kind of a vision of some sort of nirvana in the direction of where this is. You know, all of us kind of jamming and that kind of thing, and that still has just a kind of bittersweet irony to it."

Bob Rock, the observer of all these changes and the author of some of them, was interviewed in the next issue of *So What* and explained at length how the timeline from his first work with the band had flowed. "It's almost like forming a band again, you know, that's really what has happened here in my opinion, is forming a band again," he said. "Getting together and laying a whole pile of ideas down, and just watching as you listen to the ideas that you did last week, you go somewhere else or you feel like you have to go somewhere else." This reduced the pressure on James in particular: "During the *Load* and *Reload* period there was a part where James was looking at twenty-eight-plus songs that he had to write lyrics for. It was a daunting task and it was just too much for him, you know, to look at all of those songs. That's one of the reasons why it turned into two albums, but still it was just, he was just staring at these blank pages of music that he had to write lyrics to. And so what we did right away at the Presidio as soon as we started making music was get the ball rolling right away."

So what was the new music actually like? Rock mused: "It feels . . . like a really old tough English boxer who is hard as nails and drinks whiskey and is going against a young guy that is really, really strong and really agile and stuff, but the old guy beats the absolute shit out of him. These are middle-aged guys that have a wealth of experience, that have a wealth of taste and ability, just really beating the shit out of their emotions in music and I love it . . . I think that this stuff is going to make a really big statement, that's what I would say."

As the months went on, the theme of not over-producing the album was pursued more and more in Metallica interviews. Lars told the writer Martin Popoff of *Brave Words & Bloody Knuckles* that "I think we were sort of guilty in the past, especially the *Load* and *Reload* stuff, of not editing ourselves. So we're dealing with that at the moment, which is kind of weird . . . We're trying not to beat the life out of it, which I think we had done on the previous couple of records. It got to the point where we produced all the life out of it. So there's some really great moments, some energy, some moments of people playing music together in a room, and it has a lot of soul."

As 2002 became 2003, the band focused more and more on the creation of the new album, which was mooted for a spring release. More than with any of the previous albums since *Load*, expectation was starting to build around the still-untitled album, largely due to the occasional hint thrown out by the band that it contained music which was a return to the older, faster style of the band's glory days. The website diaries hinted at this: Hammett wrote that their new songs sounded a lot like the Swedish death metal act Meshuggah, to which

Lars responded: "We had a nice ugly day in the studio. Lots of nastiness and misery. I'm psyched! BTW, I think Kirk's Meshuggah comparison is a little limiting. I hear shades of Hatebreed and Entombed in there also."

Some found this harder to believe than others. Jason Newsted, for example, told MTV News: "Kirk got quoted about their new record sounding like Entombed, how can it sound like Entombed, how? Who is playing bass to make it sound like Entombed? James is a good bass player, but c'mon dude! Lars – he hasn't practised enough drums over the years – he let his art fall away from him, he doesn't have the same finesse as he used to have, so how is it going to sound like Entombed and have that energy? And anyway if they are speaking like that how come they are not talking Entombed out on tour? Or Meshuggah – how come they are not staying true to their words? That's what really bothers me."

Newsted was more annoyed, it seemed, by the recent press statement which Metallica had issued, revealing that the 2003 Summer Sanitarium tour would be supported by Limp Bizkit and Linkin Park, two massive-selling but inoffensive nu-metal acts. "It's a joke, I think Metallica are just a joke, I don't think they have any idea," fumed Newsted. "I am a fan of Metallica again, I did my thing in there and felt good and I'm proud of that shit and I am more proud than sour. But that's the integrity down the fucking tube! Why can't they take out Strapping Young Lad, why can't they take out In Flames? What they are doing now is such an obvious cash thing and has nothing to do with the music that we're supposed to be fighting for." Jason himself had just joined the seminal Canadian progressive thrash act Voivod, and was engaged in releasing their new album through his own label, Chophouse Records. A little later he offered Metallica a 'head-to-head' contest onstage, at which, he vowed, Voivod would 'kick Metallica's ass'.

He later told *Classic Rock*: "I can't even get my breath about that. I'm absolutely flabbergasted . . . As a fan of theirs I'm very disappointed and freaked out by all this. They had the opportunity to come back as leaders, to take out bands such as In Flames, SYL and Voivod – bands that deserve to be seen. Metallica are the only ones with that kind of opportunity. Do they really think it'll sell them more than a couple of fucking thousand tickets if Linkin Park – or whoever – are on that bill?

No, there are people out there who still want metal, and it's too bad it wasn't addressed in that way."

Still others simply wanted to annoy Metallica. A punk band from Edmonton, Canada had reportedly called itself Metallica as a publicity stunt, attracting a cease-and-desist letter from Jill Pietrini of Metallica's legal representatives Manatt, Phelps & Phillips. Pietrini wrote in her letter to singer Blair William Piggot: "Your use of Metallica is particularly astonishing to the band, given that you have admitted in at least one interview that 'you know you are not allowed to use the name' . . . Metallica could recover significant monetary damages and obtain an injunction against any further acts of infringement, both in the US and in Canada."

However, nothing could hinder the real Metallica's progress at this stage, it seemed, and as fanbase awareness began to grow that 2003 could be a pivotal year for the band, the long-awaited announcement came on February 24 that a new bass player had been found. Among those rumoured to be in the frame were Kyuss/Unida bassist Scott Reeder, Nine Inch Nails' Danny Lohner, Jane's Addiction's Eric Avery and – curiously – sometime Marilyn Manson member Twiggy Ramirez had all tried out for the role, but the man eventually chosen to fill the intimidatingly large boots of Cliff Burton and Jason Newsted was none other than Robert Trujillo, formerly of the hardcore band Suicidal Tendencies and latterly the bassist in Ozzy Osbourne's band. Metallica's press release ran: "We are so psyched and proud to share the news that we are welcoming another brother to the family . . . We've all known, and have been huge fans of Rob since the early Nineties when he was a part of the legendary hardcore/metal band Suicidal Tendencies. We got to know Rob when we played together with Suicidal in Europe in 1993, during the Nowhere Else To Roam tour. We were impressed by Rob's roaring bass style and his very cool, unique vibe onstage, things we got to see again during the '94 Summer Shit tour when Suicidal joined forces with us." Trujillo himself added: "I am very stoked, excited and look forward to my new journey with my Metallica brothers. Step up!"

Lars was beside himself with excitement: "When Rob came to San Francisco the first time and jammed with us, we all felt this incredible magic between the four of us. It was just something that we could not describe, we all just knew it. Bob Rock told us right after the jam, that it sounded like a fucking 747 taking off! I am so fucking excited to be a full unit again . . . The last two years of just being the three of us have taught me so much about myself, about James and Kirk and about Metallica. And to welcome Rob into Metallica in 2003, after all the growth and soul-searching we've been through for the last two years, feels so fucking awesome. Being at full strength again is at this moment indescribable."

Kirk added, "Rob's chemistry with the band is undeniable. From the first rehearsal Rob was just mind-blowing, because he had such a huge sound and he pulled with his fingers, which is very reminiscent of Cliff Burton and we really liked that sound. He delivered on all fronts. He had a big sound and on top of that he's really a great, solid guy." As for James: "He *pounds*. The power that comes through his fingers. He's a ball of energy and he's so calm and able and balanced. He's got great stuff to offer but his personality is just right. He's on fire, he's ready, he's plugged right into the strength of Metallica and helping it shine."

The choice of Trujillo was wise. As a phenomenal player, he complements the fearsome accuracy of Hetfield's riffing and leaves space for Lars, too. Like Cliff, he has an acute ear for melody, although unlike Burton it's funk which drives him rather than classical theory. Although he is best known for the slapping style which infused Suicidal Tendencies and his side project Infectious Grooves, Rob admitted shortly after joining Metallica that the slap-and-pop method would have little place in his new band. But it seems that his musical ability is less valued by Metallica, and Hetfield in particular, than his air of solid calmness: perhaps after all the struggles the band had endured, a man who could support rather than fly artistically was the best choice.

And stories of those struggles were still coming to light, as a series of interviews which Metallica were conducting from the safety of their HQ in San Francisco were published. A key moment in James' decision to enter rehab had come, one article revealed, after a Siberian hunting trip which he had completed in 2001. He reported the trip as one of alcoholic escape in a harsh environment where the only two things to drink were melted snow or vodka. After weeks of refuge in the bottle James returned home and checked himself into a clinic, which he did not name "just in case anyone decides to dig some dirt".

He explained: "I've been in Metallica since I was 19 years old, which can be a very unusual environment, and it's very easy to find yourself not knowing how to live outside of that environment, which is what happened to me. I didn't know anything about life. I didn't know that I could come home and live a family life. I didn't know that I could live my life in a different way to how it was in the band since I was 19, which was very excessive and very intense. And if you have addictive behaviour then you can't always make the best choices for yourself. And I definitely didn't make the best choices for myself.

"But rehab is like college for your head. I really learned some things about myself in there. I was able to reframe my life and not look at everything with a negative connotation. That's how I was raised. It was like a survival technique for me. And getting into Metallica meant that initially I had to fight to survive, for food, for the towel for the shower, for everything. And then fighting to be the best band you can be, and putting other bands down. Finding fault with everything was how Metallica was fuelled. And not only did I play a part in that, I was buried in that."

One of the main problems, it seemed, had been that Hetfield was finding it more and more difficult to be James the man rather than James the star: "I felt that I couldn't show any weakness. For me, I was James Hetfield of Metallica rather than just James Hetfield. And I was trying to live that lifestyle at home; I was trying to wear that mask all the time. And it's amazing how long you can wear a mask for. We're performers who play music, I mean this is us. This isn't an act. But now I've learned how to be more congruent with where I am. Admitting that sometimes being on tour really sucks, and that I would rather go home. Or that I'm not in a good mood right now, and not worrying if people turn round and say, 'Hey, you're an asshole.' That can't hurt me now, whereas I used to be so concerned that people liked me. There's a lot of machismo in this world, but I suppose the most manly thing you can do is face up to your weaknesses and expose them. And you're showing strength by exposing your weaknesses to people. And that opens up a dialogue, it opens up friendships, which is definitely what it has done for me."

Lars admitted that at one point he had wondered if the game was up and the band was finally over: "I wanted to go and visit him. I wanted to make things better. But I couldn't. And all the time your imagination is running away with itself when you don't have any real info – we didn't hear from James for months. Your mind starts to think of the worst that can happen, and I honestly wondered if this was the end for Metallica . . . I thought, you know, we'd had a good run but that this might be it." As for Kirk, he recalled a pivotal moment when, after months of absence, James had been at a surprise birthday party held for Hammett in November 2001: "Seeing him was one of the greatest birthdays I ever had. It was just so great to see him again. I'm even getting emotional talking about it now."

All this emotion evidently provided the wellspring, the foundation, for the new music – which, as had already been hinted, was supposedly the hardest the band had made for years. The new album, it was revealed, would be called *St. Anger*, which came from James' musings inspired by a surfing St. Christopher medallion which he had seen Kirk wearing.

St. Anger still seems like an odd title today. However, the reasons for Metallica's choice would not become clear until the album itself appeared which was not until June 6, 2003, after months of speculation whether it would be leaked, 'I Disappear'-style, onto the internet. This didn't happen, probably because no promo copies were sent out, with the press invited instead to listening parties in May.

The music had become tougher, it seemed, after Lars had decided to start experimenting with double-bass rhythms and thrash patterns while rehearsing. "Suddenly we woke up and some long-forgotten feelings returned," said Hetfield. "Our fingers began to whizz faster and faster over the strings, because we wanted to lift the songs to the next level." Not that the songs were a simple return to older values: "Sometimes I think some fans would like to hear a new *Kill 'Em All* from us. Then I feel sorry for them, because we can't record another *Kill 'Em All*. We don't want to repeat ourselves."

Would the album display influences from newer bands? After all, much had happened in the world of metal since Metallica's last original studio album in 1997. James shrugged this off, saying: "A lot of musicians are afraid of being influenced too much by certain musical currents. We are not, because we don't let trends overwhelm us. Lars is interested in bands like Meshuggah, or the System Of A Downs of this world, but when Lars, Kirk and I tried to sound like a complete new band and not like Metallica, the experiment failed. We'll always sound like Metallica, because we can't do anything else."

Although they couldn't sound like any other band, Metallica had, in

effect, become a whole other band since the changes in their interaction had come about. Hetfield looked back on his old management
style with some regret, it appeared: "Lars and me came into the studio
and told the others what to do . . . Everything had to be under my
control. Totally childish." He revealed that the subject was even
addressed in one of the new songs: "In the song 'All Within My Hands'
I recognised that I choke the band to death. I had panic attacks that
Jason or even Lars would start other projects and like it better than
Metallica. To hold the band together I forced Lars, Jason and Kirk to
stay and to go on. I love Metallica so much that I almost crushed the
band with my love."

James now had completely different priorities, he said. To begin
with he would perform no more than three concerts in a row before
giving his voice a rest, although both Rob and Kirk had taken singing
lessons and would provide the backup vocals that Jason had once done
so well. Secondly, his family had re-assumed its rightful role in his life.
"My family got in the background," he said. "We couldn't go on vacation, because something could happen with the band. Home became
pure hell. Living together with my wife and my kids was a huge
problem for me in the past, because I couldn't combine family and
band." More profoundly, he added: "In some ways I'm thankful for my
addiction, because I experienced my inner self through it. Now I finally
see a happy man. I could have died or gone into prison a hundred
times. But nothing happened to me: my family is fine, I've got fans
who want to hear Metallica songs, and my band is intact. That makes
me happy – really happy."

More information on the nature of *St. Anger* came from the ever-
loquacious Bob Rock, who told *Hammer* magazine that he had chosen
to session the bass parts on the album rather than join the band full-time
for practical reasons: "I have seven children. That would only cause
problems. Aside from that I'm 10 years older than the other guys.
Robert Trujillo was a better choice. I'd rather concentrate on helping
people create music." As for the powerful new songs, he commented:
"We wanted a raw, unpolished sound. This raw sound perfectly
expresses the mood of the band right now . . . We played it all live
without overdubs. It's a liberating feeling to ignore all the rules that
exist in metal. You have to play this guitar with this amp, otherwise it
doesn't sound good, blah blah blah . . . Skip the rules and do what you

want! For example I only needed 10 minutes for the drum sound."

And so the scene was set. Even the more cynical of Metallica's old fanbase (like this author) watched with interest as the first snippets of new music began to appear on websites and in press releases. The promotional treadmill for the new album began to turn in early 2003, with Metallica filming a video for the first single from the record, the title track, on April 30. Intriguingly, the shoot took place at the dreaded San Quentin Prison in San Francisco, with the band performing the song for the inmates after being warned by a warder that the prison operated a 'no hostage policy' – in other words that if one of them was taken prisoner by an inmate, no negotiations for their release would be offered. The shoot took place without any problems, however, and the band returned the following day to perform a full set of established Metallica songs for the prisoners.

Next Metallica headed to LA for the taping of an *MTV Icon* show which, it had been announced, would be in their honour this year. It was broadcast on May 6 and was formatted as a sequence of live performances of various bands playing Metallica songs, intercut with interviews with the band-members and their reactions to the guest acts' versions of their material. Bright-eyed and speedy in the standard MTV style, the four musicians (Trujillo remained politely quiet, allowing the others to speak) seemed slightly bemused by takes on their songs by acts half their age such as Avril Lavigne and Sum 41. The former, a punk-lite teenager with an attitude, covered 'Fuel' fairly competently (James commented that it was slightly weird hearing the song sung by a woman), while the latter, a foursome driven by a doglike enthusiasm, knocked out a Metallica medley. More credible than either was Limp Bizkit's take on 'Sanitarium' and a weird version by rapper Snoop Dogg of 'Sad But True'. "They icons, you know what I mean?" Snoop said after the show. "Support them and let them know they got a rapper lovin' them and then, doin' everything that they do, you know what I'm saying?"

Nu-metal scene-leaders Korn performed a creditable take on 'One', with singer Jonathan Davis explaining: "They did exactly what we do now in this time back when they first started. We have always looked up to them in the sense that they have paved the way . . . We are just here to pay respect tonight." Chester Bennington of Linkin Park added: "I was invited to come down and do something tonight and I just jumped at the chance to show my appreciation for the band. To try to do my little thing and say thank you for all the music." The appreciation among the great and the good of modern rock continued with Blink 182 drummer Travis Barker ("I grew up on Metallica. Metallica is the shit. I grew up, like, 13 years old, learning every album"), Bizkit frontman Fred Durst ("They've been around forever and I think it's hard to stick around in a world with such a short attention span"), Papa Roach drummer Dave Buckner ("What's not to love about Metallica? I mean, dude, [they're] just kick-ass heavy metal. They kick your ass with every song. What more do you want?") and Lavigne again ("I've just started getting into Metallica in the last couple of years. I really didn't, like, grow up listening to it or anything like that. But it's great and I am really happy to be here"). Metallica themselves smiled politely and offered various pieces to camera, including one from Hammett: "I think it has everything to do with the quality of our music . . . The music speaks for itself, and to me, I think our music stands the test of time. I mean, when I hear a lot of our earlier stuff, it still sounds fresh to me, and I think it must sound fresh to a lot of people who are hearing it for the 50 millionth time."

The verdict? Moronic and nauseating. After all, where was MTV when *Master Of Puppets* came out? Playing Poison and Bon Jovi videos.

Released on June 10, *St. Anger* starts well. 'Frantic' has a staccato, immediate intro reminiscent of 'Damage, Inc.', which promises much with its dry-as-dust riff accompanied by a microsecond-sharp drum pattern from Ulrich. The scrubbed, sixteenthy riff/drum roll motif which crops up every now and then harks directly back to 'One', which is also a good sign. Although the song's main section is mid-tempo rather than satisfyingly speedy when it starts at one minute in, it's still virulent enough for approval: fans were divided by Hetfield's barked gasp of "Frantic-tick-tick-tick-tick-tick-tock", but like it or not, it's memorable. The end of the song is a surprisingly disorganised thrash shuffle which moves at the right speed, even if it lacks the sophistication we have come to expect. At almost six minutes long, 'Frantic' is a reminder of the sprawling song-lengths heard on . . . *And Justice For All*, even if the complexity of the music doesn't come close.

'St. Anger' is among the more fully formed songs on the album, with a tight, focused intro leading into – at last – a fully fledged thrash riff and a one-two drum pattern of the kind last heard on 'Dyer's Eve' 14 years ago, a lifetime for the speed-deprived Metallica fan. However, the song is shockingly pedestrian apart from this section, which reoccurs a couple more times before the end. Most of it is made up of atonal picking and a surprisingly off-key vocal from James, specifically in the "Saint Anger round my neck . . ." lines. Granted, the chorus sticks in the listener's head after a few listens, and the knowing lines (which refer back to 'Damage, Inc.') of "Fuck it all and no regrets" are toxic enough to stand out – but is this song a future Metallica classic, like the other title tracks ('Ride', 'Puppets', 'Justice') which came before it? Far from it.

'Some Kind Of Monster' is next, eight and a half minutes of plain strangeness. For starters, Lars performs a thrash pattern over a slow, almost introspective riff and even over some sections which are silent except for James' rant of "We the people . . ." It's as if all the band except Lars decided to play a slow-ish song with plenty of doomy, downtuned riffs, but Ulrich decided to speed things up without telling the others. Again, not great.

The air of all-round oddity continues on 'Dirty Window', based on a simple, three-note figure similar to, say, a Led Zeppelin riff. What's weirdest here is the drum sound: Lars' snare veers from clangingly metallic to a weird, almost drum-machine sound on the "I'm judge and I'm jury" sections. James' repeated shrill wail of 'I' and a strangely female high-pitched laugh he emits halfway through make the song slightly ridiculous. By now old-school fans are beginning to shake their heads a little.

It gets worse. 'Invisible Kid', boasting schoolyard rhyming lyrics that could have been knocked up by any eight-year-old, is plain bad. Actually the music isn't that lame: what *is* embarrassingly unacceptable is the moment at 5:06 when Hetfield attempts to sound like a whining child and squeals a kind of lament. No, James, no.

'My World' is more listenable, although it's more rock riffing than genuine metal: there's not much to say about this song, other than that a repeated growl of 'It's my world' doesn't consitute a chorus in my opinion, and that the slushy, middle-heavy guitar tone which we've had for three songs now is starting to grate. It's a collection of riffs more than a cohesive song – what happened to the supertight song structures which had made even a commercial album like *Metallica* so focused? A more powerful section at the end, led by Rock's chugga-chugga bass, is a little better, although it can't redeem the song entirely.

'Shoot Me Again' is better, largely because Metallica stick to one killer motif – Hetfield's defiant cry of the title – and because the softer, picked textures which they have tried and failed to make effective so far finally work on this song. The constant stop-start tricks which Metallica employ at the end of each verse line become a little irksome when they lead to nothing, but when they do lead into James' enraged taunts, the song is satisfying. Its last section boasts as fast a drum pattern from Lars as he'd recorded since, say, 'Fight Fire With Fire', even if it is lost in the mix with that unnecessary tin-kettle sound.

Fortunately the next song, 'Sweet Amber' is a partial return to form, at least if you play it loud enough: with a standard (i.e. not messed-about-with) thrash metal intro, it's a welcome presence among these very mediocre tunes. Even if the fast part doesn't last quite as long as it could, the song is simple and powerful enough to make it worth a listen.

'The Unnamed Feeling' is just dull. All crispy, heard-it-on-*Reload* riffing and James' complaint of "I die", it's one of the weakest tracks on *St. Anger*. The mellow, crooned chorus, however, works just fine (in case anyone thinks I'm judging this album on speed content alone). It works because it comprises a simple, droned guitar line which is both unaffected and effective. The album can work when it's left to basic principles, it seems. Too bad the rest of the song isn't too interesting.

On the other hand, 'Purify' would have worked just fine as a blast-ing, angry, unreconstructed chunk of old Metallica along the lines of, say, 'Metal Militia', if it hadn't tried to be so full-on: Lars and James are fighting with each other for space and Bob Rock's bass part gets in the way a little too. The song does show that there's virulence in Metallica yet, but unfortunately the over-reliance on stop-start sections and tweaking the main riff so it's temporarily off-beat isn't quite convinc-ing. Still, like 'Frantic' and 'St. Anger', the song is a high point of a low-ranking album.

The near nine minutes of 'All Within My Hands' are much better. Like 'Sweet Amber', the song does provide some thrills that are not down to mere speed. There's real rage here, between the lines, in the evilly echoing spaces of the verses, in the picked, almost surf-guitar tones of the guitars and – most memorably – at the end of the song.

The closing section, starting from 7:27, is huge, a malevolent, three-chord, doom-metal riff overlaid with Hetfield's insane screams of "Kill, kill, kill!" If the whole album had been as good as this, we might have had a record worth filing alongside a solid B-league Metallica record like the Black Album.

St. Anger sold respectably when released, but one million in a couple of months was unspectacular by Metallica standards. The single 'St. Anger' was similarly successful, as no doubt will 'Frantic', which is scheduled to be accompanied by a violent video shot by Jonas Akerlund. The long-term assessment of the album will probably be that it was a partially successful experiment by the band, which received split reviews (as has been the case: Metallica newsgroups and media reviews have reverberated more or less equally with scornful and rapturous critiques of the record). No Metallica album has divided the band's followers as sharply, a result which the band themselves would probably applaud as it shows that people are talking about their music, whether they enjoy it or not. Few reviewers gave the record medium or halfway-praising reviews, although in truth it contains several songs which are neither classic nor terrible but somewhere in between.

St. Anger caused much interest among musicians, too. I asked Slayer's Tom Araya what he thought of it. He explained: "I gave it one good listen, and I thought, the riffs are back, and some of the vocal is good and some of it sucks, honestly. The drum sound is terrible. The open snare is great for a part of a song or maybe an entire song – but not an entire fuckin' album. Like I said, I gave it a listen once, and I thought I could listen to it again – but I couldn't. Some of the riffs and stuff were back, but it's like . . . it's not complete. It's a good start, if that's where they're headed. But I wasn't shitting myself and doing all the things I needed to do! Nothing on them, but . . . well, they're Metallica, they do what they do now. I was amazed when I saw that the album was No. 1 here. I was amazed that it managed to stay at number one for a while, until another album came and knocked it off."

But Araya retains some affection, it seems, for his one-time colleagues in thrash: "But you know, they play these shows in Europe for like 50,000 people. That blows my mind. We did a show with them here in the States at the Giants stadium, and the place was fuckin' packed. Every seat was fuckin' banging, and every hand was up with the evil little horns!"

330

One interesting aspect of the *St. Anger* phenomenon (or debacle, if you prefer) was that Lars' long-mooted use of the internet as a distribution tool came at this point. Buyers of the CD were provided with a code that allowed them access to a website, www.metallicavault.com, which provided free downloads of live Metallica songs. Ulrich told the press: "We've always wanted our fans to experience our music online. But up until now, the existing distribution methods have not passed the kind of quality standards our fans have come to expect from us. We want the music that will be accessed . . . to be the best of the best available on the internet." Would this be the beginning of an era in which fans could access classic Metallica material online? Watch this space.

Another clever move on the band's part was the decision to include a bonus DVD with the CD version of *St. Anger*. This was a film of the band in rehearsal running through the entire album, directed by Wayne Isham and a fascinating glimpse inside Metallica HQ. As well as providing another view of the album which would not be gained either by listening to the audio or watching the band live on tour, the DVD afforded another bonus: its sound mix was audibly different to that of the album itself. Rather than just being a bonus feature for audio geeks, this was a crucial point. Why?

Because the sound of *St. Anger* is terrible. More than any other aspect of this experimental album, which showcased new composing, recording and mixing techniques on Metallica's part, this is what failed. Reviewers were quick to note this, firstly realising that Lars' snare drum sound was all wrong and then noticing that the rest of the record sounded decidedly soupy. MTV even ran a website feature entitled "What's Up With The Sound On The New Metallica Album?", in which Bob Rock defended himself with the words: "I wanted to do something to shake up radio and the way everything else sounds. To me, this album sounds like four guys in a garage getting together and writing rock songs."

It emerged that before the album sessions began, Rock told Lars that he was fed up with perfect production and wanted to try a new, rawer direction. Ulrich agreed enthusiastically. The feature went on: "Rock spent five minutes setting up the drums and recorded the rest of the band with a combination of cheap PA mikes and vintage microphones. With the bare-bones recording equipment in place, Metallica started coming up with riffs together and rocked them out like a group of friends hooking up just to mess around."

The results, from James' vocals to the other instruments, were raw (or 'sub-par' as I'd call it). "There was really no time to get amazing performances out of James," Rock told MTV. "We liked the raw performances. And we didn't do what everyone does and what I've been guilty of for a long time, which is tuning vocals. We just did it, boom, and that was it."

One startling aspect of *St. Anger* is that there are no guitar solos – not one. Apparently the solos had simply not fitted: "We made a promise to ourselves that we'd only keep stuff that had integrity," Rock said. "We didn't want to make a theatrical statement by adding overdubs. If we added something and it helped the mood or what we were trying to convey, that stayed. But if it distracted from that . . . then we killed it. Every time we tried to do a solo, either it dated it slightly or took away from what we were trying to accomplish in some other way. I think we wanted all the aggression to come from the band rather than one player."

After extended cut-and-paste sessions in which the various parts of the songs were assembled using ProTools software (a program which takes digitally recorded sound, replicates and/or edits it and places it into a song), the content of the album was complete. But the band had landed a long way from perfection: "Technically, you'll hear cymbals go away and you'll hear bad edits," said the producer. "We wanted to disregard what everybody assumes records should be and throw out all the rules. I've spent 25 years learning how to do it the so-called right way. I didn't want to do that any more."

Reviews were mixed, to say the least. Writer Bernard Doe observes: "My first reaction to the CD was to the dire drum sound . . . I am astonished that Lars would approve this! Back in 1984 Lars would spend days in the studio just perfecting the drum sound before they began recording *Ride The Lightning*. Now, it's like he doesn't care any more. The production sucks big time, and the fact that Bob Rock has had to come out and explain why the album sounds like it does speaks volumes. Having said that, it is still a very heavy album, oozing with aggression that was woefully lacking with *Load* and *Reload* . . . But long term I think Metallica's popularity will be severely damaged by this album. After all, there are other bands out there now releasing much better product than *St. Anger* and are having a far greater influence on the evolving metal genre. In 2003 Metallica are no longer an essential part of the modern-day metal scene. Sad, but true."

Elsewhere, *Terrorizer*'s Ian Glasper proclaimed the album to be 'shite', while my own review in *Record Collector* concluded that it was half good and half lame.

The day after *St. Anger* was released, Metallica played three club shows in one day, all in Paris, France: one at 1pm at La Boule Noire, another at 6pm at Le Bataclan and the last at 10pm at Le Trabendo. Not bad for a bunch of ageing metallers, no matter how poor their latest album might be . . .

In June 2003 Lars revealed that the indie-kid tendencies he had been displaying since he first admitted his love for Oasis back in 1996 continued to this day. He told the *NME*: "I have to say that I subscribe to the *NME* and after being bombarded by the White Stripes for the past year, when they came to San Francisco last month I thought, OK, I have to go see this. It blew my mind. I've never seen anything quite like that. I went down after the show, I went in and humbly professed my love for what they were doing. We had a nice few moments, shared a few cigarettes and a couple of shots of Meg's whisky. It was just the three of us for about ten minutes – it was pretty cool. So I went out and bought their record the next day and I've been playing it on CD in hotels across Europe for the last week."

As if Detroit blues wasn't enough, he also added that Antipodean garage-rock was his cup of tea: "I also love the Datsuns – they showed up on my radar about a year ago and I've been a champion of theirs . . . I've been trying to get the Datsuns for months. Schedule-wise, it hasn't worked out yet. And I was really pissed at our booking agent, because I found out that they are playing at the other day of Reading than we are. I gave my email to the White Stripes' manager because he knew Dolf De Datsun, so he passed it on. And a couple of days later there was this email from Dolf, which was very cool. We have to do something with that band real soon."

In June, the bizarre news came that the US military were using Metallica's music as a torture device while interrogating Iraqi prisoners in the aftermath of the fall of Saddam Hussein. The Iraqis, unused to the harsh sounds of heavy metal, were unable to cope with it and did in fact break down after extended exposure. Lars responded, saying in a statement to the World Entertainment News Network: "I feel horrible about this. No one in Iraq has ever done anything to hurt me, and I don't understand why we have to be implicated in that bullshit. What about firing up some Venom or some of those Norwegian death metal bands? The problem with that is then it wouldn't be a soundbite. Sometimes Metallica become the token heavy metal band that you can talk about." However, he admitted his impotence: "What am I supposed to do about it – get George Bush on the phone and tell him to get his generals to play some Venom?"

In July 2003 a Canadian rock band called Unfaith planted a fake story claiming that Metallica were suing them for using the chords E and F. In retrospect clearly a joke, the story spread rapidly, with many fans and industry observers taken in. Amazingly, it seemed that quite a few people were prepared to accept it as fact. Unfaith singer Erik Ashley told me: "The story about Metallica suing us over usage of the E and F chords is parody. They never did . . . The idea behind this parody was to gauge just how much their reputation has suffered as a result of the lawsuits. Would people go so far as to believe that something this extraordinary – this outlandish – could conceivably be true?"

The Canadian station MuchMusic later broadcast some comments from Lars regarding the Unfaith hoax. Asked what he thought about it all, Ulrich answered, "I like to laugh, myself . . . You know, I thought this [hoax] was actually quite clever. People have been taking jabs at the band for close to 20 years. It's sort of part of being Metallica . . . This one was among the better ones I heard."

Obviously the Napster-derived, sue-'em-all reputation which Metallica have gained in recent years has not dissipated yet. This extends as far as the industry, too. Before singing his band's new single, Iron Maiden frontman Bruce Dickinson told the crowd at an Oslo gig the same month: "The album isn't out yet, but please pull out your digital recorders, MP3 players, cellphones or whatever you have. Put it on the internet, spread it all over the world. But on one condition: when you hear the new album, if you like it, pay the equivalent of three beers to buy the record in the store. That is what keeps us alive. If you don't like the album, just forget it . . . We are not like Metallica."

And so Metallica toured the world, with Limp Bizkit, Linkin Park and the Deftones in tow, pulling in enormous crowds, providing metal for the masses and playing sets that included only 'Frantic' and 'St. Anger' from the new album in their current set: reportedly they still have to learn how to play the other, digitally assembled *St. Anger* tracks first.

The Metallica webmaster posted on the site that there were 250 people working for the band on this tour: "We have three different stages, with six different crews: one Universal crew that goes to all of the shows, primarily travelling on a chartered jet (the band's personal techs, etc.); two identical 'Black' and 'Blue' crews that leapfrog their way around the country, looking over the stage setup at alternating shows; and finally, three 'steel' crews who actually arrive days in advance of each gig to build the stages themselves. Throw in 36 tour buses and 50+ 18-wheelers, and you've got yourself a multi-million dollar summer entertainment package!"

Lars Ulrich, reporting from Philadelphia, was having the time of his life, it seemed, admiring the other musicians on the bill: "I'm digging trying to get up onstage and see other bands. A couple of nights ago in Toronto I went up and sat behind John Otto of Limp Bizkit, who's just the king shit drummer. All of a sudden they were playing 'Seek And Destroy' snippets, 'Master Of Puppets' and then 'Sanitarium'. Sitting there and seeing him play Metallica stuff was just so cool."

Although not everything was sweetness and light – apparently Deftones Chino Moreno told the press, "A big problem for me was opening for [Limp Bizkit and Linkin Park] – two bands that wouldn't exist if it weren't for me," and "Metallica have a vast catalogue, but live? Motherfuckers just stand there and play" – the headliners them-selves have come through the last few years, recorded a big-selling (if mixed-reviewed) album and are still taking it all in their stride. Of Moreno's comments Hetfield told reporters: "It's words on paper, that's all it is. You don't know where that came from or how out of context it was. It's stupid stuff. I think you don't take something like that personally. When someone talks smack like that, maybe it's insecurity or maybe something else is going on. And then you get on the stage and you play and it's kinda like forgotten about."

The new boy, Rob Trujillo, was respectful but happy, it seemed, saying: "The stage is big like an aircraft carrier, so you have some of your cardio there, and depending on the temperature, it can be pretty challenging. Also, Metallica's music can be pretty fast and ferocious. They're pissed off, man. They scare me up there."

Fast and ferocious? Sometimes, but only when the music is of a certain vintage, it seems. Now let us examine the truth at last.

25

The Truth About Metallica

Myth 13: Metallica are and always have been the best heavy metal band in the world.

To answer this question we have to do as Metallica did in 2001 and 2002 and dig deep into their motives and reasoning. However, you don't need a performance coach to do this. You have this book.

Metallica have now sold over 85 million albums. In another two or three years, assuming they continue the record-tour-record cycle and the reissues situation remains healthy, this figure will rise to nine figures. How has this happened? Let's ask a few people.

John Marshall, Metal Church guitarist, Metallica roadie and stand-in for James on those well-documented occasions, has several strong opinions as to why they have achieved so much success: "One reason is their complete dedication to their band. For many years the band has been their family, and each guy was fully committed to what they were doing in the same way that many people are dedicated to their own flesh and blood. A lot of musicians are committed, but these guys were intense about it. Another reason is their intense love of music. I've never seen any five guys that were more into just listening to music, checking out new music, and making music. I remember seeing Jason in the dressing room after a show once. It was the anniversary of Stevie Ray Vaughan's death. He was by himself, his head bowed between the speakers, with Stevie's music just blasting out. He was just worshipping, you know? To me, that says a lot about who these guys are."

Good points. Metallica prioritised their music above all else, with results beyond their expectations – and conflict when family commitments later arose, which (in James' case at least) were only resolved

337

through therapy. Such devotion to their art and love of their music is rare, and gives them all the more reason to deserve success.

But let us be under no illusions about Metallica's skills as business operators, either. They knew where they were going and that there would be a market for them there, as Jim Martin explains: "They had the visceral fortitude and brains to stay on top of the game. They did not stagnate; they changed but remained themselves. They crossed many roads and crushed adversity. Neither radio nor MTV made them, yet they changed the face of pop music in our generation. They opened the door to many who came after, which only reinforced their pioneering approach to modern music."

In finding a strong position and redefining the metal environment, Metallica took an inevitable step away from street level, where their old-school fans wanted them to stay. This caused tension and resentment, of course. As Thomas Gabriel Fischer says: "I believe that many fans had a hard time realising that Metallica slowly began to move away from the 'we're one of you' aura. Being a musician myself, and one who has relentlessly experimented and driven his own music to new frontiers, I know first-hand how much anybody truly creative sometimes needs to enforce a new, fresh and daring direction. I myself was somewhat taken aback too when I heard Metallica's music in the mid-Nineties, but I still felt I could understand why they did it. I believe it was something they had to do, first and foremost for their own sanity."

Fischer understands that the move couldn't possibly satisfy everybody – a realisation that less informed observers would be well advised to consider: "This whole business, the music industry, is an act of balance on a knife's edge. Metallica became successful because they represented the new, the revolutionary, the daring, yet when they again tried exactly that years down the road, their fans had made the band's original revolution something household that wasn't endorsed for change. And both 'sides', fans and the band, can easily be understood for their respective attitude."

Metallica's intellectual decision to select a route to success and move down it as efficiently as possible is a common – and much admired – one among many musicians, it seems. Silenoz of Dimmu Borgir explains: "They're determined and focused only on what they want to achieve, not what others expect from them – that's why we got the

Black Album in the first place. People seem to forget that bit when they bash Metallica. It doesn't mean that other bands don't deserve the same amount of success – there were tons of bands in the same period of time that could've made it big – but you need to be at the right place at the right time, not to forget that luck is obviously also an important ingredient to complete a journey successfully." Like the others I spoke to, Silenoz pinpoints Metallica's obvious change of strategy on the *Metallica* album: "They're intelligent people who have always done what they want, regardless. They were hardly known to anyone outside the metal community before *Metallica*. They just happened to have a great sounding album, promoted the right way at the right time, appealing to a lot of new types of audiences."

Ultimately, most agree that high-quality songs, combined with the right image, breathtaking musicianship and powerful industry backup have made Metallica what they are today. Phil Demmel of Machine Head notes that "Metallica wrote great songs: they had a nice label backing them up, great management, great booking agent," while Byron Roberts of Bal-Sagoth adds, "They were exciting, dynamic and angry; they were damn good musicians; and they had fresh ideas, enjoyed experimentation, and were a marked contrast to the more plodding and mediocre bands which were the recognised face of metal in that day." He clarifies: "Albums like *Ride The Lightning* and *Master Of Puppets* were intricate and dynamic voyages of the imagination which were wonderfully crafted. They also have a timeless appeal, which a lot of other albums of that period sorely lack. The lyrical topics were also compelling, from the songs that tackled more socio-political content like 'Disposable Heroes' and 'Leper Messiah' to the brooding, Lovecraftian atmosphere of 'The Thing That Should Not Be'."

Tony Dolan of Atomkraft and Venom says: "Hard fucking work and doing what they do well and staying true to themselves. At what point did Metallica churn out the same shit? Never! When did they stop growing? Never! When did they compromise themselves? Never! That's the key. Stay true to yourself. Metallica are one of the most honest bands I can think of, like Slayer they just do what they do to please themselves and have fun making music they like and everyone comes along for the ride. The fans know that there is no hidden agenda. When it's played from the heart, you know, and when it's not, you know that as a fan too."

Mirai Kawashima of the Japanese avant-garde metal band Sigh and keyboard player with US gore metallers Necrophagia, explains: "I am sure they deserve their success. I know you can't be successful just because you're a good musician, and I don't think you have to be a good musician to be successful. But as far as Metallica go, they're superior musicians as both composers and players. Who could write riffs that top 'Battery'? They could write songs that were catchy and musically artistic at the same time. Writing catchy songs is easy, and writing artistic stuff is not difficult. However, achieving them both at the same time is really hard."

Hans Rutten of the Gathering simply says: "Quality, until the Black Album. Then they became millionaires, and my theory is that millionaires never make classic albums any more." Herr Wolf of the black metal band Amestigon reasons: "Metallica created something new; they worked continuously and are real musicians." Mikael Akerfeldt of progressive death metallers Opeth: "Good music! No ridiculous image, just good music." Timo Kotipelto of Stratovarius is even more succinct: "Good songs. Good riffs. Good production. Own style. Hetfield."

Writer Borivoj Krgin: "Metallica were simply pioneers – the first band to take the aggression of punk and really incorporate a lot of the metal influences into it without coming across as cheesy and forced. It was done incredibly well, and they had enough insight, musically, to realise that they needed to expand their horizons a bit – without 'selling out' – in order to make their music more palatable to the masses. It was really a combination of talent, luck and an incredible amount of guts – to go against the grain of everything else that was coming out at the same time around them. They didn't give a shit about anything, and they stuck to their guns, and the mainstream eventually came to them as opposed to the other way around. I have an incredible amount of respect for those guys, and I believe they deserve every ounce of success that they are still enjoying."

Metallica's US thrash metal contemporaries aren't quite as united as their European counterparts with their opinions of the secret of Metallica's success. Jeff Becerra of Possessed says: "They were technically perfect and brought hopes to us all that metal had a chance to go mainstream. Before Metallica, mainstream metal just didn't exist." However, Tom Araya of Slayer is much more convinced that Metallica were simply more fortunate with the chances that came their way.

"Right place at the right time," he told me. "Opportunities come and go, and they seemed to get all the right ones. They did that summer tour with Van Halen in 1988, and they blew everybody away. Now things have changed – or they've changed themselves – but that was the step that they needed to get on top of that ladder. And it just took off from there. And I think it's great. It blows my mind how huge they are. It's fuckin' awesome. I guess Slayer must have this stigma, because they got offered the right tours, and we struggled doing our own tours!"

Interestingly, the concept of Metallica having enjoyed critical praise before the Black Album and commercial success after it (but not the opposite) is espoused with equal commitment by the metal musicians I spoke to as much as the fans. Mille Petrozza of Kreator views their career in simple terms: "In the beginning they were one of the most influential bands, no question. I lost interest after the Black Album, though. I guess that was the moment they broke into the mainstream. There must have been a lot of money involved, too . . . I think what they need to do right now is to write an album like *Ride The Lightning*. I think they can afford to lose some of their trendy fans." Steve Tucker of Morbid Angel evidently views those early days as long-gone, although he still has a soft spot for the early classics: "They always wrote great songs, songs that pumped you up or mellowed you out – whatever they wanted. They have a way of expressing energies through their music. Now they do it in a different format than they used to, but I will always remember them the way I loved them. They influenced me tremendously, early on."

Tony Scaglione of Whiplash has witnessed more than his fair share of classic thrash at first hand, and reasons that a major factor in Metallica's rise to the top is James' remarkable singing voice. "I believe that Metallica started out with this unique sound, built an incredibly solid foundation musically and established an extremely loyal fanbase in the beginning. They constantly toured and released albums of quality. I always believed that the main reason for Metallica's success was the fact that even though they played this heavy music they always had an extremely melodic, catchy vocal melody to go over the top of it. And of course you had Hetfield's awesome voice singing it! While other bands can write heavy riffs, the monotonous shouting over the top on it limits the music as far as the appeal to the general public. People inherently like melodies that they can remember and sing to themselves, whether they do it consciously or not. That is just my humble opinion of course!"

Zyklon guitarist Samoth, who knows much about advanced experimentation in metal from his own band and from his many years with Emperor, is in a good position to comment: "I think Metallica were always a bit ahead of their time. As far as I understand, they already had a strong following, even before they had an album out. They created their own personal sound and always went their own way. They made some pretty classic albums and they always pulled off the live aspect, which is an important factor for a band trying to get anywhere." He adds, with some perspicuity, that "The fact that they decided to use a big-shot producer on *Metallica* was probably a big factor in the success."

Writer Garry Sharpe-Young sums up Metallica's ascent in simple, step-by-step terms with a convincing emphasis: "Right time, right place with the thrash explosion. They looked the part, just as Sepultura did later. Cult fanbase, the right imagery, followed by classic song, 'Enter Sandman'. That's it. After that Mensch & Burnstein take over. Metallica is now a brand. That's fine. I tip my hat to success."

Canadian journalist Martin Popoff adds: "They had distinct personalities. They definitely had that street ethic; they dressed pretty simply in their jean jackets and what not. They came from a very enthusiastic retelling of the New Wave Of British Heavy Metal ethic. They had songs, and incredible riffs – there's a lot of variety on those second and third albums. James started to sing, which is something that was lacking in bands like Testament and Over Kill and Exodus." Like so many others, Popoff points the finger of responsibility squarely at Burton: "Apparently Cliff was very musical and would go around on tour carrying a guitar to play, rather than a bass. He was responsible for a lot of the musicality of the band; his heroes were R.E.M. and Thin Lizzy, specifically both bands' harmonies, vocal for the former, guitars for the latter."

Bernard Doe says: "Through the years bands like Black Sabbath and AC/DC have stamped their authority on the scene with their style of metal, and although many have tried to copy those styles those bands are still regarded as the pioneers, because they were the first to gain the success on a mainstream level and in turn influenced so many in the process. And that is exactly what happened with Metallica. They almost single-handedly extended the barriers of the underground movement.

Their success opened the door for so many new young bands and injected life and energy into a metal scene which was fairly stagnant at a mainstream level at the time."

But if Cliff had the musical talent, the business brains which drove Metallica all the way to the top came from Lars Ulrich – and the fact that this middle-class man from a liberal, culture-rich background should be the one to drive a brand to the top of the American business world has a logic all of its own. The secret, it seems, lies in Lars' drive to succeed, which manifests itself in his almost unstoppable enthusiasm. As Diamond Head guitarist Brian Tatler explains: "Metallica have put in a tremendous amount of work and toured everywhere. But I've never met anyone as driven as Lars, his enthusiasm rubs off on you. When he phones you up and asks you to do something, you find yourself doing it. He's always on the phone to management sorting things out. You can spend a day with Lars and you have to have the next two days off to recover, I don't know how he does it." Not only is Lars driven; it seems that he is loyal, too, and knows where his debts lie. Tatler: "He's great, always makes sure I'm on the door in the middle of a UK tour. Nothing's too much trouble. When you're on tour and you've got a million things to do, to remember that your friend has a pass and a seat and backstage access, and something to eat and somewhere to stay . . . I know Lars better than I know the others. I have more in common with him because we go back such a long way." Lars' drive to succeed is crucial to the band's success. As Iron Maiden bassist Steve Harris told me: "Bands like us and Metallica don't really get a lot of play on the radio, although Metallica have probably had a lot more than we have. But what you have to have is enthusiasm to get it through to people."

However, Lars can be stubborn, as he was during the Napster case, which would ultimately alienate many of his fans. Photographer Ross Halfin reported on this side of Lars with some disgust: "Lars? He's not a friend of mine. He's one of those people that when he's shaking your hand, he's looking over your shoulder to see if there's someone more important to talk to . . . I was very, very good friends with him. I just don't like the person he's become." Asked what it is that Metallica have become, Halfin adds: "They totally became everything they laughed at. All the bands they'd laugh at, like Journey and all the really big bands, that's what they are, and half of what brings that is money. James never

343

wanted to be photographed with a private jet at the beginning, because he said it was like shoving it in the kids' faces. But at the end of the day, they like their private jets . . . In the beginning they were interested in the fans, but now it's money-driven. They are a money-driven, money-making machine."

So, where does all this leave us when it comes to myth-making? Maybe the myth of Metallica being the greatest metal band the world has ever seen is true simply because they made so many significant changes to the scene, making them the most significant force to emerge in the genre for years.

Commercially successful metal used to be a European, notably British, phenomenon: Black Sabbath, Judas Priest, Saxon and Motör-head had the scene tied up in the Seventies, and the Iron-Maiden-led NWOBHM held the world prisoner until 1982. Since then, however – and remember, *Kill 'Em All* appeared in 1983 – the world has looked resolutely to the States for its metal fix. Much of this is due to Metallica and their relentless touring. As John Bush of Anthrax says: "I rib a lot of British people about it, I say, 'Come on, where are all the great bands nowadays?' I love Radiohead and Coldplay, and even Robbie Williams, but where's the metal bands? There's Cradle Of Filth, and there's Lostprophets, but they're emulating the American bands, whereas back then we were all copying the Brits!" His colleague Scott Ian recalls how Brit-centric the scene was back then: "The NWOBHM felt like it was my thing. My thing that I had discovered. I was into Tank and all that stuff. Anything that was on Neat Records! A lot of it doesn't really stand up nowadays, but I still love Venom, oh yeah."

Perhaps the fact is that Metallica were once the best metal band around, but fell from grace. If even their huge fan Katon DePena can tell me "Of course I love their earlier stuff the best: *Puppets*, *Ride*, *Kill 'Em All* are about all I can take. If you want honesty you're going to get that from me. They used to be one of the greatest bands in the world. But a lot of bands that were great have changed . . . Deep Purple, Motörhead, Iron Maiden, their later stuff never captured the intensity of their earlier albums. But at least Metallica gets to be mentioned with those bands. If anybody doesn't like their newer albums, they don't have to listen to them," then some kind of great-past-versus-ordinary-present perspective on Metallica has to make sense.

So if Metallica are so much less exciting than they once were, why do they remain so successful? Perhaps because the demographic which buys heavy music is so different today than it once was. As we've seen repeatedly over Metallica's two-decade career, the fanbase of heavy metal has shifted more than once in Metallica's history: the Black Album came just as Nirvana's *Nevermind* took heavy music to the people, after all. Kurt Cobain opened the door to America's living-rooms, and Lars and James walked in. The result a decade later is a metal-buying public with an insatiable appetite for extremity, partly because their eyes were opened by seminal acts such as Metallica, partly because catharsis through music is now their only option. As producer Ross Robinson told me, the lust for heaviness (which has percolated out of the Prozac Generation in the form of nu-metal) comes from cultural vacuum as much as musical availability. "There's a generation of people growing up right now that have no regard for anything. Kids that have no regard, they're microwaved consciousness. They watch TV their whole lives, they get their girlfriends pregnant and they hate everything and they just wanna fucking destroy. People are so depressed, because they're just bombarded with consumerism, it's all consuming and consuming. People don't talk when they eat, they eat fast food. [Metal is] finally giving something, after taking and consuming all your life and being programmed to consume. These bands are pretty much a ministry for these kinds of people so they can release that kind of energy without hurting people."

So there's plenty of appetite for Metallica's music among the new generation, even if many of the older fans who once marvelled over *Ride The Lightning* are no longer interested. Add to this the fact that Metallica are pretty self-aware; they know that their fanbase has changed. As their old mentor Jon Zazula remarked, "They never made a mistake until *Load*. They've been handled very well. The band is full of surprises, they're very resilient, I think they know what's going on." And this despite the phenomenal changes which have occurred in the industry, too, as Scott Ian explains: "Back in 1981 and '82 there wasn't even an MTV yet, and none of these bands were on the radio, and there were no magazines for the bands to be in, really. Bands are way too exposed nowadays – they'll be hot for two weeks and then they're gone." Bathory man Quorthon adds: "Today you can form a band in January, record a demo using digital technology in February, sign a deal in March and be in a metal magazine by April." Metallica have weathered all these changes and are still selling enormously. This must make them pretty special.

So special, in fact, that they are now what fans reverently refer to as a 'classic' band. As Deicide frontman Glen Benton told me, "No one will ever replace bands like Metallica and Slayer. They are who they are. They're like Elvis. He'll always be the King." Given this fact, perhaps more tolerance all round of their more recent music is the best way forward? As Soulfly singer Max Cavalera said, "People should be able to listen to old shit and new shit and they're both great. There is a big separation – people should be able to listen to Slipknot and Manowar. It's really stupid. The barriers have got to be broken down."

So let's try the tolerant approach. Maybe Metallica's Nineties music isn't really that bad. Maybe they've just grown up and got comfortable. Tellingly, Lars told writer Martin Popoff once that his attitude had changed as the years have passed, as Martin recalls: "It is actually one of the rarest life lessons I've ever gleaned from any rock interview . . . Lars said that as he got richer, and everybody wanted a piece of him, and he had those crazy millionaire years for the first time, and was busy beyond belief, that he would listen to music that gave him pleasure. Simple as that. He said that if something was really good, somebody would point it out to him. The way he phrased it in terms of an example was, 'I can talk to you all night long about *Wheels Of Steel*, but ask me about a recent Saxon album, and I just don't know.' So that's what led to all this simple music. He listened to a lot of AC/DC; he listened to certain music just for the pleasure of it. It's like, I've made it, I've realised my dream, I coincidentally actually play music for my dream, why can't I just listen to music I want to listen to? I've earned the right to actually stupidly enjoy music and not have to do so as homework."

The result? A desire to make simpler music. In other words, Metallica's Nineties albums: "So to follow Metallica on their journey through *Load* and *Reload*, is to understand that fact. Metallica are some-what emulating the music they grew up on, music from the pre-thrash years; general rock'n'roll with grooves, good beats, things that aren't so hard on the ears, aren't so demanding on the intellect, things with more emotion, not so much teenage aggression."

All of which is a logical explanation for the softening-up of Metallica's musical approach, it's true, but not one which explains why the supposedly much harder *St. Anger* was such a failure. Perhaps the band's credibility as a truly heavy beast is gone forever, as Karl Sanders of death metal act Nile acidly points out: "Early Metallica is when they were still a metal band, duh . . . it was obvious to anyone listening that the music Metallica was making back then was undeniably classic-quality metal full of fire and power and originality – everything we loved about metal, but distilled into a breathtakingly forceful new genre."

So what is the future for Metallica? Will they be able to follow up on the slightly half-hearted, post-therapy rebirth of *St. Anger* with a genuinely classic album? Some think so; many do not. Either way, Metallica will probably be around in some form or other for some time yet. In 2003, James turned 40, but apart from a slightly more cautious approach to touring, he still seems to be committed to the band for life. But time will catch up in the end: Dave Mustaine told the author in 1999: "If I feel right, then I'll still be doing this when I'm 50. It depends if people are saying the things about us that they say about The Rolling Stones now. If I don't look too bad, I'll still be doing it and saying, fuck you." Three years later, Megadeth announced their split.

If the same happens to Metallica, it's certainly unlikely there'll be an incarnation of the band touring the cabaret circuit, the graveyard of too many classic acts. Lars: "Metallica's the only band I've ever been in. I'm not sure that when it ends in five, ten years, I'm going to put an ad in the paper saying, 'stupid drummer looking for stupid people to play music with'. Metallica is it and I think when that ceases that's it." He also told *Rolling Stone*: "One thing you won't see this band do is go out on that one last tour, make that one last record for that extra $500,000 apiece. When the reasons of playing and having fun don't matter any more, then we will have the sense to cut it off right there."

If no more classic music can come from Metallica, then a dignified close is all that remains. But you never know. Metallica may well come back and, even if they don't equal their Eighties classics, they may well surprise us yet. Three years ago I would never have made that statement – but then, at that stage Metallica had not voluntarily put themselves through therapy at the hands of a performance coach; James was still struggling with alcoholism; and they were still a three-man team, with the recruitment of the revitalising Rob Trujillo still a long way off. By re-examining themselves in intimate, sometimes painful detail with the help of Phil Towle – whose function appears to have been primarily to lead the members to re-evaluate themselves and the inter-band relationships – James, Lars and Kirk have come up with new views of their work, their career, and in fact of the nature of that most primal, protesting music, heavy metal. Strapping Young Lad frontman Devin Townsend told me once that metal is actually full of acutely emotional people: "Heavy metal gets a bad rap because it's represented in a really fucking stupid way. At the end of the day the people who play this kind of music tend to be pretty sensitive. I think there's a lot of repressed sensitivity in metal which manifests itself as aggression." His statement encapsulates perfectly the nature of the men behind Metallica and the destination to which their therapy has brought them.

Witness an interview which Metallica gave to their own *So What* magazine in 2002 for evidence. The changes in their world-view which their counselling had wrought were there, in black and white, for all to see. After explaining that Towle had initially been brought in to try to resolve the problems which Jason had had with his bandmates ("We called a big meeting in the first week of January to figure out what was up and talk about the rest of the year and talk about the state of life in Metallica. Cliff Burnstein suggested that there be a mutual party in there to mediate"), Lars recalled that the performance coach had later been asked to help them explore more profound issues: "What we ended up doing is calling this guy, the connector, basically to reconnect us again. To help us sit down and focus on the reasons why we are together, why we play music, why we have this great love for each other, why it's been so difficult for us to share that with each other."

To take such a step takes courage, especially among men at the forefront of metal, the most macho musical genre ever invented. James: "One of the most valuable things he's taught us, I think, is listening. Actually shutting the fuck up, and listening to the other guy, letting him finish the sentence and get his point across and actually looking at each other and communicating, seeing how the guy really feels. Learning to sympathise with certain situations." Kirk, always more emotionally expressive than Lars or James, had clearly learned much, too: "He's brought out a level of intimacy between us three that we've never really experienced before. And he's also brought out in us what

348

we really, truly feel about each other, how we feel about the band and our own fears and, you know, strengths . . . It gives everyone a huge sense of security. If there was any wonder on whether or not there was another potential Jason in the group, I think we've put all those fears to rest."

When Lars explained that the sessions had gone deep into the band-members' psyches ("There is an amazing sense of intimacy, an amazing sense of brotherhood, and an amazing sense of love . . . Hearing stories, thoughts, emotions, what they feel about certain things, hearing childhood experiences and crying together and all this stuff"), James – clearly on some hidden level still a man's man – is quick to assure the interviewer that: "It might sound funny to other bands that 'they're hugging and weeping' and all this crap together, but at the end of this, this shit is making us as bullet proof and as strong as it ever has been. The strength coming out of this, and the trust, and the just pure kick ass of it all is pretty amazing."

One of the most profound shifts in the Metallica dynamic, and one which could lead to different, perhaps better, music in the future, is the widening of the Lars and James axis to include Kirk. Hammett explained: "My problem in the past was . . . I always felt comfortable about showing these guys my ideas, I just didn't feel very confident . . . So I would hold myself back. Now I don't feel like I have to, which is a big plus," and Lars added, "I spoke to our accountant a couple of days ago and said we should get together and have a meeting about some financial things. The accountant said, 'I should meet with you and James' and I said, 'No you shouldn't meet with me and James, you should meet with me, Kirk and James.'" Will the addition of Kirk, the bluesologist and world-music aficionado, to the songwriting ranks lead to a return to form? We shall see.

Other skeletons in the closet which appear to have been finally laid to rest include Jason's departure and the Napster issue. Of the former, James spoke at length about his feelings over Newsted's side project, Echobrain: "I certainly had views on it and they stemmed from other things. I felt the band was becoming weak that way, and that was always my way of keeping the band together and not fracturing any kind of family strength. That's pretty important to me I guess, and I felt when Jason was doing his side project that it was taking away from his family, his brothers. And I've come to realise that it's absolutely crazy to try and limit anyone on what they want to do and you've got to find the family strength other ways . . . So in the end, we've really both kind of met towards the middle and understood what one another were talking about. So, as far as I'm concerned, there's not really any hard feelings – we just had two different opinions."

As for Napster, James appeared to retain a little anger at the way his band had been perceived – even after hundreds of protestations from Ulrich that the suit was taking place as a matter of principle, not because of money – as cash-driven: "We'll take the hits, we're strong, it's not going to kill us, it's going to make us stronger, but all of the hits about the greediness are what kind of bugged me a little bit. Greedy? So, I'm greedy because I want to get paid for what I'm doing? It's really not greedy to go online and hoard thousands of songs just because Napster might go down?" It's at this point that Ulrich hinted that he knew that he had mismanaged the PR side of the affair: "There was a little bit of chest beating at the beginning, which I think kind of turned people off. I think, ultimately, the best thing with the whole thing is that hopefully it will get to a point where it becomes a tolerable part of the music industry for the next time frame. But I think that the greatest sense of accomplishment of the last year was basically taking part in the education of the public. It was awesome to ride the front of that wave." The 'educating the public' line may stick in a few people's throats a little, of course.

The final result of the band therapy, the one which will make the most immediate impact on observers and the only real change as far as the fanbase is concerned, is the musical evolution of Metallica. James made a point of explaining that emotions could now be flowed more easily into his band's songwriting ("There is a lot of anger but there's a lot of control at the same time. We have a whole range of emotions and we're learning how to get them out and communicate them"), while Hammett added: "It's about learning how to let those emotions, like anger, come out in a more mature fashion and using them as opposed to being controlled by them. Channelling all that stuff into the right place. We discuss channelling all that energy, and we practise it."

Lastly, the band paid tribute to their fans. James said, "There is a lot of patience out there, and the people who stick with us belong with us." Lars added: "I have to agree, it's cool that so many people have been sticking with us." Kirk concluded: "I'm just glad that they're still there after all this, and they'll be rewarded for their patience because when we go back into the studio, all that patience will be rewarded."

They were right to say these things. Metallica's fans have been through a lot: and those that have chosen to stay with their idols, whose musical output has changed almost beyond recognition, are among the most loyal (although some might say misguided) in the whole pantheon of popular music.

And so we come to the end of our long and strange story. It's fitting that the final words should go to the man who made Metallica what they were in their finest hour: Cliff Burton. "The truth is the mightiest hammer," he used to say – and applying that instrument accurately has been the goal of this book.

The greatest heavy metal band in the world? Yes – once upon a time. But no longer. The challenge that Metallica now have before them is to show us all whether they can return to their previous form: and the profound evolution which they have endured in recent years provides us with a small spark of hope.

UK Discography

ALBUMS	Label and year	Chart
KILL 'EM ALL	Music For Nations, 1983	N/A
RIDE THE LIGHTNING	Music For Nations, 8/84	87
MASTER OF PUPPETS	Vertigo, 3/86	41
. . . AND JUSTICE FOR ALL	Vertigo, 9/88	4
THE GOOD, THE BAD, THE LIVE:		
The 6½ Years Anniversary Collection		
(6 × 12″ box set plus 4-track live EP)	Vertigo, 5/90	56
METALLICA	Vertigo, 8/91	1
LIVE SHIT: Binge And Purge	Vertigo, 12/93	54
LOAD	Vertigo, 6/96	1
RELOAD	Vertigo, 11/97	4
GARAGE INC.	Vertigo, 12/98	29
S&M	Vertigo, 12/99	33
ST. ANGER	Vertigo, 6/03	3

SINGLES		
JUMP IN THE FIRE	Music For Nations, 12″, 1983	N/A
CREEPING DEATH	Music For Nations, 12″, 1984	N/A
THE $5.98 EP: Garage Days Re-Revisited	Vertigo, 12″, 8/87	27
HARVESTER OF SORROW	Vertigo, 12″, 9/88	20
ONE	Vertigo, 7″, 4/89	13
ENTER SANDMAN	Vertigo, 7″, 12″ and CD, 8/91	5
THE UNFORGIVEN	Vertigo, 7″ and CD, 11/91	15
NOTHING ELSE MATTERS	Vertigo, 7″, 12″ and CD, 5/92	6
WHEREVER I MAY ROAM	Vertigo, 7″, 12″ and CD, 10/92	25
SAD BUT TRUE	Vertigo, 7″, 12″ and CD, 2/93	20
UNTIL IT SLEEPS	Vertigo, red vinyl 10″ and CD, 6/96	5
HERO OF THE DAY	Vertigo, 12″ and CD, 9/96	17
MAMA SAID	Vertigo, CD, 12/96	19
THE MEMORY REMAINS	Vertigo, CD, 11/97	13
THE UNFORGIVEN II	Vertigo, CD, 3/98	15
LIVE IN LONDON	Vertigo, CD, 5/98	N/A
FUEL	Vertigo, CD, 7/98	31
WHISKEY IN THE JAR	Vertigo, CD, 2/99	29
DIE DIE MY DARLING	Vertigo, CD, 5/99	N/A

I DISAPPEAR	Hollywood, CD, 8/00	35
ST. ANGER	Vertigo, CD, 6/03	9
FRANTIC	Vertigo, CD, 8/03	TBA

VIDEOS

CLIFF 'EM ALL	Universal Pictures Video, VHS, 1987
2 OF ONE	Universal Pictures Video, VHS, 1989
A YEAR AND A HALF IN THE LIFE OF METALLICA: Part 1	Universal Pictures Video, VHS, 1992
A YEAR AND A HALF IN THE LIFE OF METALLICA: Part 2	Universal Pictures Video, VHS, 1992
CUNNING STUNTS	Universal Pictures Video, VHS and DVD, 1998
S&M	Warners Music Video, VHS and DVD, 2000
CLASSIC ALBUMS: Metallica	Eagle Vision, VHS and DVD, 2001

Note: all Metallica albums have been reissued on LP and CD on several occasions, most notably in 2001 on heavyweight vinyl.

Online Resources

Official sites

Main band page
www.metallica.com

Fan club
www.metclub.com

Tour site
www.metontour.com

Online music archive
www.metallicavaultonline.com

Fan sites

There are hundreds of unofficial Metallica websites, but the selection below are among the best:

www.allmetallica.com
www.chapinc.com
www.encyclopedia–metallica.com
www.encycmet.com
www.intersandman.com

www.ipom.com
www.metxxx.com
www.metallica.de
www.metallica–world.de
www.themetsource.com

Thousands of Metallica links can be viewed here:

www.netlaputa.ne.jp/~met/metlink.htm
www.grand.pwp.blueyonder.co.uk/links/metallica.htm

For the other side of the coin, see how many annoyed ex-Metallica fans exist here:

wwww.metallicasucks.com

www.killmetallica.com

Other metal–related sites relevant to this book:

http://listen.to/sigh
www.bal–sagoth.com
www.blackdevilrecords.com
www.bleedingpool.com/amestigon
www.bravewords.com
www.cadaverouscondition.com
www.dimmu–borgir.com
www.emperorhorde.com
www.gathering.nl
www.hadesusa.com
www.hardradio.com

www.hirax.org
www.kreator–terrorzone.de
www.magicelf.com
www.malevolentcreation.cjb.net
www.martinpopoff.com
www.necrophagia.com
www.nocturnalart.com
www.opeth.com
www.rockdetector.com
www.stratovarius.com

Index